MAJOR & MRS HOLT'S
Concise Illustrated
Battlefield Guide to

THE WESTERN FRONT - NORTH

Mons · Le Cateau · Notre-Dame de Lorette, Artois ·
The Yser · 1st Ypres · Neuve Chapelle · 2nd Ypres
(Gas Attack) · Aubers Ridge · Festubert-Givenchy ·
Loos · Fromelles · Vimy Ridge, Arras · 3rd Ypres
(Passchendaele) · 4th Ypres (The Lys)

Tonie & Valmai Holt

For Leo Cooper
for his faith and support

Pen & Sword
MILITARY

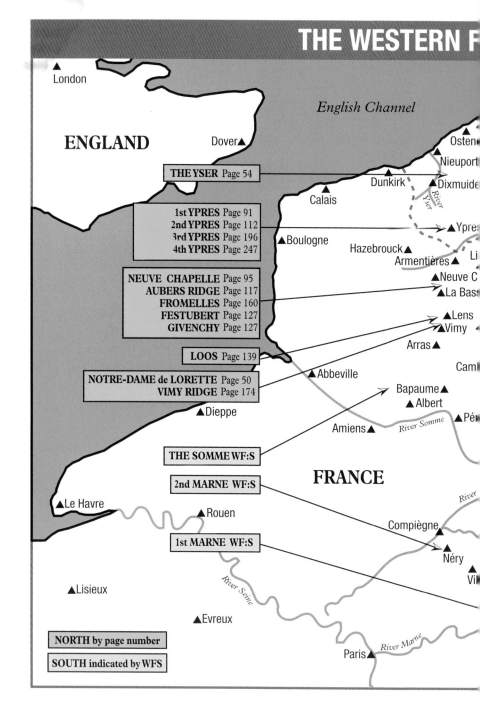

THE WESTERN F

English Channel

ENGLAND

London ▲

Dover ▲

THE YSER Page 54

Osten ▲
Nieuport ▲
Dunkirk ▲ ▲ Dixmuide
Calais ▲
River Yser

1st YPRES Page 91
2nd YPRES Page 112
3rd YPRES Page 196
4th YPRES Page 247

▲ Boulogne

▲ Ypre

Hazebrouck ▲
Armentières ▲ ▲ Li

NEUVE CHAPELLE Page 95
AUBERS RIDGE Page 117
FROMELLES Page 160
FESTUBERT Page 127
GIVENCHY Page 127

▲ Neuve C
▲ La Bass

▲ Lens
▲ Vimy
Arras ▲

LOOS Page 139

Cam

NOTRE-DAME de LORETTE Page 50
VIMY RIDGE Page 174

▲ Abbeville

Bapaume ▲
▲ Albert

Amiens ▲ River Somme ▲ Pé

▲ Dieppe

THE SOMME WF:S

2nd MARNE WF:S

FRANCE

River

▲ Le Havre

▲ Rouen

Compiègne

1st MARNE WF:S

▲ Néry

Vi

▲ Lisieux

River Seine

▲ Evreux

NORTH by page number

SOUTH indicated by WFS

Paris ▲ River Marne

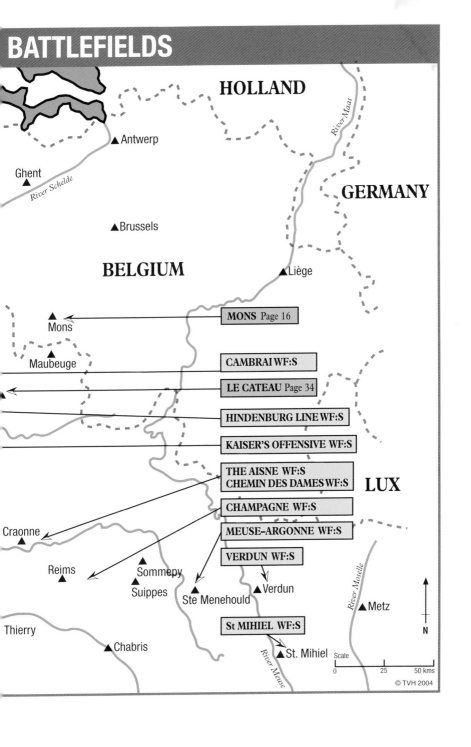

BATTLEFIELDS

HOLLAND

River Maas

GERMANY

▲Antwerp

Ghent
▲
River Schelde

▲Brussels

BELGIUM

▲Liège

▲
Mons

MONS Page 16

▲
Maubeuge

CAMBRAI WF:S

LE CATEAU Page 34

HINDENBURG LINE WF:S

KAISER'S OFFENSIVE WF:S

THE AISNE WF:S
CHEMIN DES DAMES WF:S

LUX

CHAMPAGNE WF:S

MEUSE–ARGONNE WF:S

Craonne▲

VERDUN WF:S

Reims
▲

▲
Sommepy
▲
Suippes

Ste Menehould
▲

▲Verdun

River Moselle

▲Metz

N

Thierry

▲Chabris

St MIHIEL WF:S

▲St. Mihiel

Scale

River Meuse

0   25   50 kms

© TVH 2004

By the same authors:

Picture Postcards of the Golden Age: A Collector's Guide
Till the Boys Come Home: the Picture Postcards of the First World War
The Best of Fragments from France by Capt Bruce Bairnsfather
In Search of the Better 'Ole: The Life, Works and Collectables of Bruce Bairnsfather
Revised edition 2001
Picture Postcard Artists: Landscapes, Animals and Characters
Stanley Gibbons Postcard Catalogue: 1980, 1981, 1982, 1984, 1985, 1987
Germany Awake! The Rise of National Socialism illustrated by Contemporary Postcards
I'll be Seeing You: the Picture Postcards of World War II
Holts' Battlefield Guidebooks: Normandy-Overlord/Market-Garden/Somme/Ypres
Visitor's Guide to the Normandy Landing Beaches
Battlefields of the First World War: A Traveller's Guide
Major & Mrs Holt's Concise Guide to the Ypres Salient
Major & Mrs Holt's Battle Maps: Normandy/Somme/Ypres/Gallipoli/MARKET-GARDEN
Major & Mrs Holt's Battlefield Guide to the Ypres Salient + Battle Map
Major & Mrs Holt's Battlefield Guide to the Normandy Landing Beaches + Battle Map
Major & Mrs Holt's Battlefield Guide to Gallipoli + Battle Map
Major & Mrs Holt's Battlefield Guide to MARKET-GARDEN + Battle Map
Violets From Oversea: Reprinted 1999 as Poets of the Great War
My Boy Jack: The Search for Kipling's Only Son: Revised limpback edition 2001

In Preparation

Major & Mrs Holt's Concise, Illustrated Battlefield Guide to the Western Front – South

First published in Great Britain in 2004 by
Pen & Sword MILITARY
an imprint of
Pen & Sword Books Limited
47 Church Street, Barnsley, South Yorkshire, S70 2AS

ISBN 0 85052 933 6

Typeset in 9pt Palatino by Pen & Sword Books Limited

Printed and bound in Singapore by: Kyodo Printing Co (Singapore) Pte Ltd

For a complete list of Pen & Sword titles please contact
Pen & Swordd Books Ltd, 47 Church St, Barnsley, S. Yorkshire, S70 2AS, England
email: enquiries@pen-and-sword.co.uk
website: www.pen-and-sword.co.uk

CONTENTS

ABOUT THE AUTHORS

Respected military authors Tonie and Valmai Holt are generally acknowledged as the founders of the modern battlefield tour and have established a sound reputation for the depth of their research. Their *Major & Mrs Holt's Battlefield Guides* series comprises without doubt the leading guide books describing the most visited battlefields of the First and Second World Wars. They have a unique combination of male and female viewpoints and can draw upon over a quarter of a century's military and travel knowledge and experience gained in personally conducting thousands of people around the areas they have written about.

Valmai Holt took a BA(Hons) in French and Spanish and taught History. Tonie Holt took a BSc(Eng) and is a graduate of the Royal Military Academy, Sandhurst and of the Army Staff College at Camberley. They are both Fellows of the Royal Society of Arts and Science and have made frequent appearances on the lecture circuit, radio and television.

Their website is: **battlefields@guide-books.co.uk**

LIST OF MAPS

Legend for Maps

Bunkers	●	Place names	▲
Demarcation Stones	●	Sites of Special Interest	○
Memorials	●	War Cemeteries	●
Museums	●		

INTRODUCTION

The Next War

The long war had ended.
Its miseries had grown faded.
Deaf men became difficult to talk to,
Heroes became bores.
Those alchemists
Who had converted blood into gold
Had grown elderly.
But they held a meeting,
Saying,
    'We think perhaps we ought
    To put tombs
    Or erect altars
    To those brave lads
    Who were so willingly burnt,
    Or blinded,
    Or maimed,
    Who lost all likeness to a living thing,
    Or were blown to bleeding patches of flesh
    For our sakes.
    It would look well.
    Or we might even educate the children.'
But the richest of these wizards
Coughed gently;
And he said:
    'I have always been to the front
    – In private enterprise –,
    I yield in public spirit
    To no man.
    I think yours is a very good idea
    – A capital idea –
    And not too costly...
    But it seems to me
    That the cause for which we fought
    Is again endangered.
    What more fitting memorial for the fallen
    Than that their children
    Should fall for the same cause?'
Rushing eagerly into the street,
That kindly old gentleman cried
To the young:
    'Will you sacrifice
    Through your lethargy
    What your fathers died to gain?
    The world *must* be made safe for the young!'
And the children
Went...

                         Osbert Sitwell, 1931

The tombs were indeed put up, the altars erected, the children were educated and continue to be as the Great War features in school syllabi to this day. And not once, but many times again, the children 'went'. The idea that we should learn from history that war was too terrible ever to countenance again after the Great War has been dispelled many and many a time. Yet still we strive to make sense of the greatest conflict that the world had ever seen before 1914.

After over a quarter of a century of studying that war, travelling thousands of miles over its battlefields, leading thousands of people around them, talking to scores of local experts and, above all, interviewing veterans and reading personal accounts, we are convinced that the closest we can ever come to understanding what it may have been like to take part in it and what it was in aid of, is to walk its haunted sites while studying the accounts of those who were there.

For wars are fought by human beings, not arrows and blue and red lines on maps. Their currency is human lives, of boys of 14, of men of 68. Their blood and bones, their memories and experiences impregnate the ground they fought for, in the shallow zigzags of trenches and the grassy or water-filled hollows of mine craters, in dank underground tunnels and chambers and musty bunkers – even below peaceful townships and rolling hills and beautiful thick woods. There we may occasionally glimpse a hint of their pain, hear echoes of the humour that sustained them, feel their longing for home and loved ones, sense their fear and patriotism.

Hence this guidebook, which, with its companion volume, *The Battlefield Guide to the Western Front - South*, is the culmination of our years of involvement in the Great War. They are written as a tribute to those special people of '14-'18, so different from us today because of their culture, their mores, their attitudes of a truly bygone age, and in the hope that it will help you, the reader, to get nearer to an understanding of what it was all about by getting to know where it all happened. They are written from personal experience and are designed to be simple to use, practical and informative. If we mention a bunker we have explored it, a trench we have walked through it, a memorial we have seen it, a cemetery we have visited it...

This first volume closes the gap left between our detailed guidebooks to the Ypres Salient (also included in more concise form in this book) and The Somme (where the second volume begins geographically). It visits the areas of the briefer, smaller-scale but highly significant battles at Mons and le Cateau, the desperate efforts of the Belgians on the Yser, the battles of Neuve Chapelle, Aubers Ridge, Festubert, Givenchy, Loos and Fromelles and the long struggles of the French in Artois at Notre-Dame de Lorette and Vimy Ridge. Each has its own fascination and sites where one can still relate to the conflict that took place at them.

The second volume will cover the Somme battlefields, move eastwards and southwards through Cambrai, the Marne, the Aisne, Champagne, the Meuse-Argonne and St Mihiel to Verdun, covering American, Commonwealth and French campaigns. Together they will form a comprehensive guide to the major battlefields of the Western Front and hopefully lead the reader to visiting new, extremely interesting areas where, in several cases, recent developments have opened up sites that have remained 'dormant' for many years.

Since our first tour in 1977, when no other post-WW2 organised tours existed for the general public, the battlefield scene has changed beyond all recognition. Then we would stand alone with the faithful buglers at the Menin Gate, be the sole signatories in remote cemetery registers, place our poppy tributes on rarely visited memorials. It was a very privileged time. Gradually the interest and momentum rolled on. Local authorities realised that battlefields could equate to tourism. Designated routes were devised and signed, sites were refurbished, made safe for visitors, car parks were constructed, small museums with superb personal exhibits but little professional curatorship skills were expanded and 'modernised'. Perhaps a little of the 'soul' was lost in the process but now, as battlefield touring has moved from the exclusive realms of the 'buff' or the 'pilgrim' to that of the 'student' and the 'tourist', the benefit is that so many more people are able to be exposed to the lore of the Great War and who can contribute to keeping the memory alive.

The ever-continuing research by armchair historians and energetic local enthusiasts alike has led to a flood of new information and the discovery and opening up of new sites to visit. In the Ypres Salient 'The Diggers' (qv) have discovered the treasures under the developing industrial estate at Boezinge; one of the great craters has been opened to visits at St Eloi; the fascinating Canal Bank site at Essex Farm has been exploited; Talbot House in Poperinge is opening a Visitor Centre in the old adjacent Hop Store; Zonnebeke is completely remodelling the Streek Museum and opening up the historical remains at Bayernwald; new parking facilities are being created behind Tyne Cot Cemetery. Dedicated research associations in Aubers and Fromelles are discovering more and more about the war on their land. The expansion seems never ending.

What is important is to keep alight the flame thrown to our hands by John McCrae in the best-known poem of the Great War: *In Flanders Fields*. In writing this book – the fulfilment of so many years of studying and visiting the battlefields – we have endeavoured to hold it high and now pass it you.

Tonie and Valmai Holt,
Woodnesborough, 2004

ABBREVIATIONS

Abbreviations and acronyms used for military units are listed below. Many of these are printed in full at intervals throughout the text to aid clarity. Others are explained where they occur.

A/	Acting	KOYLI	King's Own Yorkshire Light Infantry
ASH	Argyll & Sutherland Highlanders	KRRC	King's Royal Rifle Corps
BCA	*Battaillon de Chasseurs Alpins*	L/	Lance
		Mia	Missing in action
BCP	*Battaillon de Chasseurs à Pied*	MC	Military Cross
		MiD	Mentioned in Despatches
BEF	British Expeditionary Force	MM	Military Medal
		MoH	Medal of Honour
Brit	British	OP	Observation Point
CAP	*Chasseurs à Pied*	OR	Other Rank(s)
CGS/H	*Conseil Général de la Somme/Historial*	ORBAT	Order of Battle
		POW's	Prince of Wales/Prisoners of War
C-in-C	Commander-in-Chief	Pte	Private
CO	Commanding Officer	RF	Royal Fusiliers
Comm	Communal	RE	Royal Engineers
Coy	Company	RI	*Régiment d'Infanterie*
CWGC	Commonwealth War Graves Commission	RIDG	Royal Irish Dragon Guards
		RIR	Royal Irish Rifles
Ger	German	RoL	Regiment of Line,
GHQ	General Head Quarters	RWF	Royal Welsh Fusiliers
Gnr	Gunner	SGW	Stained Glass Window
HAC	Honorable Artillery Company	SMLE	Short muzzle Lee Enfield
HLI	Highland Light Infantry	T/	Temporary
IWGC	Imperial War Graves Commission	VC	Victoria Cross
		WFA	Western Front Association
K	Kitchener (as in Division)		
Kia	killed in action		

HOW TO USE THIS GUIDE

This book may be read at home as a continuous account, used en-route as a guide to specific battles and battlefields, dipped into at any time via the Index as a source of fascinating detail about the First World War or kept as a reminder of past visits to the sites described.

The most significant WW1 battles of the Western Front fought to the north of the Somme and Paris are included in chronological order. Each battle is separately described under the headings 'A Summary of the Battle', 'Opening Moves'and 'What Happened' to remind readers of their historical significance, so that the details may be more readily understood and to provide a framework upon which the accounts that follow may be hung. Each battle described is accompanied by an especially drawn map and the conduct of the battles can be more easily followed by constant references to the appropriate map.

At the front of each chapter are one or more quotations from people who were involved in the war and these have been chosen to give a relevant personal flavour to the detailed accounts. Those already familiar with the First World War will find the chapter quotations apposite before reading further, while those less familiar may well find it worthwhile to read the quotations again at a later stage.

MILES COVERED/DURATION/OP/RWC/ TRAVEL DIRECTIONS/EXTRA VISITS

The battlefield tours cover features that during our many years of guiding parties across them and writing about them have been the most requested, as being the best-known, the most important, the most emotive... Added to them are the new sites that have recently been opened up. None is exhaustive – this is a *condensed* battlefield guide – but in combination with the specially drawn maps for each battle they provide a compact and hopefully illuminating commentary upon the events of the time, from glimpses of the Grand Designs, through individual acts of heroism to the memorials that now mark the pride and grief of a past generation.

A start point is given for each tour from which a running total of miles is indicated. Extra visits are not counted in that running total. Each recommended stop is indicated by a clear heading with the running total, the probable time you will wish to stay there and a map reference to the relevant sketch map and, in the case of Ypres, to *Major & Mrs Holt's Battle Map of Ypres*. The letters OP in the heading indicate a view point from which salient points of the battle are described. RWC indicates refreshment and toilet facilities. Travel directions are written in *italics* and indented to make them stand out clearly. An end point is suggested, with a total distance and timing without deviations or refreshment stops. 'Base' towns or cities are suggested which can provide convenient and comfortable accommodation and restaurants.

In addition **extra visits** are described to sites of particular interest which lie near to the route of the main itineraries. These are tinted light grey and boxed so that they clearly stand out from the main route. Estimates of the round-trip mileage and duration are given.

It is absolutely essential to set your mileage trip to zero before starting and to make constant reference to it. Odometers can vary from car to car and where you park or turn round will affect your total so that it may differ slightly from that given in this book. What is important, however, is the distance between stops. Distances in the headings are given in miles because the trip meters on British cars still operate in miles. Distances within the text are sometimes given in kilometres and metres as local signposts use these measures.

Stout waterproof footwear and clothing, binoculars and a torch are recommended. Make sure you take adequate supplies of any medication that you are on. Basic picnic gear is highly recommended for remoter areas where restaurants are virtually non-existent or which close for lunch on unexpected days (and there is no greater pleasure than a crusty baguette filled with creamy cheese washed down with a drop of the beverage of your choice consumed on a sunny bank in a quiet corner of a battlefield). The boutiques in motorway stops can provide the wherewithal for a picnic if you are unlikely to pass a local supermarket or village shop (many now sadly permanently closed). It is also important to make sure that you have a full tank when you leave the motorway. Petrol stations are very rare in some localities. A mobile phone is a reassuring accessory.

Maps/Choosing Your Routes/Particular Visits

There are recommended commercial maps for each tour and it is suggested that the traveller buys them, or their nearest updated equivalent, and marks them before setting out. These maps, used in conjunction with the sketches in this book, make it possible not only to navigate efficiently but also to understand what happened where - and sometimes 'why'. For the battlefields of The Four Battles of Ypres reference is made to the very detailed *Major & Mrs Holt's Battle Map of The Ypres Salient*. The sketch maps which accompany each battle described in the book use the same **colour coding system of mauve for war cemeteries, yellow for memorials, blue for museums, pink for bunkers and craters, orange for demarcation stones.**

For an excellent overall view of all the battlefields in this book the **Michelin 236 Nord Flandres-Artois Picardie** 1/200,000 – 1 cm : 2kms is highly recommended.

The battles are arranged chronologically and their descriptions are self-contained so that any individual battlefield may be visited in any order. An approximate distance from Calais is given to the start point of most battlefields. If they are to be visited in geographical sequence, then the large sketch map on pages

2 and 3 will help you plan your route. The nearest Autoroutes linking the battlefields are indicated.

There are many options for the visitor in choosing his or her itinerary, depending upon interest, time available etc. For practical reasons the geographical constraints will probably have to take precedence over the chronological order of the battles and it would obviously take several weeks thoroughly to tour in one long journey all the battlefields described. Studying the campaigns in any sort of meaningful order is further complicated by the fact that many of the battlefields overlap and were also fought over at several different periods. This particularly applies to the area covered by the Four Battles of Ypres, the battles of Neuve Chapelle, Aubers Ridge, Fromelles and Festubert. Specific places to be visited may be found by reference to the Index and if a particular grave is to be located you should consult **the Commonwealth War Graves Commission Debt of Honour website** or **the American Battlefield Monuments Commission website** before you set out (see below).

At the end of the book the 'Tourist Information' section gives tips on how to prepare for your journey, where to eat or stay, and where you will find information and help. The 'War Graves Organisations' section describes in brief the dedicated associations which tend and administer the war cemeteries and memorials that you will visit following the tours. Other Commemorative Associations are listed.

PLACE NAMES

Note that there is considerable and often confusing variation in place names created by the disparate Flemish and French versions of the same place name, e.g. Mesen and Messines, Ieper and Ypres, Kortrijk and Courtrai, Rijsel and Lille, Doornik and Tournai, Nieuwkerke and Neuve Eglise, Waasten and Warneton etc. Also the names of CWGC Cemeteries tend to employ the French version of place names used in the war. Thus we have 'Wytschaete' Mil Cemetery in Wijtschate, and 'Westoutre' Cemeteries in Westouter. During the war Elverdinge, Geluveld, Hooge, Poperinge, Vlamertinge had an 'h' after their 'g'. Nieuport was Nieuwpoort, Diksmuide was Dixmude, the Ijzer was the Yser - and so on.

TELEPHONING

When calling Belgium from the UK the '+' indicated in the phone number = 00 32.
When calling France from the UK the '+' indicated in the phone number = 00 33.

COUNTDOWN TO WAR

'The lights are going out all over Europe,
we shall not see them lit again in our lifetime'
Edward, Viscount Grey of Fallodon

On 28 June 1914 Archduke Franz Ferdinand and his wife were assassinated at Sarajevo in Bosnia. The Archduke was the heir apparent to the throne of the Austro Hungarian Empire, then ruled by the Emperor Franz Josef. He had gone to Austrian-occupied Bosnia on a tour designed to bolster up the Empire which was cracking under a rising tide of ethnic nationalism. The assassins were Serbs and the Austrians immediately accused the Kingdom of Serbia of harbouring the killers and others like them, and determined upon revenge. It also seemed an opportunity to crush the growing strength of the Serbs.

On 23 July the Austrians sent an ultimatum to Serbia demanding that anti-Austrian propaganda should be banned in Serbia and that the man behind the assassination be found and arrested. To these points the Serbs agreed, but they did not agree to having Austrian officials in their country to supervise the proceedings. On 28 July the Austrians, considering the response to be unsatisfactory, declared war on Serbia.

Now the dominoes began to fall as old loyalties, tribal relationships and treaties toppled country after country into one armed camp or the other. Germany sided with Austria, Russia with Serbia. The French, still hurting from their defeat by Prussia in 1870 and determined to regain from Germany their lost provinces of Alsace-Lorraine, saw a victorious war as a method of achieving that objective.

On 31 July Russia ordered general mobilisation followed that same day by Austria. The British Foreign Secretary, Sir Edward Grey, asked both France and Germany if they would observe Belgian neutrality. France replied 'Yes'. The Germans remained silent and the Belgians ordered that mobilisation should begin the following day.

On 1 August the French ordered mobilisation, Belgium announced her intention of remaining neutral and Germany declared war on Russia. On 2 August German troops invaded Luxembourg and made small sorties into France. Belgium refused to allow German forces to cross her soil with the object of 'anticipating' (as the Germans put it or as in the case of Iraq in 2003 making a 'pre-emptive strike') a French attack and the King of the Belgians appealed to King George V of Britain for help.

On 3 August, Bank Holiday Monday, Germany declared war on France, while in Britain bright sunshine warmed the holiday crowds and Sir Edward Grey told Parliament, that 'we cannot issue a declaration of unconditional neutrality'.

On 4 August, just after 0800 hours, German forces crossed into Belgium. The British issued mobilisation orders and the British Ambassador in Berlin told the Chancellor that unless Germany withdrew her troops by midnight their countries would be at war with one another.

The Germans did not withdraw. It was war.

THE SCHLIEFFEN PLAN

The German plan for the conquest of France began to evolve in the early 1890s under the direction of the chief of Staff, Field Marshal Count von Schlieffen. France and Russia were allied against possible German aggression under the Dual Alliance of 1892 and so Schlieffen had to devise a plan that avoided fighting both enemies at the same time. According to German military intelligence estimates the Russians would be unable to mobilize fully for six weeks after the beginning of a war. Therefore, reasoned Schlieffen, if France were to be attacked first and defeated within six weeks, Germany could then turn around and take on Russia. That logic, however, only moved the goal posts to uncover another challenge: how to defeat France in six weeks?

Schlieffen had the answer to that too. The key element to a quick victory was surprise and simplistically the plan aimed to convince the French that they should maintain their major forces in the area of Alsace-Lorraine to counter an invasion directly from Germany around Metz, while the actual assault descended on France from the north via neutral Belgium.

Ten German divisions were nominated to keep an eye on the Russians, while 62 were assembled to take on the French. Of these latter, five armies were assembled in a line facing west and stretching northwards from Metz (see **Map 1**, page 18) to form a door hinged upon Switzerland. This door was to swing in a massive anti-clockwise movement through Belgium. At the top of the door was von Kluck's 1st Army and von Schlieffen had enjoined that the very last soldier at the end of the swing should 'brush the Channel with his sleeve'.

Von Schlieffen died in 1912, saying on his deathbed, 'Above all, keep the right wing strong'. His successor was Helmut von Moltke, nephew of the von Moltke of the 1870 War and made of different stuff to his eminent ancestor. A cautious man, lacking the ruthlessness upon which Schlieffen's plan depended and frightened by the possibility of a strong counter-attack by the French in the area of Alsace-Lorraine, he strengthened the hinge end of the door, weakening the force that was planned to sweep through Belgium.

Nevertheless, when the invasion began, von Moltke had almost 1½ million men forming his door and at the far end of his extreme right wing, there was the 1st Army, commanded by General von Kluck, who saw himself as Attila the Hun. On 4 August 1914 the door began to swing and Attila invaded Belgium.

MONS

23 AUGUST 1914

'Our men have come to believe that every one of you
carries a portable Maxim with him'
A German officer to an 'Old Contemptible'.

'I suppose that in the first place it was to comfort myself that I thought
of the story of "The Bowmen" and wrote it in the early days of September.
And perhaps I had better go into the box for the last time and
answer once more that the tale is mere and sheer invention.'
Arthur Machen, whose story in the *Evening News* of 29 September 1914
gave rise to the legend of '*The Angels of Mons*'.

SUMMARY OF THE BATTLE

This was the first battle of the war for the British Expeditionary Force (BEF), which faced the invading German armies along a defensive line based upon the Condé Canal running through the northern outskirts of the Belgian town of Mons. The German attack began at 0830 from the north and by mid-afternoon the British were forced to withdraw with 1,600 casualties. German casualties are variously estimated at between 3,000 and 15,000.

OPENING MOVES

On 4 August 1914 the Germans invaded Belgium and headed for Liège, expecting only a token resistance. They were wrong. The forts around Liège held out until 7 August, the same day that advance parties of the BEF began to land in France en route to Belgium.

On 20 August the Germans marched through Brussels and headed onward towards Mons and the Franco-Belgian border, less than 40 miles away. Early on the morning of 23 August their artillery came within range of the Mons-Condé Canal, which lay between them and France, and they began shelling the crossing points. Along the canal, unknown to the Germans, waited the men of the BEF.

Following the order to mobilize on 4 August, the British knew exactly what to do, because everything was written down in the 'War Book'. In anticipation of future conflicts, political and radical thinkers had envisaged as many different scenarios as they could and recorded in millions of words of instructions just what was to be done when any particular prediction came to pass. Thus, in August 1914, the section of the War Book entitled *In the Event of War with Germany* was opened and its instructions concerning the BEF were followed.

The Expeditionary Force (EF) was one of the three elements of the Army that came out of the Haldane Reforms of 1906/7. The other two elements were the 'Forces Overseas' and the 'Territorial Force' designated for Home Defence. The EF was made up of a core of Regular units stationed at home, but trained and prepared to move overseas to any trouble spot. Militia battalions of men having six months' training formed a 'Special Reserve' to fill out the EF in the event of general war, 70,000 Special Reservists being recalled in August 1914.

The Allied plan required the British to take up a position at the extreme left of the French line and to assemble in the area of the old fortress of Maubeuge, some 12 miles south of Mons. Following the War Book instructions, training and equipping (only one pair of boots) of militia reinforcements began immediately and in Britain on 9 August the main bodies of the BEF marched to their local train stations early in the morning to catch the evening boat from Southampton to Boulogne, Le Havre or Rouen. The movements of one battalion over this period were:

9 AUG:	7 am March to station
	Afternoon. Arrive Southampton
	Evening. Sail from Southampton
10 AUG:	Afternoon. Arrive Le Havre
	March to rest camp
11 AUG:	Midnight. March to station
	Slow trains north for the next five days
17 AUG:	7 mile march to Maubeuge area
20 AUG:	15 mile training march
21 AUG:	18 mile training march
22 AUG:	11 mile training march
23 AUG 0100 hours:	14 mile march to Mons to take up defensive positions.

The promised strength of the BEF was six infantry divisions and one large cavalry division, but Lord Kitchener, appointed Secretary of State for War on 5 August, mistrusted the French plan and kept back two divisions so that, when concentration of the BEF was complete at Maubeuge on 20 August, the force under Sir John French's command totalled about 80,000 men divided into two corps of two divisions each, plus an independent brigade and a cavalry division.

Early on the morning of 23 August, the BEF made its final moves into its defensive positions along the Mons-Condé Canal. I Corps, under General Douglas Haig moving well to the east of Mons, and II Corps, under General Smith-Dorrien, a survivor of the massacre at Isandhlwana in the Zulu War, covered the canal west from Mons to Condé, Mons itself and the canal to Obourg (see **Map 2**, page 19). Then they waited for von Kluck's legions to arrive. It wasn't a long wait.

MAP 1: THE ARMIES MOVE TO MONS – AUGUST 1914

ENGLAND London HOLLAND GERMANY

Southampton

The Swinging Door

Boulogne Brussels BELGIUM

BEF MONS

Maubeuge

English Channel

Le Havre BEF

Rouen

① 320,000
② 260,000
③ 180,000
④ 180,000
⑤ 200,000

LUX

Metz

R. Seine *R. Marne*

PARIS

R. Seine

Legend
1. German 1st Army of 320,000 men
2. German 2nd Army of 260,000 men
3. German 3rd Army of 180,000 men
4. German 4th Army of 180,000 men
5. German 5th Army of 200,000 men
6. German 6th Army of 220,000 men
7. German 7th Army of 125,000 men
BEF = British Expeditionary Force
········ Movement of BEF
◆◆◆◆ Movement of Germans

⑥ 220,000

⑦ 125,000

N

FRANCE

SWITZERLAND

Scale

0   50   100   200 kms

The Hinge © TVH 2004

WHAT HAPPENED

Von Kluck's troops were moving, fast. The II (Ger) Corps at the end of the swinging door had marched 140 miles in 11 days. Just after first light on the morning of 23 August German divisional cavalry were tapping at the British II Corps forward positions. At 1030 hours the IX (Ger) Corps artillery opened up in the area of Obourg and together with the III (Ger) Corps artillery quickly dominated the British line through Nimy along the canal towards Jemappes in the west.

At 1100 hours a massed infantry attack was made towards the canal bridges at Nimy, held by the 4th Royal Fusiliers and at Obourg, held by the 4th Middlesex (the 'Diehards', a name derived from the exhortation of their dying CO at Albuhera in 1811), both of the 3rd Division. This frontal assault by the 18th (Ger) Division, coupled with a flanking movement by the 17th (Ger) Division which had crossed the canal at an undefended spot east of Obourg, forced a British withdrawal to begin at around 1300 hours to intermediate positions in and around the town of Mons.

Along the canal to the west the Germans made multiple small crossings and at mid-afternoon another major attack developed, forcing further withdrawal along the whole British line. It was the beginning of the 'Retreat from Mons'.

THE BATTLEFIELD TOUR

• **The Route:** The tour begins at the Canal at Nimy then visits the plaque to 4th Royal Fusiliers, 4th Middlesex, 2nd RIR and 56th Coy RE at Masières; the memorials to the first and last British actions of the war; the sites of the actions of the 4th Royal Fusiliers and the 4th Middlesex at Obourg; Mons General CWGC Cemetery; the memorials at the Binche (la Bascule) crossroads and ends at the Saint Symphorien CWGC cemetery.
• **Extra Visits** to Villers-St-Ghislain (Gen Allenby 1914 HQ)/Ville-sur-Haine Memorial to Pte Price and Mons Town Centre.
• **Total distance:** 12.8 miles
• **Total time:** 2 hours 30 minutes
• **Distance to Calais from start point** 117 miles. Although it is motorway all the way to Mons note that there are **No Tolls**.
• **Base town:** Mons
• **Map:** IGNB M736 Sheet 45. 1:50,000
   From Calais take the A16/A26 direction Paris, then A16/E40 direction Dunkerque/Lille. Take Exit 28 to Lille/Ypres on the A25/E42. Note that navigation is tricky around Lille and take the A1 direction Villeneuve d'Asq, then the A27/E42 direction Bruxelles/Tournai.
At approx 79 miles the border into Belgium and Wallonia is crossed and the road number changes to the E42.

Continue round Tournai, crossing the Escaut Canal, and join the A7/E19. Continue to Exit 23/23bis from the E19/E42 and take the Exit N6 SHAPE/Nimy. **Set your mileometer to zero.** *Follow signs to Mons/Nimy on the N6 straight over the traffic lights. Cross the Canal* (now called the Canal du Centre and on which there is a sign 'Point 1' on the 'Mons Battlefield Tour', a local signposted route) *and immediately turn right into the square in front of the town Hall. Take the small road to the right of the Town Hall (ignoring the No Entry sign) and turn left along the Canal to the railway bridge. Stop.*

• *The Nimy Canal Bridges/4th RF & VC Memorial/0.9 miles/15 minutes/Map 2/1/OP*

Stand on the bank to the west of the bridge with your back to the canal. You are facing away from the enemy who approached from the other side of the river.

The railway bridge and the road bridge up the canal in the direction from which you came were the responsibility of the 4th Royal Fusiliers to defend and were given to C Company commanded by Captain Ashburner. Following some casualties from the Germans' early shelling, the Company had a brief encounter with a German cavalry (Uhlan) patrol and took prisoner Lieutenant von Arnim, son of the general commanding IV (Ger) Corps.

Shortly after the skirmish with the patrol the German infantry attack began. A solid mass of soldiers in columns of fours came on towards the canal from the north. The Tommies were astounded. Their opponents moved as if on parade, as if taking part in some Napoleonic war game. They were ducks in a shooting gallery to the riflemen of the BEF who were trained to fire fifteen aimed rounds a minute and capable of almost double that with such a target. Although their first attacks failed, the Germans came on, pausing to direct machine gun fire on to the Fusiliers' positions and to co-ordinate their attack with artillery fire. The two machine guns commanded by Lieutenant Dease, sited on the top of the embankment where you are standing at the southern end of the bridge, wreaked terrible havoc among the grey horde, but the Fusiliers were suffering too.

Captain Ashburner was wounded in the head and, despite reinforcements brought up from the battalion reserve in the Nimy Square, by midday the situation was becoming serious. Only one machine gun was now operating and that was being fired single-handed by Lieutenant Dease, despite his having been hit three times. Inevitably Dease died (he is buried in St Symphorien cemetery, which is visited at the end of this tour) and Fusilier Private Frank Godley volunteered to take over the weapon. For a whole hour he held off the German attack as the Fusiliers began a withdrawal down the road to Mons. He too was wounded and just before being overwhelmed by the Germans he dismantled the gun and threw it into the canal. Three months later, while in POW camp, **Frank Godley** learned that he **and Lt Dease had each been awarded the Victoria Cross (VC)**, the first ones of the Great War. After the war Godley, who had a large 'walrus' moustache, dressed as Bairnsfather's 'Old Bill' and raised funds for the Royal British Legion. At the end of the day the Fusiliers had some 250 casualties, about half the number of Germans they had killed.

Below the bridge on the southern side is a **bronze plaque** commemorating the action and the VC awards. It is Point No 2 on the Mons Tour. The French blew up the bridge in 1940 damaging the plaque which was recovered by a villager from Nimy who looked after it until the end of the war. The bridge was blown up again in September 1944 and the plaque was placed on the present bridge on 12 November 1961.

By walking to the bend in the Canal the Belfry Tower of Mons can be seen in the distance (an Extra Visit can be made to it at the end of the tour) and to its right some slag heaps. The large expanse of water is the lake and pleasure port formed in 1970 when the Mons-Condé Canal was closed to make way for the motorway.

Return to the main road and turn left back over the Canal. Continue on the N6 under the motorway to Maisières. Continue on the dual cariageway to the second of double traffic lights and turn right immediately past the church. Park behind it. On the church wall is

• Plaque to 4th RF, 4th Middlesex, 2nd RIR and 56th Coy RE/1.3 miles/5 minutes/Map 2/15

The stone plaque bears the legend in French, 'This plaque was erected with humble respect and thanks by the British and Belgian Veterans and their families in memory of the British Officers and Soldiers who were killed here in battle 23 August 1914 in the Battle of Mons and who were buried in the cemetery of Maisières. Their bodies now rest in the Military Cemetery of St Symphorien but their memory will always be honoured in this place. 56 Coy Royal Angineers [sic], 4th Bn R Fusiliers, 2nd Bn RIR, 4th Bn Middlesex Regt.' Indeed a wreath is still laid here every 11 November by local authorities and members of SHAPE.

*Continue on the N6 through Maisières following signs to **SHAPE** (which you will pass on your left). After **SHAPE**, and immediately following a crossroads controlled by overhead traffic lights, is a rise with a large building on the right, the Restaurant le Medicis. Stop beside it and carefully cross the busy road to the memorial opposite.*

• The First and Last Shots Memorials/4.3 miles/10 minutes/Map 2/2 and 2/3

This is Point No 3 on the Mons Tour. It was near this spot that Corporal E. Thomas of C Squadron 4th Royal Irish Dragoon Guards (4th RIDG) fired the first British shot of the war, an event commemorated by the monument which was unveiled on 20 August 1939, less than 2 weeks before Germany invaded Poland. Not since Waterloo had the British fired a shot on the Continent of Europe. The memorial, by Mons architect Bertiaux, stands where the 4th RIDG began their charge upon the enemy. Too often British visitors come away from this spot with the idea that the first shots of the war were fired here. Not so: the first *British* shots were indeed sounded here but by 20 August Belgium had essentially been over-run and in a series of encounters generally known as the Battles of the Frontiers the French had already suffered some 300,000 casualties.

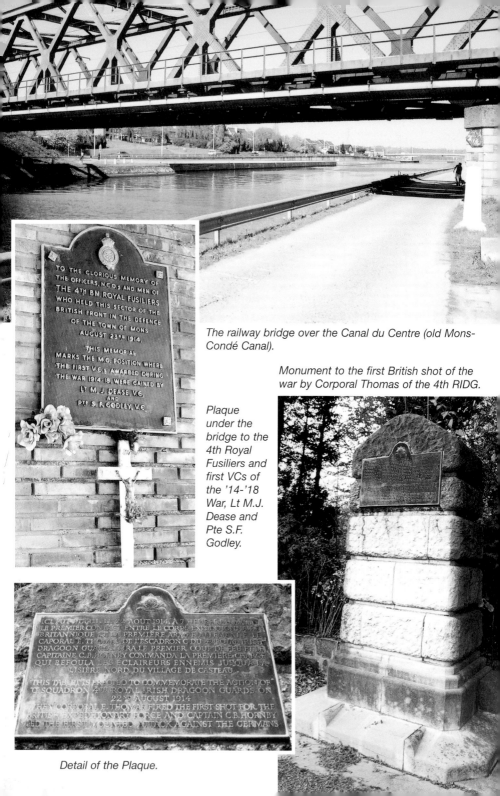

The railway bridge over the Canal du Centre (old Mons-Condé Canal).

Monument to the first British shot of the war by Corporal Thomas of the 4th RIDG.

Plaque under the bridge to the 4th Royal Fusiliers and first VCs of the '14-'18 War, Lt M.J. Dease and Pte S.F. Godley.

Detail of the Plaque.

Detail of the Plaque.

Site where the 116th Canadian Infantry Battalion welcomed the cease-fire on 11 November 1918.

Plaque to commemorate the stand of the Middlesex at Obourg Station.

General Allenby's cavalry had crossed into Belgium on 21 August and at about 0700 hours on 22 August while riding out from Mons the RIDG, part of the division, made contact with the enemy along this road. Two troops of the Dragoons were involved – 1st Troop who engaged with sabres and 4th Troop who used their rifles. Corporal Thomas, who was in 4th Troop, described what happened:

'I saw a troop of Uhlans coming leisurely down the road, the officer in front smoking a cigar. We were anxiously watching their movements when, quicker than I can write here, they halted, as if they had smelt a rat. They had seen us! They turned quickly back. Captain Hornby got permission to follow on with the sabre troop and down the road they galloped.'

Hornby's 1st Troop charged into the middle of the Germans, who included three cyclists, Hornby himself running a German lieutenant through with his sabre. Meanwhile, as the enemy dismounted and scattered, 4th Troop came up and dismounted too. Corporal Thomas's account continued:

'Bullets were flying past us, and possibly because I was rather noted for my quick movements and athletic ability in those days, I was first in action. I could see a German cavalry officer some four hundred yards away standing mounted in full view of me, gesticulating to the left and to the right as he disposed of his dismounted men and ordered them to take up their firing positions to engage us. Immediately I saw him I took aim, pulled the trigger and automatically, almost as it seemed instantaneously, he fell to the ground, obviously wounded, but whether he was killed or not is a matter that I do not think was ever cleared up.'

In all eight Germans were killed. There were no British casualties and **Captain Hornby** was awarded the **DSO**.

Cross the road back to the plaque on the restaurant wall.

The plaque commemorates the place where, at 1100 hours on 11 November 1918, an advanced post of the 116th Canadian Infantry Battalion welcomed the cease-fire. The Canadian Corps had liberated Mons earlier that day and had continued their advance to this spot where Corporal Thomas had fired the first shot four years before.

Return to your car. Drive back to the first traffic light junction and turn left on Rue Brisée direction Obourg and then take the fourth turning to the right on the Voie d'Hayon, signed Obourg. Continue downhill and turn sharp right following the road under the motorway on Rue St Denis signed Obourg. Continue through Mons-Borinage to Obourg. Continue into the village on a section of cobbled road and at the crossroads turn left on Rue de l'Yser to Obourg Centre and then right on Rue de Portugal. Continue straight through and over the roundabout and follow signs to Mons on the N539. Drive over the canal and the railway and take the first left sharply backward to the railway station. Stop. Walk over the footbridge (and because of its good vantage point the account of the action here is best read from the bridge) to the centre platform. The cement works is on the canal to the west of you from the footbridge. Go down the steps to what seems to be an isolated square brick wall. There is a plaque on the northern face.

• Plaque to the Action at Obourg Railway Station/8.2 miles/15 minutes/Map 2/4

The plaque was unveiled on 9 September 1951 on the old railway building, erected in 1849 and demolished in 1981 when the line was electrified. It was then moved to this brick memorial which is Point 4 on the Mons Tour. It commemorates the stand of the 4th Middlesex here and the bravery of a lone British soldier who held the Germans at bay from the roof of a building which once stood on this spot. The area has changed greatly since 1914 but the line of the old houses on the northern bank and the line of the road on which you have parked give a clear indication of the position of the original bridge.

The Middlesex had taken up fire positions all around the village on 23 August. D Company commanded by Captain Glass covered the bridge and B Company in the station was commanded by Lt Wilmot-Aliston following the death of the company commander and his second in command in the storm of German artillery fire that began around 0800 hours. It was probably in this area that Private J. Parr, the first British soldier to be killed, met his fate. He is buried in St Symphorien cemetery (qv). Lt Wilmot-Aliston became the first British soldier to be taken prisoner by the Germans.

The Middlesex machine guns and rapid fire caused appalling casualties in the thickly packed grey ranks of the six assaulting battalions. As at Nimy, the Germans paused and regrouped, adopting tactical movements co-ordinated with machine gun and artillery fire. Despite support from two companies of the 2nd Battalion RIR at around midday, the Middlesex were forced to withdraw shortly afterwards. Latest reports of Captain Henry Glass were that, despite two legs shattered by machine gun bullets, he remained propped up against a wall of the railway station overseeing the withdrawal of his men. The unknown soldier on the roof covered his comrades as they moved out until he was killed by the advancing Germans. The Middlesex had suffered badly. At the beginning of the day they had been almost one thousand strong. At evening roll call under three hundred answered their names.

Return to the N539, turn left and continue into La Sablonnière. Turn right on the N538 and at the next traffic lights turn right on Rue de la Procession, signed Crematorium. Continue to the large cemetery on the right and stop in the parking space. Walk to the entrance.

• Mons General Cemetery, Belgian Mil & CWGC Plots/10.0 miles/30 minutes/Map 2/5

To the right of the entrance is a **plaque to 24 Heroes of the Resistance, 1940-1945** and to the left the CWGC sign. The cemetery is open 1 March-15 November 0800-1700 and 16 November-29 February 0900-1600. The CWGC plot (P1) is signed to the left inside the entrance and leads one upwards by a series of signs to the plot at the top of the cemetery (a good steep 5 minute walk). A plan of the cemetery may be obtained from the office to the right of the entrance.

At the top the Belgian Military plot is first reached to the left and now also extending to the right for new burials, for this is a cemetery like many American ones (such as Arlington in Washington) where ex-servicemen have the right to be buried with their comrades and the burials are in date order. The majority bear a

Mons General Cemetery, CWGC Plot.

Celtic Cross to 2nd Royal Irish, la Bascule.

Detail of Plaque.

Monument to First and Last Battles, la Bascule, with detail of plaque.

German Memorial to 'Royal' Middlesex, St Symphorien Cemetery.

Headstones of Lt Dease, VC, Pte Parr, Pte Price, St Symphorien Cemetery.

Detail of German Headstone, German Plot, St Symphorien Cemetery.

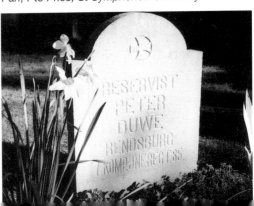

touching photograph of the soldier, often in his wartime uniform. There is a memorial with a fine bust of King Albert at the top of the plot on the left.

The CWGC plot was designed by Sir Edwin Lutyens in a unique and imaginative style. Between the Cross of Sacrifice and the Stone of Remembrance is a row of splendid gold-topped flagpoles and a ceremony takes place here on 11 November each year. The Cemetery Report and Visitor's Book are set in a circular stone seat to the right. There is a fascinating mixture of nationalities and dates of burial here – from 1914-1919 (although the majority seem to be from 1918 and 1919). The later dates were of casualties from the appalling flu epidemic which swept through civil populations and servicemen mal-nourished from four years of deprivation or from men who died as prisoners of war. There are 393 Commonwealth, with 11 unidentified, a Special Memorial to 3 men and 1 WW2, 72 Russians with 2 Unknown, 16 French, 8 Romanian and 1 German with 2 Unknown. They range from **Pte E.B**. **Quinton**, Norfolk Regt, 28 September 1914 and **Cpl R. Richardson**, RFA, 4 October 1914, age 28, to **Maj H.H. Robinson, MC + Bar**, RAMC, 3 May 1919, age 29 'on active service from August 1914'. **Sapper Clifford Lawrence Cashmore**, 4th Can Div, 1 December 1918, 'age 26 years and 11 months', has a distinctive, non-standard headstone. The burials are from the various military hospitals, CCS and Field Ambulances in Mons and include **Major John Southern Maidlow**, 49th Bty, RFA, age 39, one of only two fatal casualties from the burning of the first aid post in Gendebien Château (qv), la Bascule on 23 August 1914.

In the 12 months to April 2003 only 15 visitors had signed the Visitor's Book, only 4 from the UK. This remarkable plot deserves more visitors and the caring CWGC gardeners should have more proof that their dedicated work is seen and appreciated.

Return to the traffic lights, turn left and take the first right turn on Chemin des Mourdreux. Continue to traffic lights at a crossroads. This is la Bascule. Turn left and stop as soon as you can. Walk back to the large memorial.

• The La Bascule Memorials/10.5 miles/10 minutes/Map 2/7 and 2/6

As the BEF fought their way back from the canal line they made a stand here around the crossroads. The keystone of the defence was a small group of some 40 men gathered together by RQMS Fitzpatrick of the 2nd Battalion Royal Irish Regiment and this key crossroads position, so important to the safe withdrawal of the BEF, was held until nightfall. At midnight RQMS Fitzpatrick and 18 survivors continued the withdrawal, thus completing an action for which **Fitzpatrick was later awarded the DCM.**

The memorial was inaugurated in 1952 by Field Marshal Lord Alexander of Tunis and commemorates the two battles of Mons: 1914 and 1918. The architect was Edmond Bertiaux, Director of Mons Municipal Works, who had designed the First Shots Memorial. It consists of a memorial panel flanked by two Tuscan pillars. It claims that 'here' the forces of the British Empire fought the first and last battles of Mons. It was originally in the Belfry garden in the centre of Mons and was moved here in August 1986 when there was another unveiling ceremony.

The junction is sometimes referred to as the 'Binche crossroads'.

Cross the road to the other memorial.

This Celtic cross was unveiled by Sir John French on 11 November 1923. It commemorates the actions of the 2nd Royal Irish (18th Foot).

On the corner diagonally opposite are the grounds of Gendebien Château, now the residence of the C-in-C at SHAPE. At the time of the battle the building was used as the first aid post of the 2nd Royal Irish under the command of their medical officer, Major Long. It was set alight by German shelling but all save two of the wounded were evacuated safely. One of the fatalities, Major J.S. Maidlow of 49th Bty, RFA, is buried in Mons Communal Cemetery (qv).

Return to your car and continue into St Symphorien and at the roundabout follow the signs to the CWGC and German cemeteries. There is a further sign to the left. The cemetery is then on the right.

• Saint Symphorien CWGC Cemetery and Memorials to Middx, R. Fusiliers, R. Irish/12.8 miles/25 minutes/Map 2/12 and 2/13

This is one of the, if not *the*, most unusual and lovely cemeteries on the Western Front. It was begun by the Germans immediately after the battle in the remains of an old potash mine and the layout of the cemetery follows the contours of the spoil heaps, with trees and bushes forming leafy glades connected by small paths. The land was the gift of a local resident, Jean Honzeau de Lehaie, and the architect was W.H. Cowlishaw who, among many other works, also designed the Pozières Memorial and worked on the world's first Garden City at Letchworth.

At one side of the entrance is the bronze box which contains the visitors' book and the Cemetery Report listing all the British soldiers buried here and on the other side is a box containing German information, for men of both sides lie in this cemetery – true 'comradeship in death'. After the Armistice there were 245 Germans and 188 Commonwealth burials. Further graves were then added to make a total of 284 German and 229 Commonwealth (of which 65 are unidentified).

The German graves have grey granite markers grouped regimentally, often with different headstones for officers and men, while the British have the standard white Portland stone headstone. (Harder Italian Carrera-style stone is now used when headstones are replaced.) Among the British are some graves of particular note: **Lt Maurice Dease, VC,** generally accepted as having won the first VC of the war, though four **VCs** were won on the first day of the battle; **Pte J. Parr**, said to be the first British soldier killed in the war. [There is considerable argument about the date of his death: whether it was 22 or 23 August, the date on the headstone having been altered. Two RFC men buried in Tournai Commonwealth War Graves Commission cemetery, 2nd Lieutenants Waterfall and Bayley, were killed on 22 August 1914. Bayley was a distant relative of Gordon of Khartoum and a friend of Lanoe Hawker.]; **Pte J.L. Price** (qv), the last soldier to be killed in the Great War. He was shot by a German sniper at 1058 hours on 11 November 1918 while holding flowers given to him by Belgian civilians grateful for their liberation (he was Canadian); **Pte G.E. Ellison** of the 5th Royal Irish Lancers, who was the last British soldier to be killed in the War, also on 11 November 1918 and whose grave is almost directly opposite Parr's.

The Germans erected a number of distinctive memorials in the cemetery – to the 'Royal' Middlesex Regiment (a column surmounted by a sphere), to the Royal Fusiliers (a curved stone seat), to the Royal Irish Regiment, and an obelisk to the dead of both armies. Details and locations of all of these are given in the cemetery register.

• *End of Mons Battlefield Tour OR*

Extra Visit to Villers-St-Ghislain (Gen Allenby 1914 HQ)/Ville-sur-Haine Memorial to Pte Price (Map 2/14) Approximately 5.1 miles. Approximate time: 20 minutes

Return to the main road and turn right on the N90 to Villers-St-Ghislain.
In the school and teachers's house of this village (which remain much as they were in 1914) **Gen Allenby had his HQ in August 1914.**

Continue through the village and at the crossroads turn left to Havre. In the village continue downhill to the church and turn right. Continue over the railway line and two canals, turning left into the village of Ville-sur-Haine. Turn left at the crossrods just before the Town Hall on the right and drive down towards the canal.

On the right is a red brick memorial with a bronze plaque 'To the memory of 256265 **Private George Lawrence Price**, 28th North West Bn, 6th Can Inf Bde, killed in action near this spot at 10.58 hours, November 11 1918. The last Canadian soldier to die on the Western Front in the First World War. Erected by his comrades on November 11 1968.'

The memorial was originally erected on the wall of a house on this spot but moved to this brick frame when the house was demolished. It is in a very sad state, covered with graffiti.

You could now finish the tour in the town of Mons by following signs to the E19/E42, direction Mons/Paris and coming off at Mons, following signs to Centre Ville/Grand Place.

Extra Visit to Mons for R/WC and a walking tour of battlefield interest (Map 2/8, 9, 10) Approximate time: 1 hour 30 minutes

Note that there is now no parking in the Grand' Place but there are several well-signed parking areas within easy walking distance. Park as near as you can to the Square.

It is thoroughly recommended that you go first to the Tourist Office (qv) (which is between the magnificent theatre building and the fine Gothic 15th Century Town Hall) to pick up a town plan and lists of restaurants/hotels etc. There is a variety of restaurants around the typical Flemish square – from the cheap and cheerful to the gourmet. And it makes a good lunch stop. Be conscious, however, that the status of the Mons battlefields seems to have diminished of recent years. Monuments are neglected, what was once a superb war museum in the prime site of the Town Hall is now difficult to find and its exhibits sadly depleted.

Walk to the Town Hall.

TO THE MEMORY OF
256265 PRIVATE
GEORGE LAWRENCE PRICE
28TH NORTH WEST BATTALION
6TH CANADIAN INFANTRY BRIGADE
2ND CANADIAN DIVISION
KILLED IN ACTION
NEAR THIS SPOT AT 10.58 HOURS
NOVEMBER 11TH 1918
THE LAST CANADIAN SOLDIER TO DIE
ON THE WESTERN FRONT
IN THE FIRST WORLD WAR
ERECTED BY HIS COMRADES
NOVEMBER 11TH 1968.

A LA MÉMOIRE DU SOLDAT
GEORGE LAWRENCE PRICE
MATRICULE 256265
DU 28 ÈME BATAILLON (NORD OUEST)
6 ÈME BRIGADE, 2 ÈME DIVISION CANADIENNE
TUÉ AU COMBAT EN CET ENDROIT
LE 11 NOVEMBRE 1918 A 10H58
IL FUT LE DERNIER SOLDAT
DU CORPS CANADIEN TUÉ AU
FRONT OUEST DU COURS DE LA
PREMIÈRE GUERRE MONDIALE.
ERIGÉ PAR SES CAMARADES
LE 11 NOVEMBRE 1968

Detail of Plaque.

Memorial to Pte Price, Ville-sur-Haine.

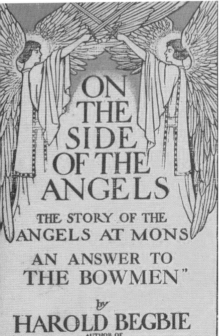

ON THE SIDE OF THE ANGELS

THE STORY OF THE
ANGELS AT MONS
AN ANSWER TO
THE BOWMEN"

by

HAROLD BEGBIE
AUTHOR OF
'BROKEN EARTHENWARE'

ODDER & STOUGHTON . PUBLISHERS . LONDON . E.C

Cover of Harold Begbie's book on the Angels of Mons.

Gun which fired the last shot of WW1, Mons War Museum.

Extra visit continued

Mons Town Hall Plaques (Map 2/8). In the archway of the entrance porch of the Town Hall are **memorial tablets** to the **5th Royal Irish Lancers** who fought in both battles of Mons, unveiled in November 1922 and to the **Canadians** whose **3rd Division** liberated Mons on the morning of 11 November 1918. This was unveiled in 1926. There is also a bronze **plaque to the United States of America**, sculpted by Gustave Jacobs. This is in thanksgiving for the food brought to Belgium from the USA during WW1.

To the left of the archway is an iron monkey, known as the 'Grande Garde' which dates from the Middle Ages but whose origins are shrouded in mystery. Its smoothed surface bears witness to the fact that is considered good luck to touch it.

Walk on to the corner of the square and follow signs uphill via the Rue des Clercs to the Belfry (Beffroi). It is a five-minute puff up a steep hill to the area of the Belfry tower, which stands on the Castle Hill behind the Town Hall.

The Belfry Tower and *Château* Gardens (Map 2/9). The 87m high seventeenth century flamboyant baroque style belfry and the area around it have been undergoing extensive renovations for many years and may not be fully accessible for some time to come. In 1999 UNESCO classified the area as a site of world-wide historical heritage. When finished it is hoped that it will once more be possible to visit the top of the tower which had a lift leading to a panorama describing the battles of 1914, 1918, 1940 and 1944. In a cavity at the base of the tower was buried some soil taken from graves of British and Canadian soldiers killed at Mons in the First World War. During the ceremony, on 3 November 1935, a small silver replica of the tower was given to the British Ambassador as a gift for HM King George V.

Face north beyond the tower.

The overview of the battlefield depends upon the foliage on the trees and general ambient visibility. On the horizon is the east-west motorway that runs from Liège to Valenciennes. At this point it runs parallel to and just behind (north of) the line of the canal defended by II Corps. Straight ahead, i.e. at 12 o'clock, a pool beside the canal may be visible. That is the area of Nimy defended by the Fusiliers where you were at the beginning of the tour. To the right, at 2 o'clock, a cement factory on the horizon marks the canal site defended by the Middlesex.

In the grounds the British and Canadian War Memorial, now moved to the Binche crossroads because of all the renovation work, was unveiled in 1952 by Lord Alexander of Tunis in a ceremony attended by King Baudouin and many other dignitaries. Alexander was then the British Minister of Defence but he had served as a Lieutenant in the 1st Irish Guards at Mons in August 1914.

Return to the rue des Clercs and follow signs to Place du Chapitre and

Extra visit continued

St Waudru's Church. This historic 15th Century church (which has a fascinating and valuable collection of treasures and relics relating to Saint Waudru) contains one of the series of over 30 Commemorative Tablets, designed by Lt Col M.P.L. Cart de Lafontaine, FRIBA, executed by Reginald Hallward and with an inscription by Rudyard Kipling, that were erected in cathedrals and important churches in Belgium and France, with replicas at CWGC HQ at Maidenhead, in Westminster Abbey and at Delville Wood.

Return to the Grand' Place and exit from it on rue de la Clef and turn right on rue de Houdain. Continue to the museum on the left.

The War Museum (Map 2/10)

The original War Museum was established by the Mons local authority in 1930 and occupied an important position on the ground floor and third floors of what was, in 1625, the town pawn shop in the grounds of the Town Hall. It has now been relegated to this somewhat difficult to find site and many of its fascinating exhibits have disappeared. At its entrance is the gun which fired the last shot of WW1.

Inside the entrance is a copy of the large oil painting which used to hang in the old museum depicting the legend of the **'Angels of Mons'**. During the evening of 23 August, bowmen 'angels' allegedly appeared in the sky over Mons and prevented the Germans from annihilating the British. Although many sworn affidavits from highly respectable 'witnesses' were produced verifying the heavenly intervention, it was all an invention of Arthur Machen, a journalist with the *Evening News*, which published the story on 29 September 1914. He wrote it to relieve his despair at the retreat of the British Army. Later he admitted that the stories of the angels were 'every one of 'em lies, sir'. However, this did not deter the believers. Harold Begbie wrote a book, *On the Side of the Angels*, maintaining that they had indeed appeared and offering various 'eye witness' accounts. By Christmas 1915 the book was in its third edition.

Some of the famous collection of 26 drums, four of which were found on the battlefield, the other 22 being presented by Regiments which fought at Mons, are still on display, as is the original headstone of Pte Price (qv), last Canadian soldier to lose his life on 11 November 1918.

There is also a Second World War section which covers the Occupation, the Resistance and the Liberation by the Americans on 2 September 1944.

There is a small entrance charge and opening hours are published as Tues-Sat 1200-1800 hours, Sun 1000-1200 and 1400-1800. Tel: + (0) 65 33 52 13. Check current times with the Tourist Office (qv).

NB. At the junction of the Boulevard Dolez and Avénue des Guérites is a grey granite obelisk to the **'Big Red 1' (Map 2/11)**, similar to that overlooking OMAHA Beach in Normandy, commemorating the liberation battle by the US Division of 2-4 September 1944.

LE CATEAU

26 AUGUST 1914

'Early on that memorable day the Cornwalls, after a
wretched night, stood to arms.
It was still dark and their clothes were sodden with rain:
many had not slept at all. Stand To was the worst hour
of the day: chilled through and drowsy.'

DCLI Regimental History.

'When men are too tired to march, they must lie down and fight.'

Gen Sir Horace Smith-Dorrien, GCB, DSO, Commanding II Corps.

SUMMARY OF THE BATTLE

Following its defeat at Mons on 23 August 1914 the BEF fell back to the south, pursued by the Germans. Just after dawn three confused days later, on the anniversary of the Battle of Crécy, von Kluck's army caught Smith-Dorrien's tired II Corps at le Cateau from where, after a morning's battle, the retreat continued. British casualties were about 8,000 men and 38 guns. German casualties are estimated at 9,000.

OPENING MOVES

The plan of the French Commander-in-Chief, General Joffre, to counter the German invasion was known as 'Plan 17'. Its essential idea was that of a massive counter-attack through the German centre to the south-east of Belgium. What came out of Plan 17 was a series of four major engagements known as 'The Battle of the Frontiers'.

In three of the battles in Lorraine, the Ardennes and on the Sambre, the French, following their tactical doctrine of *l'attaque à l'outrance* (attack to the extreme), threw themselves forward into the maelstrom of German machine-gun and artillery fire without apparent regard to tactical caution.

The French offensive stopped in bloody confusion with over 300,000 casualties and the armies began to withdraw.

The fourth 'Battle of the Frontiers' was the stand of the BEF at Mons on 23 August and as night fell Sir John French, the British Commander-in-Chief, had in mind to continue the defence the following day.

The French 5th Army to the immediate right of the BEF was under the command of the 62-year-old General Lanrézac who, believing that the security of his whole army was threatened, that same night of 23 August gave the order for a general retreat without telling Joffre – or the BEF. Fortunately there was a British liaison officer with

MAP 3: II CORPS STAND AT LE CATEAU, 26 AUGUST 1914

Legend Map 3
1. l'Arbre Rond
2. International CWGC Cem
3. Suffolk Mem
4. 66 Div Mem
5. Gun in library
6. Highland CWGC Cem

Legend Map 3a
1. Ors Communal Cem
2. Wilfred Owen WFA Mem
3. 1Div Mem
4. Mazinghien Communal Cem

MAP 3A

Bazuel
D160a
Ors
D360
Catillon
N43
D160
Mazinghien
Châpeau
Rouge

N
Scale
0   2kms

GER 8 DIV   IV CORPS

GER 7 DIV

Mons
55kms

D932

Le Cateau

2 Suffolk
2 Manch
2 ASH

14 Bde

GER 27 IR
4pm-7pm

River Selle

St Benin

III CORPS
GER 5 DIV

D12

D21

D932

Roman Road

5 DIV
Area

13 Bde

N43

15 Bde

Troisvilles

HQ II CORPS

Bertry

HQ 5 DIV

Reumont

D98

Honnechy

N

Scale
0   800m

© TVH 2004

the 5th Army who brought the news of the withdrawal to Sir John in his HQ at le Cateau just before midnight. Orders were sent immediately for the BEF to retire.

General Haig's I Corps, which had not been in action, received its orders by wire at 0200 hours on 24 August and was underway before dawn. General Smith-Dorrien's II Corps HQ was not in telegraphic contact, having been in battle all day at Mons, and its orders did not arrive until 0300 hours. As II Corps began to move it was once more under fire.

Sir John French oscillated between innocent optimism and extreme pessimism about the military situation. The British High Command did not trust the French and Lanrézac's retreat reinforced that attitude. When Lord Kitchener had briefed the British C-in-C on the responsibilities of the BEF he had said that it was 'to support and co-operate with the French Army' but had added 'You will in no case come in any sense under the orders of any allied general'. Sir John had met Lanrézac on 17 August, a week before Mons. Neither spoke the other's language and the meeting ended uncomfortably. Thus nation to nation there was hardly accord in the adjoining allied forces.

Yet things were just as bad within the BEF. Douglas Haig, commanding I Corps under Sir John, wrote in his diary, 'I know that (Sir John) French is quite unfit for this great command', while Sir John was not at all pleased at the appointment of Horace Smith-Dorrien to command II Corps. He had named General Plumer to take over after the original Corps commander died, but Kitchener chose Smith-Dorrien, who himself wasn't the greatest fan of the C-in-C. These antipathies laid reins over the course of the coming battle and led to unpleasant post-war altercations as to whether the battle of le Cateau need ever have been fought.

At 2025 hours on 24 August Sir John French issued 'Operation Order No. 7'. It said in part:

'The army will move tomorrow, 25th inst, to a position in the neighbourhood of le Cateau, exact positions will be pointed out on the ground tomorrow. '

It was a long march. I Corps was to take the eastern half of the position and II Corps the western. On average the troops had to march between 20 and 25 miles. I Corps routes were very complex, crossing and recrossing the River Sambre, and they were also occupied here and there by the retreating French. Thus I Corps fell behind II Corps and communication between the Corps was lost.

At 2100 hours on 25 August Smith-Dorrien received orders from GHQ to continue the withdrawal on the following day and not to make a stand. Yet II Corps actually stood and fought. The reader is invited to consider the circumstances in which the decision to fight was made and for that purpose should now assume the identity of General Smith-Dorrien. Imagine that it is 0200 hours on the morning of 26 August. Your Corps has been on the move for 24 hours, marching along roads thick with refugees. It is dark. It is raining. You have no communications with I Corps but you have heard rumours that they are behind (to the north) of you and that they are under pressure from the Germans.

Your troops are tired and are now approaching the town of le Cateau, which offers a certain solidity for defence and some comfort from the elements. You may get an idea of the conditions from this account by Frank Richards, a soldier in the

Royal Welch Fusiliers, who described in *Old Soldiers Never Die* how he got to the town from Mons:

'We marched all night and the greatest part of the next day and dug trenches. We were only in those trenches a few hours before we were on the march again... We marched all night again and all next day. We arrived in le Cateau about midnight, dead-beat to the world. I don't believe any one of us at this time realised that we were retiring, though it was clear that we were not going in the direction of Germany. Of course the officers knew, but they were telling us that we were drawing the enemy into a trap. Le Cateau that night presented a strange sight. Everyone was in a panic, packing up their stuff on carts and barrows to get away south in time. The Royal Welch camped on the square in the centre of the town. We were told to get as much rest as we could. The majority sank down where they were and fell straight asleep.'

General Allenby suddenly arrives at your HQ and says, in effect, 'The high ground before le Cateau that I planned to hold to cover your retreat tomorrow has been taken by the enemy. I cannot contact General French and in my opinion the Germans will attack you at first light unless you can get away now and in the dark.' You are also out of contact with GHQ which has moved back to St Quentin. It is up to you alone to decide what to do. You call in your divisional commanders to report to you. They virtually say, 'Many men are separated from their units', or 'The men are too weary to move before the morning', or 'The roads are jammed with refugees', or 'Some roads have been washed out by the storm.'

What would you decide to do? Would you obey your order to continue to retreat? Smith-Dorrien decided to disobey his orders and to stay and fight on the ridge which runs behind the town and roughly parallel to the le Cateau-Cambrai road.

WHAT HAPPENED

Shortly after dawn on 26 August, German troops of the left hand column of III (Ger) Corps entered le Cateau and came up against elements of 5th Division – the Duke of Cornwall's Light Infantry (DCLI) and East Surreys – near the railway bridge, when after a short fire fight conducted from the windows of the houses the British withdrew to the high ground behind the town.

Realising that the British meant to stand and fight, von Kluck decided to mount a frontal attack with IV (Ger) Corps behind an artillery barrage on the main British line behind the Cambrai-le Cateau road, and to send III (Ger) Corps to the east to outflank the BEF (see **Map 3**). The British line consisted of 5th Division on the high ground astride the Roman road covering from le Cateau to Troisvilles, 3rd Division to the west up to Caudry and the newly arrived 4th Division beyond that.

An early German cavalry attack on the extreme left of the BEF was checked and German small arms activity then focused upon the 5th Division area through the morning, with infantry pressing forward tactically across the broken ground with machine guns, and using the spire of le Cateau church as an Observation Point (OP). By mid-morning the Germans controlled the high ground to the east of the River Selle and had uncovered the end of the British position.

The morning had been an artillery battle above all else, with some 230 Royal

Artillery pieces ranged against about 550 of the enemy along the total frontage of about 13 miles. The 5th Division area from the le Cateau spur to Troisvilles was about 4½ miles and consisted mostly of cut cornfields with patches of beet and clover, dramatically different to the houses and slag heaps of Mons. With the exception of the broken ground behind the railway station the general aspect was one of gently rolling Atlantic waves of open fields. There was little opportunity to find cover for guns or for men.

The Germans continued to concentrate their efforts upon the le Cateau spur across which the Roman road struck straight through to St Quentin. A breakthrough at le Cateau could divide and perhaps destroy Smith-Dorrien's Corps. The main strain of the attack fell upon the King's Own Yorkshire Light Infantry (KOYLI) and the Suffolks and an attempt to reinforce them by the Manchesters and two companies of the Argylls failed. Nevertheless, at midday the British line still held.

Inexorably von Kluck's forces built up against the open right flank and by 1300 hours the British on the exposed spur were under artillery fire from three German divisions and under frontal and flank attacks by a dozen infantry battalions. It was time to get out.

Smith-Dorrien decided to withdraw by divisions from right to left, i.e. 5th Division would be the first to move. His order was issued at 1340 hours but much of the line communication had been destroyed by the artillery bombardments and the message had to be delivered by runner. 5th Division HQ received the order at 1400 hours, forward units got it at 1500 hours. 2nd KOYLI and 2nd Suffolk never got it at all and by 1600 hours they were surrounded and wiped out.

The Royal Artillery had suffered badly. Not a single Battery left on the ridge was capable of sustained action, being damaged or without horses or ammunition. But some guns could be saved – *had* to be saved – and, in volunteering to return to the ridge and recover the remaining two guns of 37 (Howitzer) Battery, **Drivers Fred Luke and Job Drain, as well as their officer, Captain Douglas Reynolds, won the VC**. Luke survived to serve with the RAF Regt in WW2. Drain also survived and formed part of the Honour Guard at the burial of the Unknown Soldier at Westminster Abbey on 11 November 1920. Both he and Luke attended the VC Reunion Dinner given at the House of Lords on 9 November 1929. On 9 September Reynolds silenced a battery which he had discovered while reconnoitring, was severely wounded on 15 September and killed at Le Touquet on 23 February 1916. He is buried in Etaples Mil Cemetery.

Thus II Corps withdrew from le Cateau, having stopped the German advance for half a day in a battle that many, including Sir John French, said should never have been fought. Others believed that the fight had saved the BEF and even the C-in-C in his Despatch dated 7 September 1914 wrote, 'I cannot close the brief account of this glorious stand of the British troops without putting on record my deep appreciation of the valuable services rendered by General Sir Horace Smith-Dorrien. I say without hesitation, that the saving of the left wing of the Army under my command on the morning of August 26 could never have been accomplished unless a commander of rare and unusual coolness, intrepidity and determination had been present to conduct the operation personally.'

Later French was to vilify the II Corps Commander (who was extremely popular with his men and whose cheery smile was recorded as being a great morale-raising factor during the Retreat) and accuse him of disobeying orders at le Cateau. In 1915 he had Smith-Dorrien recalled to England.

However, contact with the Germans had been broken. They did not immediately pursue and the BEF was able to breathe a little more easily as it fell back towards Paris and the Marne. Le Cateau cost over 8,000 casualties and 38 guns.

THE BATTLEFIELD TOUR

L'Abre Rond.

- **The Route:** The tour begins near the 'Arbre Rond', then visits the International Cemetery, continues through le Cateau to the 66th Div Commemorative Horse Trough. It then visits Ors on the Sambre-Oise Canal where the poet Wilfred Owen was killed – his grave in the CWGC Comm Cem and the WFA Memorial; the 1st Div Memorial at La Groise; the Highland Cemetery and the Suffolk Memorial on the le Cateau Ridge.
- **Extra Visit** to 5th Div Battle HQ, Reumont.
- **Total distance:** 27.9 miles
- **Total time:** 2 hours 30 minutes
- **Distance to Calais from start point** via Cambrai: 105 miles. Motorway Tolls
- **Base town:** Cambrai
- **Map:** IGN 2607 Est Le Cateau 1:25,000 and 2707

From Calais take the A26/E15 and then the E17 to the junction with the E19/A2. Take the Cambrai direction and come off at Exit 14 on the N30. Follow signs to Cambrai Centre then follow signs to Valenciennes around the town and pick up signs to F[aubour]g du Cateau and then le Cateau on the N43. Continue through Beaumont. As the Roman road rises to a crest after Inchy you are effectively in No Man's Land with the German assaults coming from your left towards 5th Division positions on your right.

Turn right just before the restaurant 'Le Pendu' on the D98. **Set your mileometer to 0.** *Continue to Troisvilles to the large calvary in the village. Keep left and continue to a crossroads with another calvary.*

N.B. In the **Troisvilles Communal Cemetery** ahead are 30 British WW1 burials, over half of whom are Unknown and which include 5 Special Memorials to men who fell on 26 August 1914. The cemetery was first used by the Germans in August 1914 and by British units in 1918.

Turn left along a track which is driveable if reasonably dry. Continue to the lone tree to the right of the electricity pylons.

• L'Arbre Rond/1.7 miles/5 minutes/Map 3/1

This is Point 138, l'Arbre Rond, on the IGN map. At the time of the battle trees were few and far between in the area and the tree that stood here was about 40 ft high. It was marked on the maps that the Germans had and they used the tree as a marker on which to range their artillery.

The 15th Brigade of 5th Division held this area with Brigade HQ nearby in the cutting. The 1st Norfolks were tasked to prepare the defences – and they wanted the tree down so that the German guns could not range upon it. They set about sawing it through but never quite finished the job.

There are various accounts about the fate of the tree and the reported planting of a sapling in the late 1950s, but the romantic can scrutinize the gnarled trunk and be convinced that healed saw cuts can still be discerned.

Return to the N43 and turn right. Continue to the crossroads and turn left signed to le Cateau Mil and German Cemetery. Continue to the cemetery on the right.

• Le Cateau CWGC International Military and German Cemeteries/5.4 miles/20 minutes/Map 3/2

This is also known as the International Cemetery because of the considerable number of British, German and Russian burials. The ground was laid out by the Germans in February 1916 with plots for their own and for the British dead which have separate entrances and visitors' books. There are over 5,000 Germans buried here (most in a mass grave) including some females. There are a number of large German memorials including a pyramid structure on which is embossed *See Getreu bis den Tod* (Faithful unto Death). Curiously a very similar pyramid is to be found on the 1942 battlefield of El Alamein to commemorate German fighter pilot Captain H. J. Marseille. Also in this cemetery is a memorial column erected by the Leibkurassier Regiment which names its casualties on the day of the battle. Thirty-four Russian prisoners lie together in a separate plot.

The British burials number some 640, buried in sections representative of 1914 and 1918 and include 3 UK Navy, 473 UK Army, 1 UK Airforce and 182 Unknown, 6 Australians, 2 Canadians and 1 Unknown, 2 New Zealanders, 24 South African and 4 Unknown and 2 German. The CWGC Plots were designed by Charles Holden. There is also a French plot at the back which is not listed in the Cemetery Report.

Here is buried **Lance Corporal John William Sayer, VC,** 8th Queen's R W Surreys, who won his award for an action on 21 March 1918 at Le Verguier where he held on to his post under heavy fire until nearly all the garrison was killed. He was captured and died of wounds incurred on that day on 18 April 1918. Also buried here is **Capt the Hon Robert Bruce,** 34, 2nd ASH, 26 August 1914, 'Master of Burleigh' and **Capt Archibald Kennedy,** 2nd ASH, 26 August 1914, brother of Capt P. A. Kennedy, who has a Private Memorial (qv) in Fromelles.

This general area formed a focus for the attacks of the 7th (Ger) Division and from here the German artillery had clear views over the British positions.

Walk to the southern border of the cemetery.

The view to the south is directly towards the high ground of the le Cateau ridge beyond the town and over which runs the Roman road (a southern extension of the road you have just used) and on which 5th Division made its stand. Note the white water tower on your left. It is a useful reference point.

Return to the N43, turn left and continue into le Cateau, uphill past the splendid Matisse Museum on the left to the Mairie on the left with some parking.

On the *Mairie* wall is a list of citizens shot by the Germans, including seven who were executed for flouting the prohibition on keeping carrier pigeons [and there is a major memorial to the pigeons and a similar martyr in Lille]. Beside it is the **Tourist Information Office** where leaflets listing the town's hotels and restaurants may be obtained. Sadly the Hotel Mouton Blanc, where the patronne hid several wounded British officers in August 1914, is no more.

During the Retreat Sir John French had his advance HQ in the *Mairie* at Bavay but visited le Cateau (where his main GHQ was situated) briefly on 24 August 1914 when he was gratified to see the leading elements of 4th Division. He then moved GHQ to St Quentin on the evening of the 25th.

Continue uphill and turn left on the N43 signed Toutes Directions. Continue to the first traffic lights at a crossroads.

N.B. To the right is the Rue du Marché aux Chevaux in which is the town Library. In it may be found one of the **British field guns (Map 3/5)** that took part in the 1914 action. By turning left at the end of the road is the Rue de Fesmy on which is the local Cemetery. Incorporated into it is the **British Le Cateau Communal Cemetery** which was used by the Germans to bury British dead in August and September 1914 and by the British in the last three months of 1918. In it there are some 150 burials including thirteen Australians. The Germans used le Cateau as a railhead and had a major hospital in the area. It is likely that the British had medical facilities here too as many of those buried in the cemetery died after the Armistice, including **Chaplain 4th Class Ernest Edward Johnson** on 1 December 1918.

Drive straight over and park as soon as you can. Walk back to the crossroads.

• 66th Division Commemorative Horse Trough/6.9 miles/5 minutes/Map 3/4

At the corner on the right as you walk back is a horse trough with a plaque in memory of the members of the 66th Division of the BEF who 'fell in the liberation of le Cateau from German occupation in October 1918'. The town was entered late on 10 October 1918, after four years of occupation, by the 5th Connaught Rangers.

Return to your car and continue on the N43 under the Cambrai-Ors railway and through Bazuel. Just before the Poilu Memorial fork left on the D160A to Ors. Turn left on the D160B following green CWGC signs to Ors Communal Cemetery. Stop at the local cemetery on the right. Walk through the local graves to the hedge-enclosed CWGC plot at the rear.

German Pyramid Memorial,
International Cemetery, le Cateau.

JOSEF MEISSNER
GEFREITER
† 26.8.1914

PAUL HAUKE
GEFREITER
† 26.8.1914

BERNHARD BITTNER
KÜRASIER
† 26.8.1914

2/708 UND 749

Headstone of L/Cpl Sayer, VC

German grave marker,
26 August 1914.

66th Division Commemorative Horse Trough, le Cateau.

IN MEMORY OF THOSE OF THE 66TH DIVISION
OF THE BRITISH EXPEDITIONARY FORCE
WHO FELL IN THE LIBERATION OF LE CATEAU
FROM GERMAN OCCUPATION IN OCTOBER 1918

• Grave of Wilfred Owen, Ors Communal Cemetery/11.5 miles/15 minutes/Map 3A/1

In the back row is a headstone inscribed '**Lieutenant W.E.S. Owen, MC**, Manchester Regiment, 4th November 1918. Age 25.' A somewhat reluctant soldier – he didn't join up (in the Artists' Rifles) until 15 October 1915 – Owen was commissioned in the Manchester Regiment on 4 June 1916. He arrived in France in January 1917 and saw action near Serre on the Somme. In March he was concussed but rejoined his battalion in April at Savy where he was shell-shocked. Then followed the famous episode at Craiglockhart War Hospital near Edinburgh where he met Siegfried Sasson and Robert Graves and wrote some of his most searing war poetry. He rejoined the 5th Manchesters in November and the following month was promoted to full Lieutenant. In August 1918 he arrived at Etaples and subsequently rejoined the Manchesters at Amiens. For his part in an action at Beaurevoir-Fonsomme Owen was awarded the MC. The reluctant soldier had become a fine regimental officer. In October his battalion took over the line west of the Sambre-Oise Canal and by 2 November they had cleared the west bank at Ors of the last enemy. Owen was detailed to lead his company in the dangerous canal crossing by raft with orders that there should be 'no retirement under any circumstances'. At 0545 on 4 November the Manchesters pressed on despite murderous fire from the heavily defended German bank. At 0700 hours, under swirling mist and gas, the attack was aborted. Among the dead were Owen, **2nd Lt James Kirk** and **A/Lt Col John Neville Marshall, CO** of the nearby Lancashires. Both the latter were awarded the **VC** for their gallantry and cool leadership during the costly crossing

Headstones of Lt Wilfred Owen, VC and 2nd Lt James Kirk, VC, Ors Comm CWGC Cemetery

WFA Plaque to Crossing of the Sambre-Oise Canal.

Detail of Plaque.

and their graves are in the same row as Owen's.

In one of the war's tragic ironies, his beloved mother, Susan, received the telegram informing the family of his death as the Armistice bells were ringing in his home town of Shrewsbury.

Owen's short military career provided him with the material for the unforgettable poetry, such as *Anthem for Doomed Youth, Dulce et Decorum Est* and *Strange Meeting*, that make him probably the most read of all the Great War poets.

The D160B on which you are parked is a no-through road. Beyond in the forest is the old military camp (marked on local maps) where the Manchesters gathered before the attack on the canal. At the far end of the forest, approached from the D959 le Cateau-Landrecies road, is the 'Forester's House'. On 31 October Owen wrote home from 'The Smoky Cellar of the Forester's House' an upbeat, but sadly ironic, letter, warmly and enthusiastically describing the camaraderie of the officers and their servants. 'It is a great life.... There is no danger here, or if any, it will be well over before you read these lines'. There are now plans by the local authorities to create a **Wilfred Owen Museum in the old Forester's House**. This will be part of an ambitious 'Cité de la créativité' cultural project for the site. For details contact the *Mairie* (Monsieur Duminy) at Ors, Tel: + (0)3 27 77 62.

Turn round, return to the main road and turn left into Ors, passing the Mairie on the right. Drive over the canal and park immediately on the right. Walk back over the bridge to the memorial on the left as you walk.

• *Wilfred Owen WFA Memorial, Ors/12.1 miles/10 minutes/ Map 3A/2*

The handsome black WFA plaque was unveiled by the Chairman of the Wilfred Owen Association in 1991. It commemorates the crossing of the Sambre-Oise Canal by 32nd Division on 4 November 1918 during which four VCs were won and amongst whose casualties was the poet Wilfred Owen, killed on the towpath about one kilometre to the north of the bridge.

The surviving **VCs were Res Maj Arnold Horace Santo Waters (later Sir Arnold) and Sapper Adam Archibald.**

Return to your car and continue to the next turn to the right on the D360 signed Catillon/La Groise. Continue to the junction with the N43 and turn left signed La Groise. Follow signs to Guise and continue to the traffic lights. Turn sharp left on the D934 and stop immediately by the memorial on the right.

•*1st Division Memorial/15.6 miles/5 minutes/Map 3A/3*

This handsome memorial was erected 'To the Glory of God and to the abiding memory of the 1st Division of the BEF which from August 1914 to November 1918 served and suffered in France and left there close upon 160,000 dead'. It bears the quotation 'Who [sic] stands if freedom fall, Who dies if England live?' from Rudyard Kipling's 1914 poem, *For All we Have and Are*. It shows the figure of St Michael.

A plaque bears the ORBAT of the Division and a further plaque records that the memorial was re-erected by 32nd Eng Regt and blessed in the presence of the

Mayor and Citizens of La Groise and officers and Maj-Gen Alexander-Sinclair and men of the 1st Division based in Germany on 28 August 1977. At that time it was moved back from the roadside where it had been hit several times by passing cars. Since that time the memorial has been maintained by the CWGC for the MOD. It stands at the crossroads where at noon on the 26 August 1914 the Division was first attacked and compelled to fall back and where on the morning of 4 November 1918 those crossroads formed the centre of its line of consolidation seven days before the Armistice. It is, therefore, rather like the 'First and Last Shots' memorials at Mons (qv). The original memorial was sculpted by R. Goulden in 1926 and cast by A.B. Burton. It was inaugurated on 17 April 1927 in the presence of Marshal Foch, Lt-Gen Sir Arthur Holland and Sir Peter Strickland.

Return to Catillon and continue on the N43, over the Sambre-Oise Canal and turn left to Maizinghien on the D160. At the crossroads in the town turn right on the D115 signed le Cateau.

On the right is the **local Maizinghien cemetery with a green CWGC plaque (Map 3A/4)** on the wall. It contains a line of headstones from 4 November 1918, including 7 Loyal North Lancs buried shoulder to shoulder and 1 Unknown German from the same date.

Turn right on the D12 to le Cateau. Continue to the cemetery on the left. Stop and walk to the back wall of the cemetery.

• Highland CWGC Cemetery/24.3 miles/15 minutes/Map 3/6/OP

At the back of the cemetery look right along the wall and just to the left on the skyline are two distinct poplar trees. This is the area of le Cateau Station where the first German attacks began. Left of the poplars is a line of trees and just on their left, as they end, the Suffolk Memorial may be visible on the skyline.

Further left is a factory complex which indicates, to a first approximation, the route of the valley of the Selle and left again a large single bushy-top tree on the skyline indicates the village of Reumont where 5th Division had its HQ. It is readily seen from here how the German 5th Division's advance from the railway station area up the Selle River Valley outflanked the Suffolk's position. The skyline running right to left is the route of the Roman road and indicates the line taken by the British 5th Division as it retired on the afternoon of 26 August.

Rudyard Kipling called these military cemeteries 'Silent Cities' and a look at a number of graves here shows the diverse nature of some of them: **Pte Osborne**, an Australian, was wounded, commissioned, invalided out, rejoined and then killed; **Rfmn King**, a deacon, the son of a priest, who had to obtain his Bishop's permission to enlist; **Lt Skemp**, Professor of English at Bristol University; **Pte Supple**, a 19-year-old boy; **Pte Torgerson**, an American from Minnesota.

The cemetery was begun by the 50th (Northumbrian) Division in October 1918 and the name comes either from the high ground on which the cemetery stands or the 32 graves of the Black Watch that are contained within it. Altogether there are some 620 burials.

1st Division Memorial, la Groise. *The Suffolk Memorial, le Cateau.*

Highland CWGC Cemetery, le Cateau.

Continue towards le Cateau under the railway bridge.
To the left is the le Cateau Railway Station.
Continue to the traffic lights and go straight over on the D21 following signs downhill to J. Rostand College to the main road and turn left on the N43. Continue uphill to the traffic lights and turn left, still following signs to the College. Continue past the hospital on the right and bear left and then right until you reach the College. Just before it is a bumpy track to the right. This can be negotiated by car if dry (if wet 4-wheel-drive would be advisable) and you have good ground clearance. Keep to the right at the fork at the top of the hill and continue to the memorial in the clump of trees.

• *The Suffolk Memorial/26.6 miles/15 minutes/Map 3/3*

You are now on the high ground of Point 139. This marks the centre of the Suffolks' position, one of the four infantry regiments that made up 14th Brigade, part of 5th Division. The other regiments were the 1st East Surreys, the 1st Duke of Cornwall's Light Infantry and the 2nd Manchester Regiment.

The original II Corps order issued from Corps HQ at 2215 hours on 25 August, just over an hour after Sir John French's withdrawal order arrived, envisaged the retreat continuing on 26 August and early that morning the Suffolks had already started to withdraw when, at 0600 hours in thick morning mist, they were stopped and told to hold the spur. Half of the Brigade did not receive that order and were in the skirmish action near the railway station. The Suffolks, therefore, had no choice of position and had to scratch shallow trenches where they stood, taking up thin firing lines on the forward slope of the feature you have just climbed and facing in an arc generally to the north and north-east.

The supporting artillery, 11th, 52nd and 37th (Heavy) batteries of 15th Brigade Royal Field Artillery (RFA), was lined up some 200 yards behind the Suffolk's trenches but in front of reserve troops so that the guns were actually sited among the infantry. As you can see the position is totally exposed. The only camouflage available to the gunners were stooks of corn which they lashed to the gun wheels.

By facing north you can see the white water tower referred to at the International Cemetery, and to the east the skyline marks the high ground beyond the valley of the River Selle, ground that the Germans occupied very early in the morning and thus opened II Corps' right flank. The initial forward movement of von Kluck's forces was towards you from the right of the tower as you look at it and German forces worked their way south along the valley of the River Selle. German machine guns were sited in the area of the tower.

Lt Col Stevens commanding 15th Brigade RFA told 52nd Battery, 'We will fight it out here and there will be no retirement', and before the guns could be properly dug in they came under rifle fire. Soon after 0600 hours German artillery opened up causing considerable casualties among the gunners and the drop-shorts fell on the Suffolks in their shallow trenches.

At about 1000 hours a German infantry attack began to develop from the area of the River Selle (see **Map 3** for orientation) just south of le Cateau and 52nd Battery inflicted considerable damage on the enemy despite having several limbers set on fire by a German HE shell. Another infantry attack began at noon from the ground left and inclusive of the white water tower. Once again it was discouraged by the artillery. The gunners' fire controller had his OP well forward in the front line of the Suffolk trenches and his instructions to the guns were relayed back by a chain of orderlies lying out in the open because all telephone wires had been destroyed.

The volume of noise beating down on the trenches was horrendous. German HE shells from some one hundred guns were bursting overhead and our own guns, between 100 and 200 yards away, added their own cacophony as they returned fire.

Despite attempts at reinforcement by the Manchesters and Argyll and Sutherland Highlanders, the courageous tenacity of the gunners and the steady markmanship of the Suffolks, the German effort built up steadily against this flank, moving ever closer and at mid-morning an aerial observer reported that a 6-mile long column of German infantry was moving down the Roman road towards the crossroads (near the International Cemetery which you visited earlier).

As targets appeared the artillery engaged them but, of the four British batteries supporting the positions on the ridge, only one remained intact at the end of the morning and most of the ammunition in the lines had been used. The 52nd Battery fired over 1,100 rounds in the action. At 1330 hours a message was received ordering the guns to withdraw, but heavy casualties among the horses, let alone both men and guns, made this no easy task.

'One of the saddest things I have seen was the wounded horses trying to keep themselves on their legs by leaning against the stooks of corn', said one Sapper officer.

Lt Col. Stevens who had earlier told 52nd Battery that there would be 'no retirement' (the word 'retreat' had not yet come into use in the BEF) decided that he needed confirmation of the order to withdraw before acting upon it and it was not until 1400 hours that the guns of the Brigade were told to move. There was no escape for the 52nd, however, because their CO, Major A. C. R. Nutt, did not receive any order at all.

German infantry were attacking to the right of the Suffolks and working clear round them. A hail of machine gun fire poured down from the guns near the water tower. The British field guns fired singly as best as they could, most of the men being dead or wounded, and the last minutes were described by Lt Col Stevens as follows:

'About 2.40 pm some cheering was heard on our right about 300 yards away and over the crest. About five minutes afterwards we heard 'Stand Fast' and 'Cease Fire' sounded and whistles blown. Then it was shouted down the line from the right, 'You are firing on friends'. All firing stopped at once. On standing upright and looking just over the crest we found everyone standing up and the firing line being rounded up by Germans. The position was lost, considerable numbers of the enemy being round our right and right rear.'

The fight had lasted eight hours. The memorial, a cenotaph, commemorates the actions of the Suffolks, the Manchesters, the Argylls and the supporting batteries of the Royal Artillery. It bears the names of the Officers, NCOs and Soldiers who were casualties of those regiments on 26 August 1914, many of whom are buried in the International Cemetery, such as Capt the Hon Bruce (Master of Burleigh), 2nd ASH. There are 3 Drummer Boys: L. C. Hill, D. Yeatsley and A. Offley.

Return to the traffic lights on the main road and turn left on the N43 to Cambrai. Continue to the junction with the D932 below the International Cemetery (27.9 miles).

Extra Visit to 5th Division Battle HQ, Reumont
Round trip: 4.5 miles. Approximate time: 20 minutes

Turn left on to the D932 Roman road. Drive into Reumont and stop at the first building on the left – a pair of semi-detached cottages.

5th Division Battle HQ. The second house of the pair (No 41) was used by the divisional commander, General Sir Charles Fergusson, as an HQ. Until a few years ago the building was marked with a plaque which has since been stolen. General Fergusson watched most of the battle from the roof of this house, from where he could clearly see the parlous state of our right flank as the Germans worked forward along the Selle Valley.

At noon Smith-Dorrien arrived here and the commanders discussed the possibility of retirement. One hour later General Fergusson sent a message to II Corps HQ at Bertry saying that 5th Division could not hold out much longer and at 1320 hours added that he ought to begin to move unless reinforced.

General Smith-Dorrien ordered the move of two reserve battalions to Bertry to come under Fergusson's command and told the divisional commander to withdraw when he thought fit, after which 3rd and 4th Divisions would follow. Fergusson issued his orders around 1400 hours. Forward battalions did not get them until 1500 hours. Some never got them at all, in particular the KOYLI of 13th Brigade who, despite an heroic stand by **Major Yate** for which he was awarded the **VC**, were overwhelmed, only eight officers and 320 men answering the roll that evening.

By 1700 hours the whole of II Corps was in retreat - but in good order with flank guards established. At 1800 hours darkness and rain settled over the long moving column and the German pursuit lost contact.

Return to the N43.

- *End of le Cateau Battlefield Tour*

OR return to le Cateau or Cambrai for RWC.

NOTRE-DAME DE LORETTE, ARTOIS

OCTOBER 1914-OCTOBER 1915

'She must become the voice which weeps for her youth cut down in its
flower, the voice which prays for the eternal rest of their souls, the voice
which talks of hope to the widows, fiancées, parents, the voice which calls
tomorrow's generations to pilgrimages of remembrance and pity.'
Monseigneur Julien, Bishop of Arras
writing about the monument at Notre-Dame de Lorette.

SUMMARY OF THE BATTLES

There are three distinct French actions around Notre-Dame de Lorette which can
be identified as the battles of Artois though their precise dates and results differ
according to the French or British accounts. We give a median interpretation.

The **first** began on 26 October 1914 following the German threat to Arras and
the occupation of Notre-Dame de Lorette and the Ablain St Nazaire heights by the
Bavarians. It ended in French losses of some 125,000 and no gains.

The **second** began on 9 May 1915 (the British Aubers Ridge and Festubert
attacks were part of the same overall offensive) and lasted until 24 June with
estimated losses of 140,000. The French re-took Ablain St Nazaire and the heights
of Notre-Dame de Lorette and Neuville St Vaast but not Souchez or the ground
commanding it. **See Map 4.**

The **third** battle was launched on 25 September 1915 (the British Loos attack was
part of the same overall offensive) and lasted for about three weeks. The French gained
a foothold on Vimy Ridge, took the Labyrinth (qv) and re-captured Souchez at a cost
of 135,000 casualties. German losses were estimated as 178,00. There the lines stayed
until the Arras offensives of April 1917, by which time the battlefield 'resembled a
furious sea, a veritable chaos, the image of the earth after the flood' (Galthier-Boissière).

OPENING MOVES

The war was barely two weeks old when in the middle of August 1914 General
Galliéni began building barricades in Paris against the rapidly approaching
invader and at the end of the month advancing German forces reached Arras,
plundering it on 6 and 7 September but leaving a day later. French resistance before
the Marne was stiffening and as Moltke urged on his troops around Arras to push
on to the French capital, Galliéni and Foch launched surprise attacks against the
Germans. The invader recoiled and thus began the 'Race to the Sea' as the Germans

Lens ▲

To Exit 6.1

D937

A26 E15

Liéven ▲

Aix-Noulette ▲

D58E2

Notre-Dame
de Lorette ▲

D58E

Ablain St
▲ Nazaire

D57

Givenchy-en-Gohelle ▲

D51

N17

Souchez ▲

D58

D55

Carency
▲

Hill 145
Highest point
Vimy Ridge ▲

Vimy ▲

D937

Legend
Approx Front Lines

——— After the First Battle
– – – After the Second Battle
•••• After the Third Battle

Hill 140 ▲

Farbus ▲
▲ Thélus

La Targette ▲

D49

Mont St Eloi ▲

D49

Neuville
St Vaast ▲

D49E

Exit 7

N

Scale
0   2 kms

Site of the
▲ Labyrinth

A26 E15

To Arras →

© TVH 2004

Roclincourt ▲

See also Map 14

were pushed back north. But here they held on to Notre-Dame de Lorette, Ablain St Nazaire, Souchez, Givenchy, Thélus and Vimy – just about all the high ground before Arras – though not Arras itself. That high ground held the key to the Douai plain, its coal mines and industry, and in the next twelve months the French would make three desperate attempts to take it back.

WHAT HAPPENED

The progress of the three battles may be more readily followed by reference to **Map 4**.

The first battle, a series of German attacks and French counter-attacks, followed the advance of the Crown Prince of Bavaria's 62nd Army moving down from the direction of Armentières, which headed for Arras intending to take both the town and its road and rail network as well as the high ground around it.

On 16 September, after the massacre of General d'Amade's territorials at le Transloy on 27/28 August (now commemorated by a significant memorial) the first French troops moved in to defend Arras and some two weeks later, on 2 October, von Arnim's IV Corps moved towards Arras along the Cambrai road, causing many civilians around Givenchy to flee to the west. On 5 October, after a number of cavalry engagements with the French, the Germans occupied Ablain St Nazaire, Aix Noulette, Givenchy, Liévin, Lens, Monchy le Preux, Souchez, Notre-Dame de Lorette and Vimy, effectively cutting Arras off from the north and east. They immediately set about preparing defensive positions with strongpoints and trenches. At about the same time at Feuchy, just below the River Scarpe and some 3 miles due east of Arras, General Barbot and his Alpine troops of 77th Division held the German advance, forcing it to swing to the north and thus saving Arras from immediate occupation. The city then came under the care of General d'Urbal with a defensive force of General Fayolle's 70th Infantry Division (Fayolle would command the French 6th Army on the Somme on 1 July 1916), General Barbot's command (Barbot moved into Arras from Feuchy) and the Zouaves of the 45th Division. Throughout the whole of this period the French mounted counter-attack after counter-attack suffering heavy losses.

On 5 October plans were being made to evacuate the city but General Foch, who the night before had been made Commander-in-Chief of the French forces, arrived and forbade it. General Barbot, despite the fact that his Alpine Division had been reduced to a quarter of its full strength, is reported as having said with great élan, 'While I still live there will be no retirement!'

Taken aback by the stubborn defence of Arras the Germans began to bombard the city at 0930 on 6 October, an artillery offensive that continued day after day including the use of big 210mm and 280mm guns. The attacks intensified. Between 21 and 23 October they were particularly virulent and were watched by the Kaiser, the Germans taking as a target the Belfry tower in the middle of the city. At 1120 on 21 October the 69th shell found its target and to paraphrase a French account, 'The Belfry's cry of agony echoed around the whole town like a plaintive scream of a soul leaving its body.' On the 22nd a determined attack on Arras through St Laurent Blangy, barely a mile and a half north-east of the city, was held by Barbot's Zouaves and Chasseurs so once again the General saved the city.

Arras did not fall and the opposing sides settled down to face the cold wet winter in trenches, much as was happening at Ypres and just like that city Arras, although under siege, would never fall, defended and held by the French (under Pétain who replaced d'Urbal) until March 1916 and thereafter by the British.

The second battle, an attack by the French, was prompted by the fact that the Germans on the high ground were able accurately to direct their artillery fire upon Arras and the French lines. Between Arras and Notre-Dame de Lorette General Foch assembled five Corps of the 10th Army, all full of enthusiasm for the affray despite the formidable German defences of fortified villages, shelters, barbed wire and re-inforced machine gun positions. On the Notre-Dame de Lorette hill were five lines of deep trenches with multiple rows of barbed wire while the old chapel itself (on the site of today's basilique) had been turned into a fortress with machine guns, sand bags and metal plates.

At 0600 on 9 May 1915 the preliminary bombardment began and four hours later the infantry attacked. Between Souchez and Neuville St Vaast XXXIII Corps under Pétain made rapid progress and the Moroccan Division reached the heights of Vimy. In Lille the Germans of Prince Rupert's 4th Army prepared to evacuate but Pétain had gone too far too fast, nearly three miles in one hour, and his exhausted troops were stopped and then pushed back by German reinforcements brought up in lorries.

At Notre-Dame de Lorette, where XXI Corps under General Maistre had been repeatedly attacking and encroaching upon the hill since December 1914, the area of the chapel was finally gained on 12 May after hand to hand fighting in the ruins, but it was ten more days before all of the Germans were pushed off the hill. On the first day French troops reached the Labyrinth, an especially constructed and formidable fortress of underground works, trenches, and wire, heavily armed with machine guns, but not until 17 July, following a French bombardment said to consist of 300,000 shells, would the whole position be cleared. Two days later the second battle came to an end after fighting whose intensity was matched only at Verdun. Souchez remained in German hands.

The third battle, which began on 25 September, was in conjunction with a British attack at Loos (qv) to the north. The French 10th Army was tasked to take Vimy Ridge but first it had to take Souchez below Notre-Dame de Lorette. The artillery preparation, more calculating than previous efforts and re-inforced with weapons brought up from Verdun, lasted for five days with particular concentration upon road junctions and any features that might represent fortifications. The Germans, however, replied with fierce fire upon the forward trenches, filling parts of them with the dead and churning up the ground over which the French planned to attack. The infantry of Fayolle's XXXIII Corps (he had taken over from Pétain) went in at mid-day on the 25th, the men weighed down in clothes soaked from heavy rains of the night before. Captain Humbert in *La Division Barbot* described their passage thus, 'Our own artillery roared behind us, the shells flying above our heads and bursting everywhere. One could see nothing, understand nothing ... the men went blindly on'. Souchez, the objective of 77th Division, cost many French lives and it was not fully cleared until the following day while at Cabaret Rouge Humbert records, 'Each night ... the dead were loaded on carts while the companies going up the line passed by long rows of other dead awaiting their turn to be removed.'

Meanwhile little else was achieved though parts of Vimy Ridge were reached as far as the Arras-Lens road (now the N17) but these advances were temporary, furious German counter-attacks forcing the French back into their own trenches. Souchez had been taken, Vimy had not and once more the front settled into trench warfare. Vimy Ridge would not be taken until April 1917 and then by the Canadians

THE BATTLEFIELD TOUR

This is made in conjunction with Vimy Ridge, Arras – see page 177 and Map 14, page 175.

THE YSER

16-29 OCTOBER 1914

'The fate of Europe, up to the time of Waterloo, has always been
decided in Belgium. It is difficult to escape from this idea.'

Marshal Foch. 19 November 1914.

Ce n'est qu'un bout de sol dans l'infini du monde...
Ce n'est qu'un bout de sol étroit,
Mais qui renferme encore et sa reine et son roi,
Et l'amour condensé d'un peuple qui les aime...
Dixmude et ses remparts, Nieuport et ses canaux,
Et Furnes, avec sa tour pareille à un flambeau
Vivent encore ou sont défunts sous la mitraille.

Emile Verhaeren.

It's only a piece of earth in the infinity of the world...
It's only a narrow piece of earth,
But which still contains its king and its queen
And the concentrated love of a people who love them...
Dixmude and its ramparts, Nieuport and its canals,
And Furnes, with its tower like a flame,
Still live or are slain by the machine-gun.

[**Emile Verhaeren**, born on 21 May 1855, was Belgium's best-known French language poet. Original, vital, lyrical, his three main themes were the improvement of humanity's lot, love of his wife, and of Flanders. Deeply moved by the outbreak of war, yet too old to fight, he lectured extensively throughout France on Belgian's cause. He was accidentally killed boarding a train after a rally in Rouen on 27 November 1916. After the Armistice his remains were transferred to his native town of Adinkerke.]

SUMMARY OF THE BATTLES

This is the story of a river and a railway. By the end of October 1914 following the struggles around Liège, Namur and Antwerp the exhausted Belgian army had fallen back onto a ten miles long line of defence based on the Yser River between the North Sea at Nieuport and the town of Dixmude. On 21 October the Germans crossed the Yser at Tervate (see **Map 5**) and a probable German advance to the Channel Ports was only prevented by the flooding of vast tracts of land and

MAP 5: THE BATTLES OF THE YSER: 16-29 OCTOBER 1914/1917

To the sea
Yser (Ijzer)
Nieuwpoort
N

Ostende
Raversijde
Middelkerke
Slijpe
Sint-Pieters-Kapelle
Nieuwpoort
Ramskapelle

GERMAN FORCES

BELGIAN FORCES

River Yser

Tervate

GERMAN BREAKTHROUGH

Pervyse
Old railway line
Kaaskerke
Vladslo
Diksmuide
Esen

Legend
1. Yser Tower Museum & Mem
2. Admiral Ronarc'h & Marines Mem
3. Trenches of Death Museum, Mem, Marker Stone
4. Albertina Marker
5. Vrouwekerke chapel, Mems, Marker Stone
6. Albertina marker, Heron stream
7. Käthe Kollwitz Mem
8. German Cem Vladslo
9. Albertina Viconia Château
10. Albertina marker Tervate Bridge
11. 2nd Bn 1st Grenadiers Mem
12. 3rd/23rd Infantry Regt Plaque
13. Pervyse old station house
14. Flying Officer Robertson grave
15. Albertina Marker Pervyse
16. Observation tower Pervyse
17. Bunkers in railway embankment
18. 16th French Chasseurs & 6th Belg Regt Mems
19. 14th Inf Regt & old station Mems

Legend continued
20. Belgian Cem, Ramskapelle
21. Ramskapelle Road CWGC & Comm Cems
22. 3rd Carbiniers & Lt Gen Baron St George Mems
23. CWGC WW2 graves
24. 14th Inf Regt & 7th Inf Granite Soldier Mems
25. Demarcation Stone, Witte Brug
26. Lt Calberg Mon
27. Yser Mon
28. Albertina Marker, Sluizenbrug
29. 1942 WW2 Mem
30. Taverne de Gansepoot
31. Bust of H Geeraert
32. French Mem
33. Brits Mem to the Missing
34. King Albert 1 Mem
35. Raversijde WW1/WW2 Museum
36. Ostende New Comm CWGC Cem
37. HMS *Vindictive* Mem

Flooded area

0   2kms

© TVH 2004

the adoption of a defensive line based on the Dixmuide to Nieuport railway embankment which ran behind the river. After 15 days of continuous struggle the front held. The lines would hold for four years.

OPENING MOVES

Closely involved in their nation's bitter struggle were King Albert and Queen Elisabeth of the Belgians. Albert was a monarch of the old school, seeing himself as a conscientious and active Head of State and Head of the Armed Forces. Born in Brussels on 8 April 1875, the younger son of Philip, Count of Flanders, and brother of Leopold II, he succeeded to the throne on 23 December 1909, through a series of premature deaths. A graduate of the Brussels *Ecole Militaire* he served as an officer in the Grenadiers. In 1900 he married Elisabeth, second daughter of the Duke of Bavaria and they had three children: Leopold, Duke of Brabant (the future Leopold III), Charles, Count of Flanders, and Marie José.

On his accession, Albert was particularly concerned with social reforms, the patronage of arts and literature and, especially, the organisation of the Army. In May 1913 he consented to the raising of the Belgian Army to a strength of 350,000, but in July 1914, when World War I was moving inexorably to its outbreak, Belgium was still dangerously unprepared for war. She depended for her survival on the treaties signed by Great Britain, France, Prussia, Russia and Austria to preserve her neutrality – notably the 1839 Treaty of London, the famous 'Scrap of Paper'. It had been tested, and held firm, in 1870 during the Franco-Prussian War. But Leopold II mistrusted the strength of the protective treaty and reinforced the forts of Liège and Namur as a failsafe. Neither the treaties nor the forts were to save Belgium from German invasion in August 1914.

On 31 July Albert wrote to the Kaiser, in a letter carefully translated by his German-born wife, reminding him of the respect due to Belgian neutrality. Wilhelm replied with the ultimatum of 2 August and hostilities began when Germany's demand for free passage of her troops was refused.

At 0800 hours on 4 August the Germans invaded Belgium. The fortified city of Liège was reached on 5 August, its last fort surrendering on the 16th; Brussels surrendered on 20 August, Namur capitulated on 25 August. Nearly 2,000 civilians were killed, 3,000 houses destroyed. The historic city of Louvain, with its famous library and cathedral, was destroyed, 79 inhabitants were shot. The Provinces of Brabant, Hainault and Antwerp were occupied and many more civilians executed.

Tales of German atrocities, many of them exaggerated, abounded, fuelling the propaganda campaign for the Allies to come to the help of 'Poor Little Belgium'. The concept of German *Kultur* equating to barbarism was perpetuated by the Dutch artist, Louis Raemakers, in a series of harrowing cartoons that chart the Germans' bloody progress through Belgium. Elsie Knocker, one of the 'Two at Pervyse' (see below) reported in her memoirs,

'Atrocities were at their height in those first months of the war, when the Germans were in a hurry to terrorise their way to a quick finish. Every unexpected resistance of the Belgian Army brought immediate reprisals against the civilian population... I did see Belgian children with their hands and feet cut off, and I saw one baby nailed to a door. The Germans forced Belgian civilians to walk ahead of them as they advanced to form a living screen... By the beginning of October nearly 1,500,000 people, or 20 per cent of the population, had left Belgian territory: a million went to Holland, 250,000 to Britain and over 100,000 to France.'

A committee under Viscount Bryce, former Ambassador at Washington, was set up to investigate the conduct of German troops in Belgium. The conclusions of the committee were that there had indeed been systematic massacres of civilians; that looting, wanton destruction and incendiarism had occurred; that the rules and usages of war had frequently been broken, particularly in the use of women and children as shields; that the Red Cross and White Flags had frequently been abused; that 'murder, lust and pillage prevailed over many parts of Belgium on a scale unparalleled in any war between civilised nations during the last three centuries.' The report even contained details of gross individual atrocities of the type reported by Elsie Knocker. Yet when the Belgian Cardinal Mercier held an enquiry in 1922, no substantiation of these atrocities were found and any real supporting evidence for them had mysteriously disappeared. No matter: mere belief in them served to fuel the Allied fervour for the war.

WHAT HAPPENED

The Belgian Army fell back on Antwerp, from which it made sorties on 25 August and 9 September to divert the Germans from their main thrust, which was now into France. During the latter sortie the Belgians lost 6,000 men. On the 26th the Germans attacked Antwerp and again on 3 October. On the 9th the port surrendered. Winston Churchill's gallant attempt to relieve the Belgians in Antwerp (qv) with an expedition by the newly-formed Royal Naval Division (amongst them an excited Sub-Lieutenant Rupert Brooke) was too late, and a miserable failure. They left Dover on 4 October and were back in the port on the 9th.

Now the whole country, with the exception of the small area around Ypres in South West Flanders, was under German occupation. King Albert had withdrawn his army (now comprising four divisions in line and two in reserve) along the Yser River, from Nieuport on the coast to Ypres. General Foch, having visited the King at Furnes, wrote in his memoirs of the Belgian Army that 'the nervous force of its soldiers was all that remained to replace the deficiencies of their equipment'.

On 14 October the King issued a last ditch command to his troops, comparable to Haig's 'Backs to the Wall' Order of the Day of 12 April 1918 (which in turn seemed to presage Churchill's stirring 'We shall fight them on the beaches' speech of 4 June 1940):

'You will now find yourselves alongside the gallant French and British Armies. Our national honour is at stake. Face to the front in the positions in which I shall place you, and let him be regarded as a traitor to his country who talks of retreat.'

His divisional commanders were then personally visited and given the following instructions:

1. Any General whose Division gives way will be relieved of his command on the spot.
2. Any officer whose men abandon their trenches will be relieved of his command.
3. Under no pretext whatsoever, even if the line is broken, is there to be any retirement.
4. Officers of the General Staff will be distributed among the troops of the front line. They will remain there during the fighting encouraging others instead of grumbling themselves.

King Albert and Queen Elisabeth installed themselves in a modest villa at La Panne (de Panne) on the coast to the east of Dunkirk, refusing to move with their Government to Calais and then to le Havre. From La Panne the King continued to play an active role as the leader of his Army and Elisabeth, who had been medically trained, took a practical interest in the care of the wounded in hospitals close to the front line. She was the active patron of the hospital that bore her name near Poperinghe and visited Ypres under severe shellfire. The dedication of this family was further proved when on 8 April 1915 the King made an 'Easter Present' of his 13-year-old son to the 3rd Division of the Belgian Army. The delicate-looking Prince Leopold was to act as a Private, getting his hands blistered by digging (alternating with term-time spent in the rarefied atmosphere of Eton).

On 6/7 October the British 7th Division landed at Zeebrugge and Ostende, and '... moved off for its nine or ten mile trek to Bruges. With elastic step and cheery voice the men swung along to the inspiring strains of "Tipperary" (*With the Immortal Seventh Division*, A. J. Kennedy). The Seventh ended up in Ypres and took part in the **First Battle**. After Mons, le Cateau and the Marne, and with the Aisne Line stabilised, the BEF was moving northwards to cover the Flanders crisis. After two months of mobile warfare and the 'Race to the Sea', the front line was soon to settle down into the stalemate of trench warfare.

On 16 October the Battle of the Yser opened. Rear-Admiral Hood brought up a Royal Naval flotilla to Middelkerke and bombarded the German coastal batteries. Naval activity heightened and on 31 October a German submarine sank the British seaplane carrier *Hermes*.

Meanwhile repeated, inexorable, German attacks in the Nieuport and Diksmuide areas continued through to the 23rd. Supported until this time only by 6,000 French Marines, the small Belgian force, deploying its entire army, was expected to hold a 22-mile front, from the sea to Zuydschoote (8km north of Ypres). And hold they did, until by 24 October the Belgian resistance started to fail. The troops were exhausted and running out of ammunition. Reinforcements in the shape of the renowned French 42nd (Grossetti) Division arrived to relieve them but the line was too thin. The Allied defences were on the point of breaking and then, at the suggestion of General Foch who declared, 'Inundation formerly saved Holland, and may well save Belgium. The men will hold out as best they can until the country is under water', Belgian engineers saved the day by opening the floodgates at Nieuport thus letting in the sea and swamping the crisscrossed drainage system of canals and ditches (watergands). Behind the river the engineers dammed twenty-two culverts under the Nieuport-Diksmuide railway embankment forming a catchment area for the coming floods. The railway, Line 74, is now a cycle path, thus the battlefield can be defined by the lines of the River Yser and the railway embankment which became the Belgians' defensive line.

By 30/31 October the operation, assisted by the high tides caused by the full moon of 29 October, was successfully concluded. The Battles of the Yser were over, ending with a furious bayonet charge to the sound of bugles which repulsed the enemy at Ramskappelle. The Belgian Army, with 20,000 casualties in this battle alone, was reduced to 65,000 men. In one regiment only six officers remained.

According to the King's ADC, General van Overstraeten, the French feared their Belgian brothers lacked 'both ability and energy' and urged the distribution of the weak Belgian remnant amongst French units. As General Pershing was to dig in his heels later in the war, about the dispersion of his American forces, Albert 'would neither agree to being deprived of his constitutional prerogatives, nor let his army be split up.' They continued to hold the line between Diksmuide and the sea. The conditions they had fought in were horrendous (see the section on Diksmuide and Vladslo below). The land itself was forbidding:

'Water is everywhere: in the air: on the ground, under the ground. It is the land of dampness, the kingdom of water. It rains three days out of four. The north-west winds which, breaking off the tops of the stunted trees, making them bend as if with age, carry heavy clouds of cold rain formed in the open sea. As soon as the rain ceases to fall, thick white mists rise from the ground giving a ghost-like appearance to men and things alike,'

wrote the Belgian author, le Goffic, in Dixmude. Add to these natural miseries the man-made horrors of modern warfare and it is little short of a miracle that they held on so long.

But now the Germans diverted their attention southwards towards Ypres.

THE BATTLEFIELD TOUR

• **The Route:** It is recommended that the tour begins from Ypres at the end of the Salient tour. It then visits the Gas Memorial at Steenstraat, Belgian Memorials to the 3rd Regiment, 3rd Division, Armand Van Eecke and Albertina Marker at Kippe; Houthulst Belgian Cemetery and Albertina Marker, 22nd Regiment Memorial; Pilot W. Coppens Memorial, Klerken; Diksmuide: Statue of Gen Baron Jacques de Dixmude, Ijzer Tower, Trenches of Death, Demarcation Stone; Albertina Markers at the Old Railway Line and the Heron Stream; Memorial Chapel, O-L Vrouwekerke and Demarcation Stone; Viconia Château and Tervate Bridge Albertina Markers; Memorial to 1st Grenadiers; Pervijze OP Tower and Albertina Marker; Ramskapelle Franco-Belgian Memorial and Old Station; Ramscapelle Road Mil and Nieuwpoort Comm CWGC Cemeteries, Demarcation Stone and Albertina Marker; Nieuwpoort Monuments to the Yser, Lt Calberg, Albertina Marker, Monuments to Hendrik Geeraert, Monument to King Albert I, British Memorial to the Missing.

- **Extra Visits:** Vladslo German Cemetery; Monuments at Uniebrug and St Joris; Coxyde Mil CWGC Cemetery; Atlantic Wall Open Air Museum, Raversijde; Oostende New Comm CWGC Cemetery and Monument to HMS *Vindictive*.
- **Total distance:** 40.1 miles
- **Total time:** 5 hours, 15 minutes
- **Distance from Calais:** see 1st, 2nd, 3rd Ypres Tour
- **Base towns:** Ieper, Dixsmuide, Ostende
- **Maps:** Belgian Survey 1:50,000 11/12 and 19/20

*From the Grand' Place **set your mileometer to zero** and drive out round the Cloth Hall and turn left past St George's Church on Elverdingsestraat, passing the **HQ of the CWGC** on the right at No 82. Continue to the first roundabout and turn right signed A19, Veurne. Continue to the next roundabout and turn right on the N379 signed Centrum and turn left at the next main junction signed Diksmuide on the N369. Continue under the motorway bridge past Essex Farm CWGC Cemetery on the right. Continue on the N369 direction Diksmuide to the large cross on the left.*

• *Memorial to the 1st Victims of Gas/6.1 miles/5 minutes*

This 15m high Cross of Reconciliation commemorates the victims of the 22 April 1915 gas attack. It replaces the original 1929 memorial which was blown up by the Germans in 1942 as they objected to the inscription (which referred to them as 'Barbarians').

Continue 200m to just before the large Steenstraete building on the right before the bridge over the Ieperlee Canal.

• *Memorial to Belgian 3rd Infantry Regiment 6.2 miles/5 minutes*

Here is the large white cross surmounted by a Crusader's sword which is the memorial to the 162 officers, NCOs and soldiers of the Regiment who fell at Steenstrate from 24 April to 10 May 1915, in the later stages of the German gas attacks.

Continue towards Kippe, crossing three 'beeks' (streams), the Lobeek, the St Jansbeek and the Langewadebeek.

• *Memorial to Belgian 3rd Army Division/8.2 miles/5 minutes*

On the left is a large concrete memorial, which looks like a chunk of a pill box, with the Division's battle honours and ORBAT.

Continue to the Kippe crossroads, signed to the right to Houthulst.

• *Albertina Marker/9.1 miles/5 minutes*

This is one of the series of stone markers inaugurated on 17 February 1984 at Marche-les-Dames 50 years after the death of Albert 1 (and also 70 years after the start of the Great War) as a reminder of the events of that war. They bear the official monogram of the King and the shield of the Province of West Flanders. They were designed by Pieter-Hein Boudens.

The marker is to the left of the crossroads and commemorates the one-day battle of 17 April 1918 when the Belgian forces succeeded in halting the German offensive. There were heavy losses on both sides.
Continue straight on for some 0.3 miles to the statue on the left.

• Memorial to Armand Victor Van Eecke/9.4 miles/5 minutes

This fine statue of a young Belgian soldier age 22, killed on 9 September 1918, and erected by his parents, is surrounded on three sides by a tall hedge. On the base are his many honours and medals and a poem describing the loss of this young ex-student of Leuven High School who became an Adjutant (Officer Cadet) in the 5th Coy of the 3rd Inf Regt.
Turn round and return to the Albertina crossroads and turn left direction Houthulst.
In the centre of Houthulst (13.7 miles) turn right on the N301 signed Militaire Begraafplaats and continue towards the forest.
The forest, which Napoleon called 'the key to the Low Countries', saw fierce action by the retreating Belgian army in 1914, when they suffered heavy losses. The occupying Germans strongly fortified the forest and from there directed their heavy artillery on the Allied lines. There was more fighting here in 1917 and finally in September 1918 when it was retaken by the Belgians. Large parts of the forest are restricted military areas, some used by the Belgian Army Disposal Service which carries out controlled explosions of the Iron Harvest that is still being dug up by the ton.
Continue to the large cemetery on the left at the edge of the forest.

• Belgian Military Cemetery, Houthulst, Albertina Marker/14.5 miles/15 minutes

As well as containing 1,723 Belgian graves (the majority of whom fell in the 28/29 September 1918 liberation offensive), concentrated here in 1923-4 and of which 493 are unknown, the cemetery contains the graves of 81 Italian prisoners of war working in German labour camps. The other Belgian casualties in the area were repatriated to their home villages. The cemetery has an elaborate and imaginative lay-out which from the air would appear as a six-pointed star, within which are many circles, crescents and lines. Outside the wall at the end of the cemetery is an **Albertina Marker** to the Battle of Houthulst Forest of 28 September 1918.
Turn round and return to Houthulst. Continue towards Diksmuide on the N301.

N.B. Just before leaving the village (15.4 miles) is a grey stone marker stone to the right to the **Belgian 22nd Inf Regt.**

Continue to the village of Klerken.

N.B. On the right in W. Coppens Plein (17.4 miles) is a small grey marker to **Heldhaftig Piloot W. Coppens** van de Belgische Luchtmachl 1914-1918, erected on 13.8.1967. Coppens started his career in 1912 with the 2nd Grenadiers who were to play such a large part in the defence of the Yser and then joined the Belgian Air Service, paying for his own training at a school in Hendon. On 14 October 1918 in a dog fight in which he was credited with his 37th victory he was shot down and suffered injuries which resulted in his losing his left leg. He later served as a military attaché. He died on 21 December 1986.

Continue to the junction with the N35 (20.1 miles).

Extra Visit to the German Cemetery at Vladslo (Map 5/7/8). Round trip: 9 miles. Approximate time: 35 minutes.

Turn right to Esen and then left towards Vladslo. Continue through Vladslo and keep on the same winding road over the N363 following signs to Deutscher Soldaten Friedhof to the cemetery on the left.

By the forest known as the Praetbos, this cemetery contains 25,664 burials. Many soldiers were buried in the surroundings and in 61 small German Military Cemeteries in Belgium. In 1956 the *Deutsche Kriegsgräberfürsorge* undertook a huge programme of concentration and the original 3,233 remains buried in the cemetery beside a German First Aid Post in the woods were moved into the present cemetery of Vladslo. Because of the density of burials in such a small space, the cemetery is virtually one mass grave. Around the graves with their standard flat marker, each listing several names, are some of the original, non-standard headstones of the early days of the war.

The burial ground is enclosed by a beech hedge, the height of a man. Oak trees are planted amongst the ten plots. The visitor enters through a brick

entrance hall where the roll of honour, in parchment books, is kept. At the back of the cemetery is the famous pair of statues, 'The Grieving Parents', created by the well-known artist and sculptress Käthe Kollwitz in memory of her son Peter, who is buried under the flat gravestone in front of the statues. For many years Kollwitz's original wooden cross was preserved in Roggeveld cemetery, Esen.

Born in Königsberg on 8 July 1867, Käthe, married to a doctor, was a graphic artist, specialising in etchings, woodcuts and lithographs. On 23 October 1914 her 18-year-old musketeer son, Peter, who had volunteered in Berlin, was killed near Esen, attacking the 11th Belgian Infantry Regiment holding the Yser at Diksmuide. It was a dreadful night. A Belgian officer described the seemingly suicidal attacks of the mainly young German forces in his diary:

"The enemy has concentrated many fresh troops opposite Diksmuide and given the order to take the town, cost what cost. Scarcely an assault has been beaten off, when they arrive again, with ever-increasing strength. What have they been promised

Statue of Armand Victor van Eecke, Kippe.

Extra visit *continued*

to let themselves be killed in such large numbers? What strong drinks have been poured out to give them such a wild courage? Drunk from blood, with devilish faces and howling like beasts, they charge again and again, falling over the heaps of dead, trampling down the wounded with their heavy boots. They are mown down by the hundreds but are coming on again. Some of them are able to reach the breast-works where it comes to cruel hand-to-hand fighting, striking with rifle-butts, sticking with bayonets. Skulls are smashed, bodies are torn open apart; but all in vain, nowhere are they able to break through. Eleven times in the northerly and easterly sector, fifteen times in the southerly sector, the waves were smashed to death."

No wonder the Germans called these battles 'The Massacre of the Innocents'.

Käthe sought to express her personal grief in a tangible, artistic form, but anguished for years over the form it should take. Should it be a monument for her son alone, or for the entire grieving legion of mourning parents? Should it be one figure or two, should the figure of the dead child be included? Käthe became bitterly anti-war and her art expressed her strong pacifist feelings and her revulsion to bloodshed. Her style and beliefs were anathema to the rising National Socialist movement after the war in Germany and, when the group of figures was reaching completion in 1932, its final form was reviled by the Nazis. The father's tight-lipped expression, the way he clutches his body with his arms to comfort himself: the mother's attitude of total sorrow, her head bowed, her hand pressing her long gown to her cheek – all were perceived as expressions of weakness by the new regime. German parents should be proud to have sacrificed their son for the Fatherland. The statues were erected in nearby Esen, where Peter was originally buried, in July 1932, probably just in time to prevent their destruction by the Nazis. In 1956 the 1,539 Germans, among them Peter Kollwitz, were moved here from the small cemetery called Roggeveld near Esen. The statues moved with them.

There has been much dispute between the German and Belgian authorities over the statues, now highly regarded as a work of art. Their soft stone is deteriorating and the Germans wished to remove them back to the Fatherland. The Belgians refused and are deciding how best to preserve the grieving pair. In the meantime, the statues are encased in green wooden boxes during

The Grieving Parents by Käthe Kollwitz.

Extra visit continued

the potentially damaging winter months.

A little further on and to the right in the Praetbos is a house built in typical German style. Now a farmhouse, it served during the war as a rest house for German soldiers returning from the front line, much as did Talbot House in Poperinghe.

Nearby is the Käthe Kollwitz Tower in Koekelare which contains an exhibition of her life and work. **Open** Tues-Fri 0930-1200 and 1400-1700. Also Sat-Sun and holidays in July/Aug.

Return to the junction with the N301.

Turn left at the T junction on the N35 to Diksmuide. Continue to the traffic lights in the town centre by the church on the left and turn right. Continue to the Grote Markt Square (20.6 miles).

Diksmuide. On 25 January 1920, Diksmuide was presented with the *Croix de Guerre* by President Poincaré, as it 'Won undying fame in the first days of the War by heroic, never-to-be-forgotten combats. Proved herself worthy of this glory by the fortitude with which she daily supported bombardments and fires, confident that her sacrifices were helping to save the Country and the Common Cause.' The award was well-deserved.

Dixsmuide was the scene of bitter fighting from 15 October to 10 November 1914. Here the 6,000 men of the French Naval Brigade *(Fusiliers Marins)* under the formidable Admiral Ronarc'h with the 5,000 strong Brigade of the Belgian 3rd Army under General Meiser held out for a month against a vastly superior enemy force. When they arrived in the pouring rain against the tide of retreating refugees the Yser was the only defence against the Germans. They immediately organised the construction of trenches around the town and fortified the bridges and dykes of the Yser Canal. They then sustained particularly violent attacks on 16-17 October and on 20 October heavy shellfire began to fall on the town and the civilians were forced to evacuate. Fires broke out and soon the town was in ruins. The Marines mounted heroic efforts to repel the attacks which culminated in the desperate battles of 24 October when the repeated German assaults resulted in hundreds of casualties on both sides. But still the heroic Marines stood firm until the advancing floods caused the Germans to turn their attention towards Nieuwpoort.

In November, however, the Germans renewed their attack on Dixsmuide. Some of the Belgian defences crumbled in the southern sector and the Germans entered the town through the breach when house-to-house fighting ensued. The Germans then placed unarmed prisoners at their head as they attacked the positions on the Yser. Among them was the Naval Lieutenant St Sérieyx who had fought with his men to the last cartridge. Asked by the Germans to point out a fordable place over the river and then to ask the remaining defending forces to surrender he defiantly jumped into the river, followed by his men, and swam to the other side.

That night the bridges and the Flour Mill *(la Minoterie)* on the banks of the river were blown up by the defenders who withdrew behind the embankment and Dixsmuide was then occupied by the Germans. For 4 years the French and Belgians in the opposing sector mounted continual attacks on the occupiers until on 29 September 1918 the ruins of Dixsmuide were finally retaken by the Belgians.

Continue to the Grote Market.

• Diksmuide Market Square/22 miles/15 minutes

In the square is the Tourist Office (at No 28, open 1000-1230 and 1300-1730, Tel: + (0) 51 51 91 46), the picturesque Town Hall and a statue to Gen Baron **Jacques de Dixmude**, who as Col J. Jacques commanded the 12th Belgian Inf Regt which defended the town at the end of October 1914. He went on to command the 3rd Division and was ennobled after the war. The statue was sculpted by Alfred Courtois and stands on a pedestal with statues at the four corners sculpted by his son, Antoine. There is a variety of attractive restaurants in the Square.

A square called Place d'Italie recalls that Diksmuide was the only town to receive the *Grande Croix d'Italie* from Mussolini in 1922. In the public park is a **marker to the French Marines** and their Admiral, Ronarc'h, who defended the town from 16 October to 10 November 1914. It was erected in 1963.

Return to the traffic lights and turn right signed Veurne on the N35. Continue to the canal.

N.B. On the left is the Hotel Sint Jan. This is on the site of the *Minoterie* (qv). Until the German occupation of World War II, there were preserved trenches here, which were destroyed when all metal was sent back to Germany to make munitions.

Cross the canal and turn left and follow signs to Ijzer Tower.

• Ijzer Tower/22.2 miles/30 minutes/Map 5/1

Listed as an International Peace Centre, the tower is a symbol of Flemish nationalism, which came to a head during the First World War. Its history is long and complicated and goes back to the 18th Century when the rich vein of Flemish culture – art, music and literature, which had been influential for centuries throughout Europe – was suppressed by the French-speaking regime. During this century not one book was printed in Flemish. After Waterloo, new links with the Dutch promised a 'window' of Flemish renaissance and King William 1 of Orange permitted a Dutch-speaking University in Ghent. But the 1830 Revolution, led by the French-speaking nobility, closed the window and set the clock back. During the 19th Century, Flemish intellectuals began working to build up a renewed Flemish identity, but when the First World War broke out in August 1914, all education was still being conducted in French and during the Yser campaign, 80 per cent of all officers in the Belgian army were French-speaking. The soldiers on the other hand were predominantly Flemish-speaking and resented their orders being given in French. Intellectuals, teachers, students and priests, disturbed by the situation, started a movement for Flemish identity that went far beyond the linguistic problem. To them it became a matter of human rights. At first the soldiers expressed their misery about the war in general through the medium of their desire for Flemish recognition, but soon the movement became more intensely nationalistic. In 1917 they addressed an open letter to the King expressing their unhappiness.

Although Albert was a fair and human man, he was above all a Belgian, and a French-speaking one at that. His advisers warned him that he had to keep his country together at all costs – it was the period of general unrest and dissatisfaction: the Russian Revolution, mutinies in the French army. The Germans, occupying 90 per cent of Belgium, were deliberately attempting to inflame the two different linguistic elements. In 1916 they had allowed the re-opening of the Flemish University at Ghent.

The letter was ignored. Outspoken Flemish soldiers were penalised by their French officers with heavy oppression. 'Martyrs' were created, as explained in the crypt of the Tower. The Flemish artist Cpl Joe English, born in Bruges in 1882 of Irish antecedents, became the artist of the Yser Front and dedicated his art to the emancipation of the Flemish. There are many examples of his work in the Tower. English, who was an active member of the Association of Flemish Catholic Students, designed the provocative headstones in the shape of a Celtic cross with the inscription *Alles Voor Vlanderen: Vlanders Voor Kristus* ('All for Flanders: Flanders for Christ') that were erected on Flemish martyrs' graves to replace what was thought to be the inappropriate official cross with a French inscription. You will see them in and around the crypt and also above the crypt in Zonnebeke local cemetery. The military authorities defaced these 'Joe English' stones, which after the war could be seen in many local churchyards, by covering the inscription with concrete, or blowing them up and using the resultant rubble in road-building.

After the Armistice Flemish soldiers threatened to refuse to hand in their arms unless something was done about the language problem and a direct appeal was again addressed to the King. He promised palliatives but died in 1934 having done nothing radical to improve the situation. Flemish resentment ran high and what was to become an annual pilgrimage began in Diksmuide, the land around which was literally drenched with the blood of dead Flemish soldiers of the Yser campaign. What was originally a pilgrimage to commemorate the sacrifice of the Flemish soldiers of the Yser gradually took on a more political flavour. In the late 1930s language laws were passed to diffuse the situation.

On 16 March 1946 the opponents of Flemish nationalism blew up the 50 metre high tower that had been built in 1930 on the pilgrimage ground containing the graves of the most famous Flemish martyrs. The present 84 metre high tower – like a giant Joe English headstone – was soon built and a great Pax Gate erected using the rubble of the original tower. The new Crypt was inaugurated in 1958 and the Tower in 1965. It is still the focal point of an annual pilgrimage in the last Sunday in August which unfortunately has also occasionally been used by European right-wing extremists as a meeting point.

Today the country is still split between the more prosperous northern Flemish speaking area (about 60 per cent) and the southern French-speaking Walloons (about 40 per cent). In the middle is the uneasy capital Brussels, mostly French-speaking, but with bi-lingual street signs and duplicated ministries.

Belgian Memorial at the Trenches of Death.

The Ijzer Tower and the Joe English Stone seen through the Pax Gate.

The Trenches of Death on the banks of the Yser.

Extensive renovation has taken place over the past few years and the entire grounds are now enclosed and entry is through a turnstile. Iron wreaths at the entrance are a reminder of the prison camps at Arne and Avours where Flemish soldiers were incarcerated for their beliefs.

Open: Daily in Jan, Feb, March, Oct, Nov, Dec 1000-1700. April, May, June, July, Aug, Sept 1000-1800. **Closed** Dec 24-26, 31, Jan 1,2 and for three weeks after the Christmas Holiday. Tel: +(0) 51 50 02 86. Fax: +(0) 51 50 22 58. e-mail: ijzertoren@unicall.be.

As you enter through the Peace Gate you will approach the Crypt, at whose entrance is a Calvary, which has push-button talking machines in several languages which tell the story of the martyrs (Joe English, Renaat de Rudder, the brothers Van Raemdonck, Frans Van der Linden, Frans Kusters, Bert Willems and Juul De Winde) buried there. Above the crypt are the words, 'Here are our bodies, like seed in the sand, hope for the harvest, oh Flanders.'

The tower, which was declared 'A Memorial to Flemish Emancipation' on 23 December 1986, has a large entrance hall with an audio-visual presentation of *In Flanders Fields – WW1*, a Chapel with stained glass windows by Eugeen Yoors (mainly from Joe English drawings) and a shop. On the lower floor is a reconstructed dugout. A lift takes you up to the Panorama hall on the 22nd floor with its 144 windows with magnificent views over the battlefield of the Yser, extending as far as Mount Cassel on a clear day, and a 67 square metres painting. Each floor on the way up has a different exhibition. They deal with the fight for the Dutch language, the Student Movement, the conduct of that they call the 'Stupid War', the Armistice, the consequences of War and growing Flemish power.

Return to the crossroads and go straight over.

N.B. On the left is a large white **Calvary,** a religious monument that was dedicated to all the soldiers and civilians who died in the Great War. It was a National statement to counter the very Flemish statement made by the Ijzer Tower. On 23 September 1928 it was solemnly blessed by the Bishop of Bruges in the presence of the Duke and Duchess of Brabant, the future King Leopold III and Queen Astrid. The Calvary was once the object of large pilgrimages.

Continue and stop at the large red brick building on the right.

• *Trenches of Death, Demarcation Stone/23.3 miles/20 minutes/Map 5/3*

The old entrance building erected by the Touring Club of Belgium, which bore a plaque proclaiming it was a listed building, underwent extensive rebuilding and modernising in 2002 when it changed from private to provincial ownership. It contains many fascinating original photographs which graphically show the horror of life in the trenches in this sector. Stairs lead to an upstairs room which gives good views over the battlefield.

Behind it is an imposing **memorial** proclaiming 'Here our Army held the invader in check 1914-1918'.

Open April-11 November every day. 12 November-April weekdays only. Tel: + (0)3 51 51 94 19.

The trenches themselves are marvellously preserved in concrete and one can walk through them to the Demarcation Stone at the end and then return along the parapet. Its galleries, shelters, firesteps and chicanes, concreted duckboards and sandbags give a realistic idea of a working trench.

This was the Belgian forward defence line throughout the whole of the Yser battles (see 'Battles of the Yser' above) separated from the enemy only by the River Yser itself. For fifty months the men in it were subjected to attack by shell and mine, grenade and bullet. Sometimes the Germans infiltrated the trench and there was hand-to-hand fighting. Death was never far away, hence the sinister name, *'Boyau de la Mort'*.

After the land between Diksmuide and Nieuport had been deliberately flooded at the end of October 1914 to halt the Germans, the trenchline was dug by soldiers totally exposed to German fire. Progress was then continued by saps. Sentry boxes and observation points were set up, the most famous being the Mousetrap, with loopholes on three sides of its concrete walls, which was erected in 1917. The trench line was exposed to the Germans on three sides. Lethal snipers from the trenches on the German bank were particularly effective. The Germans also built strong fortifications on their side of the river, one of the most notorious being the 'Flour Mill' *(Minoterie)* on the right bank opposite the present Ijzer Tower, with machine-gun and grenade launchers permanently targeted on the trench.

After the war the first Belgian **Demarcation Stone** (qv) was unveiled here on Easter Sunday 1922 by King Albert of the Belgians. Their Touring Club had raised the necessary 250,000 Francs for the erection of the Belgian stones. It was a glorious occasion, with flags and garlands, a huge crowd including many veterans and war wounded, and, according to the magazine, *Le Courrier de l'Armée*, 'vibrant' speeches from the representatives of the French and Belgian Touring Clubs.

Communications to the Belgian rearlines were made by two footbridges, well known to the Germans. One led to Kaaskerke, the village whose spire can be seen to the left. Over this bridge under the cover of darkness soldiers brought sacks of earth to repair their parapets. The other led to Lettenburg on the Nieuport road and this was used to carry wounded to the rear and to bring up supplies and ammunition. A Decauville narrow gauge railway (like those built on the Somme) was constructed to bring up the heavy mortar shells.

The soldiers manning the trench spent three days in its hell to be followed by three days of rest in the rearline villages.

Continue past the trenches and keep left at the Y junction signed to O-L [Our Lady] Vrouwhoekje, with the Yser to the right. Continue to the right turn signed to O-L Vrouwhoekje. Do not turn right but continue to the left to an Albertina Marker on the left.

• Albertina Marker, Old Railway Line/24.2 miles/5 minutes/Map 5/4

The old railway line, now a cycle path, is to the left. An Information Board describes the importance of Line No 74, the 13.5km track from Diksmude to Nieuport, which marked the Belgian front line after the flooding. The Albertina Marker commemorates the Battle of the Yser, 18-31 October 1914.

It is now possible during your tour to clearly identify the land that was flooded. The cycle track forms the left hand or western boundary and the Yser the right hand or eastern boundary.

Turn round and turn left on Dodengangstraat and follow signs to O-L Vrouwekerke to the Chapel and tower on the left.

• O-L Vrouwekerke (Our Lady of the Victory) Memorial Chapel, Memorials, Observation Tower, Demarcation Stone, Oud-Stuivekenskerke/25.6 miles/20 minutes/Map 5/5

This chapel, inaugurated on 6 September 1926, was built on the site of the old church. All but the tower was demolished and this was fortified and used by the Belgians as an OP and shelter. In the ruins of the tower stairs lead up to an Orientation Table and superb views over the battlefield. On the tower wall is a **Plaque to Martial Lekeux**, who commanded the shelter. Beside it is a **Demarcation Stone** inscribed 'Dixmuide' in remarkably pristine condition, the legend 'Here the Invader was brought to a halt' still clearly readable. The legend goes that it was not defaced by the Germans during WW2 as were most of the Markers because the local farmer hid it in a pile of sugar beet!

Between the tower and the Chapel is a **Monument to the Cyclist Carabiniers**, christened by the Germans 'The Black Devils' as their dark green uniforms appeared almost black, and beyond it a **Memorial to the 5th Lancers**. Around the Chapel are 41 stone markers with Belgian Regimental badges. Inside it are several memorial tablets and the most beautiful **stained glass windows** including remarkable portraits of the Belgian King and Queen, the Patron Saints of the Infantry (St Maurice), the Artillery (St Barbara), the French Army (St Ludovic), the French Airforce (N-D de Lorette) and St Martial etc. Two windows commemorate Edouard Lekeux, one showing him as an artillery officer, the other describing the incident when a shell entered the shelter but did not explode. This was ascribed to the presence of a statue of the Virgin Mary and Child, a large version of which stands in the centre of the windows. Lekeux was in a Seminary before the war, enlisted when it broke out and after the war became a Franciscan Monk with the name Martial.

The chapel is open during the summer months but if locked the key is held in the house opposite. A ceremony of remembrance is held here each year on the last Friday in August. Attached to the farm behind the Chapel is an original **bunker.**

Return to the junction and turn right. Continue to the Albertina Marker on the right.

• Albertina Marker, Heron Stream/25.9 miles/5 minutes/Map 5/6

This is to the Reigers Vliet (Heron Brook), The Great Watch 1914-1918. Herons are occasionally seen here today.

Continue.

You are now driving through the area that was flooded in 1914 with the Heron Brook (which is parallel to the Yser) on the right and the railway line to the left.

The King and Queen of the Belgians.

Our Lady's Memorial Chapel complex from the ruined tower.

...keux in his OP.

Lekeux with the famous unexploded shell.

St George.

Demarcation Stone with inscription 'Here the Invader was Brought to a Halt'.

Continue following signs to Viconia Kleiputten.

The village was destroyed during the war and rebuilt further along the road after the war.

Fork right and continue to the Château.

• Albertina Marker, Viconia Château /27.3 miles/5 minutes/Map 5/9

After crossing the river (see below), the Germans' first action was to take the Château. The Albertina marker records that this was a forward post (actually of course a German one) as it was on somewhat higher ground than its flat surroundings. The Château is now an hotel.

Continue.

The German advance was towards you as you drive, still in what was the flooded area. Ahead is the Yser Dyke (Ijzer Dijk). The Germans were on the other side of the Yser.

Turn left at the dyke and stop on the left at the Albertina Marker by the bus stop.

• Tervate Bridge Albertina Marker/28.0 miles/5 minutes/Map 5/10

On the opposite bank of the Yser the remains of the old bridge can be made out. This is where the Germans crossed having repaired the small bridge that was partially destroyed by the Belgians. The Albertina Marker to the left records the events of 21-23 October 1914 here. It was this crossing that threatened the whole of the Belgian defences and was only stopped by a combination of the flooding and the determination of the 2nd Battalion of the 1st Grenadiers (qv). The German attack, made at night, had been a surprise, and if it had succeeded it would have outflanked Dixmuide and Nieuport, the two keys to the defensive line. Oddly, in 1940 as the British prepared a defensive perimeter around Dunkirk, the Germans found a small unguarded sheep bridge over the Dunkirk-Veurne canal and crossed it, nullifying the British defences.

Continue to a right turn to Nieuwpoort. Turn right and continue.

N.B. To the left is a **Monument to the 2nd Bn, 1st Grenadiers** (28.3 miles), an elite regiment commanded by Major d'Oultremont which held the Germans here and at Tervate. Meanwhile its sister regiment the 2nd Grenadiers were fighting below Ramskapelle (qv). Both had been in the conflict from the beginning and their soldiers, a mixture of professionals and militiamen, were cold and tired. But they held on.

Continue along the Yser Dyke under the Tervatebrug to the junction with the N302.

N.B. On the bridge ahead is a **Plaque to the 3rd/23rd Regiment of Line** who defended it in 1914.

Turn left on Schoorbakkestraat to Pervijze. Continue to

• The Old Station House, Pervyse/32.8 miles/5 minutes/Map 5/13

Now a private house but still with the original 'PERVYSE' white sign clearly visible, this is on the line of the old railway (running left to right over the road) and there are Information Boards beside it. During the war there was an OP on top of the station

and the houses on the edge of the village were made into machine gun shelters.
Continue to the village church.
There is a green CWGC sign on the entrance and buried in the churchyard **is Flying Officer A. Robertson**, R. Can Airforce, 29 November 1943 (**Map 5/14**).
Turn left on the Dixsmuide N35 road and some 400 yards later on the right is an Albertina Marker.

• *Pervyse Albertina Marker and Observation Tower/33.1 miles/5 minutes/Map 5/15/16*

Behind the Albertina is the ruin of the WW1 OP Tower. The upper brick-built section was constructed by the Germans in WW2. It is the ruined tower of St Nicholas Church, used as an OP in 1914 after it was dynamited by the Belgians in October.

Here in Pervyse a pair of extraordinary women known as 'The Two', Elsie Knocker – later Baroness T'Serclaes – and Mairie Chisholm, Chief of her clan – set up, against all odds and much opposition, their first-aid post to support the Belgian Army. They had met before the war through their shared passion for motorbikes and again when they joined in August 1914 Dr Hector Monro's volunteer Ambulance Corps. The eccentric Scottish doctor gathered together a piece-meal force of two doctors, a Padre, three male stretcher bearers and a bevy of enthusiastic women with a mixture of nursing, driving and organisational skills. Rejected by the War Office the British, French and American Red Cross they were eventually accepted by the Belgian Red Cross and permitted to travel to the fluctuating Belgian front. From Ghent they were driven back to Dunkirk by the advancing German tide through streams of refugees and the wounded, all the time giving what assistance they could.

When the Allied defensive line was formed along the Yser they returned to Belgium and worked wherever they saw a need. They set up temporary bases in and around Dixsmuide and Furnes (Veurne). Eventually 'The Two' established themselves in a cellar in the shattered village of Pervyse. From there they sallied forth at night, often under fire, to bring in the wounded to tend.

Although disapproved of by many of the British 'top Brass' their bravery and fortitude soon became legendary. They were visited by a succession of VIPs including Marie Curie (who was running an X-ray unit at Furnes), Sir Bernard Dawson (Chief Medical Officer of the BEF), the King and Queen of the Belgians (who created them Knights of the Order of Leopold II), Prince Alexander of Teck and Bruce Bairnsfather (who drew a cartoon specially for Elsie).

Elsie (who was divorced after an unhappy first marriage and with a child who was to be killed as a pilot in WW2) managed to snatch the time to marry a Belgian pilot, the Baron Harold de T'Serclaes, but he was killed soon after their brief honeymoon. The Two were eventually accepted by the Establishment and awarded the MM and the Order of St John of Jerusalem. When the British took over the Pervyse sector in July 1917, however, they were again under threat of ejection by Gen Sir Henry Rawlinson. Elsie stood her ground: 'The General had to admit defeat', she reported, and they were allowed to continue.

Remains of the old bridge across the Yser.

Albertina Marker at the Tervate Bridge.

VAN 16 TOT 24-10-14
WERD DEZE IJZEROEVER
VERDEDIGD DOOR DE
3/23 LINIEREGT.

DU 16 AU 24-10-14
CETTE RIVE DE L'YSER
FUT DEFENDUE PAR LES
3/23 REGT. DE LIGNE

Plaque to the 3rd/23rd Regiment of Line, Schoorbakkestraat.

The Old Station House, Pervyse.

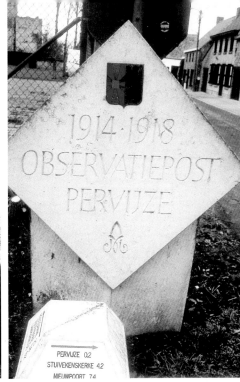

OP Tower and Albertina Marker, Pervyse.

Cartoon drawn for the Baroness de T'Serclaes by Bruce Bairnsfather.

The Ruined Station, Ramskapelle.

Their truly horrific and remarkable wartime experiences are graphically described in the Baroness's biographies, *The Cellar House at Pervyse* and *Flanders and Other Fields*.

Turn round, return to the church and follow signs to Nieuwpoort on the N355. Fork right on the N356 signed to Ramskapelle.

To the right along the embankment of the old railway lines the vestiges of many Belgian shelters or bunkers can clearly be seen. Most of them were built in brick from the ruins of local houses destroyed during the combat but there are the occasional concrete ones.

Continue into Ramskapelle.

Ramskapelle was strategically placed on the railway to Dixsmuide and on the edge of the flooded area. On 30 October it was captured by the Germans just as the flood waters reached it. Its loss was crucial as there were no lines of defences in its rear. A desperate counter-attack was mounted preceded by a fierce artillery bombardment followed by a bayonet charge to the sound of bugles by the remnants of the Belgian 6th, 7th and 14th Regiments and the 2nd Grenadiers, all supported by the French 42nd Infantry Division. The enemy was thrown into disorder, Ramskapelle was recaptured and as the flood waters crept slowly forward the line re-established.

Continue to the main square and stop on the right by the churchyard wall.

• *Franco-Belgian Memorial/36.2 miles/5 minutes/Map 5/18*

The monument commemorates the bayonet charge of 31 October 1914 by the French 16th *Chasseurs à Pied* (Light Infantry) and the Belgian 6th Regiment (the 'Blue Devils'). It was erected on 30 October 1938.

Turn immediately right past the churchyard signed to the Station on Hemmestraat.
Continue to the ruins on the right adjoining a modern house.

• *The Old Station, Ramskapelle/36.5 miles/5 minutes/Map 5/19*

The station which played an important part in the battle has been left as it was when abandoned in 1918. It had served as an observation point for the first line. Beside it is a **Plaque to the 14th Regiment of Line**, October 1914. There are Information Boards here.

Return to the church, turn right and continue to the cemetery on the right.

• *Belgian Cemetery, Ramskapelle/37.2 miles/10 minutes/Map 5/20*

There are 632 graves, 400 of which are unknown, concentrated here after the war.

The old railway ran from behind the cemetery across the road ahead.
Continue under the E40 motorway.

We are now back in the flooded area.

Continue over the Noordvaart Bridge.

It was at this point that the water flooded in from the sea.

Continue to the T-junction with the N367.

Extra Visits to Unie Bridge Memorials, St Joris Memorials (Map 5/23/24/22) Round trip: 3.0 miles. Approximate time: 30 minutes.

Turn right and continue through St Joris to Oud St Joris. On the right is the local cemetery with a green CWGC sign.

In it is a row of **9 CWGC WW2 graves**, including an RAF Crew of six, 13 March 1942.

Continue under the motorway to just before the bridge over the Ijser and stop just before the Mannekensver sign on the ramp to the right.

To the right is a grey stone semi-circular **Memorial to the 14th Regiment of Line** who 'defended the last tattered remnants of their Fatherland on 22nd, 23rd, 24 October 1914.' In front of it is a polished black marble column.

Cross the road and walk down to the statue by the bank of the Ijzer.

The fine statue of a **Granite Soldier** mounts guard over the river. He represents the 7th Regiment of Line who lost heavily to artillery and

machine-gun fire. They held the line here until the 25th when they were relieved by the 14th Regiment. The bridge is called the 'Unie' or 'Union' Bridge and was taken by the Germans on 24 October. The Belgian artillery, often working without any cover, stubbornly resisted the German assaults, hauling guns up on the river bank into the infantry lines. They then scored some direct hits on the houses in which the Germans concealed their machine guns. However the Germans outflanked the bridge and the 14th had to withdraw beyond St Joris (St George) where you go next.

Turn round and return to the church on the right in St Joris.

On the roadside just before the church is a **Monument to the 3rd Carabiniers** who distinguished themselves here against Units of the German Navy on 22 April 1918. By the church is the **Tomb of Lt-Gen Baron Dossin de Saint-George** (1854-1936) who on 20 October 1914 ordered the flooding of the Nieuwendamme Polder, a week before the flooding of the Yser Plain.

Return to the T junction.

The Granite Soldier standing guard by the Unie Bridge.

The Belgian Cemetery, Ramskapelle.

Turn left direction De Panne on the N367. On the left is

• *Ramscapelle Road Military CWGC Cemetery/Nieuport Communal CWGC Cemetery 38.4 miles/20 minutes/Map 5/21*

Most of Plot I of the cemetery was made in July and August 1917 when the British XV Corps held the front line from St George's (now Sint Joris) near Ramskapelle to the sea. It was considerably enlarged after the Armistice from isolated graves and small cemeteries in the surrounding battlefields. Here are now 841 WW1 burials, 312 of whom are unknown. There are two Special Memorials to men originally buried at Nieuport whose graves were destroyed by shell fire and who are known to be buried here. The cemetery was designed by Sir Edwin Lutyens.

Just beyond it past the petrol station is the vast **Communal Cemetery** which contains 70 WW1 burials in two lines by a Cross of Sacrifice, mostly from June-August 1917, 3 of them unknown, and in a separate plot by the rear left hand hedge 31 WW2 graves from the withdrawal to Dunkirk in 1940.

To the right of the WW1 Plot is the imposing **Memorial to Hendrik Geeraert**, 'the hero of the flooding', the lock keeper who actually opened the flood gates in Nieuport.

Continue to the Demarcation Stone on the left.

• *Demarcation Stone/39.2 miles/5 minutes/Map 5/25*

This stone by the Witte Brug is in excellent condition and still bears its inscription.

Opposite is the Hotel Martinique (3-star with restaurant – superb cuisine –, 5 en-suite bedrooms, Tel: + (0) 58 04 08. Fax: + (0) 58 24 04 07).

Ramskapelle Road, CWGC Cemetery.

WW1 Plot, Nieuport Comm CWGC Cemetery.

Monument to the Hero of the Flooding, Hendrik Geeraert, Nieuport Cemetery.

Continue on the N367 to the T junction and turn left signed De Panne into Nieuwpoort.

Note that the spelling of the town is now variable between 'Nieuwpoort', the modern day spelling and 'Nieuport', the '14-'18 version!

Immediately park on the right in front of the bridge ahead. In the small park to the right is

• Monument to Lt Calberg, Monument to the Yser/39.4 miles/10 minutes/Map 5/26/27

On the small brick monument is a plaque that commemorates the special engineer company (*'Sapeurs et Pontonniers'*) that was formed on 2 September 1915 to continue to control the flood plains of the Yser. Calberg was mortally wounded here at the lock on 16 October 1917 and died in hospital.

The remarkable Yser Monument, designed by Pieter Braecke, is in the form of a woman (*La Belgique*) who turns away from the enemy protecting the Belgian crown in her hands. Around her are a blind soldier, a wounded soldier, a sick soldier and a fit soldier, representing the resistance.

It was inaugurated on 26 October 1930 by the League of National Souvenir, whose President was Prince Mérode and whose bust is shown in *bas relief*. The monument overlooks the Albert I Memorial (visited later) and the complicated complex of sluices.

The sluice gates at Nieuport control the amount of water that is allowed to remain in the polder (reclaimed land) that lies between the town and Dixmude. The arrangement is referred to locally as the Goose's Foot. A simpler analogy might be to imagine that one's arm represents the channel from the sea to Nieuport, one's wrist the lock gates and one's spread fingers the waterways that spread across the land. Thus by opening the gates at the wrist the flood waters can spread over the polder.

Cross the first of the 6 waterways.

This is the **Veurne Ambacht**.

Immediately after the bridge on the right is

• Albertina Marker/39.5 miles/5 minutes/Map 5/28

This stone at the Sluizenbrug marks the flooding of 29 October 1914.

Cross the second waterway.

This is the **Veurnevaart Veurnesluis.**

Continue to the T junction. Straight ahead is

• Bust to Hendrik Geeraert/39.6 miles/5 minutes/Map 5/31/30

This small head is on the wall of the Café De Schhuiswachter.

Turn right.

On the left is the Taverne De Gansepoot (Goose Foot) where there is a blind alcove on the facade. This is where Geeraert's bust should have been erected (and which still bears the inscription to 'H. Geeraert, *Batelier Chef Eclusier, Inondeur Yser'*

– Chief Lock Keeper and Flooder of the Yser – 1914-1918), but in a splendid piece of lateral thinking it was decided to place it on the other café, one of his favourite drinking holes. Geeraert ,who was a ship's captain, died in 1925 and was buried in Nieuport Communal Cemetery (qv) with great pomp.

Opposite it on the right is a 1942 **WW2 Memorial** (**Map 5/29**).

Turn right and drive onto the roundabout. Watch out for the priority markings.

Extra Visit to Coxyde Mil CWGC Cemetery. Round trip: 10 miles. Approximate time: 40 minutes.

From the roundabout take the road leading towards the coast at Nieuwpoort Bad, with the tramline to the left, and then turn left at the traffic lights onto Astridlaan. Some 500m later turn right on the N396, Canadalaan, to Oostduinkerke. Continue to Koksijde on the N396.

Coxyde, as it was known during the war, was some 10 kilometres behind the front line (although occasionally shelled) and the village was used for rest billets. Here the cartoonist **Bruce Bairnsfather**, who had just been created the first ever 'Officer Cartoonist', was attached to the French when he was requested by their Intelligence Department to come and draw the *Poilu* in the trenches. They had seen the extraordinary effect that his collection of cartoons, *Fragments From France*, had had on British morale. Based at the French HQ Bairnsfather was taken round their trenches day after day – an experience that he found depressing in the extreme, compounded by his inability to communicate in their language. Nevertheless he found the French mess devoid of 'that frigid atmosphere which some of our headquarters can and do assume'.

In Koksijde centre continue some 500m beyond the village on the N396 towards de Panne and then cross the Zeelaan on Houtsaegerlaan, where it changes its name to Robert Van Dammestraat, and continue 1 km along the road. On the right is

Coxyde Military CWGC Cemetery

The cemetery was started by the French and was reasonably sheltered from the shelling. When the British took over from the French in this sector in June 1917 it became one of the most important Commonwealth cemeteries along the coast and was used at night for the burial of the dead brought back from the front line. The French took over again in December 1917 and continued to use the cemetery. During 1918 British Naval casualties from Dunkirk were buried here. It was again used in WW2 during the defence of the Dunkirk-Nieuport Perimeter in May 1940. It now contains 1,507 UK burials of WW1 and 154 from WW2, 22 of them unknown. The French graves have been removed. The cemetery was designed by Sir Edwin Lutyens. Here the critic, philosopher and poet **Lt T[homas] E[rnest] Hulme** (qv), killed on 28 September 1917 at Nieuport with the RM Artillery, is buried.

Return to the roundabout in Nieuwpoort.

Detail of the Yser Memorial.

The figure of La Belgique on the Yser Memor[ial]

The Bust of Hendrik
Geeraert, Hero of
the Flooding.

Where the
Bust should
have been.

N.B. By turning down Koningen Elisabethlaan from the roundabout two more memorials may be visited. The street changes its name to Willem de Roolan at the junction with Langestraat. At this point on the wall on the left is a small bronze **Plaque to the site of shelter for 10 men of the Sapeurs and Pontonniers.** Further down Willem de Roolaan on the right is the ruin of the St Laurent Tower, also known as the Dove Tower. This 13th Century tower was part of a church. It was destroyed in 1916 by enemy fire. On it is a large bronze **Plaque to the Sapeurs and Pontonniers** and commemorates the flooding of the Yser at Nieuport, 1914-1918.

Plaque to the Sapeurs and Pontonniers on the Dove Tower.

The Albert I Monument in all its glory at night.

The British Memorial to the Missing with one of Jagger's superb Lions.

Go right round the roundabout. Return over the Veeurnevaart and left over the next waterway. This is the Ijzer and the bridge is the Ieperbrug.
Cross the next waterway.
This is the **Kreek Nieuwendamme**.
Continue past the obelisk on the right.
This **Memorial is to several French Regiments** of the Infantry, the Artillery, the Cuirassiers and the Engineers.
Continue over two more waterways.
These are the **Plassendalevaart and the Nieuw Bedelf**.
Continue to the large parking area and stop.

• *Memorial to King Albert 1/40.1 miles/20 minutes/Map 5/34*

The impressive King Albert I Memorial, erected on the initiative of Belgian veterans, is beside the lock gates at Nieuwpoort. The brick rotunda was designed by Julien De Ridder. It surrounds a mounted statue of the king sculpted by Karel Aubroek and was inaugurated on 24 July 1938 in the presence of the Royal Family. On the wall behind the equestrian statue of the King is a bronze plaque to the German-born Queen Elisabeth (which was damaged by a bomb at the end of WW2) and around the rotunda are panels representing the spiritual and industrial life of Belgium and within are inscribed two poems by August Van Couvelaert. A lift (which is closed over the lunch-time period) takes one to the balcony at the top of the memorial from which there is a panoramic view over the Ijzer and Nieuwpoort. The monument was restored in 1974. At night it looks spectacular when floodlit.

Beside it is:

• *British Memorial to the Missing/40.1 miles/5 minutes/Map 5/33*

The British Memorial in the form of a pylon of Euville stone, 8 metres high is guarded by three recumbent lions. Bronze bands around the pylon record the names of 566 officers and men (notably of the RND) who lost their lives in the Antwerp Raid of 9 October 1914 and who died in later actions along the Belgian coast from July-November 1917 and who have no known grave. The memorial was designed by W.B. Binne with the sculptor C.S. Jagger (qv) and was inaugurated in 1927. Around it are the words by Laurence Binyon known as 'The Exhortation'.

Nieuwpoort (or Nieuport as it was then known) formed the extreme left of the Allied line on the North Sea. In an attempt to relieve Antwerp the 87th French Territorial Division and the French Brigade of Fusiliers Marins plus the British 3rd (Cavalry) and 7th (Royal Naval) Divisions arrived on the coast in early October 1914. Alone the RND reached Antwerp where they made their famous but abortive raid (qv). The French Marines and the two British Divisions covered the retreat of the Belgian forces from Ghent. On 9 October the British were placed under Sir John French's command and the whole British Army was withdrawn to Ypres and la Bassée.

The British 4th Army (1st and 32nd Divisions followed by the 66th (E Lancs) Division) took over the sector again in June 1917 and held it throughout the German attacks of July until November 1917. By then Nieuport was virtually razed to the ground but the remains were riddled with trenches made by the French. Australian and British Tunnelling Companies had moved into the area in June but offensive tunnelling proved to be impracticable. The Companies, therefore, concentrated upon the construction of tunnelled dugouts, wells, subways and covered elephant shelters.

On 10 July 1917 the Germans mounted a fierce bombardment followed by a major offensive. Remnants of the 1st Division were cut off and annihilated when bridges were demolished save for 70 men who managed to swim the river. The 32nd lost its advanced trenches but retained the bridgehead. Although bitter fighting continued until the 17th the thin new line held, although the 1st Division sustained over 2,000 casualties and the 32nd nearly 1,000. The 49th (W Riding) Division then took over the sector, followed by the 33rd. No large offensives then ensued although monthly casualties remained heavy as the Divisions were rotated. In mid-November the 41st Division left for the Italian Front and the remaining British forces were relieved by two French Divisions. So ended the British occupation of Nieuport.

- *End of Yser Battlefield Tour*

OR

Extra Visit to WW1/WW2 Museum, Domein Raversijde (Map 5/35), Ostende New Comm CWGC Cemetery (Map 5/36), HMS Vindictive Memorial (Map 5/37). Round trip: 23 miles. Approximate time: 3 hours 15 minutes

From the King Albert 1 Monument, keeping to the right on to Westendlaan direction Oostende on the N318, continue to the large sign to the Domein and the Restaurant Walrave on the left. Park by the modern reception building of the Domein, opposite the airport.

The Domein Visitor Centre houses some temporary exhibitions and a book and souvenir stall. The Domein itself is a unique complex, a royal estate originally of King Leopold II and then after WW2 that of Prince Charles (Karel), King Albert 1 and Queen Elisabeth's second son. Charles was a Cadet at the British Naval Colleges at Osborne and Dartmouth and served on HMS *Renown* with the British Navy in the Far East. During the two World Wars the Domein was incorporated into the German coastal defences. Charles served as Regent from 1944-1950 whilst Leopold III was imprisoned in Germany and afterwards settled permanently in this charming, 50-hectare coastal hideaway. In 1981 he sold it to the Belgian State which has since developed and expanded it into an area of historic and touristic interest. Part of it, known as 'The Memorial', perpetuates the memory of Prince Charles, including his

Extra visit continued

personal Pavilion, a simple fisherman's hut. There is also an Archaeological Site and a WW2 Enigma Machine – the only one in Belgium – a natural park and pond system, sporting facilities and a restaurant. During the summer months many interesting events and temporary exhibitions are staged.

A path leads from the Reception via the Prince's quarters (some of them German buildings dating from the WW2 period) to the Open Air Museum which consists of two exceptionally well-preserved series of German coastal defensive systems – one from WW1 and the other from WW2.

One may visit each one separately or make a long visit to cover them both. Visitors are equipped with audio machines (choice of 4 languages) for a self-guided tour. Expert guides can be hired by prior appointment at an extra fee. Allow 90 minutes for a thorough tour of each set of bunkers.

The WW1 bunkers are the only well-preserved '14-'18 coastal defences remaining today. The main site is the Aachen Battery, dating from 1915, containing a wonderfully original communication centre, a bomb-proof shelter, observation posts, and the remains of huge gun emplacements – all looking unbelievably modern in design and conception. The circular gun emplacements housed 15cm Naval guns with a 360° field of fire mainly targeted at the Yser Front towards Nieuport. The bunkers are inhabited by the most life-like figures dressed in authentic uniforms and surrounded by original equipment. The bunkers were manned by German Naval personnel who controlled the Naval guns but who, unusually, were dressed in field grey. Some of the uniforms, notably that of one of only 6 Generals of the Coastal Artillery, are quite unique and rare.

Atlantic Wall Museum, WW1 Section. Gun emplacement for 15cm Naval gun – the Aachen battery.

Atlantic Wall Museum, WW1 Section.
Bomb-proof Shelter.

Telephone Exchange
manned by Germans
in rare Field Grey
Naval Uniforms.

The Aachen Battery, 1919.

Extra visit continued

In the inter-war years the structures were the subject of many military lectures on successful coastal defences. Several of the young German officers who served here in WW1 came back to advise on the new construction of coastal defences in WW2. It is thanks to Prince Charles, who resisted any attempt to demolish them (as has systematically been done to the extraordinary series of bunkers in Calais) that this marvellous 2 kilometre stretch of WW1 and WW2 history has been preserved in its integrity in the dunes between Middelkerke and Oostende. This is a fantastic site which deserves a visit.

Contact: Atlantic Wall Open Air Museum, 636 Nieuwpoortsesteerweg, 8400 Ostende.

Tel: + (0) 32 59 70 22 85. Fax: + (0) 59 51 45 03, e-mail: www.domeinraversijde.be
Open: 1 April-11 November 1400-1700 (earlier for groups by appointment). 1 July-31 August 1030-1800.

From the Domein parking turn left and continue on the N318 and keep left at the junction with the N341 through Mariakerke. Continue to the traffic light junction with the R31 and turn right signed E40 Brussels. Continue to the church on the left and turn right at the traffic lights beside the church onto Stuiverstraat and continue to the cemetery on the right.

Ostende New Communal CWGC Cemetery

This is a vast and impressive local cemetery with an imposing entrance with tall obelisks at each side. On entering, straight ahead up the central aisle is the Oostende Memorial and behind it Belgian military graves with flat white headstones bearing a simple cross and the name of the man buried below. To the right is the CWGC Plot with its Cross of Sacrifice. The cemetery was used by the Germans from October 1914 to October 1918. It now contains 50 WW1 burials, 27 of them Navy, including men from HMS *Vindictive*, *Prince Eugene* and *Sir John Moore*.

There are 366 WW2 burials, including Polish, French and Dutch, of which 75 are unknown. They include **Pilot Officer Donald Gordon Cobden**, who played rugby for the New Zealand All Blacks in 1937. In 1938 he came to

Headstone of Commander A.E. Godsal, DSO, RN, Croix de Guerre, HMS Vindictive, 1918.

Extra visit continued

England and joined the RAF (for whom he played rugby). On 11 August 1940 during the Battle of Britain Cobden was engaged in a dogfight with a large group of Messerschmidt BF 110s off the coast of Harwich during which he went missing – on his 26th birthday. His body was later washed ashore on the Belgian coast and buried here. There are also 8 non-war burials and 8 non-UK burials. The Cemetery Report and Visitor's Book are housed in the shelter at the end of the WW2 Plot.

Continue to the roundabout and turn left on Zilverlaan. Continue to the next crossroads and turn left on Gistelsesteenweg. Continue over the dual carriageway and follow the road left and right to the ring road, Verenig de Naties Laan. Continue to the roundabout and take the first small exit to the right and turn left on Perronstraat. Continue to the next main crossroads, turn right and continue to the ornate bridge over the railway. The memorial is just over the bridge beside the dock to the right. You may have to walk from here because of construction work.

HMS *Vindictive* Memorial

For a few days in October 1914 Ostende was the seat of the Belgian Government but by 14 October the port was closed and the town was occupied by the Germans the following day. Thereafter Ostende was periodically bombarded by ships of the Royal Navy and bombed by Allied airmen. The town was finally entered by the British on 17 October 1918 without opposition.

In a small park beside the basin of the dry dock is the bow section of HMS *Vindictive* sunk inside Ostende Harbour on 10 May 1918. The *Vindictive* had been part of the audacious raid on the German Submarine Base at Zeebrugge.

By 1917 German submarine warfare was having a serious impact on food and materiel supplies to the UK. Many of the submarines were based at Zeebrugge and supplied via Bruges. Zeebrugge is at the end of an 8 miles long stretch of canal from Bruges and Admiral Roger Keyes decided that if the canal could be blocked it would seriously disrupt the German campaign. Three old ships, the *Thetis, Iphigenia* and *Intrepid* were filled with concrete to be sunk across the canal beside the Mole while with them was HMS *Vindictive* carrying a raiding party aboard. The raiders were to land in darkness and with the added cover of smoke provide a diversionary attack to occupy the defenders. Additionally, the submarine C5, filled with explosives, was to be blown up under the approach to the Mole to prevent the arrival of reinforcements.

As planning progressed it was clear that more transports would be needed to carry the raiding party and by the time the assault force set sail, led by Roger Keyes, it numbered over 70 vessels.

Extra visit continued

The *Vindictive* arrived at the Mole just after midnight on St George's Day, 23 April, 1918 and the raiding party, while suffering heavy casualties, managed to create the needed diversion, C5 exploded as planned, the block ships were sunk and barely an hour after she had arrived HMS *Vindictive* pulled away en route to Dover. The results were patchy. Submarine activity was inconvenienced rather than hampered though some German vessels were trapped in the canal for the remainder of the war. Of the assault force some 180 men were killed and another 400 wounded or captured. Keyes was knighted and eight VCs were awarded.

Just two weeks later the *Vindictive* returned to Belgium and was sunk as a blockship across the harbour entrance during the night of 9 May, sealing the port and effectively preventing its use as a submarine base.

The Royal Marines Museum in Portsmouth has one of *Vindictive's* anchors and in St Ann's Church in the town is a memorial cross to an unknown stoker from the May attack. *Vindictive* remained a tourist attraction after the war but apart from the bow section which now remains, it was cut up and many pieces made into souvenirs. In 2003 the American auction house George Glazer had on offer a bronze golf club made from a *Vindictive* propeller and inscribed to Admiral E. G. Pallot DSO. Price $950.

Return to the King Albert Monument in Nieuwpoort.

The bow section of HMS Vindictive.

FIRST YPRES

18 OCTOBER-11 NOVEMBER 1914

'Shall I ever forget this day?
It will be indelibly stamped on my memory.
How anyone survived to tell the story is a mystery to me.'
An infantry Captain at Gheluvelt.

'You see why you should walk lightly if you ever go to Ypres,
the very stones of which are memorials to men
who perished on the Field of Honour.'
Maj J.M. Halley, 62nd Field Coy, RE.

SUMMARY OF THE BATTLE

In an attempt to break through the rapidly stabilising allied line and to reach Calais, von Falkenhayn launched the 4th and 6th (Ger) Armies against the BEF at Ypres on 18 October 1914. The fighting, toe to toe, staggered on with no real advantage gained by either side until heavy rains brought the contest to an end on 11 November. The British lost 2,350 officers and 55,800 soldiers. German losses were more than 130,000.

OPENING MOVES

Following II Corps' brief encounter at le Cateau the BEF continued its retreat from Mons and crossed the River Marne on 3 September. Von Kluck, believing that the Allies were beaten, altered the main thrust of his attack to come east of Paris and crossed the river only a day after the BEF. This change of direction exposed his right flank (doubtless von Schlieffen turned in his grave) and on 6 September the French 6th Army struck at it with 150,000 men, while the remainder of the Allies, including the BEF, about faced and drove the Germans 40 miles back to the Aisne River. The Schlieffen Plan was finished. Its failure was probably due to Von Moltke's steady weakening of the German right wing, contrary to Schlieffen's death-bed plea to 'keep it strong'. On 14 September he was replaced by General Eric von Falkenhayn.

That same day, 14 September, General Joffre began an attack on the German positions beyond the Aisne with the BEF and the French 5th and 6th Armies. The gains against the well-entrenched Germans were small and after two days Joffre began moving forces to the north-west in an attempt to get around the end of the German line. Von Falkenhayn responded by moving reserves to outflank the outflankers who responded in similar measure. The line grew and grew in a 'race to the sea' which ended when the Allies reached the coast at Nieuwpoort in Belgium in the first week of October 1914.

The BEF moved north in the 'race' in two parts. II Corps went directly to la Bassée and immediately came into action on 11 October in the 25-mile gap south of Ypres and I Corps went first to St Omer where the C-in-C, Sir John French, had to make a choice. Either I Corps should go further to the north where thinly stretched French forces together with the recently arrived British 7th Division were maintaining their hold on Ypres and their contact with the Belgians on the coast, or he should reinforce II Corps at la Bassée. He sent I Corps to Ypres and the First Battle began.

WHAT HAPPENED

Le Cateau was the last of the old-style one-day battles. The fighting at Ypres was never so simple. The title 'First Ypres' seems to describe a clear-cut contest, over a set period, with an agreed victor, yet by the end of 1914 the measure of victory was changing. It was no longer 'he who held the ground' but 'he who had the will to fight' who prevailed, and the will depended upon many things, including national reserves of manpower. 'Kill the enemy' became not just a tactical requirement but a strategic necessity. Everywhere, all the time, each side was intent upon killing the other. 'All Quiet Along the Potomac Tonight', goes the haunting song from the American Civil War, which goes on to intone that the loss of 'a private or two now and again will not count in the news of the battle'. That daily loss, even when there was no official 'battle' in progress, became significant during the First World War.

It was never 'All Quiet on the Western Front'. The BEF would lose hundreds of men by 'natural wastage' every day from 1915 onwards, yet every so often the enemies lumbered dinosaur-like into battle against each other and engaged in periods of ferocious killing that were graced with distinctive names. So it was with 'First Ypres', where the blood of a quarter of a million soldiers began etching a line of trenches that would stretch from the North Sea to Switzerland. Yet when the battle began (and historians cannot agree on the exact date) the leaders were still hoping for a great victory, a decisive battle. It was not to be.

The armchair analyst can divide First Ypres into neat and separate parts:

Battle of Armentières	13 Oct-2 Nov
Battle of Messines	12 Oct-2 Nov
Battle of Langemarck	21 Oct-24 Oct
Battle of Gheluvelt	29 Oct-31 Oct
Battle of Nonne Boschen	11 Nov

These classifications are geographical and the actions associated with them are best described during the battlefield tour below which, to simplify touring, covers First, Second and Third Ypres simultaneously. Running together the October and November actions, the 'First' Battle of Ypres is generally accepted to have opened on 18 October 1914 when the Germans began a three-week period of repeated mass attacks against the British positions. The British occupied a salient which bulged forward with a 16 mile-long perimeter into the German line (see **Map 6**). The heart of the Salient was Ypres, its defence now the responsibility of I Corps, and German attacks were concentrated along the axis of the Menin Road which enters Ypres from the east, passing as it does so the hamlet of Gheluvelt, barely 8 miles from Ypres Cathedral.

On 31 October Gheluvelt was lost and the Germans were on the brink of breaking through the line, outflanking the BEF and making a run for the Channel Ports. In one of the most remarkable actions of the War the 2nd Worcesters charged the enemy at Gheluvelt and saved the day. The Germans made one more major effort along the same axis when on 11 November 12½ divisions attacked across a 9-mile front with almost 18,000 men against 8,000. It wasn't enough. On that day, weighted down with mud and casualties, the First Battle of Ypres ended. The Salient perimeter had shrunk to 11 miles, but Ypres had not fallen. It never would.

THE BATTLEFIELD TOUR

This is done in conjunction with Second and Third Ypres. See **Map 6**, page 94 and page 200.

Legend for Map 6

1. The In Flanders Fields Museum
2. St George's Memorial Church
3. The Menin Gate Memorial
4. Essex Farm CWGC
5. John McCrae and 43 Div Memorials
6. John McCrae's Dressing Station
7. Yorkshire Trench
8. Breton Memorial
9. Hedd Wynn Memorial Plaque
10. Cement House CWGC
11. Steenbeek Albertina Memorial
12. 20th Light Div Memorial
13. German Cemetery Langemarck
14. Canadian Brooding Soldier Memorial
15. New Zealand Memorial
16. Tyne Cot CWGC
17. Memorial Museum Zonnebeke
18. Polygon Wood CWGC Cem
19. Buttes New British CWGC Cem
20. Australian 5th Div Memorial & New Zealand Memorial to the Missing
21. Black Watch Corner
22. South Wales Borderers & 2nd Bn Worcesters Memorials
23. 18th Eastern Div Memorial
24. Gloucester Regt Memorial
25. Kings Royal Rifle Corps Memorial
26. Hooge crater and trenches
27. Hooge Museum
28. Hooge CWGC Cem
29. Sanctuary Wood Museum and trenches
30. Hellfire Corner
31. Hill 60 Museum
32. 14th Light Div, Queen Victoria's Rifles & 1st Australia Tunnelling Coy Memorials
33. Tunnellers Memorial St Eloi
34. Crater St Eloi
35. Museum Messines
36. New Zealand Kowhai tree, Ross Bastiaan plaque and Mie Tabe Peace Post
37. Island of Ireland Peace Tower
38. Hyde Park Corner CWGC Cem
39. Ploegsteert memorial & Berkshire CWGC Extension Cem
40. Hollandseschuur Craters
41. Croonaert Chapel CWGC Cem
42. 1st CAP Mem
43. Bayernwald Trenches etc
44. Wytschaete Mil CWGC Cem
45. 16th Irish Div Mem
46. Spanbroekmolen Crater
47. Lone Tree CWGC Cem
48. Kruisstraat Craters
49. Messines Ridge Brit CWGC Cem
50. NZ Mem
51. London Scottish Mem
52. NZ Mem Park

MAP 6: FIRST YPRES 18 OCTOBER - 11 NOVEMBER 1914

See page 93
for Legend

© TVH 2004

0   3 kms

N

──────── The front line at the start of the battle, 18 October 1914

• • • • • The front line at the end of the battle, 11 November 1914

NEUVE CHAPELLE

10-13 MARCH 1915

'The attack which we are about to undertake is of the first importance to the Allied Cause. The Army and the Nation are watching the results, and Sir John French is confident that every individual in the IVth Corps will do his duty and inflict a crushing defeat on the German VIIth Corps which is opposed to us'.

> Written note from General Rawlinson, commanding IV Corps, given to every soldier before Neuve Chapelle.

'The G.O.C. the Division desires me to convey to you and all ranks under your command his deep appreciation of the splendid work performed by your battalion during the last few days' hard fighting. For my own part I find it difficult to express adequately my admiration for the way in which you have fought. I mourn with you for our gallant comrades who have fallen, but the splendid cause for which they have fought, and the brave way in which they have died, must always be the greatest comfort to those whom they have left behind, and stimulate them to fresh efforts'.

> Message passed after Neuve Chapelle to the 13th Bn London Regiment ('The Kensingtons') by Brigadier Lowry-Cole commanding 25th Brigade.

We licked 'em on the Marne
And whacked 'em on the Aisne
We gave 'em hell at Neuve Chapelle
And we'll bloody well do it again

> Anon.

SUMMARY OF THE BATTLE

This was the first British-initiated offensive of the war and was prompted by French doubts about British commitment to the conflict. Following a massive but short bombardment, General Haig's 1st Army attacked the village of Neuve Chapelle which was taken on the first day. However, von Falkenhayn's rapid movement of reserves and a British shortage of ammunition prevented a breakthrough. British casualties were about 13,000, the German 14,000.

OPENING MOVES

On 15 February 1900 General French led a dashing cavalry charge to complete the relief of Kimberley after a 5-month siege by the Boers. Fifteen years later, now commanding the British Expeditionary Force on the continent of Europe, he once again seemed to have in mind a cavalry charge through enemy lines, something which, like the Kimberley affair, he hoped would have great publicity and morale benefits.

By the end of 1914 the trench system behind which each opposing army sheltered was well defined along the Western Front and the prospect of huge casualties from frontal attacks had been signalled by First Ypres. Fertile minds like Winston Churchill were seeking alternatives to mutual mass bludgeoning in Europe as a way of settling the war and by 1915 the Gallipoli alternative was taking shape. The French, however, unlike the British, had the enemy on their soil which concentrated their minds to a much shorter focal length and in January and February they engaged in aggressive and successful operations in Champagne, retaking important ground from the Germans.

The Champagne offensives generated benefits in that large bodies of German troops were diverted from the Eastern Front, but they also had a tactical lesson that was to colour the next four years of warfare. The French had won back territory by a new and sophisticated use of artillery. First they chose a sector to attack where surprise was possible. Then, by massing their artillery, they pounded the enemy front line into oblivion. At a pre-determined hour, the barrage lifted and moved behind the front line to drop between it and the German reserves. Thus reinforcements were prevented, by a curtain of steel, from moving to the front. Meanwhile the French infantry advanced and captured the German front line positions.

At the beginning of March 1915, the Belgians held the line from the North Sea to Dixmuide and the French from Dixmuide to the top of the Ypres Salient. West of Neuve Chapelle were IV Corps under General Rawlinson and the Indian Corps under General Willcocks, both part of the 1st Army. The BEF had expanded to some 18 divisions, three times its original strength of August 1914 and was now divided into two armies. Sensitive to French innuendo that the British were not pulling their weight, the C-in-C decided to mount the first British offensive of the war, an attack with General Haig's 1st Army. He gave as his reasons for offering 'a vigorous offensive movement', 'the apparent weakness of the enemy in my front... holding as many hostile troops as possible in the western theatre (and)... the need of fostering the offensive spirit in the troops under my command'.

It was decided to attack the German salient at Neuve Chapelle with a view to taking the high ground around Aubers Ridge to the east of the village and to effecting a breakthrough. There were to be two phases: (1) take the village and the line known as 'Smith-Dorrien trench' to the east of the village (see **Map 7**); and (2) enlarge the gap in the enemy line and make towards the Aubers Ridge. On 9 March General Haig finished his Special Order for the Day with these words, 'To ensure success each one of us must play his part and fight like men for the honour of old England.' At least half of the fighting, however, was to fall to the Indian Division and not the men of old England.

WHAT HAPPENED

At 0730 on 10 March almost 500 guns opened fire on the German lines over a length of 2 miles. Thirty-five minutes later the guns lifted and the iron curtain fell across the village of Neuve Chapelle itself. Simultaneously the Garhwal Brigade, the assault formation of the Indian Corps, 'swarmed over the parapet and doubling over the intervening space of from 100 to 200 yards reached (except one battalion) its first objective without a check'.

On the north western flank of the salient the assault by 8th Division met with similar success, only the Middlesex being held up just south of the Moated Grange. Complete surprise had been achieved and the village and Smith Dorrien trench were taken. Now was the time for urgency, to move on quickly to Phase 2, but communication between the two Corps commanders was confused, each waiting for the other to act, and it was five hours before General Haig ordered the attack to continue. The Germans had reacted quickly, bringing up reinforcements through thin British artillery fire. It was thin because the front had been widened but mainly because the British did not have enough ammunition to continue the bombardment at an effective rate. The shortage developed into a public outcry known as 'The Shell Scandal', which led to the appointment of Lloyd George as Minister of Munitions with the task of sorting things out. One of his actions was to introduce liquor licensing laws in an attempt to reduce absenteeism due to alcohol. Even today, therefore, some effects of the battle of Neuve Chapelle remain.

The results at the end of 10 March were, however, considerable. A front of 4,100 yards from Port Arthur to just beyond the Moated Grange had been taken and to a depth in places of 1,200 yards. The whole of Neuve Chapelle village had been captured. Little more was thereafter gained. The Germans mounted a counter-attack at dawn on 12 March with 16,000 men against the Indian Brigade and the front of 8th Division, but this failed to make any advance. It did, however, pre-empt any further offensive action of substance by 1st Army so that on 13 March both sides settled down to consolidate the positions that they held.

The battle was over, but now the British felt themselves to be more substantial than just an adjunct to the French forces, the French had proof that the British were willing to fight, the Germans began to strengthen their lines opposite the British and everyone adopted the destructive artillery barrage as being standard practice for the battles to come.

THE BATTLEFIELD TOUR

• **The Route:** The tour begins at Béthune, visits the Portuguese Cemetery and Memorial; Port Arthur, The Indian Memorial; Private Memorial to 2nd Lt Crichton; the Moated Grange; the Quadrilateral; Layes Bridge; Neuve Chapelle British and Farm CWGC Cemeteries; the le Touret CWGC Cemetery and Memorial to the Missing and ends at the house with WW1 Statues

• **Extra Visits** to La Couture Portuguese Memorial, La Vieille Chapelle Communal (with Memorial to 1st King Edward's Horse) and New and Zelobes CWGC Cemeteries.

MAP 7: NEUVE CHAPELLE 10-13 March 1917

1. Portugese Mem Chapel
2. Portugese Cem
3. Indian CWGC Mem
4. 2nd Lt Crichton Mem
5. The Moated Grange
6. Bunker
7. Bondar Mem
8. Layes Bridge
9. Neuve Chapelle British CWGC Cem
10. Neuve Chapelle Farm CWGC Cem
11. Le Touret CWGC Mem Cem
12. Maréchal Foch Statue
13. Portuguese Mem La Couture
14. La Vieille Chapelle CWGC Cem
15. 1st King Edward's Horse Mem
16. Zelobes CWGC Cem

© TVH 2004

- **Total distance:** 13.3 miles
- **Total time:** 2 hours 30 minutes
- **Distance from Calais to start point** via Béthune: 59 miles. Motorway Tolls.
- **Base towns:** La Bassée, Béthune
- **Maps:** IGN 2404 Est 1:25,000 plus IGN 2405 Est 1:25,000

From Calais take the A16/A26 direction Paris/Reims then the A26/E15 direction St Omer. Take Exit 6 to Béthune and the N41 to La Bassée and drive into the centre. Set your mileometer to zero.

• *La Bassée/0 miles/RWC*

La Bassée has no hotels but makes a good lunch break. There is a variety of restaurants, pizzerias and brasseries in and near the main square, Place du Géneral de Gaulle.

In 1914 la Bassée was a thriving town of small industry and agriculture when on 11 October 1914 their peace and prosperity was shattered by the occupation of the Germans when their front line was established two kilometres away. There followed four years of shattering fire and the town gradually disintegrated, the church being hit in the first days of the bombardment and the surrounding roads engulfed in flames. On Easter Sunday 1915 the German High Command ordered the evacuation of the civilian population – other than those who could be of practical use to them, like bakers, nursing sisters, but they too were finally evacuated on Saturday, 3 July 1915.

On 10 October 1918 the British took what remained of the devastated town. Between 1919 and 1933 the Mayor Alexandre Crespel oversaw the rebuilding of his town and the magnificent Town Hall was rebuilt, albeit some distance from the original, electricity and running water and wider streets were installed.

Once again, on 27 May 1940, the Basséens knew German occupation and damage to their buildings – until they were liberated in September 1944.

Drive north from la Bassée on the D947 signed to Estaires for 3 miles until you reach the clearly signed Portuguese Cemetery on the left. There is a chapel opposite. Stop and beware of the traffic.

Portuguese Headstone.

Entrance to the Portuguese Cemetery, with Memorial in the background, la Bombe.

• The Portuguese Cemetery and Memorial/3.3 miles/15 minutes/Map 7/2/1

This has no connection with the battle of 1915 but relates to the Kaiser's Offensive of 1918. Since the memorial is on our route, and the Portuguese did come into action here on 9 April 1918, it has been included.

The two-division Portuguese Army was dispirited by 1918. A change of government had meant that they no longer had political support at home and their morale was low. Anticipating a German offensive, the British area commander withdrew one of the Portuguese Divisions and before it could be replaced by a British force, the enemy struck directly at the one remaining Portuguese Division, now holding a double frontage. Unlike their forebears at Busaco in 1810, they broke, some taking the machines of a British cyclist battalion and pedalling their way to safety, others purportedly shooting a British driver and commandeering his vehicle to make their escape. Many others, however, fought hard against overwhelming odds when placed in a situation for which they were untrained to exploit. Brigadier F.P. Crozier in his 1930 memoirs, *A Brass Hat in No Man's Land*, was somewhat brutal in his descriptions of the Portuguese whom he found to his right on the line on the night of 7-8 April. To start with their equipment was 'all rusty and useless', while 'practically all the front line sleeps heavily and bootless in cubby hole covered with waterproof sheets, while their equipment hangs carelessly about'. Crozier's concerns about their lack of training and preparedness were justified. The attack was a disaster. 'It has been a ghastly let down', he commented, 'If the Portuguese had never entered the line it would not have been so.' One of the problems was that 'the uniforms of the Germans and Portuguese are not dis-similar. Hundreds of Portuguese were mown down by our machine guns and rifle fire.' Crozier hinted that the 'political considerations' were behind the decision to use what GHQ perfectly knew to be ill-prepared Portuguese troops.

Their losses were indeed heavy – some 7,000 were killed in the action known as the Battle of the Lys during which Neuve Chapelle was lost – and they are commemorated with pride by their countrymen. A ceremony of remembrance is held at the cemetery, usually on the Saturday nearest the anniversary. It ends not with the customary *'vin d'honneur'*, but a *'porto de honor'!*

Contact: Union Franco-Portuguaise, 61 rue des Haies, 62136 Richebourg. Tel: + (0)3 21 26 23 69.

The cemetery, which is now in pristine condition, contains 1,831 burials, of whom 239 are unidentified. It was constructed between 1924 and 1938 with bodies brought in from cemeteries in Ambleteuse, Brest and Tournai in Belgium as well as from Le Touret. The superb ornamental wrought iron entrance gates, inspired by Leal de Camara, open on to the ranks of grey headstones inscribed *'Morto de la Patria'*. Many are *'Desconehcido'* (Unknown). At the rear is a fine stone monument with battle honours.

Over the road is a small chapel to Notre Dame de Fatima, built in the 1970s by the local Portuguese immigrants' association to honour their compatriots killed during the First World War.

During the Battle of the Lys the Portuguese, for divine protection, carried into their trenches a damaged statue of Christ, with legs broken off at the knees, the right arm broken and the chest wounded. When they were forced to leave the trenches they abandoned the statue and it was later retrieved by the Bocquet family who had originally erected it in 1877. When the village of Neuve Chapelle was rebuilt, the old statue was propped up beside a new calvary, and remained in situ throughout the Second World War. In 1958, on the 40th anniversary of the Lys battle, the French Government awarded Portugal's Unknown Soldier with the *Croix de Guerre* and the *Légion d'Honneur* and the Bocquets agreed to allow the statue to travel to the commemorative monastery of Bataliha (founded in 1385). Great ceremony and pomp attended the delegation (which included Portuguese veterans who had settled in France) which flew to Lisbon on a military plane bearing a message from President René Coty to President Salazar. On 9 April 1958 the 'Christ of the Trenches' was erected in Bataliha above the tomb of the Portuguese Unknown Soldiers (one from the First World War, one from Africa) where it remains to this day.

Continue north to the next crossroads. The Indian memorial is on the left. Stop.

• *Neuve Chapelle Indian Memorial/Private Memorial to 2nd Lt Crichton/3.4 miles/20 minutes/Map 7/3, 7/4*

This is Port Arthur crossroads, Richebourg, the southern end of the Indian Corps' front on 10 March 1915. The intended main thrust of the attack here (by the 1/39th Garhwalis) was west to east, enveloping the entire crossroads. The 1/39th was the one Indian battalion which didn't make its objective. Immediately on leaving the trenches the attack veered right towards the Portuguese memorial area and entered part of the German line which had not come under the preparatory bombardment. The 1/39th suffered heavy casualties, all six British officers who were in the assault were killed. The Indian Corps consisted of two divisions, the Lahore and the Meerut, both of three brigades. Each brigade contained one British and three Indian battalions, a total Corps strength of some 24,000. The Corps had seen action at Neuve Chapelle in October 1914 and by the end of the year had suffered 9,500 casualties, 7,100 from Indian units. In the 1915 battle the Corps lost one-fifth of its strength and this is therefore an appropriate site for their memorial.

Designed by Sir Herbert Baker with Charles Wheeler, it is circular, with a lotus-capped 50ft high column flanked by two tigers, the whole complex acknowledging the connection with India, from the screen wall to the two domed chattris (loggias). It adds an exotic note to the somewhat featureless surrounding northern French landscape. The names of over 5,000 dead with no known grave are carved on the semi-circular wall, arranged in unit order. There is a special bronze panel adding 210 servicemen of Undivided India who died 1914-1918, whose graves at Zehrensdorf in E. Germany were unmaintainable, and a 1939-45 Cremation Memorial.

Here is commemorated **Lt William Bruce**, 59th Scinde Rifles, who was awarded the **VC** for his action on 19 December near Givenchy, who, though himself

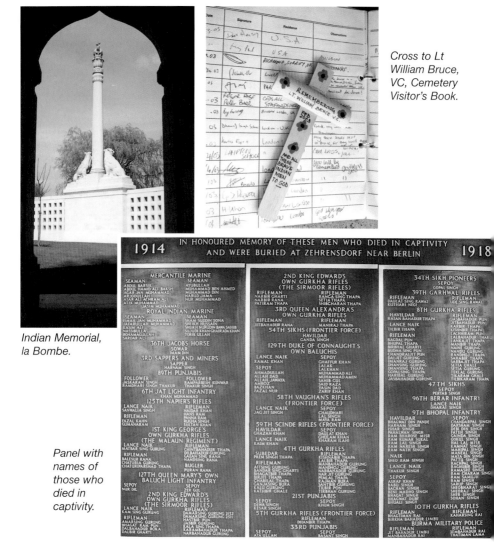

Cross to Lt William Bruce, VC, Cemetery Visitor's Book.

Indian Memorial, la Bombe.

Panel with names of those who died in captivity.

IN HONOURED MEMORY OF THESE MEN WHO DIED IN CAPTIVITY AND WERE BURIED AT ZEHRENSDORF NEAR BERLIN 1914 — 1918

wounded, walked up and down his trench encouraging his men under heavy attacks until he was killed.

The Cemetery Report should be read for the evocative and colourful names of the Regiments, many raised by Nizams and Maharajahs, and the ranks, e.g: risaldar = major, jemadar = lieutenant, kot daffadar = quartermaster-sergeant, havildar = sergeant, naik = corporal, sepoy = infantry private, sowar = cavalry sergeant.

Walk round the outside of the memorial on the D171 Le Touret road.

On the grassy bank is the **Stone Memorial to 2nd Lt Cyril Alfred William Crichton,** 3rd Bn London Regiment, RF who died here on 10 March 1915. The eulogistic inscription is summarised in French. Crichton joined the HAC while studying law at the Inner Temple and went to Malta with his battalion before coming to France in January 1915. He was killed leading an heroic charge of the old school on 'an obdurate trench that made a gap in the line'. His parents made strenuous efforts to find his grave as they wished to purchase the land on which it was sited. The story of their quest, the erection of the memorial and the subsequent discovery of Crichton's body in a different location in 1925 when it was removed to Le Touret CWGC Cemetery, visited later, is told in Barrie Thorpe's *Private Memorials of the Great War*. This rare private memorial was moved from the Estaires Road opposite the café to this safer spot in 1965. It was carefully repaired after the damage it sustained by bullets in 1940 and from being struck by a car. The CWGC has maintained the memorial since 1923 at the request (and subsequent bequest) of the family.

Private Memorial to 2nd Lt Crichton, la Bombe.

Turn right at the crossroads towards Neuve Chapelle, passing the Auberge de la Bombe on the left.

• *Auberge de la Bombe/3.4 miles/RWC*

The café's name has nothing to do with the war. Studious research at the bar (and with the local history society) by the authors established only that the name originated in the Middle Ages and has some connection with the smuggling that went on at that time. However, over the door of the café is the name 'Port Arthur' and the date '10 mars 1915', the opening day of the battle.

It is now a very popular lunch stop.

Continue through the village and just after a sharp bend right at the junction of the D171 with the D170 there is a small courtyard farmhouse on the right with iron gates. On current maps it may be called 'Ferme de Lestre'. Stop.

• *The Moated Grange/5.0 miles/10 minutes/Map 7/5*

This is not the original building (known as Ferme Vanbesien in 1914), though it is on the original site and broadly to the same design and of the same size. It is the northern (left hand) end of the attack frontage for 10 March 1915. At the time of the

The Moated Grange.

battle it had been a strongpoint in the German line. The trenches in front of the Middlesex, just below the Grange, held by the llth Jäger Battalion were not bombarded effectively, owing to the late arrival of the artillery. The leading waves of the Middlesex were cut down and the battalion had to be reinforced with two companies of the West Yorks for a later attack.

The orchard (see **Map 7**) immediately south of the Moated Grange (the orchard is no longer there) was, however, finally taken by the Middlesex and the West Yorks just after noon on 10 March. During the morning, 24th Brigade Trench Mortar Battery had dropped over 230 mortar bombs on to the Grange and when the West Yorks worked north from the orchard the German survivors surrendered. Two days later the 13th and 15th (Ger) Infantry Regiments counter-attacked the Grange but were held off, in great measure due to the activities of the newly trained 'bombing' (grenade-throwing) detachments. One bomber, **Corporal W. Anderson** of the 2nd Green Howards, won the **VC** for his part in the action for leading three men in a bombing raid against a large group of the enemy.

Another **VC** was awarded on 12 March 'at Neuve Chapelle' to **L/Cpl Wilfred Dolby Fuller** of the 1st Grenadier Guards who saw a party of the enemy trying to escape along a communication trench. Running towards them he killed the leading man with a bomb when the remainder (some 50 men) all surrendered to him. He was quite alone at the time. Fuller, was later treated for his wounds at No 3 Base Hospital, Sheffield where King George V awarded him with the Cross of the Order of St George (3rd Class) conferred upon him by the Tsar.

Continue to the next crossroads and turn right [along what was known as Winchester Road] towards Mauquissart and Piètre on the Rue des Lirons, D168.

• *The Quadrilateral/5.5 miles/5 minutes*

One hundred yards to your right, two hundred yards along the road, was the German defensive area known as the Quadrilateral which was taken by the 2nd Scots Guards on 12 March together with 400 prisoners. It was sadly one of the few places where the pressures of war and harsh military discipline led a soldier to desert. Private Isaac Reid left the forward areas the day before the Quadrilateral action, he was caught, court-martialled and executed in front of the Regiment on 9 April 1915. Reid is buried in Longuenesse (St Omer) Souvenir Cemetery.

One hundred yards further on was a line of a dozen or more craters, stretched across the road, created in later fighting.

Continue to the small stream.

This is **Layes Brook**. In 1915 it was known as the Rivière des Layes, a tributary of the Lys or an old artifical drainage channel which, the *Official History* complains, was 'said to have been dug by the farmers without expert assistance. As a result it has not a proper flow, the water sometimes going north, sometimes south'. The drainage was 'got under control' by the British during the winter of 1915-16. Then it was a considerable obstacle, 'about ten feet broad with nearly vertical banks and three or four feet of water in it'. It was crossed on 8 light bridges brought forward by the leading battalions to enable the advance on the Bois de Biez to continue. The Germans had constructed a second line of defence along the eastern side of the stream with strong bridgeheads and today a large **bunker** in good condition can be seen to the left.

In the attack which began at 0530 hours on 10 March over the stream to the Bois de Biez, Maj D.M. Watts of the 2/2nd Gurkhas was awarded the DSO and Capt A. Dallas Smith and and Lt (and Adjutant) E.J. Corse-Smith were awarded the MC. Four Germans were captured here by No. 4 Coy and another 'who had lost his way, walked into the middle of No. 2 Company and was made prisoner'!

By about 0800 hours the Germans had rushed up reinforcements. The attack had been brought to a standstill and a withdrawal was ordered by Gen Jacob, commanding the Dehra Dun Brigade, to the western bank of the stream where the wounded were collected and retired. Gallantry awards were won by Riflemen Manjit Gurung, Partiman Gurung, Ujir Sing Gurung and Jagtea Pun of the 2/2nd Gurkhas for attending the wounded under fire and bringing them back.

Continue.

To the left the farm complex which is on the site of the Moulin de Piètre can be seen. The German defences were strong here and held up the 10 March attack by the Ghurkas

At the Piètre crossroads turn right.

Many more bunkers can now be seen in the fields to the right as one drives along, and the Memorial to P.O. J. Bondar (**Map 7/7**) see page 12.

Take the next right just before the Bois du Biez.

In 1915 the wood consisted mainly of young trees with with a thick undergrowth. After the fighting of October 1914 around Givenchy and la Bassée the Germans gained a foothold in the wood here and then established a stronghold. It was one of the objectives of the Dehra Dun Brigade 10 March 1915 attack. On 11 March their advance was stopped by thick fog and heavy fire from the wood. On 12 March it was the second objective of a further attack by the Sirhind and Jullundur Brigades. The artillery kept up a fierce bombardment on the wood, with it is thought, great success as 'for days afterwards the enemy was observed to be removing bodies from the wood for burial in the fields behind it.'

After 200 yards there is a small bridge over a stream.

• Layes Bridge/7.3 miles/10 minutes/Map 7/8

This is the centre of the battlefield, the British attacks coming from directly ahead of you, and the line of the stream, Layes Brook, which features strongly in detailed accounts of the fighting, can be seen clearly to north and south. The Germans had turned this area into a redoubt with barbed wire and 15 machine guns. On 12 March, under the impression that the German line had been broken, General Haig brought up cavalry units and ordered that the infantry attack be pressed forward 'regardless of loss'. It was pressed, but the soldiers were tired, ammunition was short and the German defenders were fresh reinforcements. The Layes Bridge redoubt was never taken and the attack petered out overnight and during the following morning.

Continue to the crossroads with the D171. Turn left and just before the church in Neuve Chapelle turn right down the Rue du Moulin to the British cemetery sign to the right and turn up the track to the grass track leading to the cemetery on the left.

Layes Brook looking towards the site of the Moulin de Piètre.

Bunker beside the brook.

Headstones of Capt. A. Prismall and 17-year-old Pte A. G. Gordon.

Neuve Chapelle British CWGC Cemetery.

Neuve Chapelle Farm CWGC Cemetery.

• *Neuve Chapelle British CWGC Cemetery/8.4 miles/15 minutes/Map 7/9*

The cemetery was begun during the battle (when it was known as Moggs Hole Cemetery) and used until the following November. It now contains some 50 burials. There is a special memorial to five men of the Rifle Brigade, killed on 10-14 March 1915, (with headstones behind) who were originally buried in Neuve Chapelle Churchyard and whose graves were destroyed by shell-fire and buried here is **17 year old Pte M. Walsh** of the Manchester Regiment, 25 July 1915.

Return to the main road and continue to the next CWGC sign to the right. Park on the left and walk up the grassy path to the cemetery.

• *Neuve Chapelle Farm CWGC Cemetery/8.7 miles/15 minutes/Map 7/10*

There are 35 identified British soldiers buried here and 21 of them are from the 13th Battalion the London Regiment, known as 'the Kensingtons'. The Regiment was typical of the proud Territorial forces that came to the Colours, its origins deriving from the Volunteer forces of 1859. Like most, its gestation was complex. However, the Haldane reforms of 1908 created the Battalion via the amalgamation of the Kensington Rifles (4th Middlesex) and the 2nd (South) Middlesex and in 1913 it became 'Princess Louise's Kensington Regiment'. On 2 August 1914 the Kensingtons arrived at Salisbury Plain for their annual training. That night they

Decorative Column.   The entrance to the Colonnade.

Le Touret Memorial and CWGC Cemetery.

were woken up and ordered to return to their drill hall immediately. There they were told to be ready for mobilisation, which came two days later. Over the next fortnight the battalion was equipped and brought up to strength and on 16 August it left with other Territorial units for war training in Hertfordshire. Early on the morning of 3 November 1914, led by the band, they marched to Watford station and at 1100 entrained for Southampton. After a long wait they sailed on the *SS Matheran* at 0100 hours on 4 November, reaching le Havre that same afternoon and marching to St Martin's rest camp on the hill. By foot and train they moved to the area of Laventie and spent the winter manning trenches in what was known as a quiet sector, even exchanging souvenirs with the enemy during an unofficial truce on Christmas day. Nevertheless, by the beginning of March the battalion had 96 casualties, 27 of whom were killed. Then came Neuve Chapelle.

The Kensingtons were in reserve with 25th Brigade. Their task was to follow up the assault battalions. They had a hot meal with the rest of the brigade at Rouge Croix, filled their water bottles with tea and with two extra bandoliers of ammunition each and their rations in a sandbag, marched forward in great anticipation 'of making a decisive step towards the winning of the war'. They never came into contact with the enemy because after the first day the attack made no progress, though they began to suffer casualties from enemy artillery fire. On 11 March they were reinforced with a draft of 133 men, including Lt M. A. Prismall, son of **Captain A. Prismall** commanding B Company. For three more days they suffered under continuous bombardment and then came the order to move out. As the battalion was about to leave Captain Prismall was killed by a shell on 14 March. He lies in this cemetery with the other volunteers. He was 53. A **17 year old, Pte A.G. Gordon,** R Berks, 10 March 1915, is also buried here, among the 60 graves (nearly half unidentified) in this small cemetery surrounded by a beautiful stone wall.

Another battalion which suffered severely and with bravery in the Battle of Neuve Chapelle was the 2nd Scottish Rifles, who went into the battle on 10 March some 900 strong of whom 700 went 'over the top'. Six days later, only 143 were fit enough to parade for roll-call after the battle. The story is well-documented in John Baynes' book *Morale: A Study of Men and Courage.*

Continue to the T junction. Turn left and left again and return to Port Arthur. There turn right on the D171 (the Rue du Bois). Continue to the first turning to the right.

This was known as Chocolat Menier Corner and it was in this area that another spontaneous manifestation of that curious phenomenon the **Christmas Truce** took place on 25 December 1914. The sector was held by the 39th Garhwal Rifles and at dawn the Adjutant of the 2nd Bn, Capt E.R.P. Berryman, noticed that no shots were being fired and then heard the Germans (of the 16th Westphalian Regiment) singing and shouting in their trenches. Before long German and Indian were shaking hands and gifts of biscuits, cigarettes and cigars were exchanged for brandy, plum pudding and whisky. The Germans allowed the Indians to bury some of their dead. The jolly scene was stopped by Maj Keith Henderson of the 1st Bn who blew his whistle 'and signalled and shouted for all to come back'. [*Christmas Truce*, Malcolm Brown & Shirley Seaton]. When the affair was reported to the commanding officer leave for all officers taking part in the truce was stopped. Two of them, Capt William George Stanhope Kenny (age 33) and Lt John

Charles St George Welchman (age 26), were killed on 10 March in the Battle of Neuve Chapelle, the only officers to reach the German trench they were attacking. Kenny was killed in the trench which he held for some time 'with superb courage', despite being twice wounded. They are both buried in Laventie Mil Cemetery.

Continue to the large memorial on the left.

• Le Touret Memorial and CWGC Cemetery/12.7 miles/20 minutes/Map 7/11

This is probably the most elegant and elaborately designed memorial and cemetery complex on the Western Front. It comprises a loggia surrounding an open rectangular court encased by three solid walls and a colonnade on the east. Small pavilions mark the end of the gallery and there is a fascinating round tower at the back. It commemorates those missing with no known grave in this area over the period from the arrival of the BEF to the eve of the Battle of Loos (25 September 1915). Their names are inscribed inside the colonnade in Regimental order. It does not include any Canadian names (they are commemorated at Vimy) or, in theory, Indian (commemorated at Neuve Chapelle) although there is one Indian name. On Panels 26/27 – the Sherwood Foresters panels – is the name of **Private Jacob Rivers, VC**, 12 March 1915, age 34. His VC was awarded for two acts of bravery on 12 March, when on his own initiative he advanced on the enemy and hurled bombs, causing them to retire. Also commemorated is **Pte William Francis Elmes** of the 2nd R Sussex, 9 May 1915 age 34, who had served in the S African Campaign. His two brothers also fell in the war. Commemorated on the memorial are the 25 men from Wadhurst (qv) killed in the Battle of Aubers Ridge and who inspired the twinning between Aubers and Wadhurst.

The memorial, designed by J.R. Truelove, was, according to Philip Longworth's *The Unending Vigil*, the story of the IWGC and the CWGC, unveiled at the same hour and the same day in August 1930 as the memorials at Vis-en-Artois (also designed by Truelove), Pozières and Cambrai. CWGC records now show that it was unveiled by Lord Tyrrell on 22 March 1930.

The cemetery, begun in November 1914 by the Indian Corps, was used continually by field ambulances and fighting units until taken by the Germans in April 1918. In its spacious lawns there are over 900 burials, including that of **Lt Cyril Alfred William Crichton** (qv) who, until 1925, was buried under a special private memorial (visited earlier) near where he fell opposite the Auberge de la Bombe. He was a Territorial.

Continue to the village of Le Touret to the junction with the D169. On the right hand corner is

• House With Statues of WW1 Personalities/13.3 miles/5 minutes/Map 7/12

Surmounting this extraordinary house, known as the Villa des Verdures, is a concrete equestrian statue of Marshal Foch, built by the sculptor Alphonse Wallaert after the war. Wallaert who was known as 'The Poet of Concrete', died in La Couture in 1958 at the age of 87. Other personalities commemorated around the tower are President Poincaré and the King and Queen of the Belgians.

Extra Visit to Portuguese Memorial, la Couture (Map 7/13), Vieille-Chapelle Communal (and 1st King Edward's Horse Memorial), Vieille Chapelle New (Map 7/14/15) and Zelobes Indian (Map 7/16) CWGC Cemeteries. Round trip: 7.4 miles. Approximate time: 40 minutes

Turn right direction la Couture on the D169 and continue to the church in la Couture on the right. In front of it is

The Portuguese Memorial. This impressive memorial shows a Portuguese soldier (note the distinctive ribbed tin helmet) attacking 'Death' overlooked by the female figure representing Portugal. It was sculpted by Teixeira Lopes

and inaugurated on 10 November 1928. (See page 100).
Continue on the D170 to La Vieille-Chapelle and turn right on the D182. Continue past the church to the cemetery on the right with the green CWGC Tombes de Guerre sign on the wall.

La Vieille Chapelle Communal CWGC Cemetery. There are two CWGC graves in the cemetery, both from May 1940 – **Pte A. Leitch**, R Scots and **Sgt J. Fox**, RA. To the right of the impressive local War Memorial is a stone **Memorial to the 1st King Edward's Horse, the King's Oversea Dominions Regiment** unveiled in 1921. It lists the officers and men who were killed or died on service in France 1915-1919, 'many of whom were killed in a very gallant defence of this locality, April 1915'. Over the 9/10/11 April 1918, during the Kaiser's Offensive, strong German attacks came from your right towards Vieille Chapelle. The King Edwards Horse established defensive positions around the D170/D182 junction where you last turned, here and at Fosse (about a mile up the D172 opposite). By around 2200 hours on 10 April those at Fosse were isolated and Lt Addison of the Horse organised and inspired a stubborn resistance by a mixed force despite being hampered by retreating Portuguese. Such was Addison's spirit that a German breakthrough was averted but he was killed by a shell splinter on 11 April and buried by the Germans. Lt Noel Goodricke Addison, MC, age 25, is commemorated on the Dud Corner Memorial at Loos and the CWGC lists his date of death as 9 April, which according to the Regimentals records would seem to be incorrect.

Portuguese Memorial, la Couture.

Turn round and return to the junction with the D170 signed to Vieille Chapelle. Continue to the cemetery on the left.

La Vieille-Chapelle New CWGC Cemetery. Burials started in the village in the Old Military Cemetery near the school which was closed in November 1915, when burials were made in this cemetery. It was then used by fighting units and

Memorial to 1st King Edward's Horse, La Vieille Chapelle Communal Cemetery.

Extra visit continued

Field Ambulances until March 1918 when the village and cemetery fell into German hands. When the Germans withdrew in September 1918 further burials took place here. After the Armistice British, Indian and Portuguese graves were concentrated here from the surrounding battlefieds. The Portuguese graves were later removed to the Portuguese Cemetery (qv). It now contains nearly 1,000 British and Indian soldiers, approximately one-third of which are unidentified. The original graves are in Plots I and IV, Rows A and B. Here are buried two **VCs** from April 1918. **T/2nd Lt John Schofield**, 2/5th Lancashire Fusiliers, led a party of 9 men against a strong-point at Givenchy and was attacked by about 100 of the enemy. His skilful use of men and weapons resulted in the taking of 20 prisoners. He then proceeded with a party of 10 towards the front line where he met large numbers of the enemy and opened fire on them. Under point-blank fire he climbed on the parapet and by his fearless demeanor forced the enemy to surrender. As a result 123 of them, including several officers, were captured. Schofield was himelf killed a few minutes later. **2nd Lt Joseph Henry Collin**, 1/4th King's Own (R Lancaster) Regt, after offering a gallant resistance against German attacks on his platoon position, 2nd Lt Collin, with only 5 of his men remaining, slowly withdrew, contesting every inch of ground. Single-handed they then attacked a machine gun. After firing his revolver into the enemy he seized a Mills grenade and threw it into the hostile gun team, putting the gun out of action, killing 4 of the team and wounding two others. He then took a Lewis gun and engaged a second hostile machine gun, keeping the enemy at bay until he was mortally wounded.

The village of Vieille-Chapelle was 'adopted' by Paddington after the war. *Continue on the D182 to the T junction with the D945. Ahead is Zelobes Indian Cemetery. Turn right and stop as soon as you can. Walk back to the path to the cemetery.*

Zelobes Indian Cemetery. 1914-1915. Zelobes remained in British hands from the early days of the war until 11 April 1918 when it was captured by the Germans and held by them until 30 August. The cemetery, which is approached by a long grassed path and enclosed by a beautiful dark stone wall, was used by Field Ambulances from November 1914 to October 1915 and then after the Armistice isolated graves were concentrated into it. It now contains 105 Indian and British soldiers, 73 of whom are identified. It is worth visiting to read the wonderful Indian Regimental names inscribed on the headstones.

Return to the house with the Foch statue.

• *End of Neuve Chapelle Battlefield Tour*

OR *continue into Béthune on the D945 for RWC (see Loos tour).*
OR *go on to take the Aubers or Fromelles Tours (see pages 117 and 163).*
OR *the Festubert-Givenchy Tour (see page 131).*

SECOND YPRES

22 APRIL-25 MAY 1915

'There was a curious smell, which was quite noticeable – we all remarked on it
– and then after a time the casualties started coming in.
It was most dramatic: long, long lines of Canadian soldiers, single file,
each man with his hand on the shoulder of the man in front. There would be
a man in front who could see – all these other chaps couldn't;
hundreds and hundreds of these chaps stumbling along, single file.'

A First World War Doctor.

'Of one's feelings all this night – of the asphyxiated French soldiers –
of the women and children – of the cheery steady British
reinforcements that moved up quietly past us
going up, not back – I could write, but you can imagine.'

Col John McCrea.

SUMMARY OF THE BATTLE

At around 1700 hours on 22 April 1915 the Germans attacked the north-eastern edge of the Ypres Salient using poison gas in what is generally accepted as the first major use of gas in warfare. Subsequent defensive fighting against repeated gas attacks resulted in a shortened Salient, but no breakthrough. Allied casualties were about 60,000, German 35,000.

OPENING MOVES

At the end of 1914, the German General Staff decided that, having failed to defeat France quickly and now being faced by enemies in both the east and the west, they would concentrate upon the Russian front. General Erich von Falkenhayn considered that Russia, struggling with internal political discontent, was the weaker of his two immediate protagonists and would succumb to concentrated German might. As far as the Western Front was concerned he instructed his commanders only to do enough 'lively activity' to keep the enemy occupied. One of the things that seemed likely to 'occupy' the French and British was to try out poison gas on them.

Article 23 of the 1907 Hague Convention, which Germany had signed, forbade the use of 'poisons or poisonous weapons', but before April 1915 the Germans had already tried out gas. Shrapnel shells containing a form of chemical irritant were tried out near Neuve Chapelle in October 1914 and tear gas shells had been used at Bolimow in Poland in January 1915, but neither trial produced any significant result. Von Falkenhayn was, however, supportive of the idea of developing a gas weapon and extensive testing was carried out at the Kummersdorf artillery ranges near Berlin. In the Second World War another secret weapon was tested there – von Braun's V2 rocket.

Germany possessed the most powerful chemical industry in the world and it was not difficult to consider other ways than shelling in which an enemy might be enveloped in a gas cloud. What was more difficult was to decide where to use the gas and several German commanders considered the use of such a weapon to be unethical. However, Falkenhayn persisted and keeping in mind his need to draw attention away from his intended effort in the east, he looked for a sensitive spot on the Western Front. Ypres was such a place.

The 4th (Ger) Army had been on the edge of breaking through during First Ypres (cf. Gheluvelt p.93) and the Salient was the only significant piece of Belgian soil not yet occupied. Added benefits were that the BEF had been decimated in defending Ypres and any activity there would demand wholehearted British attention as well as the fact that the French knew full well that holding Ypres was the key to keeping the Germans out of the Pas de Calais. Therefore Duke Albrecht of Wurtemberg and his 4th (Ger) Army facing Ypres were chosen to try out the new weapon. Preparations began in February 1915.

The simplest method of delivery of the gas was by cylinder, since that was the standard commercial container. Train loads of the heavy 3.5ft long objects were brought into the lines. It is estimated that some 30,000 cylinders were brought up into the forward areas and inevitably some were damaged – by accident or enemy action – so that the presence of the gas weapon was fairly common knowledge among German soldiers as time went on. Now and again German prisoners were taken who spoke about the presence of gas. However neither the French nor the British authorities took the reports seriously enough to take any precautions, though early in April Canadian troops were warned about the possibility of a gas attack following the mention of gas in the French 10th Army's 30 March intelligence bulletin.

The cylinders were dug into their firing positions in groups of 20, each group covering 40 yards of front and, 24 hours ahead of the intended assault time, the German soldiers were given their final briefings. At 0500 hours on 22 April 1915 everything was ready – except the wind. It was blowing the wrong way.

WHAT HAPPENED

As the German infantry waited, hoping for the wind to change direction, their field artillery pounded the front line defences and heavy 17-inch guns bombarded the rear areas. When the day matured it became warm and sunny, perhaps lulling the defenders into a degree of laxity and certainly making the Germans hot and uncomfortable in their heavy equipment. By late afternoon the attack was in the balance. Soon it would be dark. The offensive could not be made at night. Then, soon after 1600 hours a breeze began to develop from the north-east and one hour

MAP 8: SECOND YPRES 22 APRIL - 25 MAY 1915

Legend

Front Line BEFORE
2nd Battle of Ypres
Front Line AFTER
2nd Battle of Ypres
Area Occupied by
Germans by midnight
22 April

Scale

0   1   2   3   4 kms

© TVH 2004

Bikschote

Langemarck

Lekkerbotterbeek

Keerselare
(Brooding Soldier)

St Juliaan

Passchendaele

Tyne
Cot

N303

Steenbeek

Zonnebeke

A19

Menin

Pilckem

Evening of
22 April

AFTER

Potijze

Menin Road

N8

Gheluvelt

Sanctuary Wood

Steenstraat

Boezinge

Ypres Canal

N369

BEFORE

Hooge

Zillebeke

Ypres-Comines Canal

N331

YPRES

Kemmelbeek

N8

N333

N38

N308

→ Poperinghe

Groте Beek

N373

Dikkebus

N304

N

later the Germans opened the nozzles of thousands of gas cylinders and a fog of death rolled slowly across No Man's Land.

Below the Pilckem Ridge was the Canadian 3rd Brigade and alongside them, north of the ridge, the French Algerian 45th Colonial Division and it was upon these two formations that the fog descended. Sir Arthur Conan Doyle described what happened: 'The French troops, staring over the top of their parapet at this curious screen which ensured them a temporary relief from fire, were observed suddenly to throw up their hands, to clutch at their throats, and to fall to the ground in agonies of asphixiation. Many lay where they had fallen, while their comrades, absolutely helpless against this diabolical agency, rushed madly out of the mephitic mist and made for the rear, over-running the lines of the trenches behind them. Many of them never halted until they had reached Ypres, while others rushed westwards and put the canal between themselves and the enemy.'

By 1900 hours there was no organised body of French troops east of the Yser Canal. Between the Belgians (who held the ground north of the 45th Division's area) and the Canadian 3rd Brigade there was now a gap of 8,000 yards. The way to Ypres was open. The German advance (four reserve divisions – the 45th, 46th, 51st and 52nd) was cautious and limited. Their objective had been to take the Pilckem Ridge and no more and by the time they reached it darkness was falling. Thus it was not until the following morning that they realised how successful their attack had been and just how close they were to Ypres, which they could now see quite clearly ahead of them (see **Map 8).** The Canadians around St Julien, meanwhile, had reacted to the gas with determination despite the fact that the French panic had left their northern flank unprotected. Brigadier General R.E.W. Turner commanding the Canadian 3rd Brigade ordered his reserve battalion, the 14th, into line beside the already postioned 13th and 15th battalions and held strong German attacks north of Keerselare (cf 'The Brooding Soldier' page 213) until they finally stopped at about 1830 hours. Two platoons of the 13th fought to their last man and **L/Cpl Frederick Fisher** of the battalion won a posthumous **VC** for his actions that day. His citation as published in the *London Gazette* gives the date of his action as the 23rd, but Canadian authorities say that this is incorrect. Sir Max Aitken, the Canadian Record Officer, later (as Lord Beaverbrook) wrote *Canada in Flanders,* the story of Canadian actions to 1916, including an entire chapter, with maps, covering the gas attacks.

Curiously, the fact that the Canadians stood and fought through the gas attack meant that they suffered less from it than they might have done had they followed the example of the French colonial troops and streamed back to the rear. The *Official History* explains: 'It early became evident that the men who stayed in their places suffered less than those who ran away, any movement making worse the effects of the gas, and those who stood up on the fire step suffered less – indeed they often escaped any serious effects – than those who lay down or sat at the bottom of a trench. Men who stood on the parapet suffered least, as the gas was denser near the ground. The worst sufferers were the wounded lying on the ground, or on stretchers, and the men who moved back with the cloud.'

General Smith-Dorrien commanding the 2nd Army first heard news of the attack at about 1845 hours on the 22nd and immediate moves were made to bring up reinforcements to plug the line. General Foch heard at midnight what had happened and reacted typically with three steps that should be taken: (1) hold; (2) organise for a counter-attack; (3) counter-attack. In fact counter-attacks did begin that night and following Foch's proposals it was agreed that 'vigorous action' east of the canal would be the best way to check any German attempts to advance. The enemy, however, struck first and on 24 April following a one-hour heavy bombardment the Germans released a gas cloud at 0400 hours immediately to the north-east of Keerselare and on a front of 1,000 yards against the Canadian Division. Throughout the day pressure on the Canadians forced them to withdraw to second-line positions, Keerselare being captured early in the afternoon. The following day, Sunday, 25 April 1915, the day of the Gallipoli landings, the Germans made a fierce effort to break the British lines. They made gains, but they did not break through.

The struggle continued in a series of engagements classified as the Battle of s-Gravenstafel, 22-23 April; Battle of St Julien, 24 April-5 May; Battle of Frezenberg, 8-13 May and Battle of Bellewaerde, 24-25 May. Overall the Germans made net gains. On 4 May the British made tactical withdrawals in order to shorten their lines, reducing their frontage from 21,000 yards to 16,000 yards and shortening the greatest depth of the Salient from 9,000 to 5,000 yards. In the World of 'If', the Germans might have taken Ypres and then the Channel Ports: if they had not used the gas just as a tactical distraction, but part of a major attack; if they had had reserves ready to follow up the initial success; if the wind had been in the right direction early on 22 April they would have seen how successful the gas had been and could have called up forces to exploit the break in the French lines. If they had used their secret weapon properly, say many, they could have won the war with it. The 'after-the-event' experts say the same thing about the British use of the tank on the Somme. Perhaps the most relevant 'If' belongs to the Canadians, courtesy of Rudyard Kipling, because they kept their heads when all about were losing theirs.

THE BATTLEFIELD TOUR

This is done in conjunction with First and Third Ypres – see page 200.

AUBERS RIDGE

9/10 MAY 1915

'The Gallipoli attack 6th to 8th May could only use 18,500 shells.
Haig was expending 80,000 on Aubers Ridge for less result,
a far less object – and twice the loss of life.'

Liddell Hart, *The Real War.*

'After Aubers Ridge surprise was abandoned.'

Alan Clark. *The Donkeys.*

'When we put memorial crosses for those who had fallen in the action
of May 9 there was a sergeant-major who put a white cross on the
grave of his son, and a private who put a cross on the grave of his father.'

W. Linton Edwards , 4th Bn Black Watch,
later Editor *Leeds Mercury.*

SUMMARY OF THE BATTLE

On 9 May 1915 the First British Army made a two-pronged attack on the German line that ran from just south of Neuve Chapelle to Bois Grenier some three miles north of Fromelles. At 0500 hours six hundred artillery weapons opened fire followed forty minutes later by an infantry advance. The southern prong consisting of the Indian and I Corps aimed towards Aubers Ridge while that of IV Corps, 6,000 yards to the north, headed for Fromelles.

The barrage had been inaccurate and short of shells, the German wire had not been cut and no small-arms supporting fire had been arranged for the advance. Little or no progress was made and by 0300 hours the following morning all the British troops were back where they had started and nearly 12,000 officers and men were casualties.

OPENING MOVES

By the spring of 1915 it was apparent that the Germans were concentrating their efforts on the Eastern Front and, following the battle of Neuve Chapelle in March, General Joffre, seeing an opportunity to take advantage of the situation, asked Sir John French if he would co-operate in a combined attack towards the ridges at Vimy and Aubers. The French were to take Vimy and the British, Aubers.

The British agreed. Sir John, convinced that the short artillery preparation at Neuve Chapelle had been a success, insisted that it be repeated and set his 1st

MAP 9: AUBERS RIDGE 9 MAY 1915 (FROMELLES) (See also Map 13)

APPROXIMATE
FRONT LINE
4 MAY 1915

© TVH 2004

Scale
0   1.4 kms

N

THE RIDGE

Fournes-en-Weppes

Herlies

La Cliqueterie

FIRST OBJECTIVE LINE

Aubers

Fromelles

Delangre Farm

Rouges Bancs

La Cordonnerie Farm

Pétillon

VC Corner

Fauquissart

The Sugar Loaf

7 Div

Layes Brook

Rue du Bois

D171

Neuve-Chapelle

La Bombe

Lorgies

25 Bde
IV CORPS
24 Bde

INDIAN CORPS
Meerut Div
Dehra Dun Bde

I CORPS
1 Div   3 Bde

2 Bde

D141a

Fournes-Weppes

D141

D41

D175

D947

D171

N41

Legend

1. Aubers Ridge CWGC Cem
2. German pill box
3. Aubers *Poilu*
4. Site of proposed Aubers Mem
5. Wadhurst roundabout
6. The Kaiser's bunker
7. Aubers documentation centre
8. The Hitler bunker
9. Fromelles Museum
10. Sgt Bramble Mem
11. Site of mine explosions
12. Capt Kennedy Mem
13. Australian Mem Park
14. VC Corner CWGC Cem
15. Le Trou Aid Post CWGC Cem
16. Rue Pétillon CWGC Cem
17. Rue du Bois CWGC Cem
18. Laventie German Cem
19. House where Hitler stayed
20. Fournes-en Weppes German Cem

Army's objective as, 'to break through the enemy's line on its front and gain the la Bassée to Lille road between la Bassée and Fournes-en-Weppes.'

The plan was to attack both north and south of **Neuve Chapelle.** The Indian and I Corps were south, essentially astride the D947 at **la Bombe** crossroads heading for the ridge and **la Cliqueterie Farm.** Some 6,000 yards to the north IV Corps, centered on the D175, was to head towards **Rouges Bancs** and **Fromelles** and then swing south with 7th Division to la Cliqueterie to join up with the northern force. Thus, in theory, having broken through the German lines, the 1st Army, now in possession of Aubers Ridge, would catch the Germans in a pincer trap.

WHAT HAPPENED

The attack was planned for the early morning of 8 May. Since the success of the operation depended initially on the attacking troops breaching the German wire, trench mortar batteries were attached to the infantry brigades for close support but in the event did not materially affect the outcome. The 1st Wing of the Royal Flying Corps was given the task of aerial reconnaissance, supposedly reporting back when successive target lines were reached by the infantry, the lines to be marked with strips of white linen 7 feet by 2 feet carried for that purpose. The effectiveness of the system was not tested as none of the designated lines were reached.

Owing to bad weather the French decided to postpone the operation for 24 hours, the decision reaching General Haig at 1700 hours on the 7th, just 60 minutes before the troops were due to move into their forward positions for the attack. Inevitably forward movements had already taken place and some troops were thus stuck uncomfortably in the open for 24 hours before going into battle, but by midnight of 8 May all units were ready for the next morning's assault.

The sun rose at 0406 hours and at 0500 hours a 40-minute barrage opened, with a furious final 10 minutes. But the shells were not of sufficient calibre, the 4.7" guns had worn barrels causing faulty aim and range and the bombardment failed in its objective of destroying the German wire and prepared defences. The operation was virtually doomed from the start.

The Southern Attack

Below la Bombe crossroads no covering small arms fire was given as the leading companies of the 2nd and 3rd Brigades of the 1st Division moved into No Man's Land intending to form a line some 80 yards short of the German positions. They were met with heavy machine-gun fire. Many fell dead on the ladders and parapets. Nevertheless some men doubled forward and formed a line not far short of the intended objective.

The Indian Corps to their left across and above the crossroads fared little better – they too lacked supporting small arms fire. The leading troops were only able to advance a few yards from their own parapets and though some following troops tried to press on they were soon driven back until the trenches were blocked with casualties, though some brave men reached the enemy. A German diarist recalled a handful of Gurkhas 'running like cats' reaching the wire and attacking with knives. All were killed and buried later that day in a communal grave.

When the barrage lifted at 0540 all three brigades attempted to storm the German lines. The lifts were too quick, being made before the attacking troops were within fifty yards of the enemy, and the wire had not been cut. Small parties from the leading battalions crossed the German trenches here and there (one from the Munsters was seen waving a green flag) and then disappeared. The Munsters suffered a double tragedy. Their CO, Lt Colonel Rickard, was killed and all but three of the survivors of the green flag party were later killed by friendly fire. Within two hours 2nd and 3rd Brigades lost some 60% of their strength. The 2nd Royal Sussex and the 1st Northants were 'virtually annihilated', with 551 and 560 casualties respectively, the shallow jumping-off trenches clogged with the dead and wounded.

Inadequate efforts were made to organise further attacks, the British artillery merely prompting the Germans to rain shells down upon the men lying out in No Man's Land. General Haig, hearing that the French were making good progress on their part of the front, decided to renew the attack later in the day. He ordered the reinforcement of 2nd and 3rd Brigades and the replacement of the Dehra Dun Brigade with the Bareilly, these actions being carried out in broad daylight. The *Official History* dryly observes 'These reliefs ... were attended by much confusion and heavy losses'. Brigadier General Thesiger, commanding the 2nd Brigade, reported that his brigade was not fit to renew the offensive and it was replaced by the 1st (Guards) Brigade.

There was a succession of postponements until, eventually, the attack began at 1557 hours. The 1st Black Watch (1st Division, 1st Brigade) was the only battalion to be in position to go over the top at zero hour, some battalions arriving after it was clear that the assault had failed. The Scots moved forward with their pipes and some 50 men reached the German front line trenches to find the occupants in flight. They turned the Germans' own machine guns round to fire upon them but were subsequently surrounded and almost all killed. **Cpl John Ripley** of the 1st Battalion, who was the first man to climb the enemy's parapet, was awarded the **VC**.

In the Meerut Division the relief of the Dehra Dun Brigade by the Bareilly cost two hundred men through artillery fire and was not complete until 1600 hours. When the brigade did go over the top it came under intense direct machine-gun fire, the enemy standing on his parapets and taking aim. Finally, when all the companies in the leading battalions had been sent forward and shot down, the attack was called off. The brigade had lost over 1,000 men in a few minutes. In this action another **VC** was won by **L/Cpl David Finlay (qv)** of the 2nd Battalion Black Watch (Meerut Division, Bareilly Brigade) who led a bombing party of twelve, ten of whom fell. Finlay then went to the assistance of a wounded man and carried him to safety over the fire-swept ground. Somewhat confusingly, Finlay's action was on 9 May, therefore technically speaking it was in the Battle of Aubers Ridge. However it physically took place in the area of the Battle of Festubert (which some authorities describe as lasting from 9-27 May 1915).

The Northern Attack

The IV Corps plan was to attack with 24th and 25th Brigades of 8th Division astride the D175 road towards Rouges Bancs and Fromelles. The brigades were moved up into the forward trenches on the night of 8 May and were in position by 0230 hours. Each was allocated a small force of cyclists and mounted troops 'to assist the advance beyond the German front line'. What might appear to be a more sensible allocation were sections of mountain artillery and trench mortars intended to take on the German machine guns. The preliminary bombardment was simultaneous with that in the south.

The attack began at 0540 hours. In 24th Brigade the 2nd East Lancs were stopped before they got half way across No Man's Land though a party of one officer and thirty men of the 2nd Northants got through the German wire thanks to a field gun that had been brought up in support. At 0610 the 1st Sherwoods were sent in to help the East Lancs but were cut down like the others. Here, as in the south, the barrage had been ineffective and the Germans were choosing their targets over open sights. Despite being under direct fire **Cpl J. Upton** of the Sherwoods rescued and tended many wounded men, actions for which he received the **VC**. Meanwhile, under pressure to push on, the supporting battalions were moving into the forward trenches crowding those still there and the casualties coming back, all falling prey to the accurate enemy artillery fire.

The 25th Brigade had split its assault into two columns four hundred yards apart. The right hand column of the 2nd Rifle Brigade and the 1st Royal Irish Rifles found the wire in front of them had been cut and covered the 100 yards of No Man's Land at speed, taking over 250 yards of German front including prisoners of the 16th Bavarian Reserve Regiment. Interestingly this was Adolf Hitler's regiment. What might have been the outcome had he been there and been one of the prisoners!

The left-hand column formed by the 1/13th London (Kensington) Regiment was also initially successful. The battalion formed up at **la Cordonnière Farm** (various spellings) and was in its assault positions by 0200 hours. The preparatory bombardment failed either to cut the wire or to destroy the enemy defences. A planned 4.7" howitzer barrage on **Delangre Farm** failed to land a single shot on target. Nevertheless, at 0540 two mines of 2,000lbs of gunpowder 70 yards apart, which had been prepared by 173rd Tunnelling Company, were exploded under the German front line trenches. The Kensingtons rushed the craters. They had trained carefully for the operation and were proud to be the first TA unit to have been used as an assaulting force in a major operation. Despite the withering opposition the Kensingtons took the craters and the track leading to Delangre, but the farm possessed a number of machine guns and the Kensingtons were unable to advance further or to receive substantial reinforcements. At 0610 hours **Brigadier Lowry-Cole,** commanding the 25th Brigade, reached the German trenches to find many men streaming back towards their own lines, bringing with them German prisoners whose presence led to a bombardment by our own guns. He leapt onto the parapet intending to rally his men, but was shot and killed. He is buried in Le Trou Aid Post CWGC at Fleurbaix (qv). Elements of the 2nd Lincolns did reach the

Aubers Ridge British CWGC Cemetery.

Rue du Plouich Bunker.

Kaiser's Bunker, Aubers.

Hitler's Bunker with
detail of inscription (inset).

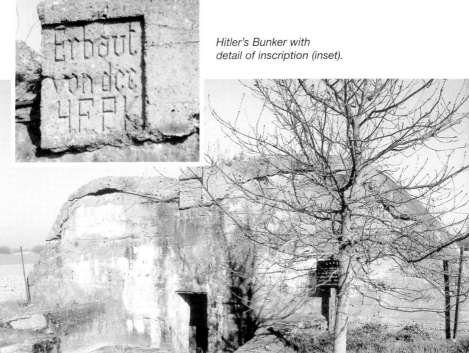

Kensingtons including **Acting Corporal Richard Sharpe** who was the first to reach the enemy line and who, using grenades, cleared 50 yards of trench, efforts for which he received the **VC**. He later became a Company Sergeant Major but was killed at Passchendaele.

When Haig heard of the stalemate he issued orders for the attack to be resumed but it became clear that, due to the severe losses already incurred and the difficulty of bringing up fresh troops, apart from the inadequacy of the artillery support, this was not practicable and during the night of 9 May the order was given to retire. Thus the remnants of the Kensingtons made their way back pursued by a strong German counter-attack around 0230 hours on the 10th. One Kensington remembered, 'We crawled about 120 to 150 yards through German barbed wire and across ground raked by a withering cross fire. It was a hailstorm of lead bullets splitting up the ground and filling the air with the buzz as of angry bees and bursting shells.' The Kensingtons had lost 13 officers and 423 other ranks. They had ceased to exist as a fighting unit.

The battle of Aubers Ridge had been a failure.

THE BATTLEFIELD TOUR

• **The Route:** The tour continues on from the end of the Neuve Chapelle Tour and starts at Aubers Ridge CWGC Cemetery, visits the Rue du Plouich Bunker, continues through Aubers village to 'The Kaiser's Bunker' and the Aubers Historical Centre and then finally looks at the so-called 'Hitler's Bunker'.
• **Total Distance:** 2.2 miles
• **Total time:** 1 hour
• **Distance from Calais to start point:** See Neuve Chapelle Tour
• **Base town:** La Bassée
• **Maps:** IGN 1:25,000 2404 Est plus 2405 Est

From the 'Foch House' (qv) return to the la Bombe crossroads on the D171. Go straight over and take the first right on the D168 to Lorgies. Turn left on the D72 to Herlies and there left on the D41. Continue to the cemetery on the right. Set your mileometer to zero.

• *Aubers Ridge British CWGC Cemetery/0 miles/15 minutes/Map 9/1*
The cemetery, which is situated right on the objective line of the first day of the battle, contains concentrations from several wartime cemeteries. It has 593 UK, 124 Australian, 1 Indian burial and 1 Special Memorial. There are also some '39-'45 graves. The burials start in 1914 and range through the dates of all the battles in the region. Many are Unknown Australians from the July 1916 Fromelles Battle in Plot I, and Plot II is almost entirely of men of the 61st (S Midland) Division from the same action. The single Indian is **Sepoy Abdullah** of 58th Vaughan Rifles, 25 September 1915 (Neuve Chapelle). **Captain W. I. Maunsell**, 2nd Cameronians, 8 February 1915, age 31, was the 'Beloved son of Surgeon General T. & Mrs Maunsell.'

In the WW2 Plot is buried **Pilot Officer Jozef Bondar** of 303 Sqn RAF, 28 June 1941, to whom a **memorial** was erected (see **Map 7/7**) in June 2003. This Polish pilot fought for his country in Poland in 1939, escaped to Rumania and thence to France where he flew a Potez 25 with the French Airforce in North Africa until the fall of France. He then joined the RAF in July/August 1940. The Sikorski Institute in London has a file on Bondar. He was shot down in a classic attack from the rear when returning from escorting a raid on the Comines electrical supply. The instigator of the memorial is Jocelyn Leclercq, who founded the research reseach group Antiq'Air Flandre-Artois (qv).

Continue towards Aubers on the D41 and after barely 100 yards turn right on Chemin de Valmondy and at the fork keep to the left on Rue du Plouich. Continue to the crossroads where, on the right, is

• *Rue du Plouich Bunker/.6 miles/5 minutes/Map 9/2*

The bunker looks remarkably like the ruins of an Irish famine cottage. The concrete structure with mesh reinforcement was in fact constructed within an existing house. It overlooked the British lines and was connected to the artillery command centre. It incorporated a telephone room and was well camouflaged.

Turn left and continue to the roundabout and turn right signed Centre Village. At the T junction turn left. In front of the Church on the left is

• *Aubers Centre & Poilu/1.1 miles/10 minutes/Map 9/3*

Records exist in the town of the original meeting on 4 April 1925 during which it was decided to employ the Parisian sculptor, Descatoires, to make the monument in the form of a 2.25m high *Poilu* on a Belgian granite base. The inscription was to be in letters of 'great character'. The monument cost 32,000 Francs.

When mobilisation was declared between 2 and 18 August 1914, men of the village left to fight. The following month refugees started to arrive from the Lille area and on 10 October a large German contingent entered the village, searching the church and many houses. On 17 October Smith-Dorrien's 9th Brigade occupied the Ridge and British soldiers were seen in the village for the first time. On 20 October the Germans launched their offensive and on 23 October the British troops were forced to withdraw. All but 200 or so inhabitants were then evacuated and the village remained in German hands until October 1918 when it was liberated by the 47th (London) Division.

[**N.B.** By continuing past the church you will pass the fine *Mairie* on the left with its elegant first floor meeting room. At the roundabout turn right and on the left, just before a right turn is the site (**Map 9/4**) where an important memorial to the Aubers Ridge Battle and the 'Men of Wadhurst' will be erected in 2005. Aubers has a very active Twinning Association with Wadhurst in Sussex. This arose because 25 men of Wadhurst, named on a Memorial in their church, were all killed in the Battle of Aubers Ridge on 9 May 1915. They are commemorated on the Le Touret Memorial (qv). The next roundabout (approximately 1 mile from Aubers Church) is called the **Rond Point Wadhurst** (**Map 9/5**).

Turn round and continue over the stop sign, direction Fromelles on the Rue Houdringue, to the smart modern dentist's surgery on the left. Just beyond and set back from the road is

• 'Kaiser's Bunker'/1.3 mile/5 minutes/Map 9/6

This ivy-covered pill-box is so called because it is said that Wilhelm II (or maybe the Kronprinz) visited the bunker during the German Occupation. It is a German third-line pill box, the top floor of which was used as a watch tower and the ground floor for stabling the horses and donkeys that the Germans used for carrying ammunition and supplies. It was also a place of rest for German soldiers coming out of the line.

Once the Germans were entrenched on the ridge they began a massive programme of defensive building in reinforced concrete. According to local historians there were between 7 and 8,000 pill-boxes and bunkers by the end of the German occupation in the 'Département du Nord', some 700 in the Aubers-Fromelles sector. Today the area still seems littered with their remains and probably some 200 exist in one form or other.

Continue to the school on the right (marked by a magnificent flowering cherry in the springtime). Beside it is

• Aubers Historical Circle Archives/1.4 miles/Map 9/7

Aubers has an extremely active Historical Circle, of which the President is the Mayor, M Pierre Descamps. His distinguished and gallant father, Henri-Clotaire Descamps, a senior officer in the Gendarmerie, founded the Resistance Cell, *Verité Française*, was betrayed, arrested by the Gestapo and beheaded in Brandenbourg-sur-Havel on 5 December 1942. He was awarded the *Légion d'Honneur*, the *Croix de Guerre* and several Resistance decorations.

The Circle's impressive archives are available to serious students on request. **Contact** the *Mairie*, Tel: + (0)3 20 50 20 38.

Continue to the T junction and turn left, direction Fromelles on the D141. Continue to the bunker on the left just before the Fromelles village sign.

• 'Hitler's Bunker'/2.2 miles/10 minutes/Map 9/8

This is so called because during his famous 1940 tour of his WW1 haunts, Adolf Hitler was said to have visited this pill-box. He fought in the Aubers-Fromelles sector as a corporal from 10 March 1915 to 25 September 1916 with the 16th Bavarian Regiment. The bunker is in a particularly fine state of preservation, with the letters *'ERBAUT VON DER 4FPIC'* (BUILT BY THE 4th FIELD PIONEERS) clearly visible above the entrance. It was on the German 5th line of 19-20 July, the Battle of Fromelles.

Continue to the T junction. Turn left and stop in the car park opposite the Mairie of Fromelles (2.6 miles).

• End of Aubers Ridge Battlefield Tour

FESTUBERT-GIVENCHY

15-27 MAY 1915

'Well lads, you may have been boys yesterday;
you're men now – yes, men.'
Col Harry Walker, Black Watch, after the Battle of Festubert.

SUMMARY OF THE BATTLE

At 2330 hours on 15 May between Neuve Chapelle and Festubert the 2nd and Meerut Divisions of 1 Corps began the first British night attack of the war followed, three and a half hours later in daylight, by 7th Division to their south. Early local success was marred by lack of materiel which had been 'loaned' to Gallipoli and inadequate artillery support. After ten days, during which time the Canadian Division became involved, the battle stalled with limited gains. British casualties were 16,648 officers and men, German about 5,000.

OPENING MOVES

As far as the French were concerned the fighting at Aubers and at Festubert was part of the same Joffre-inspired overall plan whose main objective was the taking of Vimy Ridge. General Foch, who commanded the French forces during the offensive, believed that the British short artillery bombardment at Neuve Chapelle was fundamentally ineffective and planned long systematic barrages before any French attacks. The British C-in-C, Sir John French, plagued by a shortage of shells and a proliferation of duds as well as being concerned by the situation in Ypres following the German gas attacks of 22 April and later, needed some convincing to undertake what he saw as another offensive. The battles of Neuve Chapelle in March 1915 and Aubers Ridge earlier in May had indeed suffered from too short an artillery bombardment and poorly defined daily infantry objectives, although at Neuve Chapelle the brief preliminary barrage had introduced the element of surprise into the attack.

This time, however, learning from the French successes, it was decided that a longer, two-day continuous night and day bombardment would precede the attack and that the attacking troops would be given specific objectives to be achieved on the first day. Surprise was to be gained by attacking at night.

The plan was imaginative. The night attack was to be double-pronged (see **Map 10**). One prong immediately below Port Arthur (la Bombe) was to be carried out by the Garhwal Brigade of the Meerut Division and the other, on their right, by 5th and 6th Brigades of 2nd Division. Their immediate objective was to take the first two lines of German trenches before dawn and then, at that moment, a fresh attack by 7th Division 600 yards to the south, just above Festubert, would hopefully allow some of the German defences to be taken from the rear. Once this movement was underway further limited objectives were to be attempted.

WHAT HAPPENED

The British bombardment began on 13 May between Port Arthur (la Bombe) and Festubert with a view to making the night attack on 14 May. However the assault was delayed for 24 hours because it was felt that the enemy wire had not been thoroughly cut in front of the Meerut Division. To increase the element of surprise as to the hour of the attack the bombardment programme included a number of stops and starts and cheers from front-line infantry as if they were about to go over the top.

At 2330 hours on 15 May the attack began. On the right 6th Brigade almost reached the German line before they were fired upon and quickly took and consolidated the enemy trenches, shining a pair of car headlights back towards their own lines to signal success. The 5th and Garhwal Brigades, however, were spotted and came under heavy machine gun and rifle fire, the enemy using flares or 'light balls' to illuminate the area and no progress was made. It was decided that another attempt would be made and that it should coincide with the 7th Division attack, but with the enemy artillery active upon the forward trenches this proved to be impossible and the idea was dropped.

At 0315 the 7th Division attack began, the 20th and 22nd Brigades having moved up to their jump-off positions overnight, the enemy positions being generally only around 100 yards away. The opposition was fierce and the Commanding Officers of the leading regiments of 22nd Brigade were both killed while urging their men on – Lt Col R. E. P. Gabbett, 1st Royal Welch Fusiliers (buried in the Guards Cemetery at Windy Corner) and Lt Col H. R. Bottomley, 2nd Queens (who died of wounds two days later and is buried in Béthune Town cemetery). Nevertheless the German defences were taken and the advance pushed on as far as the **Orchard** where it stopped.

In the 20th Brigade leading elements of the forward regiments, the 2nd Scots Guards and the 2nd Border Regiment, moved out into No Man's Land too early and came under 'friendly fire'. However they carried the first lines of trenches, and by-passed the **Quadrilateral,** a major German defensive position in the unassaulted area between the divisions which was firing upon their flank. The ground was difficult, including a deep dyke that had to be crossed, but finally with help from a party of 1st Royal Welch, which had drifted over from their sector, the Scots reached the area above the Orchard, an advance during which **CSM Frederick Barter** won the **VC**. Barter called for volunteers to help him extend the line when they reached the German first line trenches and eight 'bombers' responded. They then attacked the German position, capturing three German officers, 102 men and 500 yards of trenches. Barter then found and cut eleven of the enemy's mine leads. He was commissioned as a 2nd Lt on 26 August 1915, went on to become a Captain and to win the MC and survived the war to serve as a Major in the Home Guard in WW2. In an odd twist of fate, while Barter was in Palestine in April 1918, his life was saved during an action by Rifleman Karanbahadur Rana, for which Rana was awarded the VC. Barter died on 15 May 1952. Following another shelling by British guns, however, heavy machine gun fire from the flanks and a German counter-attack, the troops fell back to the captured enemy breastworks.

Thus, by 0900 hours on 16 May, looking from bottom to top (see **Map 10**), 22nd Brigade of 7th Division had advanced some 600 yards to the Orchard, 20th Brigade was at the German front trenches, 2nd Division were in and beyond the trenches but the Garhwal Brigade attack had failed. Thus the central area where the Quadrilateral posed a major threat had not been taken and during the day unsuccessful attempts were made to pinch it out by attacks from above and below.

General Haig now decided to concentrate his effort in the 7th and 2nd Divisions' areas so a bombardment of the Quadrilateral and the centre was begun at 0245 hours on 17 May. But during the night the Germans had begun a withdrawal of some 900 yards to a new defensive line towards which they were hurrying reserves, a fact that was not discovered for several days. Opposition was therefore patchy and both 2nd and 7th Divisions were able to make early advances, the Quadrilateral falling by 1015 hours. This relative success in the south led Sir John French to change the ultimate objective of the 1st Army from that of taking Aubers Ridge to that of gaining access to the canal below la Bassée, thus swinging the axis of the battle towards the south-east. However bad weather, more friendly fire, water-filled ditches, delays in getting orders to the front line, growing casualty numbers and stiffening German resistance from their new defensive line stopped all forward activity. It was decided that the Canadian Division should replace the 7th Division and the 51st (Highland) Division the 2nd Division. The 51st had been named as the 'Highland' Division on 11 May. These changes were complete by 0900 on 20 May, the two new divisions being combined as Alderson's Force after Lt Gen Sir E.A. Alderson, Commander of the Canadian Division. Immediately south of them towards the canal was 47th Division.

Over the next five days local actions were carried out to secure the positions already gained in preparation for the assault towards la Bassée, the 3rd Canadian Brigade occupying the Orchard, named thereafter the **'Canadian Orchard'**. Coincidentally it was in this area in December 1914 that the first serious British attempt to use mines had been made when the Dehra Dun Brigade attempted to drive a shallow tunnel towards the German lines, hoping to place a charge of 45 pounds of gun cotton under them, but before the mine could be fired it was detonated by enemy fire.

During 25 May the Army's only kite balloon, owned and staffed by the Admiralty, was used to direct the preparatory bombardment for the next attack and during the night the 47th and Canadian Divisions launched their assault. The 47th gained an average of 400 yards over a 1,000 yard frontage broadly parallel to the canal in the direction of la Bassée. The Canadians made little progress, due not just to the stubborn resistance of the Germans now firmly established in their new main position, but also to the shortage of artillery ammunition that prevented a substantial initial bombardment and to being armed with their Ross rifle which overheated and readily jammed with mud. It was finally withdrawn in June after

MAP 10: FESTUBERT 15-27 MAY 1915

Legend

1. Le Touret CWGC Cem and Mem to Missing
2. Post Office Rifles CWGC Cem
3. King's Post Bunkers
4. 419 Field Coy RE Bunkers
5. Brown's Road Mil CWGC Cem
6. Guards Windy Corner CWGC Cem
7. Private Mem, Lt Hill-Trevor
8. 55 Div Mem

INDIAN CORPS
MEERUT DIV

Garhwal Bde

I CORPS
2ND DIV

I CORPS
7TH DIV

Port Arthur
(la Bon·be)

Lorgies
la Tourelle

D947

GERMAN LINE

Chocolat
Menier
Corner

GER 55th Regt

2330
15 May

5 Bde

2330
15 May

6 Bde

Cour d' Avoué Farm

Canadian Orchard

Rue du Marais

D72

Quadrilateral

La Quinque Rue

0315
16 May

FINAL BRITISH LINE

20 Bde

22 Bde

Festubert

GER 57th Regt

D166

Windy
Corner

Givenchy

Violaines

La Bassée

Canal d'Aire

le Touret

D171

N

Scale
0   500m

© TVH 2004

over 3,000 Canadians had thrown away their Ross weapons and taken the SMLEs of British casualties.

It was now clear that further progress was unlikely. Sir John French, concerned about the ammunition situation at Ypres, moved much of his munitions there and in response to a French request sent the 2nd Division to relieve their 58th Division in the Vermelles area. The Battle of Festubert was over.

THE BATTLEFIELD TOUR

• **The Route:** The tour starts at the Le Touret Memorial (so could practically be done after the Neuve Chapelle Tour), visits the Post Office Rifles and Brown's Road Mil CWGC Cemeteries and two groups of 1918 British Bunkers in Festubert; Guards, Windy Corner CWGC Cemetery; the Private Memorial to Lt Hill-Trevor and the 55th Divisional Memorial in Givenchy-les-Bassée and finishes on the N41.
• **Total Distance:** 12.9 miles
• **Total time:** 1 hour 15 minutes
• **Distance from Calais to start point:** See Neuve Chapelle Tour
• **Base towns:** La Bassée, Béthune, Lille
• **Map:** IGN 1:25,000 2405 Est

*At the Le Touret Memorial **set your mileometer to zero**, return along the Rue du Bois towards la Bombe and turn right to Festubert on the D166.*
The **VC of L/Cpl Joseph Harcourt Tombs** of the 1st King's (Liverpool) Regt was won on 16 June 1915 near Rue du Bois for crawling out repeatedly under fire to bring in wounded men, one of whom he dragged in using a rifle sling placed round his own neck and the man's body. Tombs survived until 1966.

Near here, too, at Richebourg l'Avoué, in the Battle of Festubert, an interesting **VC** was won. On 18 May 1915 **Lt John George Smyth** of the 15th Ludhiana Sikhs, Indian Army, took a volunteer bombing party of 10 men who transported 96 bombs to within 20 yards of the enemy line over exceptionally dangerous ground after two other parties had failed in the attempt. Eight of the party were killed but with the remaining two (Lance-Naik Mangal Singh and a Sepoy) Smyth delivered the bombs, having swum a stream all the while under howitzer, machine-gun and rifle fire. Singh was awarded the 2nd Class Indian Order of Merit and all the Sepoys received the Indian DSM.

Smyth went on to become Brigadier the Rt Hon Sir John Smyth, Bt, was awarded the Russian Order of St George, raised the 19th London Division in India in 1941, commanded the 17th Division in Burma in 1942,

Lt John George Smyth.

was the MP for Norwood 1950-66, founder and Chairman of the VC and GC Assocation and author of books about the VC and the George Cross.

Continue to the crossroads by the church.

The church, as was practically the entire village, was razed during the war and rebuilt in 1924. It bears some traces of damage from WW2.

Turn right on the D72.

On the left is passed the village *Salle des Fêtes*, known as **The Southport Memorial Hall** as Southport 'adopted' the village after the war during the Reconstruction and paid for the building of the Hall in which a commemorative plaque was erected. The present building is modern and when it was built the plaque was moved to the right of the entrance. For many years veterans from Southport returned to Festubert and when they were no longer able to travel, members of the Sefton Dunkirk Veterans' Association continued the links on their behalf. Their last visit was in 2000 when a new plaque to commemorate their visit was unveiled on the left of the entrance.

Continue to the cemetery on the right.

• *(Post Office Rifles CWGC Cemetery/2.2 miles/10 minutes/Map 10/2*

Designed by Capt W.C. von Berg, this cemetery does not contain a War Stone. It is little-visited as the Visitor's Book in April 2003 dated back to 1993 and the fading inscriptions on the headstones are difficult to read. It was used in April-June 1915 before and during the Battles of Aubers Ridge and Festubert and originally contained 40 graves, 38 of them belonging to the London Regt (mainly the 8th Bn).

After the Armistice it was increased by concentration from surrounding battlefields, particularly from the part of the line defended by the 55th Division in April 1918. There are now 400 burials in the cemetery.

Continue to the next left turn (very quickly reached and easily missed) and turn down Rue de la Veine.

You are now entering the wooded and marshy area behind Festubert.

Keep straight on as the road narrows, follow the sharp left bend and turn first right on Rue des Malvaux. Continue to house No 315 on the right.

• *King's Post Bunker/3.4 miles/10 minutes/Map 10/3*

On private ground to the left of the house is the impressive bunker known as the King's Post after the King's (Liverpool) Regiment who fought in this area in April 1918. It clearly bears the insignia of the Lancashire Rose, the divisional sign of the East Lancashires, and the imprint of the Royal Engineers. It was designed as a brigade headquarters.

Turn round, return to the T junction and turn right and then next right Rue du Plantin. Continue to house No 337 on the right

• *Group of 1918 British Shelters/4.0 miles/10 minutes/Map 10/4*

On private ground behind the house is a complex group of shelters, many of which bear the Red Rose crest of Lancashire and 55th Division. They were built by 419th

Field Company, Royal Engineers in June 1918 following the battle which halted the German advance here in April 1918.

Turn round, return to the T junction and turn right. Continue to the cemetery on the left.

• Brown's Road Military CWGC Cemetery/4.7 miles/10 minutes/ Map 10/5

The cemetery (which has a lovely holly bush in the corner) was begun in October 1914 and used by fighting units and Field Ambulances until November 1917. It then contained 299 graves. After the Armistice it was enlarged by concentration from small cemeteries and isolated graves from the '14-'15 and '18 battles. It now contains 1,071 burials of which 407 are Unidentified. There is a Special Memorial to 3 soldiers. There are 21 Canadian and 6 S African burials here. In a row containing 9 Cameronian Officers all killed on 10 March 1915 lies **Lt Col Wilfrid Marryat Bliss**, age 49, OC 2nd Cameronians. The brother of **Pte J.C.C. Milne, Black Watch,** age 22, 23 November 1914, Pte A.J. Milne, 2nd Black Watch, age 32 was killed in Mesopotamia on 21 April 1917 and is commemorated on the Basra Memorial (qv).

Continue to the main road and turn right on the D166.

Shortly after on the left hand side and almost impossible to spot is a small dense Leylandia rectangular enclosure at the edge of a private garden. This is all that remains of the famous **Tramways House bunker**. It was illustrated in the 1970s editions of Rose Coombs' *Before Endeavour Fade* and described as having 'two chambers and an outside shelter and ... is the end of a light railway and the bunker was a ration point and officers' dugout. From January 1919 until the early seventies it was occupied by a Frenchwoman who said it made an ideal home.' During the defence of Festubert by the 55th Division in April 1918 it was known as 'Tramways House' and was probably constructed by 427th Field Coy, RE. It played a major role in the 155th Bde defeat of a German attack.

Continue.

To the left of this road was the site of the action which gained **CSM Frederick Barter** of the RWF the VC (qv).

Continue to the crossroads.

This was **Windy Corner**, so called as German shells were ranged on the crossing and to venture over it would certainly make one 'windy'.

Turn sharp right signed to the Guards Cemetery and follow the road round to the cemetery on the right.

• Guards CWGC Cemetery, Windy Corner/5.8 miles/10 minutes/ Map 10/6

The cemetery was begun by 2nd Division in January 1915 beside a house used as battalion HQ and dressing station. It was used by 4th (Guards) Brigade from February 1915 and was closed at the end of May 1916 when it contained 681 graves. It was enlarged after the Armistice when 2,700 bodies were brought in from the

Post Office Rifles CWGC Cemetery, Festubert.

King's Post Bunker with detail of Lancashire Rose on Bunker.

419th Field Coy, RE Bunkers, Festubert.

Brown's Road CWGC Cemetery, Festubert.

Row of Headstones, Brown's Road CWGC Cemetery

Windy Corner, Guards CWGC Cemetery.

Placing a flower ...

Row of HLI headstones.

surrounding battlefields and small cemeteries. It now contains 3,442 burials (including 31 Canadians and 9 Indians) of which 2,196 are unidentified. There are Special Memorials to 6 men buried in Indian Village North Cemetery and to 5 Indians originally buried here but afterwards cremated 'in accordance with the requirements of their faith'. The cemetery was designed by Charles Holden. In it are some groups of touching headstones, several of the HLI of 9 July and 25 September 1915 and of the Queens of 25/26 September 1915. Here is buried **Major John Mackenzie**, 1st Beds, age 44, 17 May 1915, who won the **VC** in Ashanti in 1900, and **Guardsman G.E. Kelsall,** Coldstream Guards, age 22, 11 August 1915 whose headstone bears the moving message, 'In a grave that we may never see. May someone place a flower for me.' Like other cemeteries in the area it is rarely visited and the visitor's book extends back several years.

Return to the crossroads, go straight over into Givenchy-les-la-Bassée and turn right past the church on Rue du Moulin. Continue to the white stone statue on the right.

• Private Memorial to Lt H. G. E. Hill-Trevor/7.4 miles/10 minutes/Map 10/7

This impressive statue, surrounded by a well-tended area of granite chippings enclosed by a low stone wall, is to Lt Hillyar George Edwin Hill-Trevor, 1st Scots Guards, age 18, died on 21 December 1914. He was the only son of the Hon George Hill-Trevor and a direct descendant of the Duke of Wellington. He was educated at Wellington and the RMC, Sandhurst. He was commissioned in the Scots Guards in August 1914 and promoted to Lieutenant in November.

On 21 December the Scots Guards were given the objective of capturing some trenches along the Rue d'Ouvert (to the east of Givenchy). The attack started in darkness at 0415 and at first met no opposition. When they reached Givenchy, however, the right flank of the Cameron Highlanders lost direction and nearly engaged the Scots Guards. In the few casualties that were incurred that day, the young Hill-Trevor was killed in his first, and last, action. He is commemorated on the Le Touret Memorial (qv).

The memorial, incorporating a mourning female figure on an ornate base with an inscription describing Hill-Trevor's death, was erected after the war near where he died. In 1927 General du Cane, whose wife was Hill-Trevor's aunt, funded minor repairs and arranged for the IWGC to care for it. In 1998 the Battlefield Memorials Project Fund of the WFA (qv) paid for major work to the memorial and its foundations and it is now in perfect condition.

Return to the main road and turn right.

Givenchy was 'adopted' by Liverpol after the war and the village *Salle des Fêtes* is known as 'The Liverpool Memorial Village Hall'.

Continue to the large memorial at a junction.

• 55th W Lancs Div Memorial/7.9 miles/5 minutes/Map 10/8

The inscription below this large cross with the Divisional badge describes how around this site from 9-16 April 1918 the Division was continuously attacked along the Canal to Festubert by 3 German Divisions. With its left flank turned, the Division held its ground and inflicted severe loss upon the enemy. 'This most gallant defence, the importance of which it would be hard to estimate', wrote Sir Douglas Haig in his Despatch of 20 April 1918. The Division's Battle Honours (Somme 1916, Ypres 1916-17, Cambrai 1917, Givenchy-Festubert 1918 and the Advance in Flanders 1918) are inscribed on the memorial and it also describes how units of the W Lancs Division Territorial Force were formed in 1918 and fought in France and Belgium from November 1914 onwards. On 3 January 1916 it was reassembled as the 55th (W Lancs) Division and served under that title throughout the remainder of the campaign. At each corner is a post with the attractive Divisional badge of a red rose and the words, 'They win or die who wear the rose of Lancaster'.

Continue on the D167 and at the first crossroads turn left by the water tower signed to Violaines on Rue d'Ouvert, the D167e. Continue on the winding road through Violaines and turn left signed Lorgies-Chef-Lieu.

You are now approximately at the limit of the British advance (it came towards you). After some 1.9 miles from the last stop and some 100m short of the T junction ahead is the site of **Canadian Orchard** (qv), now a caravan park and lake surrounded by trees. At this point the Lantern Tower of Notre-Dame de Lorette on the ridge can clearly be seen to the left.

Continue to the T junction and turn left towards Festubert.

You are now driving along what was the **Quinque Road**. Here on 29-30 October 1914 the 2/8th Gurkhas, shivered in the unaccustomed cold, in trenches half full of mud and water and which were too deep for the tiny men to be able to fire over the parapet. Nevertheless they held on despite repeated enemy artillery and howitzer fire, driving back several enemy attacks. It was, however, a costly affair for the battalion who lost 5 British and 2 Gurkha officers and 37 ORs killed, 3 British and 1 Ghurka officer and 61 ORs wounded with 1 British and 2 Ghurka officers and 109 ORs missing – 'buried by shell fire'. Again on 19 December the Ghurkas (the 2/2nd) came under severe trench-mortar fire and were forced to withdraw to a new line slightly further back.

Return to Festubert Church (12.9 miles).

• *End of Festubert-Givenchy Battlefield Tour*

AROUND THIS SITE FROM THE 9TH TO THE 16TH APRIL 1918 THE DIVISION CONTINUOUSLY ATTACKED FROM THE CANAL TO FESTUBERT BY THREE GERMAN DIVISIONS AND WITH ITS LEFT FLANK TURNED, HELD ITS GROUND AND INFLICTED SEVERE LOSS UPON THE ENEMY.

..."THIS MOST GALLANT DEFENCE, THE IMPORTANCE OF WHICH IT WOULD BE HARD TO OVERESTIMATE"....

SIR DOUGLAS HAIG'S DESPATCH DATED 20-7-18

Details of inscription on the 55th W Lancs Div Memorial, Givenchy.

55th W Lancs Div Memorial, Givenchy, with detail of Red Rose insignia.

Private Memorial to Lt Hill-Trevor, Givenchy.

LOOS

25 SEPTEMBER 1915-8 OCTOBER 1915

'Our new armies entered into action for the first time and
fought with conspicuous valour, and tens of thousands of
them fell in the futile carnage of the Loos offensive.'
Lloyd George, *War Memoirs.*

'I had come to the conclusion that it was not fair to the Empire to
retain French in command. Moreover, none of my officers
commanding corps had a high opinion of Sir John's military ability.'
General Haig in his Diary.

'My Darling Darling we've had such terrible losses
which made me very depressed and sad. . .'
General French in a letter to his mistress during the battle.

'What's happened?" I asked. "Bloody balls-up,"
was the most detailed answer I could get.'
Robert Graves, *Goodbye to All That.*

SUMMARY OF THE BATTLE

On 25 September 1915 as part of the French Artois offensive, Douglas Haig's 1st Army attacked German positions at Loos. The British used gas for the first time causing many casualties to their own side. There were no significant positive results and the affair provoked the forced resignation of Sir John French. British casualties were 43,000, German 20,000.

OPENING MOVES

Even halfway through 1915 it had not been a good year for the Allies. There had been the heavy British casualties at Neuve Chapelle, the disaster at Gallipoli and the steady reverses on the Russian front. General Joffre had prompted his forces into a number of attacks along the Western Front in what he called the 'war of stabilization'. This could perhaps be likened to a boxer moving around the ring, feeling out his opponent's strengths, before attempting a knock-out blow.

In June 1915 Joffre proposed his knock-out blow: a two-pronged offensive. One attack, the main one, was to be in Champagne and entirely French. The other was a joint Franco-British affair in Artois. Each prong was to break through the German lines. A general offensive would follow along the entire Franco-British front that Joffre believed could 'possibly end the war'. The Artois offensive was also to be a two-pronged affair with the British 1st Army attacking just north of Lens at Loos and the French 10th Army just south of Lens.

General Haig toured the area allocated for the 1st Army's attack and declared it to be unfavourable because the flat open ground would be swept by machine gun fire from the enemy's front trenches. Joffre refused to change the plan and Kitchener, visiting Sir John French in August, told him that co-operation was essential and that 'we may suffer heavy losses'. Haig, conscious of what had happened at Neuve Chapelle because of the shortage of artillery, decided that the only way in which he could get enough concentration of fire to neutralize the German machine guns was by adopting a very narrow frontage for the attack.

Accordingly he planned to attack with two divisions only, the 15th and the 9th. While the two division assault was being planned a new weapon became available – British poison gas. Haig immediately saw gas as a means of neutralizing those enemy defences that he did not have enough artillery to take on and extended the attack frontage to six divisions in line, their flanks to be protected by smoke screens. On 16 September he wrote to Sir William Robertson, General French's Chief of Staff, 'In my opinion under no circumstances should our forthcoming attack be launched without the aid of gas.' He was over-ruled and told that because of the need to co-ordinate the offensive with the French 10th Army the attack had to be made and that it would go in on 25 September. Haig therefore produced a plan with two options: one for a wide front, one for a narrow front.

1. Wide Front. If the weather conditions were favourable on 25 September the attack, with gas on the whole front, would take place on that day with 6 divisions.

2. Narrow Front. If the wind did not permit the use of gas a two division assault would be made, the wider attack with gas to be postponed until favourable conditions on the 26th or 27th or not at all.

All that remained was for the Allies to agree the time that their infantry would assault. The British wanted to go over the top as early as possible in the morning so that positions gained could be consolidated by nightfall. The French didn't want to leave their trenches before 1000 hours, so that they could visibly control the last phase of their bombardment. In the event the French attack went in $5^1/2$ hours after the British. Something similar would happen again on 1 July 1916 on the Somme.

WHAT HAPPENED

The preliminary bombardment which covered the 18-mile frontage of the 1st Army (i.e. covered the main assault and diversionary actions north and south of it) was carried out by 110 heavy guns, and 84 guns and howitzers and began at first light on 21 September. It continued day and night until the moment of the assault on 25 September. As a precaution against the enemy finding out about the gas it was given a codename – 'the accessory'.

In England and along the front line observers anxiously monitored the wind direction. Four times a day the Met Office in London sent reports and 40 specially trained gas officers stationed along the assault trenches sent in hourly reports during the night of 24 September. The required wind direction for a gas attack was from somewhere between north-west and south-west and at 2145 hours on 24 September, having received a favourable forecast, Haig ordered that the gas attack should take place on the morrow. The exact time would be 'notified later during the night'.

Early on the 25th, although the general forecast remained favourable, things looked changeable and the meteorologist, Captain E. Gold, attached to Haig's staff, advised that the sooner the gas was released the better. At 0500 hours Haig went on to the battlefield rear area and asked his ADC Major Alan Fletcher to light a cigarette. The smoke drifted north-east, a borderline but acceptable direction. Fifteen minutes later the General ordered the attack to go ahead. Robert Graves, who was in the battle (see below) wrote that one front-line report at 0530 said, 'Dead calm. Impossible discharge accessory', to which the reply was, 'Accessory to be discharged at all costs.' At 0550 hours the gas was released, emissions continuing on and off for 40 minutes. As there wasn't enough gas available to allow a continuous gas cloud, the gas cylinders were turned on and off and smoke candles burned in between to fool the enemy.

At 0630 hours the infantry scrambled out of their trenches and headed across No Man's Land in a haze of smoke and gas. There were six divisions in line, the 2nd, 9th (Scottish), 7th, 1st, 15th (Scottish) and 47th (London Territorial). Two separate divisions, the 21st and 24th, were kept back in reserve, but they were not under command of General Haig. General French kept them under his control. On the extreme right 47th Division rapidly reached the area of the Double Crassier (slag heaps) while on its left the 15th Division made spectacular progress, advancing completely around Loos to the north of, then later taking, the town after all-night street fighting. The remaining division of Rawlinson's IV Corps, the 1st, had mixed fortunes. Some units reached as far as the village of Hulluch and others retreated under enemy shell fire. South of the corps boundary, the Vermelles to Hulluch road, the gas had proven its worth, but further north in Gough's 1 Corps area alongside the la Bassée Canal the officer in charge of gas on 6th Brigade's front decided not to turn on the gas because the wind wasn't right. General Horne ordered it turned on and many men were poisoned by their own gas. Eventually Horne listened to his brigade commanders and stopped the attack.

Overall, particularly at Loos itself, the first day had gone well. There was a potential break in the German line to be exploited. Now was the time to punch through the weakened enemy defences with our fresh reserves. Where were they? They were too far away, too tired and too new to mount a successful follow-up assault. Why? Whose fault was it? The generals blamed each other.

The broad sweep of the British plan had been agreed at least one month before between Joffre and General French at a conference at Chantilly – including the formation of a two divisional infantry reserve. Yet instead of forming the reserve

MAP 11: LOOS 25 SEPTEMBER 1915

Givenchy ▲

La Bassée ▲

D167E

La Bassée Canal

D75

Cuinchy ▲

D166E

D166

D947

1

Auchy lès Mines

N41

Cambrin

2 DIV
25/9

Annequin

XX

2

XX

Cité
Madagascar

Haisnes

D163

9 DIV
25/9

Hohenzollern Redoubt

D166

XX

XX

Cité St
Elié

N43

7 DIV
25/9

Vermelles ▲

D39

5

6

Hulluch

4

1 DIV
25/9

Old rail route

Le Rutoir
Farm

24 DIV
26/9

7

8

D39

XX

15 DIV
25/9

XX

Lone
Tree

Chalk Pit
Wood

9

Mazingarbe ▲

GUARDS DIV
27/9

Bois
Hugo

12

XX

21 DIV
26/9

Puits
14 Bis

Hill 70 ▲

Legend

1. Cambrin CWGC Cem
2. Cambrin Churchyard Extension CWGC Cem
3. Quarry CWGC Cem
4. 46th Div Mem
5. Site of Worcesters' Attack, 26 Sept 1915
6. St Mary's ADS CWGC Cem
7. Ninth Avenue CWGC Cem
8. Bois Carré CWGC Cem
9. Area where John Kipling last seen
10. Loos CWGC Cem
11. Dud Corner CWGC Cem and Mem
12. Area where body claimed as John Kipling found

11

D165

11 LOOS

47 DIV
25/9

D165

10

A21

Double Crassier

Lens

British Front Line 25/9	
German Front Line 25/9	
British Lines pm 25/9	
Divisional Boundaries	XX

Scale

0   1   2km

N

© TVH 2004

MAP 12: LOOS – ATTACK OF THE 2ND WORCESTERS 26 SEPTEMBER 1915

La Bassée

D947

Cité St Elié

Hulluch

Loos

© TVH 2004

N

Scale

0   0.5   1km

The Quarries

Gun Trench 20 Bde

Track

Breslau Avenue

Track

Track

St Elié Avenue

9(BR) DIV

Slag heap now removed and built over

Fosse 8

St Mary's ADS Cemetery

Pope's Nose

2 Worcestershire deploy for attack

Cité Madagascar

Hohenzollern Redoubt

CWGC Quarry Cemetery

D39

Track

Vermelles

Le Rutoir Crossroads

Le Rutoir Farm

Legend

British Trenches

German Trenches

British gains on 25th

British gains on 26th

from seasoned divisions already in France, General French nominated two raw, untried 'K' (Kitchener volunteers) Divisions, the 21st and 24th, which had arrived in France in September. They had never been in the trenches or under fire and they were held many miles to the rear under Sir John's control as part of XI Corps, which also included the newly formed Guards Division. On the night of 24 September, the two K Divisions marched 10 miles through rain to within five miles of the front line. It took over six hours. The previous night they had rested, but on each of the two nights preceding that they had marched more than 20 miles.

Sir Douglas Haig had assumed that the two reserve divisions would move forward at 0630 hours together with the main assault and come under his control ready to follow up a breakthrough. They did not. Sir John French said that he put the divisions under Haig's command at 0930 hours. Haig didn't agree that that had been done. On 29 September he wrote to Lord Kitchener, 'No reserve was placed under me. My attack, as has been reported, was a complete success... The two reserve Divisions (under C-in-C's orders) were directed to join me as soon as the success of the 1st Army was known at GHQ. They came on as quick as they could, poor fellows, but only crossed our old trenchline with their heads at 1800 hours. We had captured Loos 12 hours previously and reserves should have been at hand THEN'.

At first, despite their tiredness, when they did eventually arrive the reserve divisions had some success but German counter-attacks forced them back, only the arrival of the Guards Division on 27 September preventing what might have been a headlong retreat of the novice soldiers. The battle ventured on without concentrated central effort or achievement until the first week in October. It had been, wrote Lloyd George in his memoirs, 'a futile carnage'. Two months later Prime Minister Herbert Asquith wrote a secret letter to Haig saying that Sir John French had resigned and 'I have the pleasure of proposing to you that you should be his successor.'

The Loos Trenches in Blackpool

After the Loos battle, the 'Divisional Military Authorities' in Blackpool built a replica of the trenches at Loos at Squire's Gate, presumably for training purposes. It was then decided to make the system open to the general public as an educational and tourist attraction and also to raise funds for the nearby King's Lancashire Military Convalescent Home. Convalescent soldiers acted as guides and pointed out features such as the defensive structure known as 'the Redoubt', the 'Telephone Dug-out', the 'Traversing System' to avoid enfilading, the 'Sentry Post', the machine gun posts, the snipers' loopholes, the sandbagged parapets, the drainage system, the Battalion HQ, the medical facilities, the cookhouse and the stores and the communication trenches. Money was also raised by selling postcards and a guide leaflet, which cost 1d, to these 'couple of miles of admirably planned and cleverly constructed Trenches, a perfect reproduction of this astonishing aid to modern warfare'.

THE BATTLEFIELD TOUR

• **The Route:** The tour begins at Annequin, visits Cambrin Military CWGC Cemetery and the Churchyard Extension CWGC Cemetery; Auchy les Mines and Quarry CWGC Cemetery and then follows the centre line of the British attack from Vermelles; the 46th Division Memorial; the Rutoir Crossroads; St Mary's Advanced Dressing Station CWGC Cemetery; 9th Avenue and Bois Carré CWGC Cemeteries; Hulluch – passing Puit 14 and the Chalk Pit; Loos and the British CWGC Cemetery (site of 'London Bridge'); the area of Hill 70 and the Double Crassier, ending at Dud Corner north-west of Loos.

The battlefield has changed very little in the intervening years and particularly rewards the use of a good map and binoculars.

• **Total distance:** 14.4 miles`
• **Total time:** 3 hours
• **Distance from Calais to start point:** 56 miles. Motorway Tolls.
• **Base town:** Béthune
• **Map:** IGN 2405 Est. Lens 1:25,000

From Calais take the A16/A26 direction Paris/Reims then the A26/E15 direction St Omer and take Exit 6 to Béthune. Follow signs to Centre Ville and the Grand' Place.

Béthune. Ninety per cent of the town was destroyed in 1918. The Town Hall (like many other buildings around the centre) was rebuilt in 1920 by J. Alleman, its stonework depicting events of the town in WW1 when it won the *Croix de Guerre* and the *Légion d'Honneur* (the town lost 557 of its sons in battle and 97 civilian casualties in the war). It is listed as an historic monument and houses the municipal archives. There is parking around the famous belfry (qv) which also houses the Tourist Office (qv).

In the 14th Century Church of St Vaast (rebuilt by the architect Cordonnier) is one of the **Commemorative Tablets**, designed by Lt Col M.P.L. Cart de Lafontaine (qv), executed by Reginald Hallward and with an inscription by Rudyard Kipling, commemorating the sacrifice of the British and Dominion troops in the diocese. Like Arras, Béthune has underground chambers known as *boves* which were used as shelters during the war.

There are many accounts of WW1 life in Béthune, non more vivid than Robert Graves's in *Goodbye to All That*. His 1915 memories include the queues of up to 150 men at the Army brothel, 'The Red Lamp' (fee 8 francs or 8s.). Graves also met the Prince of Wales (who was billeted in the Hotel de France and whose favourite restaurant was The Globe) in the public baths. 'Dressed in nothing at all, he graciously remarked how bloody cold the water was.' When not in reserve Graves had 'a beautiful Louis XVI bedroom at the *Château Montmorency.'*

The Indian GHQ was housed in the *Château* in October 1914 and the town remained in Allied hands throughout the war. It was continually shelled and bombed by Gothas and Taubes and then on 9 April 1918 in the German Offensive the town was again under imminent threat. On the 18th the population was evacuated and the bombardment redoubled. Fifty thousand incendiary shells and gas shells rained down on the town. Nine hundred houses were destroyed, the Church of St Vaast and the Town Hall in ruins. Finally, on 28 August 1918 the Allies began to drive the Germans from the Lys Salient. By 2 October the remains of Béthune were no longer under threat.

Take the N41 direction Beuvry/Annequin.

Just before entering Annequin there is a convenient Courte Paille restaurant (part of the great Accor chain) on the right. Varied menu, will do speedy service on request.

*Enter Annequin and **set your mileometer to zero** when passing the Mairie on the right.*

• *Annequin/0 miles/RWC*

Here in September 1915 was the principal British and French artillery observation station on the dump of Fosse 9 de Béthune, then, at 135 feet high, the most prominent feature of the whole area. It was, however, some 2 miles from the front line trenches and its vision was restricted by the Cité spur and Hill 70.

Continue to Cambrin and stop on the left by the Café Beaulieu.

• *Cambrin Military CWGC Cemetery/.6 miles/15 minutes/Map 11/1*

Walk up the path following the CWGC sign to the left.

Cambrin housed brigade HQ at one time but until the end of the war it was only about 800m from the front line trenches. This cemetery was once called Cambrin Château and described as being 'behind the Mayor's House'. It was begun in February 1915 and used as a front line cemetery until December 1918. It contains many graves from the Battle of Loos and in Row D there are 57 officers and men of the 1st King's (Liverpool) Regt, who died on 25 September 1915. Designed by Charles Holden it contains 816 burials, including **Lt H.C. Soden**, King's Liverpool Regt, age 19, 3 May 1916 whose headstone bears the words, 'This memorial is substituted for one erected by officers, NCOs and men of his company RIP' and **L/Cpl W.W. Boak**, RE, 29 May 1916, 'Salvation Army Bandsman.'

Return to your car and continue to the Mairie on the right.

Outside the *Mairie* is the striking town war memorial ('chosen from a catalogue'). It is an exact copy of Bartholdi's New York Statue of Liberty by sculptor Julien Flament. It was erected in 1926 and cost 35,000 francs, raised by a tombola! There are four other replicas of the statue in France (on the Pont de Grenelle at Paris, at Roybon (Isère), Saint Etienne (Loire) and at Saint Cyr sur Mer (Var).

Turn right after the Mairie, following CWGC sign, to the church on the left and stop.

• *Cambrin Churchyard Extension CWGC Cemetery/.8 miles/10 minutes/Map 11/2*

The large CWGC plot is behind the local graves. The cemetery was taken over from French troops in May 1915 and used for front line burials until February 1917 when

Headstone of Capt A. L. Samson,
Cambrin Churchyard Extension
CWGC Cemetery.

'Statue of Liberty' Memorial, Cambrin.

Middlesex
Men
shoulder
to
shoulder.

Headstone
of three
Middlesex
Men, 25
September
1915.

15910 PRIVATE
R. A. WOOD
MIDDLESEX REGIMENT
25TH SEPTEMBER 1915 AGE 20
GONE BUT NOT FORGOTTEN

8465 PRIVATE
T. WILLIAMS
MIDDLESEX REGIMENT
25TH SEPTEMBER 1915

10004 PRIVATE
W. WRIGHT
MIDDLESEX REGIMENT
25TH SEPTEMBER 1915 AGE 29
GONE BUT NOT FORGOTTEN

it was closed (except for 3 graves from 1918 in the back row). Designed by Charles Holden it contains 1,211 Commonwealth burials and 98 French graves. The graves are grouped by battalion, with striking groups of 79 graves of the 2nd Argyll & Sutherland Highlanders, 15 of the 1st Cameronians, 35 of the 2nd RWF and 115 of the 1st Middx, all dating from 25 September 1915, the first day of the Battle of Loos, and buried shoulder to shoulder, many 2 and 3 to a headstone. Here is buried **Captain A.L. Samson** of 'C' Coy, 2nd Bn RWF, a friend of Robert Graves, killed near Cuinchy, 25 September 1915. He describes in *Goodbye to All That* how he found Samson's body 'hit in seventeen places. I found that he had forced his knuckles into his mouth to stop himself crying out and attracting more men to their death.' Graves wrote the poem *The Dead Fox Hunter* in his honour....

> We found the little captain at the head,
> His men lay, well aligned.
> We touched his hand – stone cold – and he was dead,
> And they, all dead, behind
> Had never reached their goal, but they died well.
> They charged in line, and, in the same line, fell.

Also buried here is **L/Cpl W. Pardoe,** 25 September 1915, a friend of the writer Frank Richards, also of the 2nd RWF who was killed while sniping in the Fromelles battle when officers carried their swords and **Captain the Hon Ernest William M.M. Brabazon, DSO,** age 31, Coldstream Guards, 17 June 1915, the son of the Earl and Countess of Meath.

Return to the main road and turn right.

Just after the petrol station on the right there is a group of CWGC signs to the left to Woburn Abbey, Cuinchy Communal and the Guards Cemetery, Windy Corner (qv).

Continue towards Auchy, passing on the right a **Memorial to the French 58th Division,** behind which the Double Crassier is visible.

Continue into Auchy Centre and turn right on to the D163 towards Cité du 8.

It was in this area of 28th Brigade, that the gas blew back over the British lines and caused many casualties. The failure of the brigade to advance negated the success of 26th Brigade towards whose area you are travelling. It was also in this area that the poet-author-raconteur Robert Graves, serving with the RWF, observed the muddled and tragically ineffective gas attack. His memories of the loosing of the 'accessory' are graphically and often amusingly described in his gossipy, and sometimes imaginative, autobiography, *Goodbye to All That.* It should be compulsory reading for anyone studying the Loos battle.

Continue past the Mairie and War Memorial. Eventually on the left there is a sign to Quarry Cemetery (it may appear to be pointing in precisely the wrong direction). Keep to the right. Continue to a track signed left to the cemetery and if dry drive up the track to the cemetery on the right.

As you drive up the track you are going in the direction of the attack of 26th Brigade of 9th Division on the 25th of September.

• *Quarry CWGC Cemetery/4.2 miles/20 minutes/Map 11/3/OP*

This unusual and beautiful cemetery contains burials from the fighting in the area of the Hohenzollern Redoubt and was used mostly between July 1915 and June 1916. It was badly damaged by shell fire and not all of the 140 burials are individually marked because the original graves were lost. Therefore some headstones say, 'Buried near this spot', and the register lists only 129 war graves. Many of the graves are those of cavalrymen who were used in the dismounted role and there is one German soldier. The 'Quarry' referred to is the one in which the burials have been made, which is an old chalk pit about 10 ft deep and reached by steps. It is not connected with the 'Quarries' which featured in the fighting near Hulluch.

Stand with your back to the main entrance to the cemetery.
You are standing in what was No Man's Land on 25 September. The front line of 26 Brigade was behind you. Some 300 metres straight ahead below the power lines you should be able to define a slightly higher feature of ground with some trees and bushes on it. That is the Mont d'Auchy on which was the Hohenzollern Redoubt, a major German defensive position. It was taken by 9th Division that day and they pushed on beyond, towards the village of Haisnes. This remarkable achievement was the result of careful planning and the digging forward of Russian saps (tunnels barely below ground that can rapidly be converted into open trenches) so that when these were opened, and their heads joined by a trench, the assault line was only 150 yards from the redoubt. The attack was led by the 7th Seaforths and the 5th Cameron Highlanders, all wearing glengarries. Sadly, at mid-morning, Lt Col Gaisford commanding the Seaforths was killed. The Germans recaptured the Hohenzollern on 3 October.

Beyond the Hohenzollern was the slag heap of Fosse 8 (now removed and built over). It was to this area that Maj-Gen Thesiger, commanding 9th Division (formed on 21 August 1914 and almost entirely composed of Scottish Battalions), went, on 27 September, to investigate the situation, having heard that '73rd Brigade was unsteady'. On reaching the eastern face of the Hohenzollern he was killed by a shell, together with two of his staff. Haig heard of this 'irreparable' loss whilst visiting 1 Corps HQ and ordered Maj-Gen Bulfin, then commanding 28th Division, to assume command of 9th Division. Maj-Gen Thesiger is commemorated on the Loos Memorial at Dud Corner (qv).

To your right on the skyline are the twin peaks of the Double Crassier (slag heaps) and to their left a mineshaft (*Puits*). In front of them is a road running left to right and using binoculars on a clear day it is possible to see Dud Corner Cemetery and Memorial at the bottom right hand side of the peaks. To a first approximation the peaks mark the bottom (southern) end of the Loos battlefield and the N41 road that you traveled on from Annequin to Auchy marks the top from which you can get a good idea of the frontage of the attack.

Return to the metalled road and turn left on the C6.
To the left is a straight tree-lined track on the line of the old railway.
Continue into Vermelles.

Quarry CWGC Cemetery, Loos.

• *Vermelles/5.7 miles/RWC*

Take the first left as you enter the village which is the D39 to Hulluch.
The village sits like a lollipop head at the western end of its stick the D39 Hulluch road, the Corps boundary. IV Corps were south, i.e. to the right exclusive of the road, I Corps north. It was in areas like Vermelles that final arrangements were made before battalions moved forward through communication trenches to the front line. Tea would be brewed, hot meals served (on rare occasions), orders issued, heavy kit left behind, routes signed and 'farewell' notes written. As you drive now you are following exactly the route taken by 7th Division as it moved into its forward trenches in preparation for its attack. How would you be feeling?

Continue and as you leave the built-up area there is a memorial on the right. Stop.

• *46th (N Midland) Division Memorial/5.9 miles/5 minutes/Map 11/4*

This commemorates an action on 13 October 1915, the week following the 'official' end of the Loos offensive. The 138th and 139th Brigades of the Division set off to recapture the Hohenzollern Redoubt (to the north-east). Their gas cloud was weak and the artillery bombardment had not destroyed the German wire. The Hohenzollern was not taken, though parts of it were entered by the Midlanders. The Division lost heavily – 180 officers and 3,500 men.

Continue to the next crossroads at which there is a small calvary on the right (Notre Dame de la Consolation). Stop. The farm to your right down the track is le Rutoir.

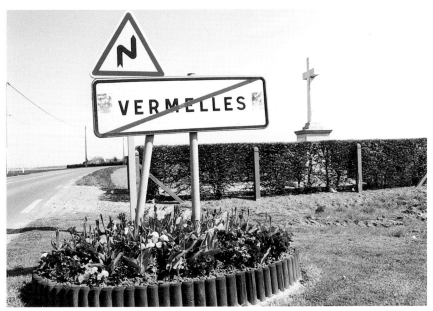

46th (N Midland) Division Memorial, Vermelles.

• *Le Rutoir Crossroads/6.7 miles/20 minutes/Map 11/5*

It is very rare to be able to identify precisely where a battalion action took place and even rarer also to have a clear account of what happened there. The situation becomes almost unique when the ground remains much the same as it was in 1915-18. Using **Maps 11** and **12** you can be in just such a unique position.

Walk 700 yards north-east up the track from le Rutoir crossroads. You are now where the 2nd Worcesters deployed for their attack on 26 September 1915.

By 26 September 7th Division was stuck in front of the Quarries. 2nd Worcesters, part of a temporary brigade under Colonel Carter of the King's Regiment, was ordered to attack the Quarries. (From where you are now they are immediately in front of a large coal heap due east – the heap was not there in 1915.) This is how the *Regimental History* tells the story:

'At 1 p.m. the Battalion filed into a big communication trench at Vermelles. This trench was a very long one and progress along it was difficult. The troops were carrying heavy loads and were hampered by wearing gas-masks, for several leaking gas-cylinders were lying in the trench. Crowds of wounded men were sheltering in the trench or making their way back, and other parties of all kinds impeded the advance. One by one the Worcestershire companies reached the forward lines, but not until 4.45 p.m. did the rearmost platoon get clear of the communication trench. Then the Battalion deployed for attack behind the original British front line. In front of them was a wide stretch of open ground – the former "No Man's Land" – on the far side of which was the old German front line, occupied by troops of the 7th Division. Still further forward on slightly rising ground a tangle of broken ground marked the near edge of the Quarries, the objective of the attack.

The Battalion deployed in four 'waves' – 'C' and 'D' Companies leading, 'A' and 'B' following, each company being formed in two lines. Colonel Lambton gave the signal, and the advance began.

With bayonets fixed, the companies of the 2nd Worcesters swept forward across the open, wave after wave, in splendid order. The platoons came under a heavy fire as they reached the old German front line. That trench was found to be wide and deep, crowded with disorganised or wounded men of the 7th Division ... **Colonel Lambton** ... coolly walked up and down the parapet under a heavy fire, directing the reorganisation of the attack. **Major-General T. Capper**, commanding the 7th Division, appeared in the trench and assisted in the direction of the fight ... Colonel Lambton again signalled the advance ... The German rifles and machine-guns opened a devastating fire. Officers and men went down in rapid succession under a hail of bullets. On the left flank **Major P. S. G. Wainman** led his men forward, waving his stick till he fell riddled with bullets. Further to the right, General Capper himself rushed forward with one of the Worcestershire platoons, cheering them on until he was hit and fell mortally wounded.

The leading groups reached a line of broken chalk, a half-dug trench within two hundred yards of the enemy's position. There they flung themselves down ... and held their ground opposite the enemy's line during the remaining hours of daylight ... Night fell amid pouring rain, and it became possible to collect the wounded and count the loss. Of the 2nd Worcestershire nearly half had fallen – 13 officers and more than 300 N.C.O's and men. The 2nd-in-Command, all four Company Commanders, the Machine-Gun Officer, the Medical Officer and three out of the four Company-Sergeant-Majors were casualties ... All through the night the stretcher-bearers worked across the field of battle, searching for the wounded ... The Chaplain, the Rev. J.R. Stewart, earned general admiration by arriving in the front-line, leading a small party carrying cans of hot tea and jars of rum, which he personally distributed all along the line.'

Maj-Gen Sir Thomson Capper is buried in Lillers Communal CWGC Cemetery. His grave stands alone near the gardener's shed. Maj Philip Stafford Gordon Wainman is buried in Vermelles British Cemetery. He is listed as Captain.

The Loos Battle was exceptional in that three Major-Generals were killed during it, within a week: Capper, Thesiger (qv) and Maj-Gen F.D.V. Wing, commanding 12th Division, killed on 2 October and buried in Noeux-les-Mines Comm Cemetery. Conan Doyle in his *British Campaigns in Europe 1914-1918* conveniently, for the sake of poetic licence, has them all dying on the same day, which he then described as the worst day for the British Army, as far as generals were concerned, since Waterloo!

Return to your car, continue along the Hulluch road.

To the left a watertower marks the top, and to the right the Double Crassier marks the bottom end, of this well-defined battlefield.

Continue to the first British cemetery on the right. Park.

• St Mary's ADS CWGC Cemetery/7.6 miles/20 minutes/Map 11/6/OP

The attack along, inclusive and immediately north of this road up to the southern edge of The Hohenzollern Redoubt was made by the 20th and 22nd Brigades of 7th Division. 20th Brigade had the area from the road to inclusive the German position known as Breslau Avenue (see **Map 12)**. The leading battalions, the 2nd Gordon Highlanders and the 8th Devons, set off at 0630 in a cloud of their own gas. They were wearing smoke helmets, but these made it very difficult to breathe, and when they took them off to draw breath, many men were overcome by the gas. Despite heavy casualties from enemy artillery Gun Trench was taken and elements of both battalions reached the Lens-la Bassée road.

The Advanced Dressing Station was set up during the battle and after the Armistice the cemetery was established on the same spot. Of the more than 1,760 burials in the cemetery (the majority from the battle of Loos) 90 per cent are unknown, evidence of the chaos that existed on the battlefield. One of them, reburied here in September 1919, was a lieutenant of the Irish Guards. In July 1992 the headstone marking his grave was changed to read **'Lieutenant John Kipling'** when the CWGC believed that it had identified the body – on the grounds that Kipling was the only full lieutenant of the Irish Guards killed or missing in the Loos battle. This late identification was particularly ironic as his father, Rudyard Kipling, who sat on the committee of the Imperial War Graves Commission, spared no efforts to find his son's body, but in vain. Following extensive research the validity of the identification is strenuously disputed by the authors and described in their book *My Boy Jack?: the Search for Kipling's Only Son.*

Stand by the wall in the back left hand corner of the cemetery.
Look over the loggia in the cemetery beyond (Bois Carré) to the tall tower in the distance. That is the area of the Chalk Pit, some 1.7 miles away, where John Kipling was reported to have been killed. Looking to the right past the Double Crassier (the double slag heaps) is a large flat-topped slag heap which appears to have a wireless mast coming out of it. The body buried under the Kipling headstone was found beyond that slag heap which is 2.5 miles from here and 3.5 miles from where he was last seen alive. On a clear day, half way between the Double Crassier and the flat-topped slag heap, the Lantern Tower of Notre-Dame de Lorette is visible on the skyline and between it and the cemetery is Dud Corner Memorial.

Continue to the next small turning to the right with CWGC signs. Drive up if dry to the immaculately maintained narrow grassed path to the right. Walk up it to

• Ninth Avenue CWGC Cemetery/7.9 miles/10 minutes/Map 11/7

This tiny cemetery contains only 46 headstones, 41 of which are of the 1st Cameron Highlanders killed in action 25-29 September 1915. They are actually buried under 'Grave No 5' (a small flat stone marker in the centre). It is surrounded by a beautiful flint wall.

Continue to the next grassy path to the right. At the end of it is

The immaculate grass path leading to the Ninth Avenue CWGC Cemetery, Loos.

Ninth Avenue CWGC Cemetery.

My Boy Jack? St Mary's ADS CWGC Cemetery, Loos.

Bois Carré CWGC Cemetery with the Double Crassier behind across the Battlefield.

• *Bois Carré CWGC Cemetery/8.0 miles/10 minutes/Map 11/8*

This cemetery contains 174 known UK and 53 Unknown burials. The name means 'Square Wood' and the cemetery actually is square. The gardener's hut is beautifully faced with flint – perhaps in reaction to Rudyard Kipling's comment when visiting St Mary's ADS Cemetery in 1924, 'Spoilt by the gardener's hut'!

Return to the track.

N.B. This track continues right to the town of Loos, passing Lone Tree CWGC Cemetery and the Chalk Pit – an interesting walk.

When the Loos battle opened at 0630 on 25 September the Irish Guards, part of the Guards Division, were 16 miles as the crow flies behind Vermelles. The Division had been formed in September and had three brigades, the old 4th (Guards) Brigade becoming the 1st Guards Brigade. The 2nd Brigade had the 1st Scots Guards, the 1st Coldstreams, the 3rd Grenadiers and the 2nd Irish.

During the day the Irish marched towards the front along roads crowded with refugees, cavalry and wounded. The *Official History* described the journey thus – 'The confusion and congestion of the traffic on the roads had been appalling.' It was a journey that took 15 hours and they finally reached billets in the area of Noeux les Mines, some 4 miles west of Vermelles, at around 0100 hours on 26 September. They were wet and exhausted. At 1330 they marched out towards the battle but when they got beyond Vermelles there was no one to tell them what to do or where to go. After discussing things with the Scots Guards on their right it was decided to occupy a line of old German trenches between le Rutoir and Lone Tree (see **Map 11**) but it was midnight before everyone was settled in, some men having had less than four hours sleep the previous night and none having had any rest during the day.

Two and a half hours later they were on the move again and occupied a line of trenches some 500 yards further on, broadly along the track where you are now and facing towards Puits 14. No 3 Company of the 2nd Battalion was on the extreme right and next to it was No 2 Company with 2nd Lt John Kipling.

At 1600 hours on 27 September the Irish left their positions and set off for Puits 14 and Chalk Pit Wood (just to the left of Puits 14), their objectives. These were virgin soldiers. This was not only their first time into battle but as they went forward they had to cope with the returning stream of remnants of the 21st and 24th Divisions whose earlier efforts had failed. At first things went well and the Irish got into Chalk Pit Wood and even across the Loos-Lens road into Bois Hugo as well as around Puits 14 with the Scots, but a storm of German machine gun fire fell on them and drove them back in a confusion which only stopped at the Loos-Hulluch road where the Coldstreams, called up to help, held firm. Rudyard Kipling summarised what had happened in *The Irish Guards in the Great War*: 'Evidently, one and a half hours' bombardment against a countryside packed with machine guns, was not enough to placate it. The Battalion had been swept from all quarters, and shelled at the same time, at the end of two hard days and sleepless nights, as a first experience of war, and had lost seven of their officers in forty minutes.' One of those officers was John Kipling, last seen alive in the area of Puits 14.

Return to the metalled road and continue along the D39 to the small crossroads just before the Hulluch sign.

To the left is the area of the Quarry and Gun Trench. With the Devons in Gun Trench was the war poet **William Noel Hodgson**, who was to be killed on the Somme on 1 July 1916 after writing the prophetic poem, *Before Action*. For his action at Loos Lt Hodgson was awarded the MC.

Continue to the roundabout with the replica pit head and turn right on the main la Bassée-Lens road (D947). In due course the road begins to rise towards Loos-en-Gohelle and on the right are the factory buildings of MEAC.

Behind them is the Chalk Pit where John Kipling was last seen on 27 September 1915 and the body that is claimed to be his was found some 3,000 yards away to your right. It seems unlikely to us.

Continue to the large mine buildings of Fosse Ernest Cuvelette on the right.

• *Puits 14/10.5 miles/Map 11/9*

A *puit* (literally a well, here meaning shaft) is a minehead and the area was once dotted with them. Most had winding gear and this, until recently dismantled, was a typical example. On the opposite side of the road is Bois Hugo and the local airfield. The hill immediately ahead is Hill 70. The area between here and Hill 70 was the secondary objective for the 44th and 46th Brigades of 15th Division who were attacking from the right starting beyond the built-up areas. As with 7th Division, the 15th Division was affected by our own gas remaining about our jumping-off trenches. To encourage the men to go forward **Piper Laidlaw**, of 7th KOSB, a leading battalion of the 46th Brigade, marched up and down the parapet as men waited to open the attack on Hill 70, playing his pipes (notably *Blue Bonnets over the Border*) until he was wounded, an action for which he was awarded a **VC**. Laidlaw later featured in the film of the Great War, *Forgotten Men*. It was also in this area that the Guards Division filled the gap left by the retreating 21st and 24th 'K' Divisions, one of the company commanders of the Irish Guards being Captain H.R.L.G. Alexander, later to become Lord Alexander of Tunis.

Continue over the roundabout on the D947 and over Hill 70, turning right at the traffic lights signed Loos-en-Gohelle. Continue to the T junction and turn left. Continue following signs to Centre Ville and A21 and at the roundabout with the Mairie to the right turn left following a sign to Loos British Cemetery. Continue uphill to just short of the railway bridge. The cemetery is on the left.

• Loos British CWGC Cemetery/12.7 miles/20 minutes/Map 11/10

This vast (11,364 square metres) cemetery contains nearly 3,000 WW1 burials, of which two-thirds are unknown, and a small number of WW2 graves. It is beautifully landscaped with spacious lawns and an ornamental wall behind the Cross of Sacrifice approached by steps. The cemetery was begun by the Canadian Corps in July 1917 and the original graves are in Plot I, Rows A and B and Plot II Row A. The other graves were concentrated here after the Armistice from battlefield graves and other small cemeteries in the vicinity. Special Memorials commemorate British and Canadian soldiers believed to be buried among them. The great majority fell in the Battle of Loos and it is sobering to read the message 'Known unto God' over and over again along the long rows of graves.

The cemetery is on the site of 'Tower Bridge', a pithead with double winding gear towers that seemed to Tommy to resemble the famous London landmark (another nickname for it was 'The Crystal Palace'). The giant steel structure dominated the area for miles around – it served as a guiding point for the British infantrymen as they attacked in the cold light of dawn of 25 September – and, despite the hurricane of shells that fell around it, Tower Bridge, albeit it in a somewhat mangled state, still stood after the battle.

Turn round and return to the roundabout. Turn left signed A21 on the D165. Straight ahead at the crossroads are the new multiple peaks of the Double Crassier. Turn right on the N43.

• The Double Crassier/13.7 miles

The attack here came from left to right, heading due east as you drive, and was by the 140th and 141st Brigades of 47th Division. The gas worked well and on the extreme right of the attack German fire was attracted off target by the use of dummy figures – heads and shoulders pulled up and down by strings. In the 141st Brigade, the lst/18th London (London Irish Rifles) Regiment which led the assault came on behind the gas and smoke cloud dribbling a football and by 0730 the trench line between the Double Crassier and the N43 had been taken. The Division advanced so well that elements penetrating into Loos village became mixed up with 15th Division north of the N43 and went on to the area of Hill 70 from where you have just come. On the first day of the battle, and mostly before 1000 hours, the 47th Division lost more than 1,200 officers and men.

Continue up the hill to the British cemetery on the crest on the right. Stop, and be careful of the fast-moving traffic.

Loos British CWGC Cemetery.

Dud Corner CWGC Cemetery and Memorial from the Observation Tower, with the battlefield behind.

• Dud Corner CWGC Cemetery & Loos Memorial/14.4 miles/20 minutes/Map 11/11/OP

During the battle of Loos many British shells that were fired were duds and on finding much unexploded shot lying around here the troops nicknamed it 'Dud Corner'. The memorial is virtually on the site of a German strongpoint (*stutzpunkte*) called the 'Lens Road Redoubt' captured by the 15th (Scottish) Division on the first day. The walls surrounding the cemetery which form the memorial record the names of almost 21,000 men with no known grave who fell in the battle of Loos 1915 and the later battles of the Lys, Estaires and Béthune. One of the names, still not removed in April 2003, was that of **John Kipling** (see above). Also commemorated on the wall is the 20-year-old, highly regarded war poet, **Charles Hamilton Sorley**, of the 7th Bn. the Suffolk Regiment. **Three VC** winners are commemorated, two from the Loos battle – **Temporary Lt Col A.F. Douglas-Hamilton** commanding 6th Cameronians for actions at Hill 70 on 25 and 26 September 1915 and **Pte G. Peachment** of the 2nd KRRC for bravery near Hulluch on 25 September 1915 – and **2nd Lt F.B. Wearne** of the Essex Regiment for actions in 1917. Also commemorated here is **Maj-Gen George Handcock Thesiger** (qv), Commanding 9th Division, age 47, 26 September 1915.

A viewing platform on the north-west pier of the memorial offers a remarkable panorama over the battlefield, as does a position near the Cross of Sacrifice at the far end of the cemetery. On a clear day all the places visited on the tour can be identified. The architect was Sir Herbert Baker and the memorial was unveiled on 4 August 1930 by Sir Nevil Macready, Adjutant-General to the BEF in 1914.

There are some 1,800 burials in the cemetery (666 UK Army and 1116 Unknown, 2 UK Airmen, 16 Canadian and 12 Canadian Unknown), including **two VCs – Capt A.M. Read** of the 1st Northants for conspicuous bravery during the attack of 25 September 1915 near Hulluch, and **Sgt Harry Wells** of the 2nd Royal Sussex for actions on the same day near le Rutoir. Shortly before he died Rudyard Kipling left an endowment to fund the nightly sounding of the Last Post here, but no such ceremony takes place.

Climb to the top of the left hand loggia.

With binoculars there are some extraordinary views of the battlefield from this vantage point. Looking across to the Double Crassier, from left to right the twin pylons of the Vimy Memorial and the Lantern tower and Basilique of Notre-Dame de Lorette may be seen.

• End of Loos Battlefield Tour

FROMELLES

19-20 JULY 1916

'Boys you won't find a German when you get there.'
Australian Brigadier-General Elliot.

'They strolled on through the grass like sportsmen after quail,
occasionally shooting at Germans who had settled in
shell holes and who now started up to run farther'.
C.E.W. Bean about the Australian 14th Brigade at Fromelles.

SUMMARY OF THE BATTLE

At 1800 hours on 19 July 1916 the Australian 5th Division which had arrived from Egypt less that two weeks earlier, accompanied by the British 61st Division, attacked German positions at Fromelles. Despite briefly entering and holding part of the German line the Australians were driven out by enemy counter-attacks and were back in their own lines the following day. The 5th Division lost some 5,500 men, the 61st about 1,500 and the Germans almost 2,000.

OPENING MOVES

On 1 July 1916 the great Battle of the Somme began and by the end of the first day the British had lost around 60,000 casualties. The Germans had suffered too and within days each side was bringing in fresh troops to replace those lost or exhausted. The British staff looked around for some way to discourage the Germans from bringing troops from other parts of the front and came up with the idea of making a massive three-day artillery assault in the area of Fromelles as if in prelude to an attack on Aubers Ridge.

Following a conference with General Haig, General Haking, the XI Corps Commander, persuaded G.H.Q. that an infantry assault should actually be made with a view to taking out the small German salient at Fromelles known as the **Sugar Loaf**.

Many staff officers expressed doubts about the idea, particularly whether there was sufficient artillery to support an attack. Haking thought otherwise and planned to use a mix of over 250 field guns and more than 60 medium and heavy weapons which would give one gun to every 15 yards of the 4,000 yards frontage of the attack. In addition it was intended that early on the day of the attack, 17 July, the barrage would lift from the German front trenches to the rear areas leading the Germans to think that the infantry assault was imminent and to come out of their dugouts to man the front line. At that point the artillery was to rapidly return its fire to the front trenches, a process that was to be repeated a number of times so that when the actual attack finally came the enemy would be slow to come out, thus enabling the attackers to cross No Man's Land unopposed.

The infantry plan was to attack the right hand (western) side of the salient using the British 61st Division and the left hand side with the Australian 5th Division, the dividing line between the divisions being roughly north to south through **VC Corner.**

WHAT HAPPENED

The bombardment began on 16 July but without the heavy guns, because rain and mist had prevented them identifying (registering) their targets. On the morning of 17 July the mist still lay over the battlefield and Haking asked for a 24-hours postponement while the 1st Army Commander, Sir Charles Monro (qv), felt that the operation should be cancelled. Haig opted for an attack at 1800 hours on 19 July 19 with the final bombardment to begin at 1100 hours on that day.

The delay at least gave the Australians some rest. They had marched for two days and nights to get to the front line and many had gone without sleep leaving them tired and exhausted. The day dawned bright and sunny and as the troops moved into their attack positions they were closely watched by the Germans in Observation Posts on Aubers Ridge (e.g. the **Kaiser's Bunker**). Early in the afternoon enemy artillery fire fell heavily upon the assembly areas, destroying communication trenches and causing many casualties. Nevertheless, at 1800 hours the infantry moved forward, some through friendly artillery fire, and the attack began. They had been told to head for the third and last line of the German front trench system.

Advancing with three brigades side by side the 61st Division came under intense artillery and machine-gun fire, both in the assembly trenches and in No Man's Land, and only on their extreme right did they reach the enemy trenches – but even there they were driven back and no permanent gains were made. German defence works were formidable. One regiment alone, the 16th opposite the 183rd and 184th Bavarians, had 75 concrete protected positions in its forward parapets and after the initial bombardment 60 of them were undamaged.

The Australians too advanced with three brigades 'up' (i.e. side by side). Right to left they were the 15th (alongside the 61st Division), the 14th and the 8th. At 1830 Brigadier-General Elliott reported that the German fire had died away and that the attack had succeeded. It was not so. The 15th had been badly cut up by the ferocious German fire and dead and wounded lay in and around **Layes Brook** and the **Sugar Loaf**. The 61st Division asked the 15th Brigade to support them in another attack at 2100 hours but this was cancelled – though not before the 15th had gone in, suffering more casualties. The 14th had crossed No Man's Land readily and went on through the German positions, moving across open fields looking for the third line, which they could not find, and then scattering into small groups of isolated posts in ditches and shell holes. It was the same story with the 8th who even took part of a communication trench that led back to **Delangre Farm**, but as night fell the Germans brought up reinforcements, gradually surrounding the separated 'Diggers' (a name given to the Australians in Gallipoli when having landed at ANZAC they were told that all they had to do was to 'dig, dig, dig'.)

Around 0330 hours the order was given to return to their old lines and for the next six hours the Australians fought their way back. At the end of the fighting the

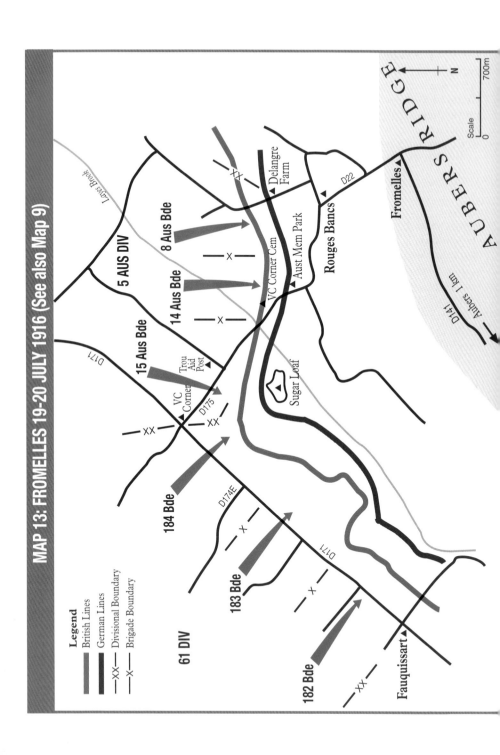

MAP 13: FROMELLES 19-20 JULY 1916 (See also Map 9)

Legend
- British Lines
- German Lines
- —XX— Divisional Boundary
- —X— Brigade Boundary

5 AUS DIV

8 Aus Bde

14 Aus Bde

15 Aus Bde

61 DIV

184 Bde

183 Bde

182 Bde

Layes Brook

D171

VC Corner

Trou Aid Post

D175

Sugar Loaf

VC Corner Cem

Aust Mem Park

Delangre Farm

Rouges Bancs

D22

Fromelles

D174E

D171

Fauquissart

AUBERS RIDGE

Aubers 1 km

D141

N

Scale
0   700m

Bavarians (the opposing Germans were part of the 6th Bavarian Reserve Division) agreed to a truce that allowed many lives to be saved but the Australians had lost 5,533 men in little over one night. No substantial effect on the movement of Germans to the Somme had resulted and the relatively poor performance of the under-strength 61st Division, which in England had been a second-line force used as a source of reinforcements, added to the Australian feeling that the British were lacking in fighting resolve.

The whole affair had been a costly failure.

THE BATTLEFIELD TOUR

• The Route: The tour presumes continuing on from the Aubers Tour and starts at the Museum in Fromelles *Mairie*. It then visits two private Memorials – a WW2 to Sgt Bramble and a WW1 to Capt Kennedy and friends; the sites of Delangre and Cardonnerie Farms; the Australian Memorial Park; the CWGC Cemeteries of VC Corner, Le Trou Aid Post, Rue Pétillon Military and Rue du Bois Military; Laventie German Cemetery. It returns to the *Mairie*. (See **Maps 9** and **13**)
• **Extra Visits** to the site of Hitler Plaque, and German Cemeteries, Fournes-en-Weppes and Wicres.
• **Total Distance:** 7.3 miles
• **Total time:** 2 hours 30 minutes
• **Base towns:** Béthune, Lille
• **Distance from Calais to start point:** see Neuve Chapelle Tour
• **Map:** IGN 1:25,000 2404 Est

• *Fromelles Museum/0 miles/20 minutes/Map 9/9*

The Museum of the *Association Souvenir de la Bataille de Fromelles* is in the attic of the Mairie, approached up a narrow wooden spiral staircase. It is visitable by appointment only (made 15 days in advance) or on certain Sundays in April, May, June and July, September, October, December and on 8 May and 11 November.

Plaque from Adolf Hitler's 1916 Billet, Fournes-en-Weppes.

Interior of Museum, Fromelles.

CWGC Stone to Australian 5th Division 19-21 July 1916.

Contact: *Mairie*, Tel: + (0)3 20 50 20 43, Fax: + (0)3 20 50 67 49. There is a small entrance fee payable.

This is a truly superb museum and very well worth the effort to visit it. It is mainly the work of ex-Mayor, Francis and his son, Benoit, Delattre, Martial Delebarre, Henri Delepierre and Carol Laignel. Many hours of loving care have been put into the cleaning, preserving, presenting and careful labelling (in three languages) of the extraordinary variety of exhibits, many of which have been found on the surrounding battlefield and a number of which are quite unique. It has a wonderful atmosphere and retains the personal feeling so lacking in some new, expensive and technology-led museums.

It features many soldiers who fought in the Battle of Fromelles of July 1916 and local men too, with photos and documents, such as local Resistance hero Henri-Clotaire Descamps (qv). There are collections of pickelhaube, grenades, maces, gas masks, binoculars, rifles, pumps, entrenching tools and other items found in the gallery beneath the bunker in the Australian Park and, rarest of all, the plaque that was on the wall of the house in Fournes where Hitler was billetted in 1916.

There is a special headstone made by the CWGC to commemorate the Australians of 5th Division killed in the 19-21 July 1916 attack.

From the Mairie take the first left on the D22, signed Mémorial Australien and continue past the Café Au Gallodrome (the social hub of the village and where the Anciens Combattants Association meets), *and the Church and turn left on the D22C, signed to VC Corner 'Australien' Cem. Continue to a sharp bend to the left and stop.*

• *Private Memorial to Sgt Bramble/.8 mile/5 minutes/Map 9/10*

This grey polished granite memorial commemorates Sgt Kenneth Walter Bramble, pilot of 609 Sqn, RAF, whose Spitfire was shot down in aerial combat by Obfw Maerz of 5/JG26 near this spot at 0830 in the morning 21 July 1941 as he returned from a bombing raid on Lille. It was erected by Antiq'Air Flandre-Artois (qv) in 1999 after research by Joss Leclercq (qv). Sgt Bramble was actually found near the row of trees that can be seen on the horizon to the left (over the fences held up by WW1 pickets) near Fauquissart. Sgt Bramble is buried in Merville Comm Cemetery Extension, 15 kms north of Béthune.

Turn right and then first left on Rue de la Cardonnerie and continue on the narrow road to the copse surrounding a modern house on the right.

This was the site of the heavily armed **Delangre Farm** and to the left were craters which had been blown by 173rd Tunnelling Coy on 9 May 1915 during the unsuccessful British IV Corps attack on Aubers Ridge. Oddly the German defenders in 1915 were the same ones as in 1916 – the 6th Bavarian Reserve Division. Delangre Farm was the final objective of the attack and there was a long German communication trench beside it which was the objective of the 8th and 14th Australian Inf Bde into which some men of the 8th penetrated briefly.

Continue round the bend and immediately up the track to the left is a farm.

This is **Cardonnerie** (sometimes marked as 'Cordonnerie') **Farm.** In driving from one farm to the next you have crossed first the German front line and the Australian front line.

Return to the Bramble Memorial and continue round the on the D22C to a Calvary on the right.

• *Private Memorial to Capt P.A. Kennedy & Others/2.5 miles/10 minutes/Map 9/12*

This perfectly maintained (by the *Association Souvenir de la Bataille de Fromelles*) memorial is to Capt Paul Adrian Kennedy, Rifle Brigade, kia 9 May 1915, also to Lt Talbot Fitzroy Eden Stanhope, 2nd Lt Henry Ralph Hardinge and Lt Edward Henry Leigh, also of the regiment. All these officers are commemorated on the Ploegsteert Memorial (qv).

Capt Paul Kennedy was the third-born of the four sons of Sir John (who died in 1913) and Lady Archibald. By the time he arrived in France in September 1914 his oldest brother, Archibald, had already been killed in the Retreat from Mons on 26 August 1914. Paul Kennedy was wounded on the Aisne but was back on active service in March 1915. He was shot by a sniper while leading 'B' Coy of the 2nd Rifle Brigade on 9 May 1915 and though brought in by his men, died of his wounds. His youngest brother Patrick was killed near Villers Bretonneux on 24 April 1918.

After the war Lady Kennedy and her one surviving son, Leo (T/Capt A.L Kennedy, MC) began the search for news of the three missing Kennedy brothers. Patrick was discovered to be buried in Crucifix Corner Cemetery, Villers Bretonneux and Archibald was buried in Le Cateau Mil (International) Cemetery.

As Paul's body was never found, Lady Kennedy purchased the small plot of land where his men told her they had laid him to his final rest. On it she placed a fine wooden crucifix carved in Austria with a marble plaque on the plinth, surrounded by a garden and iron railings. She made local arrangements for the site to be cared for and visited it regularly until her death in 1939. After WW2 the monument fell into disrepair and in 1954 the CWGC contacted both Leo Kennedy and the local Commune. They both reacted to restore the memorial. The original wooden crucifix was moved to the church for safe keeping and a new, more durable crucifix erected in its place. A beech hedge replaced the old iron railings. Leo died in 1965 but since then the Commune of Fromelles has continued to maintain the memorial to a very high standard. In 2003, to redress a certain amount of vandalism, it was refurbished and a new copper beech hedge planted.

Continue to the memorial park on the right.

• *Australian Memorial Park/2.7 miles/15 minutes/Map 9/13*

The park is situated around the remains of German fortifications on the part of their line that was captured by the 14th Australian Brigade and held overnight on 19-20 July 1916. Under the further bunker is a 25m gallery in which several of the items in the Fromelles Museum (qv) were found. The park contains a fine bronze statue entitled 'Cobbers' depicting the rescue of a wounded soldier. It also contains a battle exploit explanatory plaque. At the entrance is a Ross Bastiaan (qv) bronze plaque with a fine *bas relief* map of the battle and shows its context in relation to Ypres and other battles. This was unveiled by the Australian Chief of the General Staff on 1 September 1993. Also at the entrance are explanatory boards describing the action

Monument to
Sgt Bramble,
21 July 1941

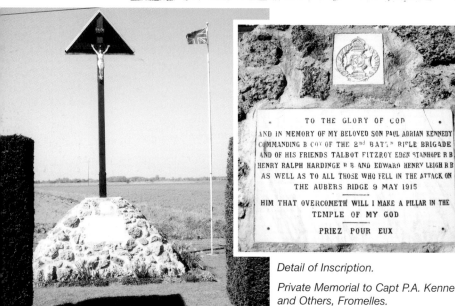

Detail of Inscription.

Private Memorial to Capt P.A. Kennedy
and Others, Fromelles.

here and at the infamous 'Sugar Loaf', with photos. The statue is of Sgt Simon Fraser, 57th Bn AIF, whose company brought in 250 wounded men during the battle as, to quote him, 'the Germans treated us very fairly'. This fine statue recalls two episodes from the Gallipoli Campaign of 1915: the story of Pte Simpson ('The Man with the Donkey') who brought many wounded men down Shrapnel Gully until he himelf was killed, and the Turkish statue of a Turk bringing in a wounded soldier on 25 April 1915. The figure here was sculpted by Peter Corlett and unveiled on 11 November 1998. Fraser, who was farmer from Victoria, went on to be commissioned but was killed at Bullecourt on 12 May 1917. He is commemorated on the Villers Bretonneux Memorial. The statue is known as 'Cobbers' as Fraser described in a letter to his family at home how he and his fellow stretcher bearers brought in the wounded and recalled a wounded man crying out, 'Don't forget me, Cobber'.

Continue to the cemetery to the right.

Detail of Statue.

Detail of Plaque.

'Cobbers' Statue on Bunker,
Australian Memorial Park, Fromelles.

• *VC Corner CWGC Cemetery/2.8 miles/15 minutes/ Map 9/14*

This unusual cemetery has no headstones and is the only completely
Australian cemetery in France. On a screen wall are recorded the names of
1,299 Australians who died in the 19-20 July 1916 Battle of Fromelles, the
Australian 5th Division's first attack in France. The unidentified bodies of 410
of the men are buried under the two lawns, each marked with a white stone
Cross set into the grass. It is situated in what was No Man's Land between the
Australian and German front lines and was designed by Sir Herbert Baker. It
is said that after the war, when the local people returned from their
evacuation, the women who lived nearby were simply able to scoop up the

VC Corner CWGC Cemetery, Fromelles.

thousands of bones in their capacious apron pockets and bring them to the newly made cemetery. The stonework in the cemetery was refurbished in 2003 and gleamed a brilliant white in the sun.

According to the book *Don't Forget Me, Cobber*, by Robin S. Corfield, the cemetery got its name from 4 VCs won in the fighting in Rue du Bois (which runs from south of here to la Bombe) and Rue Delvas on 9 May 1915. The Black Watch **VCs of L/Cpl Finlay** (qv) and **Cpl Ripley** (qv) were won there on 9 May 1915. Ripley survived until 1933 but Finlay was killed in Persia on 21 January 1916 and is commemorated on the Basra Memorial, Iraq. This Memorial bears the names of more than 40,500 Commonwealth soldiers who died in what was then Mesopotamia from Autumn 1914 to August 1921. It was originally situated within the Basra War Cemetery but in 1997 was removed, stone by stone, by 'presidential decree' – an incredible, and extremely costly, engineering feat. It is now located 32 kilometres along the road to Nasiriyah in what was a major battleground of the First Gulf War of 1990. At the time of writing this entry (Spring 2003) it was again the site of conflict and the current state of Iraqi cemeteries and memorials is the subject of a report on the CWGC website (qv). On the same day the **VC** of **Cpl James Upton** (qv) of the 1st Sherwood Foresters was won at nearby Rouges Bancs so was that of **Cpl Charles Richard Sharpe** (qv), 2nd Lincolnshires. However, in *Goodbye to the Battlefields*, H.A. Taylor maintains VC Corner has a special interest, for it would seem to have taken its name from the episode of 16 May 1915 when **CSM Barter** (qv), of the Welsh Fusiliers, won the highest award for valour.

Note that this spot is not actually 'VC Corner'. This will be passed later in the tour.

Continue until the road bends to the right and then the left, crossing Layes Brook (a wide ditch). You are now effectively on the Australian front line.

To the left is the site of the infamous **Sugar Loaf**. The object of the whole 19 July offensive was to attack what was known as the Sugar Loaf Salient in a feint to threaten Aubers Ridge and so to persuade the Germans to leave troops to defend it rather rather than transfer them to the continuing battle on the Somme. The feature lay opposite the boundary of two British Armies – the 1st and 2nd, so each of them could be expected to contribute artillery. Behind the Sugar Loaf and then crossing the two front lines ran the Layes Brook and this became a death trap for the Australians as fire rained down on it from the German defences. On the morning of 20 July the scene in No Man's Land in front of the Sugar Loaf was horrendous. During the previous day and night 5th Australian Division had lost 5,533 men and many of the wounded lay here. An Australian batman searching for his officer near the German wire was challenged by a Bavarian officer who then initiated an informal truce thereby saving many Australian lives.

The northern face of the Sugar Loaf was in the 184th Brigade sector and the 2/4th Berkshires and 2/1st Bucks were chosen as assault formations. The Bucks decided to make use of pipe-pushers (Barratt hydraulic jacks set about 5 feet underground which pushed forward a pipe full of ammonal) against the Sugar

Loaf fortifications but to no avail.
Take the next turning to the right and follow the CWGC signs on the D175. Stop at the cemetery on the left.

• Le Trou Aid Post CWGC Cemetery/3.3 miles/20 minutes/Map 9/15

The Aid Post was established early in the war and the cemetery begun in October 1914, used until July 1915 and in 1916 it was described as being 'a short distance behind the present support line'. There was an actual hole (*trou*) here, surrounded by water, at the time, clearly marked on trench maps. The cemetery was enlarged after the Armistice (when it contained 123 burials) and now contains 356 UK, Australian and Canadian burials, 207 of them unknown, 1 French burial and 5 Special Memorials. Many are officers and men from the fighting at Le Maisnil (21 October 1914), Aubers Ridge (9 May 1915), Loos (25 September 1915) and Fromelles (19-20 July 1916). It was designed by Sir Herbert Baker.

Here is buried **Brigadier-General Arthur Willoughby George Lowry-Cole, CB, DSO (qv)**, age 54, of 25th Brigade who was killed on 9 May 1915 as he stood on the parapet a few hundred from this point trying to reorganise his men as the situation around him became chaotic. He had served in the Burmah, W African and S African campaigns and was Commandant Northern Nigeria 1899-1901. Also buried here is **2nd Lt George Mortimer Langdon Goodall**, 2nd E Lancs, age 21, 9 May 1915. He was a member of the Goodall family who produced playing cards, notably sets with backs of Bruce Bairnsfather's cartoons.

Continue to the next cemetery on the right.

• Rue Pétillon CWGC Cemetery/4.0 miles/15 minutes/Map 9/16

The cemetery was begun in December 1914 and used by fighting units until March 1918. It then fell into enemy hands. At the Armistice it contained 12 battalion burial grounds made by units which had occupied HQ and Dressing Stations at 'Eaton Hall' adjoining the cemetery. It was then enlarged by concentrations and now contains over 1,500 burials, nearly 50% unidentified. There are Special Memorials to 2 Indian soldiers, 15 Canadians, 5 UK and 1 Australian. There are 4 named German graves and 8 Unknown. It was designed by Sir Herbert Baker.

Here serried rows of Unknown Australian soldiers lie shoulder to shoulder and also buried here are **Lt A.C.G. Lonsdale**, KRRC, age 23, killed on 10 March 1915 who was a 'Scholar of Eton and Radley and Undergraduate of Trinity College, Cambridge', and **Lt Col G.C. Shakerley, DSO**, KRRC, age 46, 15 May 1915. Listed as 'Major' in the *Official History*, Shakerley was mortally wounded leading the 1st KRRC in a night attack which started at 1130 on 15 May during the Festubert battle when each man wore a white patch on his back The frontage of the attack was from Chocolat Menier to la Bombe. Half of the leading companies almost reached the enemy breastworks before a shot was fired and secured it with little loss, but the initial success was not sustained.

Continue to the T junction and turn left. Continue to the crossroads and turn left direction Béthune on the D171. Continue to the cemetery on the right.

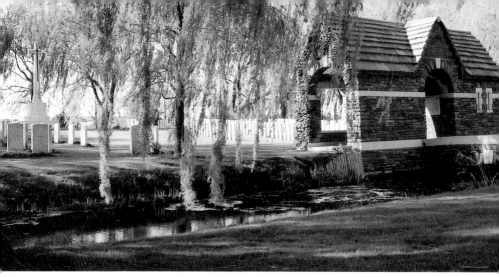

Le Trou Aid Post CWGC Cemetery, Fromelles.

Detail of Entrance Plaque.

German Cemetery, Laventie.

Entrance to Rue
Pétillon CWGC
Cemetery, Fromelles.

Site of Hitler's 1916 Billet, Fournes-en-Weppes.

The padlocked gate.

German Cemetery, Fournes-en-Weppes.

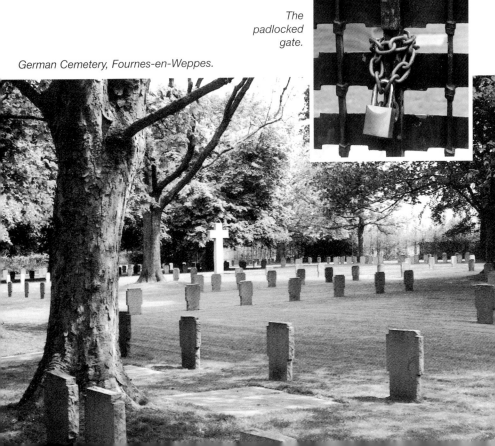

• Rue Du Bois Military CWGC Cemetery/5.4 miles/15 minutes/ Map 9/17

The village of Fleurbaix in which the cemetery is situated remained in Allied hands during most of the war until it was captured by the Germans on 9 April 1918 after a gallant defence by the 2nd Suffolks. It then remained in German hands until September 1918. The original cemetery, begun in November 1914 and used until December 1916, was then reopened in January 1918. It comprised what is now Plot I and Rows A and B of Plot II and included 27 Australians from the Fromelles Battle of 19-20 July 1916. After the Armistice the cemetery, which was designed by Sir Herbert Baker, was enlarged and now contains 844 burials, 395 of them Unknown. There is a Special Memorial to 13 men.

Buried here is **Pte Albert Drew Hughes**, age 22 of the 2nd Wilts, 25 (listed as 26 in the Debt of Honour Register) May 1915, one of 4 brothers. His brother, Rfmn Enos George James Hughes, London Regt, age 31, was killed on 1 September 1918 and is buried in Assevillers New Brit Cemetery on the Somme.

Continue to the crossroads with the D175.

This is the Pétillon crossroads. During the war this was actually known as **VC Corner** – not the area of today's VC Corner Cemetery. The D171 road ahead, which was the main road from Armentières to Béthune, was just behind the British front line and essential to their supply system. A continuous stream of soldiers, ammunition and supplies was moved along this busy road. This section of the Rue du Bois was known as Rue Tilleloy during the war. It was here, quite unusually for the second Christmas of the War, that a brief truce took place on 25 December 1915. It was described by Lt Wyn Griffith of the 15th RWF in his book *Up to Mametz*. On Christmas Eve a message forbidding fraternisation of the kind that had taken place the previous year had been read out, but towards midnight snatches of song wafted over from the German trenches and a few drunken soldiers clambered out of their trenches. A few minutes later 'there was a rush of men from both sides, carrying tins of meat, biscuits and other odd commodities for barter'. After 'a feverish exchange of "souvenirs"... an irate Brigadier came spluttering up to the line, thundering hard', throwing a "court martial" into every other sentence' and the fun was stopped dead.

Continue towrds Fauquissart.

The attack by 61st Division came from your right as you drive and occupied the entire length of this road from VC Corner to Fauquissart.

Turn right signed Cim Mil All Laventie on a very narrow road to the cemetery on the right.

• German Cemetery, Laventie/7.3 miles/10 minutes/Map 9/18

This bare cemetery surrounded by savagely pollarded trees is punctuated by stark black crosses with a larger cross in the centre. It contains 1978 German soldiers, three of them bearing Jewish headstones. The burials are mostly of June/July 1918.

Turn round and return to VC Corner. Turn right to Fromelles. Return to the Mairie (11.2 miles).

• End of Fromelles 1916 Battlefield Tour

Extra Visit to Site of Site of Hitler Plaque & German Cemeteries, Fournes-en-Weppes & Wicres (Map 9/19,20). Round trip: 12 miles. Approximate time: 1 hour.

From the Mairie take the D141 direction Le Maisnil and then next right to Fournes-en-Weppes on the D141a. At the T junction turn left on the D141 direction 'Mairie/PTT' and continue 100m to a house on the right.

On house No 966, between the *pharmacie* and the '8 to 8' store, is the house in which Hitler was billetted in 1916 (then Cordon's the Butcher) and on which the plaque, which is now in the Fromelles Museum (qv), was erected in 1942. Hitler was a company runner and each morning he would bicycle to Wavrin to get orders from Capt Wiedemann, then proceed to Fromelles and return at noon. The procedure would be repeated in the afternoon. His rest periods were spent in Haubourdin.

Turn round and turn sharp right on the D97 signed to Cimetière Militaire Allemand Fournes-en-Weppes and then first right, still following signs. Continue to a huge Essors warehouse at a dead end and stop. The holly-bordered path to the cemetery (not signed) is to the left beyond the warehouse.

Fournes-en-Weppes German Cemetery. Unusually the wrought iron gate to the cemetery was padlocked on our last visit in May 2003. The signs of graffiti on the headstones and general vandalism to be seen explain why. The cemetery is planted with some beautiful trees, including a magnificent copper beech in the centre round which the grey stone crosses, which date from 1914-1918, are ranged. There is a large stone cross to the left. The cemetery contains 1,739 named soldiers with 177 Unknown.

Turn round and turn left and then left again at the main street. Continue to the impressive Poilu War Memorial on the right.

Beyond it is the excellent Auberge les Vieilles Poutres, Tel: + (0)3 20 50 23 13. This is a typical and charming restaurant with a variety of menus to suit all pockets.

Continue to the N41, turn right and continue to the German Cemetery on the left.

Wicres German Cemetery. This is unusual in that the flat headstones are laid in flower beds which are a riot of pink in season. It contains 584 burials from 1914, 1915 and 1916. In the centre is a grey stone cross supported by two mourning figures, which is a memorial to the Prinz Friedrich der Niederlande and the 2nd Westfaelisches No 15 Regiment.

There are two other German Cemeteries in the vicinity: **Illies** (to the west of the N41 with 2,619 named burials and 255 Unknown) and **Salomé** (on the D145 with 2,548 burials).

Return to the Mairie of Fromelles, or continue to la Bassée to the left or the Commercial Centre at Englos to the right on the D7 for RWC.

VIMY RIDGE, ARRAS

9-12 APRIL 1917

'Suddenly every gun opened and the sky became one run of fire and
the hill rose up red and white and brown and gray, blown up bodily
in heaps by our shells: it was the worst shell fire ever seen ...
I believe the Somme was child's play to Vimy.'

John Masefield. Letters from France 1917.

'In the monring, tired and back from night duty, we lay down with the words,
"Now let us put the blankets over our heads and sleep."
Suddenly there was heavy drumfire. We jumped up,
all tiredness gone, for our country and our lives were at stake.'

A German Fusilier's memory of 9 April 1917 on Vimy Ridge

'Within forty minutes of the opening of the battle, practically the whole of the
German front line system on the front attacked had been stormed and taken.'

Sir Douglas Haig's Despatches.

SUMMARY OF THE BATTLE

On 9 April 1917, Easter Monday, the Canadian Corps, commanded by Lt Gen
J.H.G. Byng, attacked what was probably the strongest of German defensive
positions in northern France. They rehearsed their assault and used miles of
tunnels to approach the enemy lines. By midday only the highest point of the ridge,
Hill 145, remained in German hands and that fell the following day. German
casualties were about 20,000, the Canadian losses were half that. Four VCs were won.

OPENING MOVES

Vimy Ridge forms part of the front that was known as the 'Arras Sector'. This ran
from Lens in the north to Beaurains in the south. Arras itself was never occupied
permanently by the Germans (though they spent two days in the town in September
1914), and a salient bulged east from the city into enemy territory throughout the war.

The front formed in September/October 1914, at which time the Germans took
the heights of Notre Dame de Lorette and Vimy Ridge during struggles known as
the first battle of Artois. In May 1915 in the second battle of Artois, the French
mounted an attack towards Vimy with their seasoned 10th Army and gained the
crest of the ridge, but were unable to consolidate their positions. In September 1915
as part of the third Artois Offensive, of which the British attack at Loos was the

MAP 14: VIMY RIDGE 9-12 APRIL 1917 (NOTRE-DAME DE LORETTE OCT 1914-OCT 1915)

Exit 6.1
A21
D58
D58-E2
Aix Noulette
Notre-Dame de Lorette
Souchez
Cabaret Rouge
1 CORPS
4(Cdn) DIV
3(Cdn) DIV
Neuville-St-Vaast
La Targette
Mont St Eloi
CANADIAN CORPS
2(Cdn) DIV
1(Cdn) DIV
D55
XVII CORPS
Ecurie
D937
D341
N39
ARRAS

The Pimple
Givenchy-en-Gohelle
La Chaudière
VIMY
N17
Petit Vimy
Hill 140
Farbus
Thélus
Zivy
Front Line 9 April
Front Line 12 April
AE19 - A26
D49
D50
D919
N50
D57

Notre-Dame de Lorette
Ablain
Souchez
Vimy
Neuville
Mont St Eloi
Arras
Loos
Lens
Gavrelle
Monchy-le-Préux
Beaurains
Wancourt
Croisilles
Front Line 15 May
N
0   2.5 kms

© TVH 2004

2 kms
N

Legend for Map 14

1. 158th Regt & Sous-Lt Léon Mem
2. 174th Regt & Sous-Lt Defrasse Mem
3. Gen Maistre Mem
4. N-D de Lorette French Nat Cem
5. N-D de Lorette Museum
6. Gen Barbot & Others Mem
7. Cabaret Rouge CWGC Cem
8. Czech Cem & Mem
9. Polish Mem
10. La Targette Museum
11. La Targette Hand Mem
12. La Targette CWGC & French Nat Cems
13. Neuville-St-Vaast German Cem
14. Lichfield Crater CWGC Cem
15. Grange Tunnel & Preserved Trenches
16. Canadian No 2, Givenchy Road & Givenchy-en-Gohelle CWGC Cems
17. Vimy Ridge Canadian Nat Mem
18. Vimy Ridge Interpretative Centre
19. 5th Canadian Div Mem
20. Canadian Artillery Mem
21. Zivy Crater CWGC Cem
22. Faubourg d'Amiens CWGC Cem
23. Arras Boves (Tunnels)

Tunnels —

northern prong, the 10th Army again set their faces towards the ridge, but German counter-attacks drove them back.

Trench warfare, which had begun late in 1914, now became the order of the day and the French and Germans adopted a 'live and let live' policy. The Arras front became what was known as a 'quiet sector'. In March 1916 the British took over the Arras front from the French 10th Army which had lost a reported 135,000 men in trying to take the ridge. The British immediately set about trying to take the initiative with many patrols into German lines and J.B. Priestley who was in the Souchez area recalled in his memoirs (*Margin Released*), 'It had been quiet recently around there until we British arrived, but of course we had to hot it up for the sake of our morale, to keep our fellas on their toes ... So very soon, having asked for it, God knows why, we caught a packet. It was not long before our own B Company with a nominal fighting strength of 270 had been reduced to a grim and weary seventy.'

In late autumn the Canadians came north from the Somme to relieve the British and settled for a cold winter of strengthening defences. At the end of the year, at Chantilly, the British and French agreed to continue their policy of joint offensives, a decision unaffected by the replacement of Joffre by Nivelle on 31 December. Nivelle, the new broom, proclaimed the need for an offensive of 'violence, brutality and rapidity', and told all and sundry that his plan would end the war by breaking through the German lines. As a preliminary to his assault, planned to begin on the Aisne in mid-April 1917, the British were tasked to attack on the Arras sector with their First and Third Armies, drawing German forces away from the Aisne.

The British preparation was very thorough and included the use of tunnels to bring troops forward to the front line without being observed or shot at. Arras itself has two major cave systems dating back to the seventeenth century and in the eastern suburbs these were enlarged and connected to a series of tunnels by special Tunnelling Companies – particularly by the New Zealanders. Twenty-five large caves were excavated with room for 11,000 troops and electric light, running water and ventilation systems were installed. In order to bring forward the vast amount of supplies of ammunition and stores needed, standard and narrow gauge railways were built and plank roads laid. A very deliberate policy of achieving air superiority was maintained by offensive flying, particularly in the days immediately prior to the attack. 'Boom' Trenchard mustered some 750 aircraft against the Germans' 260 and in the four days before the battle the RFC lost 131 machines, though contemporary reports put the figure as 28 (shades of the reports of RAF losses in the Battle of Britain in 1940). However mastery of the skies gave artillery observers the freedom to register their guns effectively. Three weeks before the assault the artillery began to bombard the German wire. Heavy artillery concentrated on the rear areas, on headquarters and on communications. As the day of the attack approached, the intensity of shelling increased by night and day and at intervals along the front gas discharges were made. The total frontage of the attack was just on 15 miles from Vimy Ridge to Croisilles southeast of Arras. The southern half was entrusted to the 3rd Army under Allenby and the northern half to the 1st Army under General Horne. The assault on what General Haig called 'an important tactical feature, possession of which I considered necessary', was delegated to General Julian Byng's Canadian Corps, part of 1st Army. The feature was Vimy Ridge.

WHAT HAPPENED

At 0530 on 9 April 1917 in driving sleet the British armies emerged from their tunnels and trenches and advanced behind a rolling barrage. It was Ludendorff's 52nd birthday. What a present! He was not in the best of spirits anyway, having heard that three days earlier America had declared war on Germany. He had observed all the careful preparations and had expected the British attack, indeed he had anticipated it with confidence, but the force of the assault broke through the German positions, in places to their third lines, and Vimy Ridge was effectively lost soon after midday. It took two days of counter-attacks and movement of reserves to stem the possibility of a British breakthrough, but in the week before Nivelle's offensive on the Aisne, the 1st Army (in effect the Canadians) took 4,000 prisoners and 54 guns while in the south the 3rd Army took 7,000 prisoners and 112 guns. The penetration made and held was estimated by Ludendorff to have been '12 to 15 kilometres wide and 6 or more kilometres deep'. Ten days after the attack began there were almost twice as many infantry opposite the British as there had been at the start. Haig's men had done what had been asked of them – 'take some German forces away from the Aisne'.

The Canadian achievement here was the result of a formidable artillery preparation, intensive training, particularly in rehearsing infantry movement to keep time with a creeping barrage, and very careful overall planning combined with Canadian dash and verve.

The aerial combat over Vimy during this month of April 1917 was so costly to the British that they dubbed it 'Bloody April'. During those 30 days **Rittmeister Baron Manfred von Richthofen** increased his 'score' from 31 to 50, despite the numerical superiority of the RFC. But the Germans were flying over their own territory and their Albatross D111 triplanes were superior to the allied Spads and FEs – both in speed and manoeuvrability. One of the Red Baron's opponents that month was **Captain William Avery Bishop, DSO, DFC**, who won his **MC** on 7 April 1917 for shooting down a German balloon, and who later in 1917 was awarded the **VC** 'for most conspicuous bravery, determination and skill'.

THE BATTLEFIELD TOUR

This incorporates the Notre-Dame de Lorette, Artois Battlefield Tour (see pages 50-53)
• **The Route:** The tour starts at the 158th RI Memorial, Tomb of S/Lt Léon, Memorial to S/Lt Defrasse then visits the Memorial to Gen Maistre, French National Memorial and Museum at Notre Dame de Lorette; Statue & Memorials to Gen Barbot/77th Division/Gen Stirn/Gen Plessner/ Departmental Memorial to the War in Algeria, Tunisia and Morocco, Souchez; Cabaret Rouge CWGC Cemetery, Czech Memorial & Cemetery and Polish Memorial; la Targette-Neuville St Vaast WW1 Museum, Flame in Hand Memorial and British, French and German cemeteries; Canadian Memorial Park at Vimy Ridge; Arras – War Memorial, Boves, Faubourg d'Amiens CWGC Cemetery and Arras Memorial; *Mur des Fusillés*.
• **Extra Visits:** Lichfield Crater CWGC Cemetery; 5th 'Imperial' Div Memorial.
• **Total distance:** approx 21 miles

- **Total time:** 5 hours
- **Base town:** Arras
- **Distance from Calais to start point via A16/E15:** 61 miles. Motorway Tolls
- **Maps:** IGN 1:25,000 2406 Est Arras plus 2405 Est Lens

From the A16/E15 take Exit 6.1, the junction with the A21. Fork right and exit immediately, signed Liéven, Lens and filter to the right to Bruay en Artois, Aix Noulette, Noeux les Mines. Notre Dame is then signed on the D937.

The light tower and Basilique can now be seen on the crest to the right.

Continue through Aix Noulette, past the junction with the D51 to the Auberge de Lorette on the right. There is a memorial on the left. Set your mileometer to zero.

• 158th Regt d'Infanterie Memorial/Tomb of Sous-Lt Jean R. Léon/Memorial to Sous-Lt Jacques Defrasse/0 miles/10 minutes/ Map 14/1 and 14/2

The Regimental Memorial was erected by survivors of the Lorette sector. Before it is the tomb of Sous-Lieutenant Jean R. Léon, *Légion d'Honneur, Croix de Guerre*, killed 26 May 1915 . Up the track marked *privé* to the left is the large Memorial to Sous-Lieutenant Defrasse, age 23, killed on 16 June 1915 during the second battle of Artois, like Léon, and to the 174th Regiment. On the side is a message attesting to his courage by the General commanding his division. He was killed in the assault on La Tranchée des Saules (approximately on the line of the track). Defrasse had just put up his rank stripes on his tunic which may be seen, with other personal belongings, at the Museum at Notre-Dame de Lorette, gifts from his family. He had been commissioned on 3 May 1915 at La Tranchée de Calonne.

Continue to the junction with the seemingly defunct European Centre for Peace/tourist office (with a splendid mural) to the left and the Artisan Museum ahead and turn right signed to N-D de Lorette. At the top of the hill is

• French National Cemetery, Basilique, Memorials and Museum, Notre-Dame de Lorette/2 miles/40 minutes/Map 14/3, 14/4, 14/5/ OP/RWC

This hill and Vimy Ridge, which is to the south-east and separated from it by the motorway, are adjacent features. On a clear day Vimy Ridge, Arras to the south and the battlefield of Loos to the north-east are all clearly visible.

The hill, which is 165 m above sea level, had its first chapel in 1727 which was enlarged to a church in 1870. During the 'Race to the Sea' in 1914 the Germans took the hill and Ablain St Nazaire (see **Map 4** page 51), pushing the French lines to the west of the present Basilique which has been built on the site of the old chapel. In 1915 there were two major actions around Notre-Dame de Lorette. On 9 May the 21st Division and the 33rd Division under General Pétain attacked to the south of the hill as part of a 10th Army offensive and gains were made everywhere, but the feature was not cleared. On 16 June as part of the same offensive the same formations attacked again, but any gains they had made were wiped out by German counter-attacks on 13 July, although in both actions the Moroccan Division had distinguished

Statue to Gen Maistre and 21st Army Corps with Notre-Dame de Lorette lantern tower in background.

Memorial to Gen Barbot and 77th DI, Souchez.

The Basilique, Cemetery and Lantern Tower, Notre-Dame de Lorette.

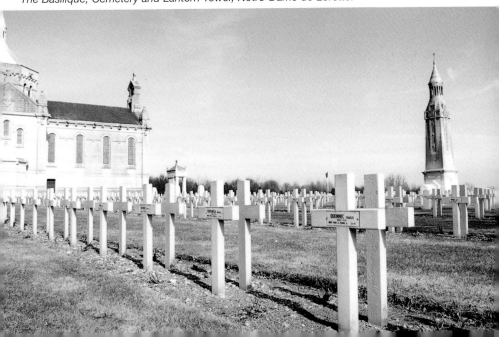

itself by its bravery and élan. The attack of 25 September 1915 was more successful. The village of Souchez was taken by the French 13th and 70th Divisions and Cabaret Rouge was cleared by the 77th Division, now sadly without their charismatic General Barbot. (See the battle of Notre-Dame de Lorette, Artois page 53)

This part of the feature where you are now was also taken but the plateau of Vimy Ridge remained in German hands and stayed with them until the Canadian assault of 9 April 1917, almost two years later.

On 12 September 1920 the Association of Notre-Dame de Lorette was founded, with the aim of building a **cemetery, an ossuary, a symbolic lighthouse and a chapel (Map 14/4)** in order to commemorate those who died. The Association has almost 3,000 members and the memorial area was officially recognized as a National Monument in 1963. Members of the *Garde d'Honneur de Lorette* man the area from 0900-1630 in March, until 1730 in April and May and until 1830 in June-Aug, then again until 1630 up to 11 Nov. The cemetery contains 19,000 identified burials and six mass graves containing more than 16,000 soldiers, all arranged around a clear central area in which is the tower and the Basilique. The first grave on the left as you enter the cemetery is that of **General Barbot** (qv) of the 77th Division who was killed on 10 May 1915, just after his division had attacked Souchez – you pass the divisional memorial later. Barbot is credited with saving Arras from occupation in 1914 not just once but twice. The tower, designed by Maître L. Cordonnier, is 205 ft high and has 200 stairs and 5 floors. At the top is a 3,000 candlepower light that rotates at 5 times per minute and when shining can be seen for more than 40 miles. In the crypt of the tower are an unknown soldier from the Second World War; the ashes of people deported to concentration camps; an unknown soldier from Indo-China and an unknown soldier from North Africa. The first stone was laid on 19 June 1921 by Marshal Pétain and the tower was inaugurated on 2 August 1925 by President Painlevé. To enter the tower there is a nominal charge which goes towards the upkeep of the memorial. On the first floor is a small museum which was opened in 1964 and (if it is not under repair) it is possible to climb to the top and to look out over the battlefield. The Basilique, or chapel, was consecrated on 26 May 1927 in the presence of Marshal Pétain and has inside, on the left, a statue of Monseigneur Julien, the founder of the Association and on the right a statue of Notre-Dame de Lorette. The stained-glass windows commemorate famous historical events.

Outside the cemetery entrance and almost opposite to it is **a Memorial to General Maistre and the 21st Army Corps (Map 14/3)**, erected in 1925. It was Maistre who had been stubbornly assaulting the hill since December 1914 and it took until 12 May 1915 before the area of the chapel was captured. There is also an orientation table detailing the Artois fighting from October 1914 to September 1915, put up in 1975.

Standing with your back to the cemetery, and looking out over the plain below, the ruined tower of the Abbey at **Mont St Eloi** can be seen, left as a reminder of the First World War, as was the ruined steeple of the church at nearby **Ablain-St-Nazaire**. Ablain St Nazaire was inside the German lines before the 9 May 1915 offensive while Mont St Eloi was just within the French and between them they indicate the maximum extent of the German salient towards the west. To a first approximation the May offensive came straight towards you from Mont St Eloi and it was over that distance that General Maistre's troops toiled for six months to

The ruins of Ablain-St-Nazaire church.

reach where you are now. On the esplanade between the tower and the chapel is a bronze *Croix de Guerre* which supports the eternal flame which is rekindled each Sunday morning after the 1030 Mass.

On the far side of the cemetery from where you are parked (you can drive round to it if you wish) is an excellent **Museum (Map 14/5),** recreating the life of the soldier on the Artois front, with many interesting dioramas with sound effects, and collections of artifacts including the tunic of Jacques Defrasse (qv), which should not be missed. There is an entrance fee and a diorama room with refreshments. Behind the museum is a recreated battlefield area.

Open every day: 0900-2000.

Tel: + (0)3 21 45 15 80.

In front of the Museum is a **Memorial to Sous-Lieutenant Henri Merlin**, age 24, of the 10th Chasseurs á Pied, 3 March 1915. His citation by the General commanding the 10th Army records that he fought to the last, overcome by the Germans, and when his last comrade died he killed himself rather than retreat.

Return down the hill with amazing views over the Douai Plain, the Loos Battlefield and Vimy Ridge, and turn right to Souchez.

As you drive down the D937 from here to the German cemetery you are driving essentially parallel to the German front line trenches of April 1917 which would have been about 1,000 yards to your left. The Canadians' northern boundary included the village of Souchez, the responsibility of the 4th Division and that line ran 4 miles south to beyond the German cemetery. Thus the Canadian build up and assault of 9 April 1917 might be imagined as 4 miles of the D936 picking itself up and hurling itself to the left!

On leaving the village is

• Statue & Memorials to Gen Barbot/77th Division/Gen Stirn/Gen Plessner/ Departmental Memorial to the War in Algeria, Tunisia and Morocco/4.8 miles/10 minutes/Map 14/6

On the large memorial which depicts General Barbot leading his Chasseurs into battle are plaques to Generals Stirn and Plessner. It commemorates the period from October 1914 to February 1915 when the division was in the Souchez sector. The General was mortally wounded near Cabaret Rouge on 10 May 1915. Colonel Stirn, promoted to replace him, was killed two days later by a shell. The sculptor was Jules Déchin.

The nearby imposing 1952-64 N. African Campaign Memorial was raised in 2002 by the survivors to their fallen comrades. It consists of large white archways joined by a pathway in which there is an eternal flame, flagpoles and a sunken pool. The names of the dead are inscribed in white on a black memorial wall reminiscent of the Vietnam Memorial in Washington DC.

Here around Souchez, particularly in the area of the local cemetery, was some of the fiercest fighting during the 1914/15 Artois battles. The Germans had fortified all the houses and built a number of strong points – the cemetery, the Cabaret Rouge – and armed them with machine guns. The heights of Notre-Dame de Lorette (visible on a good day behind the General's statue) seemed to dominate the French positions at the end of 1914, much as Monte Cassino seemed to dominate the way to Rome in 1944. During the second Artois battle from May 1915 the intensity of the struggle to clear 'the bloody hill' of Lorette, the village of Souchez and to gain Vimy Ridge, reached depths of horror and destruction only paralleled at Verdun. Even with Lorette under control Souchez stood in the way of a secure assault upon Vimy and it was not until 26 September 1915 that the village was finally re-taken. It had been in German hands for a whole year. On 23 September 1920 the village was awarded the *Croix de Guerre*.

Continue to the cemetery on the right.

• *Cabaret Rouge CWGC Cemetery/5.2 miles/10 minutes/Map 14/7*

This was started by the British 47th Division in March 1916 and used by fighting units including the Canadian Corps until September 1918. It was enlarged after the Armistice. There are over 7,000 burials and 60 special memorials. In Plot 8, Row E,

Grave 7 is a headstone recording the fact that the **Canadian Unknown Soldier** was taken from here on 25 May 2000 to the tomb of the Unknown Warrior at the National War Memorial in Ottawa. Buried in Plot XXVII, Row A, Grave 14 is **Lt Col Victor George Howard Rickard**, 2nd Royal Munster Fusiliers, age 40, 9 May 1915, who was killed leading his battalion in the Battle of Aubers Ridge (qv). In Plot XXX, Row F, is buried **Lt Col A.L. Wrenford**, 4th E Lancs, 21 March 1918, who has a **Private Memorial** near Villerets (qv).

Under the entrance arch is a **plaque to the cemetery designer, Sir Frank Higginson**, secretary to the IWGC 1947-1956, who died in 1958 and whose ashes were scattered in the cemetery.

The original Cabaret Rouge was a house between here and the Barbot statue, the area of the local cemetery.

Between the wars pilgrims to the cemetery were able to refresh themselves at a nearby café called 'The Better 'Ole' after Bairnsfather's famous cartoon. The French writer,

Former grave of the Canadian Unknown Soldier, Cabaret Rouge CWGC Cemetery.

Czech Memorial and Cemetery, Neuville St Vaast.

Polish Memorial, Neuville St Vaast.

Torch in hand Memorial, la Targette.

La Targette CWGC and French Cemeteries.

German dressing station diorama, la Targette WW1 Museum.

Cross and Jewish Headstone, with Memorial to 4th Hannover IR in background, German Cemetery, Neuville St Vaast.

Henri Barbusse, author of *Le Feu* (Under Fire) served in this area in 1915. In his diary he recorded his impressions of Cabaret Rouge. 'Never have I seen such total devastation of a village. Here, nothing with any shape left, not even a stretch of wall, a railing, a doorway left standing. It might have been a dirty, boggy wasteland near a town whose inhabitants had, through the years, been tipping on it their debris, rubbish, rubble from demolished buildings and scrap iron. In the foreground, the fog, the unearthly scene of massacred trees.'

Continue to Neuville St Vaast. On the right is

• Czech Memorial & Cemetery/Polish Memorial/6.3 miles/10 minutes/Map 14/8 and 14.9

The Czechs joined the French Foreign Legion in Paris in 1914, forming part of the 2nd Regiment of Infantry. Together with the Moroccans they fought in the May 1915 second Artois offensive as part of the French 10th Army taking this area but with heavy casualties. The memorial particularly refers to the 9 May 1915 attack towards the German strongpoint at Hill 140 (Thélus Mill) just north of Thélus village. They went over the top from this area and had 80 per cent casualties. Thélus was not taken until the Canadian attack of 9 April 1917. The memorial, sculpted by J. Hrvska, was erected in 1925 and behind it are graves from the First and Second World Wars, plus a memorial shelter put up in May 1968. Looking across the road, to the left of the Polish memorial (which was destroyed by the Germans in 1940 and rebuilt identically after the war) the tops of the pylons of the Vimy Canadian memorial on Point 145 the highest part of Vimy Ridge, can be seen on the skyline.

On the opposite side of the road is the Polish Memorial which commemorates the part played by the Poles in the Artois campaign, probably as members of the Foreign Legion. They too attacked Hill 140 on 9 May 1915. The memorial was inaugurated on 9 May 1935, twenty years after the attack.

Continue to the crossroads in the centre of La Targette village and park behind the Museum on the right on the D49.

• La Targette Memorial/Museum/7.1 miles/20 minutes/Map 14/10/11

This striking village memorial on the left of a huge hand and wrist (which bears an identification tag with the name of the village upon it) emerges from broken soil to hold aloft the flame of life – a concept explored in John McCrae's poem, *In Flanders Fields*, and in the sculpture on the Vimy memorial. It was completed on 20 October 1932. The village, within German lines after 1914, was entered on the morning of 9 May 1915 by troops of XX Corps and after five days of fighting the Germans were pushed to its far edge but the village was decimated, the destruction being completed by later French mining activities in May 1916. Over the road is the well-maintained private Museum owned by David Bardiaux (who also owns the Notre-Dame de Lorette Museum). It contains a superb collection of uniforms, Allied and German gas masks, weapons and artefacts and has several well-presented scenes of trench, aid post and dugout life. **Open every day** 0900-2000. Tel: + (0)3 21 59 17 76. Entrance fee payable.

Return to the D937, continue and then turn right on the D55 and La Targette CWGC Cemetery is signed just a few metres off the road to the right.

• La Targette CWGC/French National Cemeteries/7.4 miles/15 minutes/Map 14/12

The CWGC Cemetery, originally known as Aux Rietz Mil Cemetery, was begun at the end of April 1917 and used by Field Ambulances and fighting units until September 1918. One-third of the burials are of Artillery Units and there are 295 Canadian burials, 3 S. Africans and 1 WW2. Adjoining it is the French Cemetery built in 1919 from concentrations from the surrounding battlefields and other small cemeteries. It contains 11,443 burials (including 3,882 Unknown) from WW1 and 593 French, 170 Belgians and 4 Poles from WW2 all laid out in a perfectly symmetrical pattern which stretches up the slope to the three ossuaries.

Return to the D937 and turn right. Continue to the sign to the German Cemetery on the left.

• Neuville St Vaast German Cemetery/7.9 miles/10 minutes/Map 14/13/WC

This is the site of the heavily defended German position known as 'the Labyrinth'. It has been graphically described by two famous writers of the First World War. One was **Henri Barbusse**, a comparatively elderly (forty-one when he enlisted in 1914) socialist – some would say communist – whose uncompromisingly subjective book *Le Feu* drew heavily on his experiences of attacks like the desperate one against the Labyrinth. The book was controversial because of its brutality, but it had a profound influence on the realism of Sassoon and Owen when they read it at Craiglockhart. The other writer, also to become controversial for his supposed Nazi sympathies in the 1930s, was **Henry Williamson**, who described it in the account of his return to the battlefields after the war, *The Wet Flanders Plain*, as the scene of some of the most terrible fighting during the first two years of the war, 'An underground fortress with access to scores of ferro-concrete blockhouses, held machine-guns under steel cupolas which resisted destruction by all but the heaviest shells. Here a maze of trenches were protected by belts of unpenetrable barbed wire. The Labyrinth spread over thirty acres of chalk. . . . like the web of an immense spider.' In 1915, following almost continuous fighting for Vimy Ridge, thousands of shredded French and colonial uniforms lay on the barbed wire above heaps of bones and skulls. Williamson was appalled by the number of black crosses marking the German graves, concentrated from many areas nearby, that confronted him in 1924. These original crosses remained until the early 1960s when improvement work began. Today there are 37,000 burials here, as well as over 8,000 in one mass grave. In the entrance is a stone block on which is a *bas relief* map showing all the cemeteries in this area, including Lens. There is a WC to the left of the entrance. Opposite is a farm known as la Maison Blanche, the original of which gave its name to this sector.

Return to La Targette crossroads and turn right. Continue through Neuville St Vaast to the sign to the right to Lichfield Crater (easily missed).

Extra Visit to Lichfield Crater CWGC Cemetery (Map 14/14). Round trip: 1.4 miles. Approximate time: 15 minutes

Follow the crater sign and continue over the motorway and fork right along a deteriorating cart track (probably not driveable in wet weather) to Lichfield Crater.

This is one of the most unusual cemeteries on the Western Front. It is one of two mine craters (the other being Zivy Crater, see below) used by the Canadian Corps Burial Officer for bodies from the Vimy battlefield from 9 or 10 April 1917. Designed by W.H. Cowlishaw it was originally simply called CB-2A. The grassed circular cemetery is essentially a mass grave and contains only one headstone – to **Pte Albert Stubbs**, 8th S Lancs Regt, age 25, 30 April 1916. The Cross of Sacrifice is on a raised level and below it is a memorial wall on which are the names and details of 41 Canadian soldiers buried here. There are also 11 unidentified Canadians, 4 completely Unknowns and 1 unidentified Russian.

Lichfield Crater CWGC Cemetery.

Continue and drive into the Park.

• Vimy Ridge Canadian National Memorial, Interpretative Centre & Park/11.2 miles/60 minutes/Map 14/15, 14/16, 14/17, 14/18

Drive into the park and drive past the parking area on the right for the Tunnels/Trenches, follow signs to the Monument and park near the Interpretative Centre.

On 25 April 1915 allied landings were made in Gallipoli. The ANZAC forces landed in the wrong place and were caught and held by the Turkish defenders on a narrow beach below high cliffs where in essence they were to remain until withdrawn nine months later. The extraordinary courage and resolution of the ANZAC soldiers depicted mostly in the writings of C.E.W. Bean, the official Australian historian, led to the Gallipoli campaign becoming a focal point in the developing character of that young nation. Here too was a 'National Army'

The imposing twin pylons of the Canadian National Memorial, Vimy

Detail of Canada mourning for her dead.

fighting its first battle, the Canadian. In a way the fighting for, and the capture of, Vimy Ridge, might be seen as the Canadian's Gallipoli. Their achievement was remarkable and their pride in what they achieved thoroughly deserved. The importance of Vimy to the self-awareness of Canada is evident in that it is at the highest point of the Ridge that they have placed their most important memorial.

Opened in 1997 (as described by a bronze plaque at the entrance) the **Interpretative Centre (Map 14/18)** has informative panels and photographs, some trench periscopes, a circular audio-visual presentation of the battlefield in English, French and German and a small book stall. Open every day (except two weeks around Christmas) 1000-1800. Tel: + (0)3 21 50 68 67/68. Website: www.virtualmemorial.gc.ca. There are phone boxes and washrooms in the parking area.

This is the rear side of the **National Memorial (Map 14/17)** which is reached along a narrow stone path. When the Canadians decided to erect a national memorial here to replace the divisional memorials placed after the battle, they invited competitive designs and 160 were submitted. The winner, who said that the design came to him in a dream, was a Toronto sculptor, Walter Seymour Allward (who also designed the Superintendent's house opposite). The two tall pylons symbolize Canada and France and between them at the front, carved from a single 30-ton block of stone, is a figure of Canada mourning for her dead. Below the figure is a sarcophagus carrying a helmet and laurels and a Latin subscription commemorating the 60,000 Canadians who died during the Great War. On the wall of the memorial are the names of 11,285 Canadian soldiers who were killed in France and who have no known grave. The 90 ft high memorial stands on Point 145, the highest point of Vimy Ridge. The base was formed from 12,000 tons of concrete and masonry and 6,000 tons of Dalmatian stone was used for the pylons and the figures, of which there are twenty, all 12 ft high. Construction began in 1925 and Allward's aim was, he said, to produce 'a structure which would endure, in an exposed position, for a thousand years – indeed, for all time'. However in 2004 a 2 year programme of necessary repairs began.

When you drive off you have to follow the one way circuit. Stop below the memorial for a view of what was designed as the front of it and for a magnificent view over the Douai Plain and Loos battlefield.

When the memorial was unveiled on 26 July 1936 (it took four years longer to build than at first estimated) it was in the presence of King Edward VIII, his only overseas official engagement as King. Also present was M. Victor Maistriau, the Burgomaster of Mons, which had been liberated by the Canadian Corps on 11 November 1918. He carried with him the personal flag of Lt General Sir Arthur Currie who had commanded the Corps. The General presented his flag to the town of Mons and it is now in the Museum there. The area between where you are and the memorial was filled with pilgrims, of whom 8,000 had come from Canada.

Continue.

On the right is the **Moroccan Division Memorial**, commemorating the Division's achievements during the second battle of Artois on 9 May 1915. Bronze panels around the stone monument list the ORBAT of the Division (motto *Sans peur, sans pitié* – without fear, without mercy) and also recognise the contribution of other foreign forces, including the Jews, Greeks, Sudanese and Czechs.

Continue towards the Tunnels, passing signs to
Canadian Cemetery No 2, Givenchy Road Canadian Cemetery and Givenchy-en-Gohelle Canadian Cemetery. Map 14/16

Continue to the car park by the Lions Club International Memorial on the left.

Here is another information kiosk where enthusiastic and well-informed bi-lingual Canadian student guides may be found between 1 April-30 Nov from 1000-1800. There is fierce competition in Canada amongst young people who wish to be guides, most of whom are either students or graduates. Each year a new cadre is selected and shared with the Memorial Park at Beaumont Hamel on the Somme. There are more telephones and washrooms here.

The tour goes through a tunnel system but for security reasons only in groups accompanied by guides, for which there is no charge. A trip into the tunnel, which begins near the Canadian flag, generally lasts about 25 minutes and should not be taken by anyone who is at all claustrophobic. It is cold underground and often wet and slippery.

Beyond the tunnel, clearly signed, are the preserved trench lines formed with concrete sandbags. Work on preserving this area began in the late 1920s and was still going on in 1936 when the Vimy Memorial was unveiled. The first trenches are the Canadian line, and sniper posts, firesteps and duckboards are plain to see. Just over the top of the Canadian parapet is one of the features that makes Vimy so extraordinary – a huge mine crater.

When the British took over this 'quiet sector' from the French, (after the Artois battles of 1914/15 both sides settled for a mutually uncomfortable existence devoid of set-piece attacks) peace gave way to conflict. Fighting patrols were sent out to take enemy prisoners, raids were launched, 'nuisance' bombardments began and underground too the warfare intensified. Tunnel after tunnel was driven under the enemy trenches, packed with explosives and fired. Huge craters resulted with identifying codenames: 'Irish', 'Montreal', 'Love', 'Grange'... The crater immediately beyond the Canadian line is 'Grange' (and it is the Grange tunnel through which one walks underground on the tour). The effectiveness of the mine warfare is evident in a report from the German 163rd Regiment. 'The continual mine explosions in the end got on the nerves of the men. One stood in the front line defenceless and powerless against these fearful mine explosions.'

Both sides attempted to sabotage each other's mining by burrowing under the other's galleries and blowing them up. Miners had to stop and listen at regular intervals for the sound of enemy digging and then make fine judgements about just where the other's tunnel was and what he was about to do. The tension must have been heart-stopping. Dark cramped conditions, foul air to breathe, hot and probably wet too, trapped mole-like underground – it needed special qualities just to remain sane. Tunnels were frequently dug at different levels. Near Souchez mining went on at 110 ft and 60 ft down, and some tunnels were over 1,000 yards long. One, called 'Goodman', was more than 1,800 yards. Grange was a sophisticated tunnel 800 yards long with side-bays for headquarters, signal offices, water points, etc. and standing room. It was meant for the movement of troops. Six miles or more of such tunnels were dug before the battle. Tunnels to be used solely as a means of reaching the enemy lines in order to place explosives under them were frequently crawling-size only. There is yet another surprise in store because just across the crater, on the opposite lip, are the German trenches.

It was a remarkable feat for the Canadians to do so well here. The whole attack had been rehearsed day after day at unit level on a full-scale replica behind the front. Short, reachable objectives were marked on maps as lines – black, red, blue and brown, attacking formations only moving on or through as each line was established. The Canadians went in ten battalions abreast, fighting, for the first time as a national contingent, and working steadily forward from objective to objective.

The 0530 hours pre-assault bombardment, which had been started by the firing of a big gun from behind Mont St Eloi, was of such intensity that it was impossible to distinguish the sound of individual explosions. Those present felt that if they could reach up into the air they would touch a wall of sound. The plan was that the guns would lift at intervals and the infantry would then walk forward as if behind a curtain of steel. Gus Sivertz, serving with the 2nd Canadian Mounted Rifles, later recalled, 'We didn't dare lift our heads, knowing that the barrage was to come flat over us and then lift in three minutes. I don't think anyone was scared ... instead one's whole body seemed to be in a mad macabre dance. It was perhaps the most perfect barrage of the war, as it was so perfectly synchronised. Then suddenly it jumped a hundred yards and we were away.' (*Vimy Ridge* – Alexander McKee). Flying over the assault was Major Billy Bishop who wrote, 'The waves of attacking infantry as they came out of their trenches and trudged forward behind the curtain of shells laid down by the artillery were an amazing sight. These troops had been drilled to move forward at a given pace and from this timing the 'Creeping' or rolling barrage which moved in front of them had been mathematically worked out' (*Winged Warfare*). In fact the timing for the infantry was that they should move 100 yards in three minutes. If they were to go too fast then they would run into their own artillery fire, if they were too slow then the barrage would get too far ahead of them and they would lose its protection.

The timing of the Canadian attack went even further. The four Canadian

Grange Tunnel tour.

divisions had 35 minutes to reach the Black Line, then 40 minutes there to re-organise, then 20 minutes to get to the Red Line. There the attack was to narrow to a two division front and, after two and a half hours there, reserve brigades of the 1st and 2nd Divisions were to push on to the Blue Line, re-organise there for 96 minutes and then carry on just beyond the crest of the ridge to the Brown Line which in theory would be at 1318 hours. It was an extraordinary plan. A common military maxim is that 'No plan survives contact with the enemy' and the more complicated a plan the more likely it is to go wrong.

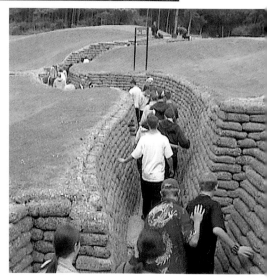

Preserved Trenches, Vimy Ridge.

There are many examples of too complicated plans going wrong particularly when they involve precise timings. A prime instance took place 27 years later on 6 June 1944 at OMAHA beach when American General Huebner's precise instructions did not survive contact with events. It worked for the Canadians in 1917 and they deserved it to do so but they had to have had an added factor – luck. Perhaps one does make one's own luck and as President Lincoln apparently said, 'Give me lucky generals'.

The Grange position was defended by companies of the German 261st Reserve Regiment of the 79th Reserve Division. When the fighting was over the 261st Regiment had lost 86 killed, 199 wounded and 451 missing – a total of 736 men. The Canadian assault here was made by 7th Brigade of the 3rd Division and alongside, to the north, 111th Brigade of the 4th Division. One of the Canadians waiting in the Grange tunnel at 0530 hours described the sound of the opening barrage as 'like water on a tin roof in a heavy thunderstorm'. Around the Grange crater area there are many other craters and paths lead off into the woods.

It was long believed that each of the trees in the park represented one of the 66,655 Canadian soldiers (their dead for the entire war) listed on the Memorial and that they came from Canada. In fact they are Austrian firs, three containers of whose seeds arrived by train after the war as part of Germany's reparations price. Beneath the trees, shell-holes, craters and lines of trenches in the Park are a series of German and allied tunnels which were packed with mines and then exploded. The 100-hectare Park is full of unexploded and highly volatile materiel and most areas are out of bounds. There is a constant threat of erosion to this historic site, presenting great problems of preservation to the Canadian Ministry of Veterans Affairs which administers it. Much dangerous work has been undertaken by the Durand Group (qv) to render known unexploded mines harmless to the thousands of visitors who walk and drive over them each year. Sadly one of the group's founders, Lt Col Mike Watkins, was killed in 1998 when one of the tunnels they were excavating collapsed.

Some parts are off limits.

Shell craters, Vimy Ridge.

Turn right out of the car park and first right signed to Vimy. Follow the road through the battle-scarred woods of the Park to a sign on the left to 5th Imperial Division Monument (12.8 miles).

Extra Visit to 5th 'Canadian' Division Monument (Map 14/19) Round trip 400m. Approximate time: 15 minutes

Walk along a track to the Monument.

This concrete Cross was erected to the men of the Division who gave their lives in defence of the line from October 23rd 1916 to February 15th 1917 and in the attack and capture of Vimy Ridge on April 9th 1917 and in subsequent operations. The Division had actually arrived to take over from the French between Arras and Roclincourt in March 1916 when they were outnumbered by the French dead that they found. The Division, which was known as the 'Imperial' Division (the Canadian version of 'British') because it was made up from British regiments, was in reserve for the initial attack, but at Farbus, where the 2nd Canadian Division attacked with two brigades up on a front of 1,500 yards, the 13th Imperial Brigade of the 5th Division had the task of following the assault brigades and consolidating the gains.

Memorial Cross to 5th (Canadian) Division, Vimy Ridge.

The brigade, which was supporting the third of the Canadian Division's brigades (6th Brigade) was made up with the 1st Royal West Kents, the 2nd KOSB and the 14th and 15th Battalions of the Royal Warwickshire Regiment, all of whom wore Canadian flashes for the attack.

Return to your car and pick up the main itinerary.

Continue to the T junction turn right on the N17(N25) signed Arras/A26. Continue into Thélus.

On the left at the cross roads is the **Canadian Artillery Memorial (Map 14/20)** unveiled by General Byng on 9 April 1918 and signed to the right is **Zivy Crater (Map 14/21).** This was used by the Canadian Corps in 1917 as one large grave and contains 50 Canadian and 3 Unknown. The Zivy Crater road, the D49, leads to la Targette, just under 2 miles away, where you were earlier. The D49 was effectively the line of advance of the 2nd Canadian Division which came directly towards you. The

Canadians, reaching here on the 9th, took many prisoners including 4 German guns which their gunners turned upon the enemy. Thus it seems an appropriate place for the Artillery Memorial.

Continue under the motorway to the centre of Arras following signs to Gare SCNF and park as near as possible to the railway station.

• *Arras Centre/Boves/19.3 approx miles/40 minutes/Map 14/23*

N.B. From here the mileage may vary depending upon exactly where you can park and if you walk or drive to the Town Hall.

Arras suffered considerable damage from long-range shells – the German front line was only some two miles east of the town. In 1916 the British took over from the French and in the days preceding the April 1917 offensive the war correspondent Philip Gibbs vividly described the scene in the damaged town: the Highlanders playing their pipe bands, the soldiers in their steel helmets and goatskin coats who resembled 'medieval men-at-arms', the dead horses lying thick on the Arras-Cambrai road, the long queues of wounded men waiting for treatment in the old Vauban Citadel – 3,000 of them on one day alone... Men and materiel poured through the town in huge numbers in the preparation for the offensive.

Opposite the railway station on the central area is the **Arras War Memorial,** with some fine *bas reliefs* of various aspects of the Great War, which shows scars from the Second World War. All around the square are numerous cafés and beyond the war memorial, in the Boulevard de Strasbourg, is the local tourist office, from which a town map may be obtained. The town has been a centre of trade and population since ancient times. It was fortified by Vauban who built the citadel. It was briefly overrun by the Germans in September 1914 but then held by the French until March 1916 and then the British until the end of the war.

The Town Hall/*Boves*. This is a five minute walk from the station area (follow signs to 'Les Places', or you may decide to drive and park under the Grand' Place). The Squares have delightful Flemish baroque facades and many restaurants. Through the Town Hall (with its impressive belfry, started in 1463, rebuilt between 1924-1932) is access to the *'Boves'* – the caves and tunnels dating from the fourteenth century that were enlarged and extended during the 1914-18 war. The soft, porous stone underlying Arras was tunnelled in deepest secrecy for 18 months before the April 1917 offensive when narrow-gauge railways were constructed to carry away the spoil. The tunnels, christened after British towns – 'Glasgow', 'Manchester' etc, were reinforced with pine logs supporting the heavy cross timbers of the roof and led to cavernous chambers. Generating stations to produce electricity were installed and miles of wiring were used in the hundreds of yards of tunnels that linked the ancient cellars, crypts and quarries. Not only were the undergrounds used as hospitals and shelters, but also to transport vast bodies of troops and material safely to the start line trenches of the offensive in open country.

The Tourist Office in the Town Hall is usually open every day except Christmas

Arras Memorial to the missing and RAF Memorial.

and New Year from 0900 to 1200 and 1400 to 1800 (no lunch time closing from 01/05-30/09) and a visit to the *Boves* may be booked here. Tel: + (0)3 21 51 26 95. It will *Arras War Memorial.* be useful for your next stop to pick up a town plan here.

Return to your car and follow signs to the Citadelle/Motorway and on the town ring road, Boulevard Gen de Gaulle, just south of the junction with the N25 to Doullens, is

• Faubourg d'Amiens CWGC Cemetery/Memorials to the Missing/Mur des Fusillés/approx 20 miles/35 minutes/Map 14/22

Despite the name, this is the Arras memorial. It takes the form of a wall carrying almost 36,000 names of the **Missing of the battles around Arras**. On it are the names of the First World War poet **Capt. T.P. Cameron Wilson** of the Sherwood Foresters, **Lt Geoffrey Thurlow** of the same regiment – one of Vera Brittain's coterie of friends, and **Captain Charles McKay** and **Private David Sutherland** of the Seaforths. David was the subject of Lt. E. A. Mackintosh's searing poem, *In Memoriam*, which describes his death during a trench raid on 16 May 1916 in which McKay also took part. Also commemorated here is **2nd Lt Walter Daniel John Tull**, Middx Regt, 25 March 1918, age 29. Tull was one of Britain's first black professional footballers and, despite his poor background, also its first black Army Officer. Tull was admitted to an orphanage in Bethnal Green when both his parents died and was signed up by Tottenham Hotspur in 1908. In 1909 he suffered appalling racial abuse during a match and was transferred to Northampton Town. On the outbreak of war he enlisted in the 17th (1st Football) Bn of the Middx Regt, was promoted to sergeant in 1916, was invalided home with trench fever at the end of the year and went to the officer cadet training school at Gailes in Scotland – despite the fact that 'Negroes' were specifically excluded from commanding as officers. In 1917 he went to the Italian Front as a 2nd Lieutenant in the 23rd (2nd Football) Bn of the Middx Regt and was MiD in the Battle of the Piave. In 1918 he returned to France and was killed in No Man's Land near Favreuil. In the mid-1990s a campaign was started to use Tull's inspiring story to help black recruitment in the British Army and to defuse racial discrimination in the world of football and on 11 July 1999 the Walter Tull Memorial and Garden of Rest was opened at Sixfields Stadium, Northampton.

The wall encloses the cemetery, begun in March 1916, and which contains 2,700 burials. At the back are separate small rows for Hindus, Mohammedans and Sikhs. Just within the entrance wall, in a space once occupied by the graves of French soldiers, is the **Royal Flying Corps Memorial**. It takes the form of a column surmounted by a globe. The flight of doves encircling the globe is following the path of the sun on 11 November 1918. It carries the names of all **RNAS, RFC** and **RAF** personnel missing on the Western Front, **including VCs Major Lanoe Hawker and Major E. ('Mick') Mannock**. Also commemorated here is **Lt Donald MacGregor**, the Red Baron's 63rd victim, shot down on 30 November 1917 during the Cambrai battle.

Outside the memorial the '*Mur des Fusillés*' is signed. This is a 1 mile round trip drive which leads to a poignant area where between July 1941 and July 1944 the Germans shot over 200 Frenchmen, including some liberated in the 'Operation Jericho' Amiens prison raid of 1944. A concrete marker indicates the execution post and memorial plaques commemorate those who were killed. Entry to the area is controlled by a gate which closes at dusk.

• *End of Notre-Dame de Lorette, Artois/Vimy Battlefield Tour*

Memorial Panels and Execution Post, Mur des Fusillés.

THIRD YPRES
Passchendaele

7 JUNE-10 NOVEMBER 1917

'Rain has turned everything into a quagmire and the shell holes
are full of water. Duckboards are everywhere leading to the front
line, but Jerry has these well taped and frequently shells them or sprays
them with indirect machine-gun fire. ... Guns of all calibres are everywhere,
in places wheel to wheel. The debris of war is lying about.
Broken guns, limbers, horses blown to blazes. But very few human
bodies, for they have all been swallowed up in the mud and water of
this horrible sector. It seems madness on the part of Higher Authority
to expect any advance over this indescribable morass.'

The diary of a Sergeant in the Somerset Light Infantry.

SUMMARY OF THE BATTLE

On 7 June 1917 the British attacked and captured the Messines Ridge, a
dominant feature that extended northwards to the German-held
Passchendaele Ridge. On 31 July, the British attacked again and floundered
in mud and rain in an assault that earned General Haig the title of 'Butcher' and
won the Passchendaele Ridge after 16 weeks' fighting. British losses were over
300,000 and German losses, never published, variously estimated between 65,000
and 260,000.

OPENING MOVES

Early in May 1917, following the bloody failure of Nivelle's attack on the Chemin
des Dames, the French Army began to mutiny until sixteen Army Corps were
involved. On 15 May, General Pétain, 'the saviour of Verdun', took Nivelle's place
and, by a mixture of personal visits to front line units and summary courts martial,
including executions, set about restoring discipline. Richard M. Watt, in his book
Dare Call it Treason, supposes that at least 100,000 men actively mutinied and even
the official figures admit that between May and October 1917 23,385 men were
found guilty of offences. Yet, extraordinarily, the news of the mutinies did not
become general knowledge.

Haig therefore realised that the French would have to be left out of any
immediate British plans for an offensive and later asserted that Pétain actually
asked him to maintain British attacks on the Germans in order to relieve pressure
on the French. Haig had fought his first battle as C-in-C the previous year on the

Somme and opinions were sharply divided about its outcome – whether it had been a strategic success in the casualties inflicted upon the Germans, or a costly failure because of our own losses. Nevertheless, Haig was still determined to prove himself as a commander. His conviction that the only way to win the war was by frontal assault remained undimmed. If he wanted to win the war alone he had to hurry, because on 6 April 1917 America had declared war on Germany and soon her soldiers would arrive to swing the balance against the Germans.

Thus to 'help' the French, to prove himself and his men, and to do it before the Americans arrived, he set about planning an attack. First though, he had to persuade a reluctant War Committee that an attack was both needed and would have positive results. The War Cabinet, which had to sanction the C-in-C's plans, was led by the Prime Minister, Lloyd George, who was very unhappy at the long British casualty lists for which he held Haig personally responsible. Haig promised that his campaign would be a limited one and proposed that it should be in Flanders in order to capture the German U-Boat bases on the Belgian coast, said by the Admiralty to be the source of the submarine offensive. In fact the U-Boats were coming from Germany and the Belgian theory surprised many people, including the chief of Haig's intelligence staff who later said, 'No one really believed this rather amazing view.'

However, Haig found it useful and when he maintained that 'if the fighting was kept up at its present intensity for six months, Germany would be at the end of her available manpower', the War Committee reluctantly agreed to his plans.

First of all the C-in-C wanted to gain a foothold at the southern end of the Ypres Salient, around a village called Messines. It was to be a remarkably successful battle that by its very success may have doomed General Gough's 5th Army to the seemingly endless slog up the slope to Passchendaele.

WHAT HAPPENED

The high ground at the southern end of the Salient had been occupied by the Germans since the British shortened their lines at the end of Second Ypres. The Messines-Wijtschate area was of particular value to the Germans because from there they could enfilade much of the British trench system. The task of dislodging them was given to General Plumer's 2nd Army. Plumer had already been preparing for an assault for over a year by tunnelling under the German lines and placing 19 huge mines in a ten-mile arc from near Hill 60 via Spanbroekmolen to Ploegsteert Wood. There were over four miles of tunnels and more than a million pounds of high explosives. The attack was planned in great detail and models of the German positions used so that formations down to company level could be quite clear what their objectives were, and those objectives were limited and precise.

At 0310 on 7 June 1917 the mines exploded following more than two weeks bombardment by over 2,000 guns. X (British) Corps and II (Anzac) Corps advanced, assisted by 72 tanks and with complete air superiority. By the end of the day the first objectives were all taken. The 36th (Ulster) Division and the 16th (Irish) Division took Wijtschate and Messines fell to the New Zealanders.

MAP 15: THIRD YPRES 7 JUNE - 15 JUNE - 10 NOVEMBER 1917

Bikschote

Steenstraat

Langemarck

N8

Boezinge

Pilckem

Passchendaele

St. Juliaan

N303

N333

Old rail route

Ypres Canal

Zonnebeke

Potijze

A19

N308

N38

Poperinghe

YPRES

Hooge

N8

N373

Zillebeke

Gheluvelt

Dikkebus

Menin →

N304

N331

N303

N375

Canal

N336

Loker

Wijtschate

Kemmel

N365

Dranouter

Messines

N58

N515

Comines

Legend

River Douve

River Lys

Front line before
Messines offensive
7 June 1917

Old rail route

Warneton

Neuve Eglise

D945

Front line after
Messines
15 June 1917

D108

Front line
10 November 1917

Ploegsteert

D933

Ground gained
in the
Messines
offensive

Nieppe

Lille →

Scale

A25

0   2   4kms

Armentières

© TVH 2004

N

So far so good. So now on to the Passchendaele Ridge while the momentum of success was still warm? No. Now a near 8 weeks delay while preparations were made for the next attack. Why wasn't the Messines attack delayed until it could be followed immediately by the second phase? Were the French in such desperate straights that we had to grasp the German's attention in June? Perhaps. Perhaps too we needed to assemble and to reposition our artillery, something not done in a few hours, but the delay was fateful. It saw out the good weather and gave the Germans time to put the finishing touches to their new scheme of defence – defence in depth. Gone now were the old linear lines. Now trenches ran backwards and forwards in great depth and within the grid so formed were disconnected strongpoints and concrete pillboxes. The manning philosophy had changed too. The ground was covered by mutually supporting machine guns and forward positions were lightly held with reserves well back and concentrated ready for counter-attack. On top of all that the Germans introduced mustard gas.

The preliminary bombardment began on 22 July 1917. Over 3,000 guns hurled almost five tons of shells at every yard of the front. Ten days later, at 0350 hours on 31 July, twelve divisions advanced on an 11-mile front in pouring rain. North of Ypres advances of two miles were made, the Pilckem Ridge was recaptured, but further south and around the Menin Road the attack quickly stuck. The preliminary bombardment had totally destroyed the water table and the rain could not run away. Shell holes filled to overflowing with water and the earth turned into a thick glutinous mud, stinking and foul with the decay of dead horses and thousands of corpses. The mud reached out and sucked under any unwary soldier who left the duckboard path. Gough advised Haig that the attack should be stopped, but the C-in-C, falsely buoyant from the success at Messines, perhaps, or determined to demonstrate what Clausewitz called the 'maintenance of the Aim', i.e. steadfastness of purpose, pressed on, through battle after battle and casualty after casualty.

The Official History records the following battles:

Messines	7-14 June
Pilckem	31 July-2 Aug
Langemarck	16-18 Aug
Menin Road	20-25 Sept
Polygon Wood	26 Sept-3 Oct
Broodseinde	4 Oct.
Poelcapelle	9 Oct
First Passchendaele	12 Oct
Second Passchendaele	26 Oct-10 Nov

In the first week of November, 16 weeks after the second phase began, the 1st and 2nd Canadian Divisions occupied the shapeless ruins of Passchendaele village. The mud and blood bath was over. It is said that Lt-Gen. Sir Launcelot Kiggell, Haig's Chief of Staff, visited the battlefield for the first time just after the fighting was over (a terrible indictment in itself) and when he saw the foul swamp in which it had been fought burst into tears saying, 'Good God! Did we really send men to fight in this?'

THE SALIENT BATTLEFIELD TOUR:
1ST, 2ND, 3RD YPRES

Although the Three Battles of Ypres are normally identified and treated separately as historical bites, it is not possible to tour them in isolation. Therefore the battlefield tour described here is a tour of the Ypres Salient and encompasses all three battles (see **Map 6**, page 94). At its end the tour which concentrates on the Fourth Battle of Ypres could then be followed (see page 249). To tour the Salient in a comprehensive manner requires at least three days and travellers with that amount of time are referred to our guide book *Major & Mrs Holt's Battlefield Guide to the Ypres Salient* with its accompanying detailed Battle Map. The following suggested tour covers the most important and easily accessible points of interest in the Salient.

The Route: The tour of First, Second and Third Ypres begins at the In Flanders Fields Museum in Ypres, visits St George's Memorial Church and the Menin Gate Memorial by foot. It then moves north and clockwise via Essex Farm; Yorkshire Trench, Boezinge; Langemarck German Cemetery; the Canadian Brooding Soldier Memorial; Tyne Cot British Cemetery (Passchendaele); the Dugout Experience, Memorial Museum at Zonnebeke; Polygon Wood & Buttes New Brit Cemeteries, Australian 5th Div Memorial and N Zealand Memorial to the Missing; Black Watch Corner; Gheluvelt Mill & Memorials; Clapham Junction Memorials; KRRC Memorial; Hooge Crater, Preserved Trenches, Museum & Cemetery; Sanctuary Wood CWGC Cemetery and Museum & preserved trenches; Hellfire Corner; Hill 60 & Memorials; St Eloi Tunnellers' Memorial & Craters; Wijtschate – Bayern Wood, Croonaert Chapel CWGC Cemetery, 1st Chasseurs à Pied Memorial, Site of Hitler Painting; Wytschaete Military CWGC Cemetery/16th Irish Div Memorial; Spanbroekmolen (Pool of Peace); Lone Tree CWGC Cemetery; Kruisstraat Craters; Messines Ridge British CWGC Cemetery/New Zealand Memorial; Messines Museum & Memorials; Island of Ireland Tower; Ploegsteert Memorial & Berks & Hyde Park Corner Cemeteries.

    N.B. At this point one may return to Ieper or continue with the tour which visits sites of **Fourth Ypres** (see page 249).

• **Extra Visits:** Talbot House, Poperinge; The London Scottish Memorial; Plugstreet Wood and St Yvon – Prowse Point CWGC Cemetery, Khaki Chums Christmas Truce Cross, Bairnsfather Memorial Plaque.

• **Total distance:** 43.4 miles

• **Total time:** (excluding time for Ypres walking tour) 9 hours – best split over two days.

• **Distance from Calais to start point:** 59 miles. No Motorway Tolls

• **Base towns:** Ieper, Poperinge

• **Maps:** Major & Mrs Holt's Battle Map of the Ypres Salient plus best of all are *the Carte de Belgique* 1:25,000 Nos. 20/5-6, 28/1-2, 28/3-4, and 28/5-6. *The Carte de Belgique* No. 28 IEPER 1:50,000 is coloured and covers the whole area and shows the road changes, including the motorway up to 1979. IGN 2 Lille/Dunkerque

1:100,000 covers the area.

From Calais take the A16/A26 signed Dunkerque. At Grande Synthe take Exit 28 to the A25 to the right signed Lille, Ypres. Take Exit 13 at Steenvoorde on the D948 signed Ypres (Ieper). Cross the border (no longer manned) and continue on the D948/N38 to Poperinge.

Extra Visit to Talbot House, Poperinge
Round trip: 2.25 miles. Approximate time: 45 minutes

Follow signs to Centrum and park in the main Market Square.

Known as 'the last stop before Hell', Poperinghe was the BEF's principal town behind the lines and was never taken by the Germans although it suffered occasional heavy shelling. The town teemed with shops, estaminets (segregated for officers and ORs), restaurants, hostels, concert halls, cabarets and cinemas, brothels and other facilities for the troops coming out of the line for rest and refreshment. The YMCA and the Church Army were well-represented. Today it makes a good base for touring the Salient.

In the square is the picturesque Town Hall with the Tourist Office in the basement. They have literature on Poperinghe (as it was spelt in 1914-18) during the Great War. Behind it is the **Execution Post** where at least 5 men were shot during the war.

Walk to the far end of the square.

On the left is the famous Café de Ranke, popular with officers during the war, mainly because of the charms of the daughter of the house, 'Ginger', and the liberally flowing champagne.

Walk up Gasthuisstraat.

At No 12 was another popular officer's club, nicknamed Skindles. It is now a pharmacy.

Continue to No 43.

Still hanging outside the elegant building where Padre Philip Byard (Tubby) Clayton started a rest house which inspired the movement which is now world-wide, is a sign which states, 'Talbot House 1915-? Every Man's Club'. This extraordinary club was named after Gilbert Talbot, son of the Bishop of Winchester, who was killed in the Salient and is buried in Sanctuary Wood Cemetery (qv). Tommy shortened the name in Army signallers' language to 'Toc H'. It had the atmosphere of a home, where the men, weary and frightened from a spell in the trenches of the Salient, could come, whatever their rank, and be refreshed physically and spiritually.

Talbot House was officially opened on 11 December 1915, in the empty house of the banker and hop merchant, Maurice Coevoet. It operated on 'the Robin Hood principle of taking from the rich to give to the poor', maintained Tubby, another of whose occasional nicknames was 'Boniface' (after the innkeeper in George Farquhar's *The Beaux Stratagem*). Tubby had a marvellous knack of wheedling supplies, furniture and other domestic items from all and sundry. According to *Tales from Talbot House*, for 5 francs officers

Extra visit continued

Talbot House.

arriving from the leave train at one a.m. secured cocoa and Oliver biscuits or before departure at 5 a.m. a cold meat breakfast. Other ranks did not pay until June 1916 when the officers were "thrown out" to Skindles (see above). Until then they (but never other ranks) could get a bed.

Only one soldier was killed in Talbot House during the war. He was Sgt G.J.M. Pegg, ASC CEF, who was mortally wounded by a shell that hit the side of The House on 28 May 1916. He is buried in Poperinghe New Mil Cemetery (qv).

From April 1918 the Germans pressed ever closer to Ypres, Kemmel fell, defensive lines were hastily built around Poperinghe, great expanses of countryside between Dunkirk and St Omer were flooded. Poperinghe was evacuated of civilians; cinemas, shops and other entertainments closed down. Alone Toc H remained open. But it was heavily shelled and eventually 'imperative orders to leave at once' were received. It closed on Whit Tuesday, 21 May to re-open on 30 September at the end of Fourth Ypres.

In 1919 Tubby founded the Toc H movement and in 1929 Lord Wakefield of Hythe, at the instigation of Major Paul Slessor (who gave his name, to the 'Slessorium' – originally a bath house for post-war pilgrims – built in the garden in 1930 and to whom there is a memorial plaque in the hall), put up sufficient funds to buy the Old House. He also bought the 'Pool of Peace' or Spanbroekmolen crater at Wijtschate (qv) for Toc H.

The Execution Post, Poperinge Town Hall.

During World War II the Germans occupied Poperinghe on 29 May 1940. One report, as yet unconfirmed, says they requisitioned Talbot House on 13 July and in 1943 used it as billets for the Kriegsmarine. On 6 September 1944, Polish troops liberated the town and all the precious contents, whisked away by local sympathisers as the Germans moved in, were soon restored. On 10 September the house re-opened, with its original purpose to act as a rest house for British soldiers.

Many original artefacts, pictures (including portraits by one of the ninety-odd official war artists, Eric Kennington) and signs remain to be seen, witness of Tubby's relaxed attitude and the sense of humour which made him so special. 'All rank abandon ye who enter here' was his motto, inscribed over his, the Chaplain's, room...'

Extra visit continued

The chapel on the top floor, with its carpenter's bench which served as an altar, looks much the same as in the days when over 20,000 officers and soldiers received the Sacrament there before going into the trenches. In 1922 Barclay Baron, a founder member of Talbot House, suggested that the form of an early Christian lamp should become the symbol of Toc H ('as dim as a Toc H lamp' was a popular post-war phrase). The lamp was first lit by the Prince of Wales in 1923. In the well-tended, tranquil garden, which gave rest to many a man from the shattered landscape of the Salient, is an obelisk-shaped Mié Tabé Peace Post (qv) inaugurated on 24 September 1988.

On 24 October 1996, the Talbot House Association finally succeeded in purchasing the adjacent old hop store which Tubby had also used.. Once more it forms an integral part of the Old House. The Association also owns and runs The House and provides guides and members of staff to look after it. Their Chief Executive is Mrs Annelies Vermeulen, e-mail talbot.house@skynet.be.

'Tubby' Clayton, the Chaplain.

The House has had a succession of wardens and guides. For many years the most knowledgeable and enthusiastic guide has been the popular Jacques Ryckebosch. Jacques has done extensive research and spent much time cataloguing the treasures that still remain in the House. Much research has also been done by The Secretary, Mr Jan Louagie and his wife, authors of *Talbot House – Poperinghe, 'First Stop After Hell'*.

Talbot House proves clean and comfortable self-catering accommodation at a reasonable price. It makes an excellent base for touring the Salient. It is extremely popular – there is something very special about staying in this Club, so redolent of the Great War and the men who peopled it – and booking well in advance is advised.

Until 2003 The House was entered through the imposing front door in Gasthuisstraat but on 15 May 2004 the new reception area with a shop and toilets and the large exhibition area was opened in the old Hop Store with an entrance in Pottestraat (turn first right after the building on Gasthuisstraat). The old building has been extensively renovated and reinforced for the purpose. The exhibition is based on 'Life in the Poperinge area during The First World War' and

WW1 Veteran, Arthur Halestrop (105 years old), being gently carried down from the Talbot House Chapel by local firemen, 12 November 2003.

Extra visit continued

is conceived as Tubby's 'photo album' showing the various aspects of life in the British sector. A new glass extension with a lift gives access to the first and second floors of the Hop Store and to the garden (in which there are some informative plaques). The Slessorium houses an audio-visual presentation in which Tubby shows the visitor around Talbot House plus some illustrations and documents on Little Talbot House in Ypres and Skindles. It includes Tubby's original 'hut' which was located at Proven in 'Dingley Dell'. On the first floor of the Hop Store the wartime Concert Hall has been restored to its 1917 aspect and shows a recreation of a wartime concert party (filmed with a live audience in January 2004). The second floor will be used as a documentation and archives area and will not generally be part of the regular visitor circuit but can be booked by school parties for lectures and working sessions.

These works have created much controversy to regular and faithful visitors to Talbot House who appreciated the delight of entering through the beautiful old front door to become immediately bathed in the warm glow of welcome created by Tubby in 1915 and which lingers still. Conscious of this, The Association gave them careful consideration but concluded that the changes had to be made for the very preservation of The House (a listed 18th Century building with a frail structure) itself. Such is the volume of visitors in recent years that the pressure has simply become too great for Talbot House to support and the Belgian Monumental Care Department seemed likely to step in to insist on the measures. The changes are also designed to improve the quality of staying in The House. It was also considered that 'many visitors are unlikely to be aware of the traditions of the house and would not have any difficulty using an alternative entrance' and that the work load of welcoming 25,000 people per year was too much for individual guides like the highly valued Jacques Ryckebosch.

On 12 November 2003 a special service was held for 105-year-old Arthur Halestrop, the only WW1 veteran who was able to travel to the Salient for the Armistice Day commemorations. It was a very moving occasion and local firemen took a day's unpaid leave to carry Arthur tenderly up the almost perpendicular staircase to the chapel on the top floor, so redolent with memories of the men who had said their last prayers in the room.

Entrance fee payable. **Open:** daily except for Mondays: 0930-1730 (last admission at 1630). Tel: + (0) 57 33 32 28. Fax: + (0) 57 33 21 83. **E-mail:** info@talbot.house.be **Website:** www.talbothouse.be Visits for groups must be booked in advance.

Continue on the N38 and follow signs into the centre of Ieper and park in the Grand' Place (Main Square) in front of the large cathedral-like building (small parking fee from meter).

This is the Cloth Hall. The actual Cathedral (St Martin's) is behind it and there is more parking in front of it. At the eastern end of the Cloth Hall are the tourist office and In Flanders Fields Museum.

• *In Flanders Fields Museum/Regional Visitors' Centre & Shop, Cloth Hall/ Map 6/1*

Walk along the façade of the Cloth Hall where there is the entrance to the Visitors' Centre. Beyond it, through the archway of the Donkere Port (Dark Gate) under the belfry tower, is the entrance to the In Flanders Fields Museum which is upstairs on the first floor of the Cloth Hall.

The museum is named after John McCrae's 1915 poem (qv), emphasising the fact that the museum extends beyond the confines of the Cloth Hall to the battlefields which surround it. Hexagonal blue and white signs mark the 82km *In Flanders Fields Route* (which has an accompanying booklet).

While incorporating some of the invaluable collections of the small but well-loved Salient Museum which it replaces, the new museum makes use of the latest state of the art technology and presentation techniques. Throughout the museum are inter-active displays and CD-Roms in four languages which examine war artefacts: their military use, the poetry, music and personal recollections of soldiers in the front line and behind it. The museum explores Ieper's current importance as a 'Town of Peace', comparable to Hiroshima and Stalingrad.

The opening section introduces the quiet rural backwater that was pre-War Ypres, then the early battles are shown through audio-visual presentations. The visitor then passes through reconstructed trenches which symbolise the stalemate that existed along the front line at the time of the Christmas Truces of 1914 which form a backdrop to a series of tableaux. *Son et lumière* is employed using the words of John McCrae and Wilfred Owen to recall the ways in which the soldier poets responded to their various experiences of war.

A dramatic 'No Man's Land Experience' portrays the horror of the Battle of Passchendaele, using the sights and sounds of battle in 'brutal reality' and with contrasting personal memories. The visitor then passes through a recreated Casualty Clearing Station where the development of medical services and evacuation routes are illustrated through the reminiscences of doctors and nurses. The different nations involved, the numbers of casualties and prisoners of war are featured here. The Germans' Final Offensive of 1918 is then examined. The final exhibition shows the rebuilding of Ypres through objects, models and archive film, the legacy of war, the memorials to the dead, the wounded and the survivors, and a section which invites the visitor to reflect on the experience of war and to compare this conflict with subsequent wars.

In Flanders Fields is intended to be a 'centre for study and discussion on the themes of war and peace ... and by using the Internet to create a kind of "virtual museum" where thoughts and opinions are constantly and freely exchanged. Visitors to the museum can also make their own contributions, using a series of computers located at the end of the route'. Areas have been allocated for temporary exhibitions. Visitor numbers to the museum have well exceeded expectation – reaching one million in less than four and a half years.

Visitors to the museum exit through the Regional Visitors' Centre and shop on the ground floor (which also have their own separate entrance on the square.) The centre describes the attractions of the Westhoek area (Ieper, Poperinghe, Heuvelland, Zonnebeke, Wervik, Langemarck-Poelcapelle, Mesen and Vleteren). There is an

In Flanders Field Museum typical interior scene.

information counter where one can obtain details of accommodation, restaurants and current events. The 50sq m shop stocks an impressive range of guide books, maps and souvenirs.

Battlefield tours may be booked here using official local guides, and trips are available on the British red double-decker 'Young Bill II' bus (named after Bruce Bairnsfather's cartoon character (qv)) for many years a familiar sight around the Salient.

Opening times: April-September 1000-1800, every day. October-March 1000-1700, closed on Mondays. Closed Christmas and New Year's Day and the first three weeks after the Christmas holidays. Ticket sales stop one hour before closing time. Entrance fee payable with special rates for students and groups.

Contact: Cloth Hall, Grote Markt 34, 8900 Ieper. Tel: + (0) 57 22 85 84. Fax: + (0) 57 22 85 89

E-mail: flandersfields@ieper.be   **Website:** www.inflandersfields.be

Leave the museum on foot via the archway at the corner of the Nieuwerke with the Kleine Stadhuis Restaurant and continue left around the building (in which, incidentally, there are good public toilets).

Opposite is St Martin's Cathedral in which there are several WW1 Memorials.

Turn right on Coomensstraat. St George's Church is on the far corner on the opposite side of the road to the cathedral.

• St George's Memorial Church/Map 6/2

The idea of having a British memorial church or chapel in Ypres was raised formally as early as 1920 when the Church Army appealed for donations to establish a building fund. In 1924 Sir John French, who had taken the title Earl of Ypres, added his voice to the call and the foundation stone was laid on Sunday, 24 July 1927. On 24 March 1929 the church was dedicated by the Right Reverend Bishop of Fulham. As a tribute to the 342 old Etonians who fell in the Salient the College provided the 'British School' which is next door to the church and is now used as the Church Hall and by the Royal British Legion as a club house. Services are held every Sunday and on 11 November each year the congregation is swelled by hundreds of people from all over Britain and spills into the nearby theatre or the Cloth Hall.

Every item in the church is a memorial, from the beautiful stained-glass windows to the chairs, on each of which is a brass plate naming the missing loved one. On the south wall of the church is a bust of Sir John French and on either side of it memorials to Field Marshal Montgomery and Sir Winston Churchill who both served in the Salient. New memorials continue to be erected, for the church now

St George's Church
with detail of the
colourful kneelers.

commemorates the fallen of both World Wars. A few minutes contemplation in this home of memory brings gentle pride in the solid beliefs of the men who fought for King and Country and there is sadness too that so many had to suffer, both on the battlefield and left alone at home. It is right to remember the sacrifice and the penalties and here it can be done without pomp or circumstance. The church is usually open and there are postcards available on a table beside the door, a visitors' book to be signed and a collection box. Tel: + (0) 57 21 56 85.

Return past the Cathedral and walk up the Menin Road to the Menin Gate.

• *The Menin Gate, Indian Memorial, RB Australian Memorial/Map 6/3*

Winston Churchill said of Ypres, 'A more sacred place for the British race does not exist in the world', and proposed that the town be left in ruins as an eternal memorial to the million men who fought in the Salient. The townspeople had other ideas and began to rebuild their homes, and it was agreed that on the site of an old

The Menin Gate.

Vauban gateway from Ypres on the road to Menin, the road taken by tens of thousands of British soldiers on their way to the trenches, a memorial arch should be constructed. Work under Sir Reginald Blomfield began in 1923. The material used was French limestone and the arch is 80 ft high, 135 ft long and 104 ft wide. It was unveiled on 24 July 1927 by Field Marshal Plumer (the same day that he laid the foundation stone of St George's Church) in the presence of the King of the Belgians and many thousands of veterans and relatives of the Fallen. The whole ceremony was transmitted by wireless by the BBC and the Last Post was sounded at the Gate for the first time. Carved over all the walls of the great gate, inside, up the stairs and around the top on each side overlooking the ramparts are the names of almost 55,000 soldiers who fell in the Salient between the beginning of the war and 15 August 1917. They simply disappeared.

In his address Lord Plumer said, 'It can be said of each one in whose honour we are assembled here today, "He is not missing, he is here".'

Among the 54,000 names recorded on its panels – each important to those who mourn – are the poets **Lt John Collinson Hobson**, MGC, killed on 31 July 1917, **Lt Walter Scott Stuart Lyon** (qv), Royal Scots, killed on 8 May 1915, **Capt the Hon C.E.A. Philipps** (qv), RHG killed on 13 May 1915, and **Lt Gerald George Samuel,** RWK, killed on 7 June 1917.

Also listed are **2nd Lt Henry Anthony Birrell-Anthony**, 1st Bn the Monmouthshire Regt, killed on 8 May 1915, who is mentioned on the Monmouth Memorial at St Julien; **Lt Aidan Chavasse** of the 17th King's Liverpool Regiment, missing in action on 4 July 1917 (youngest brother of Noel Chavasse (qv), the Double VC winner); **Lt the Hon W.A.M. ('Bill') Eden**, KRRC, killed on 3 March 1915, cousin of Anthony Eden; **2nd Lt the Hon Gerald William ('Billy') Grenfell**, Rifle Brigade, brother of the poet Julian Grenfell; **Lt Alexis Helmer**, 1st Bde Field Artillery, inspiration for John McCrae's poem *In Flanders Fields*, killed on 2 May 1915; **2nd Lt Arthur Oscar Hornung**, Attd 2nd Bn the Essex Regiment, killed on 6 July 1915, son of E. W. Hornung, creator of Raffles, the 'Gentleman Burglar' and nephew of Conan Doyle; **L/Cpl Thomas ('Pat') Rafferty** of the R Warwicks, Bruce Bairnsfather's inspiration for 'Old Bill'; three men who were executed: **Driver T. Moore**, of 24 Div Train ASC, shot on 26 February 1916, for murder, **Cpl George Povey** of the Cheshire Regt, shot on 11 February 1915, **Pte W Scotton** of the 4th Middlesex, shot on 3 February 1915.

Victoria Cross Winners commemorated are **L/Cpl Frederick Fisher** of the Quebec Regt, killed on 24 April 1915; **Brig-Gen Charles FitzClarence** of the Irish Guards, killed on 12 November 1914 near Polygon Wood commanding the 1st Guards Brigade (a Boer War VC); **Sgt Maj F.W. Hall** of the 8th Manitoba Regt, killed on 25 April 1915; **2nd Lt Dennis George Wyldbore Hewitt** of the 14th Hampshires, killed on 31 July 1917; **Capt John Franks Vallentin**, 1st S Staffs, killed on 7 November 1914; **Pte Edward Warner**, 1st Beds, killed on 2 May 1915, near Hill 60 and **2nd Lt Sidney Woodroffe** of the Rifle Brigade, killed on 30 July 1915, friend of, and subject of a poem by, the poet Charles Sorley (qv).

Pte James Smith of the 1st Bn the Black Watch, killed on 31 October 1914, has the Regimental Number '1'. **Capt A.E.B. O'Neill** of the 2nd Life Guards was the first Member of Parliament (for Mid Antrim) to be killed in the war on 6 November

1914. Brothers-in-law of the 1st Life Guards, **Capt Lord Hugh Grosvenor** (son of the Duke of Westminster) and **Lt the Hon Gerald Ward, MVO** (son of the 1st Earl of Dudley) both disappeared in the fighting of 30 October 1914, at Zantvoorde.

Note that the UK names inscribed on the wall are for the period up to 15 August 1917, after which date they were inscribed on the Memorial Wall at Tyne Cot. The names of Australians, Canadians, Indians and South Africans are for the entire duration of the war: they have no names on the Tyne Cot Memorial. There are no New Zealand names on the wall – they have their own memorials throughout the Salient.

On the town side at the top of the arch is a sarcophagus, while looking down the Menin Road is a British lion sculpted by Sir Reid Dick RA. Under each is an inscription by Kipling (after whom the street to the left beyond the arch is named).

At ground level in the pillars are the bronze boxes containing the Memorial Reports with details of those commemorated, first in regimental order and then by name. The ramparts should be visited above the Gate, access being via the stairways to each side of the centre. To the right is the **Indian Memorial** unveiled on 10 November 2002 and to the left is the bronze **Ross Bastiaan** (qv) **Australian Memorial**. It is possible to walk around the beautifully renovated ramparts to the Lille (Rijsel) Gate.

*Return to your car, **set your mileometer to zero** and leave the Square, driving out round the Cloth Hall and turning left past St George's Church on Elverdingsestraat.*

The HQ of the CWGC is on the right at no 82, with flagpoles outside. Tel: + (0) 57 20 01 18. Fax: + (0) 57 21 80 14. **E-mail:** neaoffice@cwgc.org

Continue to the first roundabout and turn right signed A19, Veurne. Continue to the next roundabout and turn right on the N379 signed Centrum and turn left at the next junction signed Diksmuide on the N369. Continue under the motorway bridge to the British war cemetery on the right with flagpoles. Stop.

• *Essex Farm CWGC Cemetery/Albertina Memorial/Dressing Station/49th (W Riding) Div Memorial/2.3 miles/20 minutes/Map 6/4, 6/5, 6/6*

Outside the cemetery is an **Albertina Memorial** to the poet **John McCrae** (qv), unveiled on 15 November 1985 by the Governor of West Flanders and executed by the sculptor Pieter-Hein Boudens of Bruges. Unlike the other Albertina Memorials (qv), McCrae's bears a poppy instead of King Albert's Royal Cipher. To the left of the cemetery is a commercial building and behind it some concrete dugouts. Between 1915 and 1917 these were used as a dressing station. The path to the canal leads to the site of the notorious 'Bridge 4'. Third Ypres casualties from the 51st (Highland) and 38th (Welsh) Divisions were treated here.

Canadian Medical Officer Colonel **John McCrae**, who had served with the Artillery in the Boer War, had written what is perhaps the war's best-known poem, *In Flanders Fields*, when he served in what was then a simple earthen dugout dressing station in the spring of 1915. On 24 April McCrae wrote home with one of the most vivid and moving accounts of the Second Battle of Ypres. He saw the 'asphyxiated French soldiers' and streams of civilian refugees – 'the very picture of debacle'. By 25 April the Canadians had lost 6,000 of their strength of 10,000. The shelling was unremitting and the small cemetery beside the dressing station grew daily. On 2 May, one of McCrae's patients and a friend, Lt Alexis Helmer, was

Essex Farm Dressing Station Bunkers.

Unknown Canadian Headstone, Essex Farm CWGC Cemetery.

49th (W Riding) Division Memorial, Essex Farm.

virtually blown to pieces by a direct hit by an 8in shell. McCrae was touched by the last words in Helmer's diary, 'It has quieted a little and I shall try to get a good sleep'. McCrae said the committal service over Helmer's body. 'A soldier's death,' he commented. A wooden cross was put over Helmer's grave and the Colonel was moved to write his famous lines,

In Flanders fields the poppies blow

Between the crosses, row on row,

That mark our place...

The poem was published in *Punch* on 8 December 1915, and became an instant popular success. From it the symbol of the poppy was taken by the British Legion to represent remembrance of those who gave their lives in the Great War and subsequent conflicts.

Helmer's grave was lost in the subsequent fighting over the ground and he is commemorated on the Menin Gate.

In the early spring of 1995 extensive restoration began in the concrete bunkers of the dressing station at the joint initiative of the Ieper Town Council, Talbot House and local school children. It was completed in time for the eightieth anniversary of the writing of McCrae's poem on 3 May 1995, when an impressive ceremony was held. Now the various chambers which housed the Officers' Mess, the wards for walking cases and stretcher cases, the latrines, the mess kitchen, the area for the wounded to be evacuated, the stores and offices – all built in 1916/17 – can once again clearly be seen. At the entrance are bronze plaques placed by the Historic Sites & Monuments Board of Canada with a brief summary of McCrae's career and his famous poem.

The sheer volume of visitors to this site was overwhelming it and in spring 2003 extensive landscaping was undertaken, leading visitors on gravel paths to the 49th Div Memorial and to the canal bank 'to spread the load' with Information Boards along the way.

The **cemetery** contains 1,088 UK, 9 Canadian, 102 Unknown, 5 German prisoners and 19 special memorials. They include **15-year-old Private V.J. Strudwick** of 8th Bn the Rifle Brigade, killed on 14 January 1916, and **Pte Thomas Barratt, VC,** of the 7th Bn the S Staffs Regt who on 27 July 1917, acted as the scout to a successful patrol, killing two German snipers and covering the patrol's withdrawal, but was killed by a shell on his return. Also buried here is **Lt Frederick Leopold Pusch,** DSO, of the 1st Bn Irish Guards, age 20, killed on 27 June 1916. A silver memorial cup, inscribed to Lt Pusch – 'M. H. 1908-1910', was found by the authors in the shop at Delville Wood Museum on the Somme. His 19-year-old brother, 2nd Lt E. J. Pusch of the 11th Bn the Royal Warwickshires, was killed on 19 August 1916, and is buried in Flatiron Copse CWGC Cemetery on the Somme. **Lt Donald Campbell** of the Coldstream Guards, killed on 19 July 1916, and buried here is the son of Capt the Hon John B Campbell, DSO, age 48, of the same regiment, who had been killed on 25 January 1915, and is commemorated on the Le Touret Memorial.

Behind the cemetery on the canal bank is the **memorial column to the 49th (West Riding) Division.** The 49th, a territorial division, came out early in 1915. It had the dubious distinctions of being, together with 6th Division, one of the first to face a phosgene attack when the two divisions suffered over 1,000 casualties from the gas alone and in the winter of 1915 having more than 400 cases of trench foot in just one battalion. Trench foot was the result of prolonged standing in water in flooded trenches. The feet swelled to football-sized proportions and became painfully sensitive to the extent that the sufferer found it virtually impossible to

Yorkshire Trench Preserved Trenches, Industrial Estate, Boezinge.

German Cemetery, Langemarck.

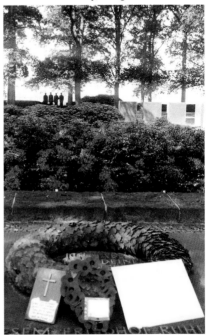

walk and hence became unfit for duty. The memorial was inaugurated in 1924.
Continue on the N6 past the turn off to the village of Boezinge and take the first turning to the right signed Langemark. Continue over the canal and take the second right signed Ieper. Continue along the canal bank to the left turn on Bargiestraat at the Biovita buildings with flags and follow the road to the left to the site.

• *Boezinge Archaeological Battlefield Site-Yorkshire Trench/5.5 miles/15 minutes/Map 6/7*

This is the site, first explored by the 'Diggers' (qv) in February 1992 of an important trench and dugout system known as Yorkshire Trench. The incredibly well-preserved 'A' frames and other original elements discovered in the retentive Flanders blue clay mud have been incorporated in a representation of the system in the In Flanders Fields Museum. At the site itself the Town of Ieper have recreated the trench and entrance to the dugout, with realistic looking sandbags and duckboards, with several explanatory panels, inaugurated in May 2003.
Turn round and return to the Langemark-Poelkapelle road and turn right on Langemarkseweg.
You are now travelling along the Pilckem Ridge. At 7.0 miles **Artillery Wood CWGC Cemetery** (where the poets 'Hedd Wyn' and Francis Ledwidge are buried) is signed to the left and the Irish flag which flies over the Ledwidge Memorial can be seen. On the corner is the **Breton Memorial (Map 6/8)**.
Continue another 1.3 miles.
On the house on the right just before the crossroads (Iron Cross) where Ruisseau Farm CWGC Cemetery is signed to the left is a **plaque to the poet 'Hedd Wyn'** (Ellis Humphrey Evans, **Map 6/9**).
Continue a further 0.8 mile.
On crossing the Steenbeek, on the bridge to the left is an **Albertina Memorial (Map 6/11)** to mark the end of the Steenbeek Offensive.
Just beyond, on the left is
The **20th Light Division Memorial (Map 6/12).**
Continue to the Langemark crossroads. Turn left (the restriction only applies to heavy vehicles) and follow signs to Diksmuide and 'Deutsche Soldaten Friedhof'.

• *Langemarck German Cemetery/10.1 miles/15 minutes/Map 6/13/WC*

This area was captured by the British 20th (Light) Division on 16 August during the Third Ypres offensive of 1917. It had been defended by the French in 1914 and lost on 22 April 1915 (Second Ypres) during the gas attack. In continuing operations in October 1917 the 4th Bn Worcester Regiment were ordered to push further north from here. On the evening of 7 October the battalion had marched out from Ypres following the route you have driven, turned right at Boezinghe and along the Pilckem Ridge via duckboards to the front line at the northern end of the cemetery. They were in position by dawn on 8 October and spent the day preparing for their assault. In the engagement that followed the next day a famous VC was won by **Private Frederick George Dancox**, a solid old soldier who captured a pillbox.

The cemetery is maintained by the *Volksbund Deutsche Kriegsgräberfürsorge* – the German People's Organisation for the Care of War Graves – and is the only German cemetery in the actual Salient. When the war was over the German dead were all amalgamated into four cemeteries – Langemarck, Menin, Vladslo and Hooglede. As the bodies were exhumed, all those that could be identified were reburied in marked graves, sometimes several inscribed on one tombstone to symbolize comradeship in death and because there simply was not enough land to bury each one individually. The unknowns were buried in a mass grave. Most of the landscaping work was completed between 1970 and 1972, much of it by international students working voluntarily during their vacations, although detailed work at Langemarck was not completed until the late 1980s.

Langemarck is one of the largest German cemeteries in Belgium, with 44,292 bodies, and has an impressive entrance with two chambers, one with the names of the missing carved in oak, and the other bearing a relief map showing the past and present German cemeteries in Belgium and containing the Visitors' book and Cemetery Register. The cemetery is planted with oak trees, the symbol of German strength, and in the communal grave rest the remains of 25,000 soldiers – half of whose names are known. The four impressive sculptures which overlook the cemetery were executed by Professor Emil Krieger and around the mass grave are the Regimental insignia of the student brigades who fought in this area. In the north wall of the cemetery are the remains of some massive German block-houses, doubtless similar to the one that Private Dancox captured. There is a WC to the left of the main entrance.

Langemarck Cemetery was on the route of Adolf Hitler's June 1940 tour of the Salient.

N.B. By continuing, and taking the first turning left along Beekstraat a **Bunker** and **the Memorial to 34th Division, RE and RA** may be reached

Drive back to Langemarck traffic lights and continue straight over the next crossroads with the N313 at which there is a tall memorial column. Stop in the carpark on the left.

• *The Brooding Soldier, Vancouver Corner/12.1 miles/10 minutes/ Map 6/14.*

This remarkable, dramatic memorial, represents a soldier standing with 'arms reversed', the traditional stance at a funeral. When the Canadian government decided to erect memorials in Europe to their war dead they initiated a competition to find the most appropriate design. This was the runner-up. The winning design was erected on Vimy Ridge. The architect here was Chapman Clemesha, from Regina, who had fought in the war and had been wounded. The 35-ft high central column of Vosges stone rises out of a circular pavement on which are marked direction indicators to other parts of the battlefield. The bowed helmeted head was carved in Brussels. At the back of the memorial is the bronze box containing the visitors' book. The inscription on the column in French and in English reads. 'This column marks the battlefield where 18,000 Canadians on the British left withstood the first German gas attacks the 22nd-24th April 1915. Two thousand fell and lie here buried.' 'Here buried' does not

THIS·COLUMN·MARKS·THE
BATTLEFIELD·WHERE·18,000
CANADIANS·ON·THE·BRITISH
LEFT·WITHSTOOD·THE·FIRST
GERMAN·GAS·ATTACKS·THE
22-24 APRIL 1915·2,000·FELL
AND·LIE·BURIED·NEARBY

The Brooding Soldier, Vancouver Corner.

literally mean on this spot, but over the battlefield. The memorial was unveiled on 8 July 1912 by the Duke of Connaught in the presence of Marshal Foch. The Canadian cedars are trimmed to represent shells.

The German gas attack launched in the afternoon of 22 April 1915 caught the Allies by surprise. The French Colonial troops on the left side of the allied line broke before the gas and the Canadians, with British county regiment reinforcements – the Buffs, Middlesex, York and Lancs, Leicesters – moved into the gap and held both that attack and the second on 25 April. The soldiers had no gas masks but discovered that, by soaking handkerchiefs in water and stuffing them into their mouths, they could get some relief. This road junction is also known as Vancouver Corner and Kerselaar.

Continue past the Brooding Soldier towards Zonnebeke. After some 200m take the small road, Vrouwstraat, to the left, past the glasshouses. This leads to the mill.

On turning, look right down the road towards Zonnebeke. Three tall chimneys are visible. One is taller than the other two. They are on the Western edge of Zonnebeke and provide an excellent reference point.

• *Totemuhle (Death Mill)/12.5 miles*

The original mill on this site earned its title during its use by the Germans as an observation post. In such flat countryside even a few metres of additional height greatly increased visibility and Forward Observation Officers directing artillery fire often carried their own step ladders to climb upon. When you are sitting in a coach you are roughly at the height of a man on horseback.

Near the *Totemuhle* served Erich Maria Remarque, author of the German classic

All Quiet on the Western Front. The mill may be visited and opening times are posted outside.

> *Continue to the right of the mill. Pass a small junction to the left and stop just before the next junction to the right opposite a calvary.*

• *Observation Point/12.8 miles/5 minutes/OP* (crops permitting)

You are in the middle of the battlefields of Second and Third Ypres. Take 12 o'clock to be your direction of travel. At 10 o'clock is the rectangular shape of Passchendaele water tower and at 11 o'clock the spire of Passchendaele Church. The Passchendaele-Messines Ridge runs from 11 o'clock to 2 o'clock. The three chimneys are at 1 o'clock. The bulk of Kemmel Hill may be seen on the horizon just to the left of Ypres which is at 3 o'clock, with the other Flanders hills behind it and Langemarck Church can be seen past the mill at 6 o'clock. On a clear day the tops of a group of four poplars may be seen between 11 and 12 o'clock through the buildings beyond the near horizon. That is Tyne Cot Cemetery. Before the beginning of Second Ypres the Germans held the ridge, the British the area you can see between Ypres and some 3km to your left. Following the success of the chlorine gas on 22 April 1915, the Germans released their next cloud at 0400 hours on 24 April in the area to your left. It swept across the road on which you are now standing, while German artillery kept up a continuous assault on British positions in the Salient. The German forces involved here were part of the 51st Reserve Division and, in particular, the 4th Marine Brigade which advanced through here on the following day. **Map 10** page 113 shows the extent of the German advance when the assault ended on 25 May. At the beginning of Third Ypres in June 1917 this spot was just to the rear of the German third main trench line.

> *Continue along the road to the next crossroads.*

• *s-Graventafel Crossroads, New Zealand Memorial/Bunker/14 miles/10 minutes/ Map 6/15*

The column on the left commemorates the men of the New Zealand Division in the battle of Broodseinde of 4 October 1917. On a front extending from around Geluveld to just short of Houthulst, an attack began at 0600 on 4 October in which Australian, New Zealand and English divisions took part. By chance the attack went in 10 minutes before the Germans planned to launch their own assault and the Germans thus

Bunker, s-Graventafel.

New Zealand Memorial, s-Graventafel.

suffered severely from artillery fire, much of the fighting then being finished off with the bayonet. The task of taking the Zonnebeke/s-Graventafel spur was given to the 2nd Anzac Corps and the stiffest opposition was faced in this area which was taken by the New Zealanders under Maj-Gen Sir A. H. Russell. By the end of the day the division had taken over 1,100 prisoners and 59 machine guns. To the right at the crossroads and some 100m down is a bunker in the right-hand bank.

Continue straight over the crossroads onto Schipstraat.Continue and turn left along Vijfwegenstraat, and then Tynecotstraat, to the cemetery.

• Tyne Cot CWGC Cemetery/15.1 miles/30 minutes/Map 6/16

On this forward slope of the Passchendaele Ridge are both the largest British war cemetery in the world and a memorial wall designed by Sir Herbert Baker on which are commemorated the almost 35,000 soldiers missing with no known grave for whom room could not be found on the Menin Gate, i.e. those killed after 15 August 1917. The local name for this area is Nieumolen, but British soldiers of the Northumberland Fusiliers, seeing on the ridge square shapes which they thought resembled Tyneside cottages called it 'Tyne Cot'. In actual fact the square shapes were the new German pillboxes and inside the cemetery on each side of the central path two of them can still be seen, now surrounded by poplar trees and at the end of the path is the Cross of Sacrifice which has been built on top of a third pillbox.

In 1922 King George V and Queen Mary toured the battlefields and, 'Tyne Cot he saw for the first time this May afternoon. He understood how appalling was the task that his soldiers faced there and turning to the great pillbox which still stands in the middle of the cemetery he said that it should never be moved, it should always remain as a monument to the heroes whose graves stood thickly around. From its roof he gazed sadly over the sea of wooden crosses, a "massed multitude of silent witnesses to the desolation of war". It is indeed fitting that this should form, as it will, the foundation for the great Cross of Sacrifice shortly to be built up as a central memorial in this cemetery.' *(The King's Pilgrimage,* Rudyard Kipling)

Today at the base of the cross a small patch of that original block-house can still be seen, contained within a bronze wreath, while on the far side of the cross, between it and the memorial wall, is a higgledy piggledy collection of some 300 graves. These are the original battle burials left where they were found after the Armistice. They included some German graves. The other, almost 12,000, graves which stand in parade ground order, were brought in from all the surrounding area. The majority of them are unidentified. The report for the cemetery is in a box under the entrance porch and the reports for the memorial wall are in the left-hand loggia. It is a sobering experience to look for one's own name in the reports and many a visitor has discovered the details of an unknown relative.

Looking back from the cross to the entrance, the chimneys of Zonnebeke should be visible well to the left and to their right on the near horizon the spires of the Cloth Hall can be seen on a clear day. The battle of Third Ypres surged up to here for three months from the direction of Ypres, the Germans holding this ridge, defending it with pill-boxes, machine guns, barbed wire and mustard gas. It was an Empire battle, the graves bearing witness to the team effort – some 8,900 from the UK, 1,350 from Australia, almost 1,000 from Canada and over 500 from New Zealand.

It was not until the end of October 1917 that the village and the ridge were taken, much of the latter in this area by the Australians and the empty village by the Canadians. In an action on 12 October the Australian 34th Infantry Battalion attacked two German pillboxes 400 yards north of here and was held down by heavy machine-gun fire. **Captain Clarence Jeffries** organised and led a bombing party against the pillbox on the right, taking 35 prisoners and capturing four machine guns. He then led a successful attack on another machine-gun emplacement and while attempting yet another he was killed. Born in Wallsend, New South Wales on 26 October 1894, Jeffries joined the militia at the age of fourteen, and was promoted to Captain four months before his death in the action which won him the **VC**. He and five other **VCs** are buried or commemorated here, including **Sgt Lewis McGee**, of the 40th AIF, who was killed taking the righthand pillbox. This is truly a 'Silent City', each headstone representing not just a life lost, but a family bereaved and generations unborn. Standing beside the white sentinels on this now peaceful hillside in Flanders, it is difficult to believe that all the suffering was worthwhile – and yet, simply to be able to stand here is a privilege won and paid for by many thousands who lost everything they had, including their name, and whose headstone reads only 'A Soldier of the Great War Known Unto God' – a phrase chosen by Kipling.

The Commune of Zonnebeke is planning (for opening in 2005) an Interpretative Centre with panoramic views over the battlefields, a large car park and toilet facilities. This will all be constructed behind the cemetery so as not to obstruct the fine approach. There will also be a memorial walk tracing the path of the Australian attack of 4 October 1917 and the linking of the cemetery with the Zonnebeke Museum via the old railway line. Funding of 1.1 million Euros is being provided for the project by the EC, the Flemish Government, the Province of West Flanders, the Commune of Zonnebeke and a private partner.

Turn round and follow Tyncotstraat round the cemetery to the junction with Passendalestraat and turn right. Continue to the next roundabout and turn right on the N332 to Zonnebeke.

The French Memorial is passed on the left. It has a sadly neglected air.

Continue into Zonnebeke.

Zonnebeke. German recce patrols were sighted in this area as early as the last week of August 1914, followed by a large contingent of regular troops in preparation for the First Battle of Ypres on 19 October. From the Second Battle of Ypres in April 1915 the area remained under German occupation until the British Offensive of July 1917 and the dreadful Passchendaele campaign. During the German offensive of spring 1918 the Allies were forced to withdraw towards Ypres

Entrance to Tyne Cot CWGC Cemetery.

Plaque to Canadian D21 Bty Field Arty Coy, Zonnebeke Church.

Trench Armourer, diorama in the, Memorial Museum, Zonnebeke.

until the final offensive of September 1918 when the village was liberated by British and Belgian forces. The Commune of Zonnebeke was completely destroyed during the war but the determined inhabitants returned and the five shattered villages in the area were rebuilt. On the church wall is a **Plaque to the Canadian D21 Bty Field Arty Coy.**

Continue past the church on the left to the Tourist Office with flagpoles on the left.

• *Memorial Museum, Zonnebeke/16.9 miles/30 minutes/Map 6/17*

In 2003 the old Streek Museum (in the 1924 Château) was closed while a major refurbishment took place. The new museum, opened on 23 April 2004, is known as the Memorial Museum Passchendaele 1917 and the visitor will enter through a German trench and down into a British 'Dugout Experience' complete with communication and dressing posts, HQ and accommodation. On the floors above will be permanent traditional-type exhibitions giving an overview of the Battles of Ypres and 'The Breakthrough' using the museums's existing fine collection of historical artefacts and ephemera, with life-like dioramas. There will also be interesting temporary exhibitions. A documentation centre will also be housed here and queries are always welcome about the surrounding battlefields or the location of relatives' graves. Well worth a visit. Open: 25 April-30 November, Mon-Fri: 1000-1800, Sat/Sun:1400-1800. Groups any time by appointment. Entrance fee payable. Tel: + (0) 51 77 04 41. Fax: + (0) 51 78 07 50. E-mail: **info@passchendaele.be** Website: <u>www.zonnebeke.be</u>

Continue to the second turn to the left and follow signs to Buttes New & Polygon Wood Cemeteries.

• *Polygon Wood CWGC Cemetery/Buttes New British CWGC Cemetery/NZ Memorial/Australian 5th Div Memorial/18.3 miles/ 25 minutes/Map 6/18, 6/19, 6/20*

This area is $1^1/_2$ miles due north of Gheluvelt (the next stop but one on the itinerary) where the Worcesters distinguished themselves in 1914. You are at the north-eastern end of the wood which in November 1914 (First Ypres) was held by 1st Kings with just 450 men and 6 officers strung along the 1 mile long southern edge and two companies of the Black Watch in the south-west corner.

Australian 5th Division Memorial and headstones, Buttes New Brit Cemetery, Polygon Wood plus detail.

The badly weathered New Zealand Memorial, Polygon Wood.

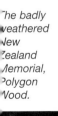

On 11 November 1914, the Prussian Guard made a determined attack in massed strength along the axis of the Menin Road moving east to west. Their efforts to break through this wood were stopped by dogged resistance by the Kings and the Black Watch. By the end of the day only one Black Watch officer was unwounded. His name was Captain Fortune! The 1st Kings had originally entered the wood during the first week in November and were told to hold it at all costs. They came under shell-fire almost immediately and that, combined with heavy rain, turned the ground into a quagmire. Trenches, such as they were, were knee deep in water and it was impossible to get warm because a fire straightaway brought down German artillery. Hand pumps were used both to draw water and to clear the trenches. Yet, despite their discomfort, the casualties which mounted steadily and being outnumbered, the Kings held on to the wood. Following the German gains made after the gas attacks of April 1915 (Second Ypres) the wood was evacuated and the Germans constructed a number of pillboxes in it as well as tunnelling into the high mound of the old musketry butte.

During 3rd Ypres the wood again featured in a named battle – the 'Battle of Polygon Wood', 26 September to 3 October 1917. The offensive opened at 0550 on 26 September being a rolling barrage with seven divisions in line on a 6-mile front. In the centre were the Australian 4th and 5th Divisions attacking west to east. The wood here and the butte were the objectives of the 14th Australian Brigade, the Australian line stretching north from here to Zonnebeke (from where you have just come).

The barrage was overwhelming. Immediately behind the Australians were the 2nd RWF and Private Frank Richards recalled the experience: 'I entered one pillbox during the day and found 18 dead Germans inside. There was not a mark on one of them. One of our heavy shells had made a direct hit on top of it and they were killed by concussion, but very little damage had been done to the pillbox'. By the end of the day the wood was taken but the two Australian divisions had 5,500 casualties.

On top of the butte is a **Memorial to the Australian 5th Division** and below are over 2,000 headstones of the Butte cemetery. This was made after the Armistice by concentrating graves from the Zonnebeke area, almost all of them from 1917. More than four-fifths are unknown, a testimony to the savagery of the fighting. At the far end of the cemetery is a **Memorial to the officers and men of New Zealand** who fell in this area and have no known graves. It has its own register. It was designed by Charles Holden in his distinctive somewhat severe style.

The small cemetery opposite Buttes is **Polygon Wood Cemetery**, begun in August 1917 in the front line, which has some 100 burials, mostly of New Zealanders. There was at one time a German cemetery at the back of it, but the graves have been moved, probably to Langemarck.

Continue along the side of the wood and turn left on Lotegatsestraat until you reach the road bridge over the motorway. Turn left and immediately stop by the gate into the wood.

• *Black Watch Corner/19.3 miles/5 minutes/Map 6/21/OP*

On 11 November 1914 began the battle known as 'Nonne Boschen' – Nun's Wood. Polygon Wood was at the northen edge of the German attack. Crown Prince Rupprecht ordered the Prussian Guard to take Polygon in co-operation with the 54th Reserve Division. Just after 0630 the German guns opened fire and at 0900 the assault began on a nine-mile front in mist and rain. The barrage had reduced the woods to a tangle of broken trees and undergrowth which impeded the German advance. On almost all of the front the attack faltered but at the southern end of Polygon Wood, between it and Nonne Boschen (where the motorway now is) was a gap in the British line for which the German 3rd Foot Guard Regiment headed. At this south-west corner of the wood, the 23rd Field Company RE under Major C. Russell-Brown had completed a strong point just an hour before the assault, and in it were forty men of the Black Watch commanded by Lt F. Anderson. The position consisted only of a trench inside the hedges of a cottage garden and a few strands of barbed wire but it provided shelter from the artillery. Anderson's party opened such an effective fire on the Guards that they broke formation and were eventually stopped and beaten back by the guns of 2nd Division. In recognition of the role that the Black Watch played here the corner was named after them. It was during this period of fighting that **Captain Brodie** (who has a Private Memorial in Nonne Boschen) of the Cameron Highlanders was killed.

The Brigade formation which had taken the brunt of the attack was the 1st (Guards) Brigade under Brigadier-General FitzClarence (qv) and, having stopped the German assault on 11 November, the Brigadier decided to mount a counter-attack to recover trenches lost to the Germans. While reconnoitring forward of Black Watch Corner he was killed. A farm to the south of the wood near Black Watch Corner is named FitzClarence Farm in honour of this popular old soldier who was affectionately known as 'GOC Menin Road'.

OP. Stand with your back to the gateway to the corner of the wood and look along the motorway. The church spire on the horizon to the right of the motorway, partly obscured by trees, is that of Geluveld. It was from this corner, on 31 October 1914, at the height of the crisis of First Ypres, that Major Hankey led off the 2nd Worcesters in an advance that would end in their famous bayonet charge into the grounds of the château. It was the church spire that they used as their marker for their objective.

Continue on Oude Kortrijkstraat/d'Hekschscheure and continue to the first crossroads then turn right on Reutelhoekstraat. Continue to the the T junction, turn left and at the next T junction turn right over the motorway.

As you drive uphill you are skirting Geluveld Château and its grounds on the right.

Continue to the church on the right and stop in the car park.

Behind the church and in front of the Château gates is an **Information Board**.

Walk towards the mill on the left.

• *Geluveld Mill/Memorials to S Wales Borderers & 2nd Worcesters /19.3miles/10 minutes/Map 6/22*

At the foot of the windmill are memorials to the 1st South Wales Borderers and to the 2nd Bn Worcestershire Regiment which commemorate a famous action of 31 October 1914. The German attacks astride the Menin Road towards Ypres began on 29 October 1914, urged on by the Kaiser, certain that he would soon address his victorious army from the Cloth Hall in Ypres. So confident was the Kaiser that he moved nearer to the front line in order to be on the spot for the triumphal entry into the town. The German Order of the Day read, 'The break through will be of decisive importance. We must, and therefore will, conquer, settle for ever the centuries long struggle, end the war, and strike the decisive blow against our most detested enemy. We will finish with the British, Indians, Canadians, Moroccans and other trash, feeble adversaries who surrender in mass if they are attacked with vigour.'

The Germans, in overwhelming strength, pushed hard against the thin line of defenders. This area was the responsibility of the British 1st Division under General Lomax (qv). At midday on 31 October Geluveld fell and shortly afterwards Lomax was killed by a shell in his headquarters at Hooge (nearer to Ypres). The game was in the balance. General Haig, the Corps Commander, was somewhere along the Menin Road at this time, but unaware of the true tactical situation. However, he did issue orders to the effect that if his Corps could not hold on where it was, it should fall back to a line just in front of Ypres. Meanwhile local commanders took matters into their own hands. The commander of the Menin Road front was Brigadier-**General C. FitzClarence** (qv), late of the Irish Guards, who had won a **VC** as a Captain in the Boer War at Mafeking for 'extraordinary spirit and fearlessness'.

A counter-attack by the 1st South Wales Borderers had made the Germans pause just past Geluveld and at 1300 on 31 October FitzClarence called upon the Worcesters, gathered at the southern end of Polygon Wood, to regain the village. The Worcesters were actually part of 2nd Division, but General Lomax had arranged that in an emergency they could be detached to 1st Division. They had been in continuous action for ten days and were down to about 500 men, little more than half of their original strength. Major Hankey, commanding the Worcesters,

sent one company to cover the Menin Road itself, lined up his three remaining companies side by side, fixed bayonets and doubled across the open ground between Polygon and the village. Just short of the village was Gheluveld Château and here the Worcesters found gallant remnants of the South Wales Borderers still hanging on.

Together they pushed forward to the village, now burning furiously and under bombardment from both German and British artillery. Brigadier FitzClarence decided to withdraw to a firmer position and at 1800 the Worcesters and Borders began a move backward to Veldhoek, just under a mile from here along the Menin Road). The German tide had been stopped, but it had cost the Worcesters dear – 187 of the 500 had been killed or

Memorial to 2nd Worcesters, Geluveld Mill.

Memorial to the 18th Division with 1st Gloucesters Memorial behind, Clapham Junction.

Detail of plaque.

wounded. The chase across the open field with bayonets may have saved Ypres, may have saved the BEF, may have saved the war. The British Commander-in-Chief, Sir John French, said that the moment of the counter-attack was 'the worst half-hour of my life'. Sadly, on 12 November, less than two weeks later, Brigadier FitzClarence was killed. His body was never found and he is commemorated on the Menin Gate.

Drive to the Menin Road and turn right towards Ypres. Continue to a crest with a garage complex on the right and the turning to Pappotstraat on the left.

• Clapham Junction/ Gloucestershire Memorial/18th Division Memorial/23.7 miles/10 minutes/Map 6/23, 6/24

This was a meeting point for roads and tracks, hence its name. The 1st Battalion of the Gloucestershires saw heavy fighting here during First Ypres and the 2nd Battalion during Second Ypres. Their memorial obelisk is on the right. Opposite on the left is a similar one for the 18th (Eastern) Division which has others in Trones Wood and Thiepval on the Somme.

To the left is the area known as Stirling Castle, named by the Argyll & Sutherland Highlanders after their garrison town and described in 1917 by Col Seton Hutchison in his book *Pilgrimage* as a 'treacherous heap of filth'.

Continue downhill along the Menin Road, to the memorial by the entrance to the car park for Bellewaerde Leisure Park on the right.

• KRRC Memorial/24.3 miles/5 minutes/ Map 6/25

The memorial, which is similar to one on the Somme at Pozières and another in Winchester, is placed here in acknowledgement of the Regiment's part in the battle of 30/31 July 1915 at Hooge Château (qv) and the later battle of Sanctuary Wood (qv) on 2 June 1916. During the war the Regiment grew to twenty-two Battalions.

Memorial to KRRC, Hooge.

• Site of Hooge Château/Crater

The leisure park is on the site of the original Château whose destruction began on 31 October 1914, when a shell fell on Maj-Gen Monro's Divisional Headquarters and several staff officers were killed. Others were wounded, including Gen Monro (qv) and Lt Gen Samuel Holt Lomax (qv), CB, of 1st Division, age 59, who was mortally wounded and eventually died on 10 April 1915. He is buried in the Aldershot Military Cemetery. Several of the casualties are buried in Ypres Town CWGC Cemetery. The crater itself was filled in during the 1920s. It was formed by a mine sprung by 3rd Division on 19 July 1915. The gallery leading to the charge of 3,500lb of ammonal was 190ft long and was prepared by 175th Tunnelling Company RE. When new the crater measured 120ft across and 20ft deep. (For those who know the Lochnagar crater on the Somme, that took 60,000 lbs of ammonal.)
Continue to the Hotel Kasteel to the right.

• Front Line Hooghe Crater/Preserved Trenches/Bunkers/24.4 miles/15 minutes/RWC/Map 6/26

To the left of the hotel, three adjoining water-filled craters (blown by the Germans in June 1916 during the attack on Mount Sorrel) and blockhouses, both in and out of the water, have been excavated and may be visited. There is no formal entrance fee but there is a box by the entrance of the site for donations to its maintenance. The area where the path runs between the craters and the fenced border of the theme park is where in a surprise attack at 0315 on 30 July 1915, the Germans are said to have first used the flame thrower against British troops. At that time the crater and its immediate surroundings were held by the 8th Rifle Brigade and the 7th Bn KRRC, and jets of flame were sent against both sides of the crater from the direction of today's theme park. The *Flammenwerfer* equipment that the Germans used was carried by one man and looked rather like a portable fire extinguisher. The liquid was ignited at the nozzle and produced a jet of flame some 25yd long accompanied by thick black smoke.

Both battalions were forced back beyond what is now the rear wall of Hooge Crater Cemetery. Despite further flame attacks that night the line was stabilised some 200yd beyond the other side of the Menin Road and in the two days of fighting the 7th KRRC lost 12 officers and 289 other ranks and 8th Rifle Brigade 19 officers and 462 other ranks.

Bitter fighting had taken place earlier in this sector in 'The Battle of Hooge' (or Belle-waerde) of 16/17 June 1915, and the Royal Fusiliers, the Royal Scots Fusiliers and the Northumberland Fusiliers, followed by the Lincolns and the Liverpool Scottish, assaulted enemy trenches between the Menin Road and the Ypers-Roulers railway line. An account of this action, which practically wiped out the Liverpool Scottish, appears in Ann Clayton's biography of **Noel Chavasse** (qv). For it was here that their Medical Officer, who was to go on to win the **VC and Bar**, won the **MC** for 'untiring efforts in personally searching the ground between our line and the enemy's [for which] many of the wounded owe their lives'.

This area is noted for another innovation. It is said that here the first experimental use of portable wireless was attempted between division and brigade HQ. It is to be hoped that the army radios worked better then than they seemed to do at Arnhem in 1944 or even in 21st Century conflicts such as in the Gulf.

The adjoining Hotel Kasteelhof 't Hooghe and Restaurant, Tel: + (0) 57 46 87 87, e-mail: kasteelhof.thooghe@belgacom.net website: www.hotelkasteelhofthooghe.be owned and run by the Loontjens family offers not the usual 'sea views' but 'crater views'!

Continue to the Hooge Crater Museum on the right.

• *Hooge Chapel Museum/24.5 miles/20 minutes/RWC/Map 6/27*

The old chapel at Hooge, built as a memorial to those who fell in the Salient, was acquired by Roger de Smul, who after extensive renovation, opened a museum in it at Easter 1994. It houses two superb private collections. One consists of World War I armour and equipment, handed down through members of the de Smul family (who during WW2 managed the Regina Hotel in Ypres in which they had a secret room where they hid downed RAF pilots and crews until they could be guided out through the German lines). The other, of uniforms and artefacts of the men who fought in the Salient, belongs to the collector Philippe Oosterlinck. There are some well-interpreted dioramas and a dramatic stained glass window of the Cloth Hall on fire. There is a 1917 German Fokker DR1 and an authentic British 1916 Ford 'T' ambulance, audio-visual presentations and a new section dedicated to the finds of 'The Diggers' (qv). British sculptor John Bunting created a statue of Madonna and Child for the museum in memory of **Pte Joseph P. Bunting**, killed 1 July 1916 on the Sommme. It stands in a niche above the doorway.

Open daily: 1 Feb-1 Dec, 1000-1800. Closed Mondays. Tel: + (0) 57 46 84 46. A small entrance fee is payable. Attached to it, on the site of a former small school, is a pleasant modern café with clean WCs. Own picnics may be consumed with the purchase of at least a drink from the café.

Walk carefully over the road to the cemetery.

• *Hooge Crater CWGC Cemetery/19.2 miles/10 minutes/ Map 6/28*

The cemetery was begun during Third Ypres by the 7th Division's Burial Officer on land that had been heavily fought over in 1915 and 1916 and extended by concentration burials from the surrounding battlefields after the Armistice. There are 5,892 graves registered here, including 2 from the British West Indies and 45 Special Memorials. Over 60% are 'Known Unto God'. The cemetery was designed by Sir Edwin Lutyens assisted by N.A. Rew.

The stone wall that encircles the Stone of Remembrance and which leads to the Cross of Sacrifice at the front of the cemetery is said to be reminiscent of the crater blown across the road on 19 July 1915.

Private Patrick Joseph Bugden, VC, of the 31st Battalion, AIF, who won the medal for his heroic actions at Polygon Wood on 26-27 September 1917, and who was killed on his fifth mission to rescue wounded men under intense fire, is buried here. In the area of the cemetery **2nd Lt Sidney Clayton Woodroffe** of the 8th Bn The Rifle Brigade won his **VC** on 30 July 1915, for gallantly defending his position against the German attack and for leading a counter-attack under intense fire,

Exterior Hooge Crater Museum.

during which he was killed. His body was lost in subsequent fighting and Woodroffe is commemorated on the Menin Gate. The VC was gazetted on 6 August and on 8 August Woodroffe's friend, the poet Charles Sorley (qv), wrote:

In Memorian S.C.W., VC
There is no fitter end than this.
No need is now to yearn nor sigh.
We know the glory that is his,
A glory that can never die.

Also buried here is **Lt Wilfrid Evelyn Littleboy** of the 16th Bn R Warwicks, killed on 7 October 1917, to whom there is a plaque in Geluveld Church (qv).

Continue down the hill for 500m and turn left up Canadalaan (Maple Avenue) by the Canada Café to the cemetery on the right.

• *Sanctuary Wood CWGC Cemetery/ 19.9 miles/10 minutes*

The cemetery contains 102 UK, 41 Canadian and 1 German burial. Here is buried **Lt Gilbert Talbot** of the Rifle Brigade, after whom Talbot House (qv) was named. Son of the Bishop of London and brother of the Rev Neville Talbot, Senior C of E Chaplain of 6th Division, Gilbert was educated at Winchester (where he became friendly with A. P. Herbert) and Christ Church, Oxford, where he was President of the Union and a brilliant debater. In the afternoon of 30 July 1915 he fell, near Zouave Wood, leading a counter-attack with what remained of his men after the brutal liquid fire attack of that morning. Near him as he was shot in the neck cutting the old British barbed wire was his servant, Rifleman Nash, who was shot through the finger as he lay Gilbert's body down. Later attempts by him to return with stretcher bearers to recover Gilbert's body failed, but Nash was later to receive the DCM for his 'devoted care and courage'. Neville Talbot crawled out through the dead of the Rifle Brigade two days later, first finding Woodroffe's body and then Gilbert's. He took his pocket book, prayer book, wrist watch and badge and gave his brother the benediction. A week later he brought the body in and buried it. Killed in the same attack, but whose body although buried and marked, could not be found after the war, was 2nd Lt the Hon G.W. ('Billy') Grenfell, younger brother of Julian Grenfell (qv), the poet. Like Woodroffe, he is commemorated on the Menin Gate. Near to Talbot's grave is that of **Hauptmann Hans Roser, Iron Cross** holder, who was the observer in an Albatross of Field Flying Section 3 which on 25 July 1915 was shot down by a Bristol Scout piloted by Captain Lanoe Hawker. Many British soldiers watched the action, including, it is said, General Plumer. Hawker won the VC for his victories that day. He brought down two other planes in the same action.

The cemetery was designed by Sir Edwin Lutyens with N.A.Rew and its fan-shaped layout is typical of Lutyens' originality.

Outside the cemetery is a **Private Memorial** to **Lt Keith Rae**, also of the Rifle Brigade, killed on the same day. He was last seen at a spot near Hooge Crater in the *Château* grounds and after the war his family erected this memorial to him on that site. When the last member of the Vink family to own the *Château* felt that the memorial could no longer be cared for it was moved here and is maintained by the Commonwealth War Graves Commission.

Continue to Sanctuary Wood Museum car park.

• *Sanctuary Wood Museum/Preserved Trenches/25.9 miles/30 minutes/Map 6/29/RWC*

The wood in which the museum is sited is on the forward slopes (Ypres side) of the last ridge before the town. At the top of the road is Hill 62, where a Canadian memorial in the form of a small garden and Stone of Remembrance commemorates the Dominion's efforts in the Salient and in particular the presence in 1914 of the first Canadian troops – Princess Patricia's Light Infantry – to fight against the Germans. During the First Ypres battle the wood still had trees, not yet destroyed by artillery, and it housed a few reserves, medical facilities and dozens of

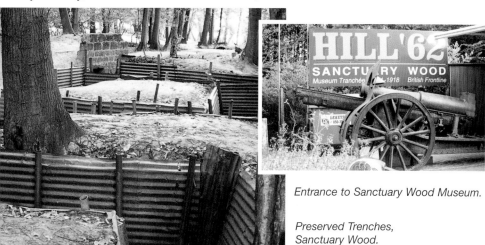

Entrance to Sanctuary Wood Museum.

Preserved Trenches, Sanctuary Wood.

stragglers. Brigadier General Bulfin, of 2nd Division, ordered that the stragglers be left 'in sanctuary' until he instructed what should be done with them – and the wood got its name.

The museum here is owned by Jacques Schier and it is in two parts – the building and the preserved trenches. The building houses the bar and bookstall, with various military souvenirs on sale, and a museum. The souvenirs are not exclusively from the First World War, although many of the artefacts on sale were actually found in the Salient. It is always sensible to be cautious about remnants of bullets and shells and collectors should *never* pick up anything on the battlefield itself. People are still occasionally killed or maimed by First World War explosives. Every year farmers plough up what is called the Iron Harvest and the Belgian Army collects it at regular intervals and blows it up in controlled explosions.

At the heart of the collection are the dozen or so 3-D wooden viewing cabinets. They are a *must*. Each one has different glass slides that when viewed with persistence focus dramatically into sharp 3 dimensions. Here in this atmospheric environment is the true horror of war – dead horses, bodies in trees, heads and legs in trenches and, everywhere, mud, mud, mud. The history of the pictures is obscure. Jacques maintains that they are Belgian, others say that they were once owned by the Imperial War Museum and disposed of during a clean-out in the 1950s. There are similar, if not identical, cabinets and slides at the Armistice Carriage Museum at Compiègne and in a stationer's shop in Verdun. They may well be of French origin. At the back of the museum, past hardware so rusty that is difficult to see how it keeps heart and soul together, are the trenches. They are original in the way that George Washington's axe, with three new heads and two new handles, is original. Yet they follow the shape and nature of the original trenches, which were designed to twist and turn so that invaders were always isolated in a short length of trench and could not set up machine guns to mow down the defenders in lines. They smell, but not with the stench of death that hung over the Salient for four long years. They are damp, probably with water underfoot, and in the middle is a concrete tunnel, passable to the wellie brigade. It defies the imagination to conjure up a picture of trenches in belts up to a mile or more wide joined in chicken-wire patterns and stretching from the North Sea to Switzerland – but that was how it was.

Open all year round during daylight hours. Entrance fee payable. Tel: + (0) 57 46 63 73.

Some 300 yards further up the road is the **Canadian Memorial at Hill 62 ('Mount Sorrel').**

Return to the Menin Road, turn left and drive to the first roundabout. Drive around it.

• Hellfire Corner Demarcation Stone/27.5 miles/5 minutes/Map 6/30

This is Hellfire Corner. It was under constant observation by Germans on the high ground and anything that moved across it was shelled. Canvas screens were erected beside the road in an attempt to conceal movement.

By the roadside as you drive round the roundabout is a **Demarcation Stone** (one of twelve surviving in the Salient) to mark the Germans' nearest point to

Ypres. It now bears an explanatory plaque. The metre-high stones, made from pink Alsace granite were designed by the sculptor Paul Moreau-Vauthier who had been seriously wounded while serving as a machine gunner at Verdun and who first conceived the stone at the *Salon des Artistes Décorateurs* in 1919. It was made by the stonemason Léon Telle and had three patterns: the Belgian, surmounted by a *Jass's* casque, with, on its sides, a typical Belgian water bottle and gas mask; the British, surmounted by a Tommy's tin helmet, with a British water bottle and small box respirator, and the French, surmounted by a *Poilu's* casque, with on its sides a typical French water (or wine!) bottle and gas mask. Beneath the helmet was a laurel wreath. All bore inscriptions in the three languages: 'Here the invader was brought to a standstill 1918'; *'Hier werd de overweldiger tot staan gebrackt 1918'* and *'Ici fut arrêté l'envahisseur 1918'* (preferred to a proposed *'Ici fut brisé l'élan des Barbares'!* 'Here the thrust of the barbarian was broken') and the name of the appropriate sector. At each corner was a palm emerging from a hand grenade.

They were erected by the Touring Club of France, supported by the Belgian Touring Club and the Ypres League and erected in the early 1920s, their sites having been decided by Marshal Pétain and his staff. They were to mark the length of the Front Line from the North Sea to the Vosges. Accounts vary wildly as to how many actually were erected – from 119 (Rose Coombs) to 280 (Swinton's *Twenty Years After*). The history of the stones is being researched by Rik Scherpenberg whose web site details his findings (www.geocities.com/demarcationstones/).

Turn left at Hellfire Corner signed Zillebeke.

Perth China Wall CWGC Cemetery is passed on the left.

Continue through the village of Zillebeke, turning left at the T junction after the church following signs to Maple Copse CWGC Cemetery, but before reaching it turn right following signs to Hill 60 just before the woods. Stop at the museum on the right.

• Hill 60 Museum/Memorials/29.7 miles/20 minutes/RWC/Map 6/31, 6/32

Here is a **Memorial to the Queen Victoria's Rifles**, plus small craters, a blockhouse and across the road a museum. This has a reasonably well-preserved collection of weapons and hardware and is run by a cousin of Jacques Schier. There is a small entrance charge and the opening hours are irregular. There is a bar to revive the weary. Tel: + (0) 57 20 62 76.

The 'Hill' was formed by the spoil taken from the cutting through which the railway runs (200 yards further up the road) and gets its name because the resultant feature is 60 metres above sea level and forms an extension to the Messines Ridge. The French lost the Hill to the Germans in 1914 and when the British took over from them following the race to the sea it was then decided that the feature must be retaken. Much of the fighting here was underground and it was probably here that the first British mine of the war was blown by Lt White, RE on 17 February 1915 – though the tunnelling had actually been taken over from the French. It was decided that a major mining operation should be undertaken and the job was given to 173rd Tunnelling Company, RE. Work began early in March 1915 and three tunnels were begun towards the German line about 50 yards away, a pit having first been dug some 16 ft deep. Almost immediately the miners came

Memorial to 1st Australian Tunnelling
Company, Hill 60.

Zillebeke Demarcation Stone.

Bunker near St Eloi Crater.

Memorial to St Eloi Tunnellers with
Krupp Kanon.

St Eloi, 7 June 1917 Crater.

upon dead bodies and quick-lime was brought up to cover them and the bod,
were dragged out. It was hot, unpleasant and dangerous work. Apart from the
constant threat that the tunnel would collapse and bury the miners alive, there was
the possibility of poison gas and not least that the enemy might break into the
tunnel or explode a mine of his own below it. By the time that the digging was
finished the tunnels stretched more than 100 yards, and dragging the ninety-four
100 lb bags of gunpowder to the mineheads, winching them down the shafts and
then manoeuvring them along the tunnels was a Herculean task. On 15 April all
the charges were ready and on 17 April at 1905 hours the mine was fired.

The explosion built up over 10 seconds throwing volcano-like debris nearly 300 ft
high and for 300 yards all around. Simultaneously British, French and Belgian guns
opened an artillery barrage and encouraged by regimental buglers the Royal West
Kents fixed bayonets and charged the dazed Germans of the 172nd Infantry
Regiment, killing about 150 for only seven casualties of their own. The Hill was won.

Three days later **Lt Geoffrey Harold Woolley** won the **first Territorial Army
VC** in resisting a German counter-attack. His citation reads, 'For most conspicuous
bravery on Hill 60 during the night of 20-21 April 1915. Although the only officer
on the hill at the time, and with very few men, he successfully resisted all attacks
on his trench and continued throwing bombs and encouraging his men till
relieved. His trench during all the time was being heavily shelled and bombed, and
was subjected to heavy machine-gun fire by the enemy.' Woolley was a member of
the 9th London Regiment, Queen Victoria's Rifles who had, with the Royal West
Kents and King's Own Scottish Borderers, taken part in the initial assault on 17
April. Underground warfare went on here for another 10 months until the
beginning of Third Ypres. Many of the men who worked and fought in those black
corridors in the clay died there and are there still. Hill 60 is a cemetery.

Beyond the enclosed area on the left are **Memorials to the 14th (Light) Division
and the 1st Australian Tunnelling Company.**

The hitherto inaccessible path to Caterpillar Crater, to the left, has recently been
opened up.

*Continue over the railway and turn right towards Ypres at the T junction. Continue
to the first left turn (Vaartstraat) with a signboard to several CWGC Cemeteries.*
Ahead Kemmel Hill can be seen in the distance.

N.B. By continuing some 400 yards to the next junction you would reach the
Zillebeke Demarcation Stone (with a Belgian Helmet) in the centre of the road. Its
'objectional' inscription concerning 'The Invaders' has been erased.

Turn left and continue.

CWGC Cemeteries **Chester Farm** and **Spoilbank** are passed on the right.

Continue to the T junction and turn left. Continue to the roundabout. Ahead is

• *Monument to St Eloi Tunnellers/Craters/32.3 miles/15 minutes/ Map 6/33, 6/34*

This memorial was erected on 11 November 2001 to 172nd Tunnelling Coy 3rd Br
Div, 2nd Can Div and 7th Belg Fld Arty. T. E. Hulme (qv) served in the trenches at
St Eloi in the spring of 1915 and wrote a poem *Trenches: St Eloi*, which expresses the

mind-numbing emptiness and apparent futility of trench warfare:
... Behind the line, cannon, hidden, lying back miles.
Before the line, chaos:
My mind is a corridor. The minds about me are corridors.
Nothing suggests itself. There is nothing to do but keep on.

Hulme was wounded in the arm here on 14 April 1915, with a 'Blighty one'. An extract from his poem is inscribed on the memorial. The British flag flies beside it and in 2003 a Krupp gun was added.

Two of the **craters blown here on 27 March 1916 and 7 June 1917** are now visitable by taking the fork to the left of the memorial. They are then one on each side of the road. On the right is an Information Board about the 7 June 1917 mine and a wooden path leads to the impressive water-filled crater where there is a seat and more Information Boards. A trail round the crater leads to a well-preserved bunker. **N.B.** You must collect the key to the complex from the Tourist Office in the Cloth Hall in Ieper and leave a returnable deposit for it. Well worth the effort. The crater to the left is up the small path to the left and easily accessible. It was created by one of six mines blown astride the old German front line at 0415 hours on 27 March 1916. Shafts dug to position the mines were up to 55ft deep and took more than 8 months to prepare. The mines were blown as part of an assault by 9th Brigade, after which most of the 4th Royal Fusiliers' objectives were still in enemy hands. Casualties were forty officers and 809 other ranks. On 3 April, 76th Brigade was brought in to reinforce a new attack. During the assault the Brigade Major, Capt Billy Congreve (qv), reached the rim of one of the craters. He wrote in his diary:

"Imagine my surprise and horror when I saw a whole crowd of armed Boches! I stood there for a moment feeling a bit sort of shy, and then I levelled my revolver at the nearest Boche and shouted, 'Hands up, all the lot of you!' A few went up at once, then a few more and then the lot; and I felt the proudest fellow in the world as I cursed them."

Congreve brought in four officers and sixty-eight men – though other accounts make it five officers and seventy-seven men – for which he was recommended for the **VC** (which he was not to receive until July 1916 and then posthumously after further acts of bravery on the Somme) and awarded the DSO.

Today the water-filled crater is stocked with fish.

Take the N365 signed to Armentières and continue to Wijtschate.

• Wijtschate

Nicknamed 'Whitesheet' by the Tommies, fighting began around here in the first year of the war. The Germans held this area of high ground despite efforts by both the British and the French to take it. In the first, Messines, phase of the Third Battle of Ypres, the village was taken by the 36th (Ulster) Division and the 16th (South of Ireland) Division. On 3 July 1917 General Plumer presented King Albert of the Belgians with the bell of the church which had been dug out of the ruins.

Serving near Wijtschate from 6 June 1917 with 224th Siege Battery RGA was the vorticist artist, writer and philosopher, **Wyndham Lewis**. On 14 June he wrote to

Ezra Pound, 'Imagine a stretch of land one mile in depth sloping up from the o German first-line to the top of a ridge, stretching to right and left as far as you can see. It looks very large, never-ending and empty. There are only occasional little groups of men around a bomb-dump, or building a light railway: two men pushing a small truck on which a man is being brought back lying on his stomach, his head hanging over the side. The edge of the ridge is where you are bound for, at the corner of a demolished wood. The place is either loathesomely hot, or chilly according to the time of day at which you cross it. It is a reddish colour, and all pits, ditches & chasms, & black stakes, several hundred, here & there, marking the map-position of a wood.' Later in June Lewis contracted trench fever and was hospitalised in Boulogne.

On entering Wijtschate take the right turn signed Kemmel. Continue into the main square and keeping to the right of the bandstand turn right direction Dikkebus/Sporthaal and then right again signed to Croonaert Chapel Cemetery. Continue to the path (which is 200m long) to the left to the cemetery.

• Memorial to 1st Chasseurs à Pied/Croonaert Chapel CWGC Cemetery/35.3 miles/15 minutes/Map/6/42, 6/41

At this point there is a grey **stone memorial to Lt Lasmer, 11 'Sous Officiers' and 174 Corporals and Chasseurs of the 1st Bn Chasseurs à Pied** who fell here in the defence of Belgium and France in the fighting of 3-15 November 1914. It was unveiled on 9 June 1935 when 90 veterans of the regiment came from all corners of France to pay homage to their old comrades with their old commanding officer, General Somon.

In **Croonaert Chapel Cemetery** there are 75 burials, seven of which are unknown. After the Armistice 51 German graves from 1917 were removed. The grave of **Chang Chi Hsuen** of the Chinese Labour Corps, 23 January 1919 lies in a separate plot just within the entrance. The cemetery, which was designed by W.C Von Berg, was begun in June 1917 by 19th Division and used until the following November. Two later burials were made in April 1918 and January 1919.

It is on the site of the original chapel painted by Adolf Hitler who fought in this area in the 16th BRIR.

Turn round and return towards Wijtschate.

• Bayernwald Trenchlines and Mine Shaft/35.4 miles/15 minutes/ Map 6/43

To the left is the area known to the Germans as Bayernwald, also known as Bois Quarante, a site owned for many years by M. Becquaert (Senior) who operated an idiosyncratic museum here. After his death the site was left to deteriorate but it has now been sold and the present owner has granted permission to the ABAF (qv) to excavate the interesting network of trenches, dugouts and the 'Frauenlob' mineshaft. Together with the Commune of Heuvelland they are restoring 4 exceptional concrete bunkers, the deep German counter-mine shaft constructed to listen for British workings, about 100m of the trench system from the main German

Kruisstraat Craters.

Memorial to 16th Irish Division
with Wytschaete Military CWGC
Cemetery behind.

line of resistance 1916-17, recreating with A-frames 320m of trenches and constructing a wooden shelter with Information Boards. For the latest situation and to make a booking to visit, contact the Tourist Office at Kemmel, Tel: + (0) 57 45 04 55.

Turn first right along Hollandseschuur (ignoring the restriction sign) to the T junction.

N.B. By turning right here and continuing some 250m to the right the **Hollandseschuur Craters** are seen to the right (**Map 6/40**).

Turn left onto Vierstraat. Continue to the farm on the right and pull in at the end of the farm buildings.

Ahead in the meadow to the right is a distinct dip leading up to 5 tall poplar-like trees. This is the site of the **Sunken Road painted by Adolf Hitler in 1914**.

Return to Wijtschate Square. Keeping right past the bandstand turn right following signs to Kemmel. On the right is

• Wytschaete Military CWGC Cemetery/16th Irish Div Memorial/ 37.0 miles/5 minutes/ Map 6/44, 6/45

Containing 486 UK, 31 Australian, 19 Canadian, 7 New Zealand, 11 South African, 1 German, 25 special memorials and 673 unknown burials, the cemetery was created after the Armistice by concentration of graves from the surrounding battlefields. Here are the graves of **Drummer James Etak McKay**, 1st/4th Gordon Highlanders, 19 March 1915 age 20 and **2nd Lt John Victor Ariel**, 45th Sqn RFC, age 20 who 'Died of wounds received in aerial combat 7 July 1916'. The cemetery was designed by Sir Edwin Lutyens with W.H. Cowlishaw. Just beyond it is the

Memorial to the 16th Irish Div who captured Wijtschate on 7 June 1917. There is a similar monument to the Division at Guillemont on the Somme. Kemmel Hill is visible on the horizon ahead.

Continue to a green CWGC sign to the left to Spanbroekmolen Cemetery.

A short distance up the road to the left (and only visible from that road) is the large water-filled **Peckham Farm Crater**.

Continue along the road (which was known as Suicide Road) to the CWGC sign to Lone Tree Cemetery to the left and turn left along Kruisstraat. Stop on the left at the entrance to the Spanbroekmolen crater.

• *Spanbroekmolen (Pool of Peace)/38.3 miles/10 minutes/Map 6/46*

Named for the windmill that stood here for three centuries until it was destroyed by the Germans on 1 November 1914, this is the site of what was probably the largest mine explosion of the nineteen blown on 7 June 1917, at the start of the Messines phase of the Third Battle of Ypres. It consisted of 91,000lbs of ammonal.

Following a seven-day bombardment the battle opened with nine divisions of infantry advancing on a 9-mile front. They came towards you from the west. They had been told to advance at zero hour, 0310, whether the mines had blown or not. Spanbroekmolen went up 15 seconds late, killing a number of our own soldiers from the 36th Ulster Division, some of whom are buried in the cemetery ahead. The war diary of the 3rd Bn Worcester Regiment, that attacked a little south of here, records for that day, 'Battalion casualties were heavy and difficult to account for – a fair proportion must have been caused by our own barrage'.

Sir Philip Gibbs (qv), the war correspondent, described the scene thus, 'Suddenly at dawn, as a signal for all of our guns to open fire, there rose out of the dark ridge of Messines and "Whitesheet" and that ill-famed Hill 60, enormous volumes of scarlet flame from nineteen separate mines, throwing up high towers of earth and smoke all lighted by the flame, spilling over into fountains of fierce colour, so that many of our soldiers waiting for the assault were thrown to the ground. The German troops were stunned, dazed and horror-stricken if they were not killed outright. Many of them lay dead in the great craters opened by the mines.'

On 12 March 1915 an attack on the mill (coming from the direction of Kemmel) then in German hands, was used by the British as a diversionary action during the Neuve Chapelle battle as a means of drawing away enemy reserves. The 1st Wiltshires and 3rd Worcesters achieved little and incurred heavy losses.

In September 1929 Tubby Clayton wrote to *The Times* to point out that the last of the big craters at St Eloi, now 'a pool of rare perfection', was in danger of being lost in plans to extend the village. Two major craters, however, still remain visible in the village today (see page 232). Tubby's letter prompted discussions which led to Lord Wakefield buying the Spanbroekmolen Crater. It was renamed 'The Pool of Peace' and then left untouched as a memorial. On 22 April 1985 (the seventieth anniversary of the inauguration of Talbot House) Princess Alexandra visited the Pool and planted two mountain ash trees. She was due to be accompanied by her husband, the Hon Angus Ogilvy, who was Patron of Toc H, but he was ill and could not travel. Nevertheless he was mentioned on the commemorative plaque that was erected at the time at the entrance. However on 2 June 1992 the site was listed as an area 'of outstanding natural beauty' and therefore subject to the attendant rules and regulations. This included the removal of this plaque. (It is planned in the future to erect one plaque which will tell the history of the Pool of Peace.) After the listing a new wooden gate and fence were erected and the perimeter cleared. Visitors can walk all the way round the original borders. Just inside the gate is a tubular metal sculpture erected in 1998 and designed by the then 16-year-old Aline Overbergh. It symbolises two timeless people reaching out to each other with the Dove of Peace between them. Sadly this memorial has twice been badly vandalised and has had to be removed for repair.

Continue a few yards to the path on the right to the cemetery.

From this point a superb view over the Messines battlefield can be seen. Looking back down the road the bulk of Kemmel Hill is clearly visible and looking forward along the road Messines Church can be seen on the Ridge. To the left on the skyline is Wijtschate Church.

• *Lone Tree CWGC Cemetery/38.3 miles/10 minutes/Map 6/47*

The cemetery contains 88 UK burials and 6 unknown, many of them of the RI Rifles (36th) Division, killed on 7 June 1917, some by our own mine.

Continue, to the next crossroads and turn right along Wulvergemstraat (once known as Pill Road). On the crest of the hill, before the house on the right are some large craters. Stop.

• *Kruisstraat Craters/38.9 miles/10 minutes/Map 6/48*

You are now standing on the German front line at the beginning (7 June 1917) Messines Phase, of Third Ypres. The attack came from the direction of Kemmel Hill (which can be seen just beyond the craters) passed over the area where you now are, down into the valley and up onto the Messines Ridge where the distinctive shape of Messines Church can be seen.

These two craters are legacies of the mines blown at the start of Third Ypres. The digging was begun by 250th Tunnelling Coy in December 1915, handed over to 182nd Company at the beginning of January 1916, and to 3rd Canadian at the end of the month. In April, 175th Tunnelling Coy briefly took charge and when the gallery reached 1,051ft it was handed over to 171st Coy who were also responsible for Spanbroekmolen.

At 1,605ft a charge of 30,000lb of ammonal was laid and at the end of a small branch of 166ft to the right a second charge of 30,000lb was placed under the German front line. This completed the original plan, but it was decided to extend the mining to a position under the German third line. Despite meeting clay and being inundated with water underground which necessitated the digging of a sump, in just two months a gallery stretching almost half a mile from the shaft was completed and a further charge of 30,000lb of ammonal placed. This tunnel was the longest of any of the Third Ypres mines. In February 1917 enemy counter-measures necessitated some repair to one of the chambers and the opportunity was taken to place a further charge of 19,500lb making a total of four mines all of which were ready by 9 May 1917.

The two craters that remain, probably the first two charges, are favourite fishing spots for licence holders.

Return to the crossroads and turn right towards Mesen (Messines). At the next T junction turn left and stop immdiately on the right.

• Messines Ridge British CWGC Cemetery/New Zealand Memorial/40.3 miles/10 minutes/ Map 6/49, 6/50

Created after the Armistice, the cemetery contains 986 UK, 332 Australian, 1 Canadian, 115 New Zealand, 56 South African, 954 unknown and a large number of special memorials. At the entrance to the cemetery is the **New Zealand Memorial**, listing 840 men killed in the Salient and who have no known graves, following their policy not to list their missing on the Menin Gate. The New Zealand Memorials are all in cemeteries chosen as appropriate to the fighting in which the men died. This cemetery and memorial were designed by Charles Holden (who also designed the New Zealand Memorial at Polygon Wood).

On 7 June 1917, during the Messines action which was the prelude to Third Ypres, one of the war's most beloved Padres was awarded the Military Cross for his work on the Messines Ridge. The citation which was published in the London Gazette of 16 August reads,

"For conspicuous gallantry and devotion to duty. He showed the greatest courage and disregard of his own safety in attending wounded under heavy fire. He searched shell holes for our own and enemy wounded, assisting them to the dressing station, and his cheerfulness and endurance had a splendid effect upon all ranks, whom he constantly visited."

This brave Padre was the **Rev Geoffrey Anketell Studdert Kennedy, Chaplain to the Forces**, then serving with 17th Bde of 24th Division and better known as 'Woodbine Willie'. This unconventional Padre endeared himself to the men for his habit of doling out Woodbine cigarettes, for using their own strong language when he felt it necessary, and because he questioned his own faith when confronted by the cruel carnage around him. His *Rough Rhymes of a Padre* expressed his love for his fellow soldiers and his understanding of their love of each other, as exemplified in the poem, *His Mate*, which describes the burial of a soldier and whose last verse is,

There are many kinds of sorrow
In this world of Love and Hate,
But there is no sterner sorrow
Than a soldier's for his mate.

Studdert Kennedy was not so popular with the Establishment. General Plumer walked out half-way through one of his sermons in ire and had Woodbine Willie removed from the 2nd Army. After the war Studdert Kennedy continued his tireless ministry, speaking on many themes that were then considered to be avant-garde – divorce, contraception and abortion. At his funeral in 1929, the two-mile cortège from Worcester Cathedral to the cemetery was lined by crowds of his old comrades and the coffin was showered with packets of Woodbines.

Buried here is **Usko Leonard Salonen** 'of Finland' serving with the 39th AIF, killed 8 June 1917 aged 29.

From the top of the cemetery the Island of Ireland Tower can be seen.

Continue along Nieuwkerkestraat to the crossroads with the N365.

Extra Visit to the London Scottish Memorial (Map 6/51)
Round trip: 1.5 miles. Approximate time: 10 minutes

Turn left and continue to the memorial on the right.

The inscription on the grey granite Celtic Cross records how near this spot on Hallowe'en 1914 the London Scottish came into action, being the first territorial Battalion to engage the enemy. The battalion lost 394 of their 700 strength in the action. It was erected to the memory of all the Officers, NCOs and men of the Regiment who fell in the Great War, 1914-1919 and shows its Battle Honours year by year.

Turn round and return to Nieuwkerkestraat and pick up the main itinerary.

Turn right at the crossroads along the N365 into Mesen and first left following signs to Bethleem Farm CWGC Cemetery. Park near the bandstand.

• Messines (Mesen)/Museum/RB/Memorials/40.7 miles/10 minutes /Map 6/35, 6/36/OP

On the left, in the Town Hall of this 'the smallest city in Belgium', is a small **Museum** only open on application (Tel: + (0) 57 44 405 11). It contains weaponry, artefacts, photos and documents relating to the war. To the right is a small group of memorials including a New Zealand Kowhai tree, planted on 11 November 1993 (the 75th Anniversary of the Armistice). The New Zealand Ambassador comes to Messines each year to celebrate ANZAC Day and Messines is associated with the New Zealand town of Featherston, where some 8,000 NZ soldiers trained before coming to the Western Front. There is also a Ross Bastiaan Australian bronze relief memorial tablet and a Japanese International Peace Post (qv) unveiled on 17 September 1989 by the artist, Miss Mié Tabé, and given to Messines by the Japanese Peace Movement. Its message says 'May Peace Rule the World'.

Mié Tabé Peace Post and Ross Bastiaan Plaque, Messines.

Turn right before the bandstand to the Church.

This was the subject of a painting by Cpl Adolf Hitler when he was posted in the area with the 16th Bavarian Reserve Infantry from November 1914 to March 1915 and purportedly treated in the crypt which served as a German Field Hospital when he was wounded in the arm. It now contains an extraordinary carillon whose bells were contributed by many Belgian and Allied organisations.

Continue back to the main road and continue on the N365 direction Armentières. After some 400m turn right following signs to the New Zealand Memorial. Park at the entrance.

• *New Zealand Memorial and Park/Bunkers/41.2 miles/15 minutes/Map 6/52*

This memorial is identical to that at s-Graventafel (qv). It was unveiled on 1 August 1924 by King Albert I of the Belgians and overlooks a memorial park at the foot of which are two large, well-preserved German pill boxes.

It was well known that the Germans were constructing numbers of pill boxes on the Messines Ridge and prior to the opening of Third Ypres frequent patrols were made into German lines in order to find out more about the defences. The New Zealanders maintained daily intelligence summaries on the current state of the defences and their engineers blew up concrete dugouts half a mile south of here at Petite Douve Farm (qv) barely two days before the offensive opened. These two pill boxes appear identical, but the one on the left was made in situ while the other was put together with concrete blocks, probably to a pre-fabricated design.

Bunker, New Zealand Memorial Park, Messines.

On 7 June the attack here was led by the 3rd New Zealand Rifle Brigade advancing broadly from the direction of Nieuwkerke and the bunkers were taken in the first hour.

From the seat between the bunkers a good view of the Messines battlefield can be had provided trees do not obscure the view. The front lines here were about 700 yards away. Take straight ahead as 12 o'clock. At 1 o'clock the church on the skyline is Nieuwkerke. At 11 o'clock on the horizon

Island of Ireland Peace Park and Tower.

are the spires of Armentières and at 10 o'clock in the middle distance is Ploegsteert Wood Military CWGC Cemetery (**Map YP R29** and **Map 6**).

Standing outside the park, with one's back to the entrance, look straight towards the hills ahead and take that as 12 o' clock. At 10 o'clock in the middle distance is the spire of Wulvergem Church roughly 1,500 yards away. Moving towards 12 o' clock is the tall wireless mast of Mont des Cats, then Mont Noir and next to it, the tallest hill, Kemmel, with a smaller radio mast. At 12 o'clock on the horizon are the bushes which surround Spanbroekmolen.

Return to the N365 and follow signs to Ploegsteert and Armentières. Continue downhill to the tower on the right.

• Island of Ireland Peace Park and Tower/41.7 miles/15 minutes/Map 6/37

For many years following the Armistice, during the turbulent period leading to the formation of the Irish Free State, men from Southern Ireland who fought with the British in the Great War were often considered as 'traitors' and their sacrifice deliberately forgotten. This imposing grey stone tower is dedicated to the memory of all those from the Island of Ireland who fought and died in the First World War in an overdue gesture of remembrance and reconciliation between nationalists and unionists. The Tower was the brainchild of Catholic Nationalist MP Paddy Harte and Protestant Unionist Glen Barr who visited the area together in 1996 and conceived the project as 'A Journey of Reconciliation'.

It was unveiled on 11 November 1998 by President Mary McAlease and Queen Elizabeth II in the presence of the King and Queen of the Belgians. This site was chosen as it stands on the Messines Ridge where men from the north and the south of the Island fought almost shoulder to shoulder in June 1917.

As one passes through the entrance in the grey stone walls there are polished granite Information Plaques in Belgian, French, English and Gaelic leading up to the tower itself. They include some moving quotations from the poets Francis Ledwidge (qv) and Tom Kettle, from the Official War Artist, Sir William Orpen, Chaplain Francis Gleeson of the R Munster Fusiliers and others who served with Irish Regiments. Other plaques salute the memory of the 10th (Irish) Division which lost 9,363 men, the 16th (Irish) Division which lost 28,398 and the 36th (Ulster) Division which lost 32,186. In the room at the base of the slim Tower, a traditional Irish form which has been built in Ireland since the 8th Century, are beautiful bronze boxes made to contain the names of the Irish casualties and a Visitor's Book.

The park surrounding the tower includes four gardens for the four Provinces with four different types of tree representing the Irish soldiers marching towards the tower. Owing to financial difficulties experienced by the originators, the park is now maintained by the Commonwealth War Graves Commission.

Continue downhill.

Just before the bottom of the hill on the right hand side is La Petite Douve Farm. Under this farm many experts believe is one of the powerful remaining unexploded mines set to fire on 7 June 1917.

Continue to a left turn to the group of CWGC signs to Mud Corner, Prowse Point etc.

Extra Visit to Prowse Point CWGC Cemetery (Map 6/53), St Yvon Christmas Truce Cross (Map 6/54) and Bairnsfather Plaque (Map 6/55) Round trip: 1.4 miles. Approximate time: 30 minutes.

Turn left and continue along the Chemin du Mont de la Hutte to the cemetery on the right.

Prowse Point Military CWGC Cemetery

Designed by W.K.Cowlishaw, this lovely cemetery with an unusual irregular layout was named after Brig-Gen C.B. ('Bertie') Prowse, DSO, who fell on 1 July 1916, and is buried at Louverval on the Somme. It was begun by the Dublin Fusiliers and the 1st Warwicks and was used from as early as November 1914 until April 1918 and contains 159 UK, 42 New Zealand, 13 Australian, 1 Canadian and 12 German prisoner burials. At the front of the cemetery is a rectangular pond with water lillies. The roof of a small bunker that existed during the war can still be seen in the lawn to the right of the graves area.

Also buried in Louverval CWGC Cemetery is the poet, Lt Roland Aubrey Leighton, probably best known for being the fiancé of Vera Brittain, author of *Testament of Youth*. On 12 April 1915, Leighton's battalion, the 7th Worcesters, reached trenches in Plugstreet Wood. Here he wrote the poem to Vera entitled *Villanelle*,

Violets from Plug Street Wood,

Sweet, I send you oversea.

(*Violets from Oversea*, the first line of the last verse, gave us the title of the first edition of our book on twenty-five poets of World War I). Leighton was killed on 23 December 1916.

Another poet was Charles Sorley (qv) of the 7th Suffolk Regt serving to the south of Ploegsteert Wood in July 1915. In his letters Sorley describes a bombing raid on a 'redoubt of some kind' the Germans were making and upon which the battalion did not have enough shells to fire. Although some bombs (grenades) were thrown, the Germans soon raked the ground 'with an absolute hail of rifle and machine-gun fire'. Many of the raiding Suffolks were wounded. Nevertheless the officer leading the raid, described only as 'C' by Sorley, was noticed the next day on trench patrol, 'dressed in summer get-up; gum boot, breeches, shirt-sleeves, sambrown belt and pistol. He had a bandage round his head, but only a very slight scratch from a fragment of bomb. He was walking along, reading from his German pocket edition of *Faust*.'

To the right just beyond the cemetery is a path which leads to **Mud Corner**, **Toronto Avenue**, **Ploegsteert Wood Mil** and **Rifle House** CWGC Cemeteries. It would take about an hour to walk to all of them and back to the road. They are in what was the infamous 'Plugstreet' Wood. The Wood is about 2,000 yards wide, east to west, and about 1,000 yds, north to south. Critical fighting for possession of it took place in 1914, between mid-October and the beginning of November – known as the Battle of Armentières. It ran, therefore,

Top of bunker, Prowse Point CWGC Cemetery.

Extra visit continued

concurrently with First Ypres and this point, of Ploegsteert, marks the bottom end of the Salient. A fine bayonet charge by the 1st Somersets (their '1st in France', as the Regimental History puts it – although they were in fact in Belgium) stopped one German attack on the village of le Gheer at the south-east corner of the wood. Conditions in the wood were abominable. The Somerset History records,

> "On 25 October ... the trenches were absolute quagmires ... the water and mud were ankle deep in the front lines; by the beginning of November the trenches were knee-deep in slime and filth. The stench from dead bodies often partially buried in the soggy, slimy ground, just as they had fallen, was awful. Unwashed, caked with mud, clothes sodden... aching with rheumatism and the early symptoms of trench feet, verminous and generally in a deplorable condition [the Somersets] held the line with a degree of staunchness, determination and cheerfulness of spirit never surpassed in the whole glorious history of the Army."

Although they made excursions into the eastern edge, the Germans never took the wood.

Continue to the cross in the bank on the left.

Khaki Chums' Christmas Truce Cross

A simple wooden cross was erected here by the Khaki Chums Association for Military Remembrance when they spent a cold Christmas in the area to commemorate the 85th Anniversary of the Truce. On 13 December 2003 a more substantial Cross was dedicated.

Extra visit continued

You are now in the village of St Yvon. Here the cartoonist **Capt Bruce Bairnsfather** (qv), then a Lieutenant, was billetted and created his immortal character, 'Old Bill'. Bairnsfather, a trained artist who had previously served in the Royal Warwickshires before the war, rejoined the colours in August 1914 and by November was with the 1st Battalion here in the trenches at Plugstreet Wood. Possessed with sharp powers of observation and a quick pencil he began to draw cartoons to amuse his men – on anything that was to hand, from ammunition boxes to walls. Just behind the regiment's lines in this village he and a fellow officer called Hudson took over the ruins of a cottage with a more or less intact cellar, which they converted into a dugout for living quarters. On the dugout's walls Bairnsfather amused himself by sketching the situations that he was experiencing in the area.

Continue, past a pond at the bend to the right, to the first house on the right.
Commemorative Plaque to Capt Bruce Bairnsfather on House No. 12 Chemin du Mont de la Hutte.

This house has been built on the very site of that billet. On one occasion when several of them were in the cottage, the Germans began to shell the village and, knowing that the enemy would have ranged his guns on the buildings, they dashed outside and took cover in a nearby ditch. At last when the shelling seemed to be over they went back into the cottage and just as they did so a heavy shell landed close by and to a man they rushed to the broken doorway and with one voice exclaimed, 'Where did that one go to?' Bairnsfather turned the situation into a cartoon of that title. It was an action that was to lead to a lifetime career built around the immortal character 'Old Bill' that emerged from his cartoons, collectively called *Fragments from France*. [It is a story that we examine in our biography *In Search of the Better 'Ole, The Life, the Works and the Collectables of Bruce Bairnsfather*.]

Unveiling of Plaque to Capt Bairnsfather on cottage wall, St Yvon.

Cottage on site of the dugout where Bairnsfather drew his first cartoon, complete with plaque.

Extra visit continued

On 13 December 2003 the authors unveiled a bronze plaque on the cottage wall to commemorate the birth of Bairnsfather's inspired creation and the seeds of his extraordinary career.

Bairnsfather also decided to try his hand at sniping, considered an 'officer's sport', and climbed onto the roof of another cottage. He had hardly done so when another German barrage began and he had to beat a hasty retreat, an experience that he turned into the cartoon, *They've evidently seen me*, which shows a startled soldier clinging to a chimney as a huge shell whistles by.

It was in this area that men participated in that curious phenomenon, 'The Christmas Truce' on 24/25 December 1914. The 1st Battalion the Warwickshire Regiment in Plugstreet Wood took part in the truce and 2nd Lt Bruce Bairnsfather, in his book, *Bullets and Billets* gives a full and humourous account of what happened. After singing and shouting 'a complete Boche figure suddenly appeared on the parapet and looked about itself. This complaint became infectious. It didn't take Our Bert long to be up on the skyline. This was the signal for more Boche anatomy to be disclosed and this was replied to by all our Alfs and Bills until in less time than it takes to tell, half a dozen or so of each of the belligerents were outside their trenches and advancing towards each other in no-man's-land.' He goes on to describe how he joined in the fraternisation and how eventually everyone returned to their trenches. 'The last I saw of this little affair was a vision of one of my machine gunners, who was a bit of an amateur hairdresser in civil life, cutting the unnaturally long hair of a docile Boche who was patiently kneeling on the ground whilst the automatic clippers crept up the back of his neck'. The experience may well have led to one of his *Fragments* cartoons entitled *Coiffure in the Trenches* where a soldier (either Alf or Bert) is having his hair cut by Old Bill as a large shell sails by. Bill is saying 'Keep yer 'ead still or I'll 'ave yer blinkin' ear off'.

Sir John French reacted quickly to the news of the truce. Units that had participated were moved out of the lines and hostilities immediately recommenced. Christmas Day 1914 was not without its official pleasures, however. Every officer and soldier in the field was given two gifts. The King and Queen sent a postcard bearing pictures of themselves, the King in service dress, and on the reverse in a facsimile of the King's hand the message, 'With our best wishes for Christmas 1914. May God protect you and bring you home safe. Mary R. George R'. Princess Mary, following a tradition that Queen Victoria had begun in the Boer War, sent an embossed brass tin containing a mixture of cigarettes, pipe tobacco and chocolate together with a small folded card wishing the recipient a Happy Christmas.

[**N.B.** By continuing along the small road to the T junction, the St Yvon craters of Trench 127 to the left and Trench 122 and Factory Farm to the right will be passed, followed by the site of the mine that blew in 1955 at Le Pélerin.]

Turn round and return to the main road, turn left and rejoin the main itinerary.

On the slope to the right is the site of the old Château de la Hutte on Hill 63 under which the British built large subterranean shelters. At one time it was planned to build the Ploegsteert Memorial here.
Continue downhill to the large memorial on the right. Stop.

• *Ploegsteert Memorial/Berkshire CWGC Cemetery Extension and Hyde Park Corner CWGC Cemeteries/Last Post/43.4 miles/15 minutes/Map 6/39, 6/38 /RWC*

Here, since 7 June 1999, the Last Post has been played on the last Friday of the month at 1900 hours by local buglers. The event was organised by the *Comité du Mémorial de Ploegsteert* with the assistance of Ted Smith of the WFA. Special ceremonies may be requested. Tel: + (0) 56 58 84 41. Fax: + (0) 56 58 75 34.

Guarded by two lions, one baring his teeth, the other looking benign, designed by Sir Gilbert Ledward (who was to do work in the World War II Reichswald Cemetery on the Dutch-German border) is the Berkshire Cemetery Extension which was begun in June 1916. The rotunda structure is the Ploegsteert Memorial to the Missing bearing the names of 11,447 officers and men from nearby battles for every year of the war and has its own registers, separate to those for the adjoining cemetery.

There are **three VCs** commemorated on it: **Sapper William Hackett** of 254th Tunnelling Coy, RE, for helping to rescue men entombed with him in a mine after an enemy explosion on 22/23 June 1916, at Givenchy, and who was killed four days later; **Pte James Mackenzie** of the 2nd Bn Scots Guards for on 19 December 1914, at Rouges Bancs, rescuing a severely wounded man under very heavy fire and who was killed later that day attempting the same act; **Capt Thomas Tannatt Pryce** of the 4th Bn Grenadier Guards for on 11/12 April 1918, at Vieux Berquin leading an attack on the village, beating off 4 counter-attacks and driving off a fifth with a bayonet charge, who was last seen, with only 17 men and no ammunition, leading another bayonet charge. The Report for the memorial shows the continuing work of the Commission. Several entries have been amended as men whose names are inscribed on the memorial have been identified in cemeteries, e.g. **Serjt J. B. Coutts**, now in Tournai Cemetery, and **Pte T. Gordie** buried in Le Grand Beaumont British Cemetery

The memorial was originally planned to stand in Lille, but the French were becoming 'disquieted by the number and scale of the Memorials which the Commission proposed to erect'. When the number of Imperial Memorials in France was reduced from the planned twelve to four (Soissons, La Ferté, Neuve-Chapelle and the Somme) extra land was acquired from the Belgians here at Ploegsteert. The names of the missing destined to be inscribed on other cancelled memorials were inscribed on memorial walls built inside the land assigned to a cemetery, e.g. Vis-en-Artois and Pozières. The disappointed architects of the aborted memorials were given other assignments. Thus Charlton Bradshaw, who had won competitions for his designs for Lille and Cambrai (another memorial which was cancelled) was allotted Ploegsteert and Louverval. This explains why the memorial commemorates the Missing of the Battles of Armentières, 1914, Aubers Ridge, Loos

Ploegsteert Memorial.

and Fromelles, 1915, Estaires, 1916 and Hazebrouck, Scherpenberg and Outtersteene, 1918. It was inaugurated on 7 June 1931, by the Duke of Brabant, later to become King Leopold III.

In 1981 a ceremony was held at the memorial to celebrate the 50th anniversary of the inauguration. It was attended by Winston Churchill, grandson of Sir Winston Churchill. His illustrious grandfather had served with the Royal Scots Fusiliers in the Ploegsteert sector after the humiliating end to the imaginative concept of the Dardanelles campaign, from 26 January to 3 May 1916. A **plaque, showing Churchill** in his WW2 attire of Homburg hat and large cigar, can be seen on the wall of the Ploesteert Town Hall.

In the cemetery are 295 UK, 51 Australian, 3 Canadian and 45 New Zealand burials, among them Anthony Eden's **Platoon Sergeant, 'Reg' Park.**

Over the road is Hyde Park Corner CWGC Cemetery which was begun during Second Ypres by the 1st/4th Royal Berkshires, remained in use until November 1917 and contains the grave of **16-year-old Pte Albert Edward French,** the subject of a BBC Radio 4 documentary in 1983. He was killed on 15 June 1916, a week before his seventeenth birthday. Apparently the War Office refused the family a war pension as Albert had lied about his age on joining up and was under the offical enlistment age when he was killed. The local Member of Parliament took up the case and eventually Albert's father received 5 shillings a week. His brother George spoke the words that gave the title to the radio programme about Albert, *He shouldn't have been there, should he?*.

There is a café on either side of the road.

• *End of 1st, 2nd & 3rd Ypres Battlefield Tour*
OR Return to Ieper for RWC
OR Continue with 4th Ypres Battlefield Tour (page 249).

FOURTH YPRES: BATTLE OF THE LYS

7-29 APRIL 1918

'The enemy has exerted all his strength in men and guns in the battle now raging from the river Lys to Wytschaete and our troops have been fighting without respite to hold him on our main defensive positions... Once again our men are outnumbered – the same men who fought until they could hardly stand in the week that followed March 21.'

Philip Gibbs, *Open Warfare. The Way to Victory.*

'There was no nobler or more decisive stand than that of the BEF in front of Ypres in April 1918.'

Brigadier General S.L.A. Marshall, American historian.

SUMMARY OF THE BATTLE

Despite the extraordinary initial success of the Kaiser's Offensive, Ludendorff did not make the gains that he had desired and when the next – Lys – phase of his plan, 'Operation George', opened on 7 April, he had to reduce the troops involved and the frontage of his attack to such an extent that one of his staff officers suggested that the offensive be renamed 'Georgette'.

After three weeks of desperate fighting as the Germans drove towards the Flanders Hills, Ludendorff's supply line became too stretched and he was exposed on three sides. April 29 became the most bloody day of all for many tired German regiments who were swept back on all sides. Fourth Ypres ended in the Allies' favour.

OPENING MOVES

Following two days of concentrated gas attacks around Armentières, nine full-strength divisions drove directly at Neuve Chapelle where a solitary Portuguese Division in the process of being relieved was no match for the Germans and the town fell, hence their memorial and cemetery (qv) there.

By the evening of 9 April the Germans had reached the Lys (see **Map 16**, page 250) and the next day they drove north of Armentières, taking the Wijtschate and Messines Ridges and Ploegsteert village, despite determined resistance by the South African Brigade. The British 34th Division just escaped encirclement in Armentières and by the end of that day the Germans had driven a 10-mile salient into the British lines and were just 4 miles south of Ypres.

WHAT HAPPENED

Below Armentières the 51st Division was saved from near disaster by the 61st, another Territorial force, and frantic phone calls from London by the Prime Minister and others called for help from the French and the Americans. Both in London and at GHQ the view was forming that the Germans were on the edge of splitting the Allies and that Ypres could well fall. Haig wrote a 'Special Order of the Day' which ended, 'With our backs to the wall, and believing in the justice of our cause, each one of us must fight to the end.' It was meant to stiffen the resolve of his troops, but it unintentionally revealed the level of his concern about the situation. The message, which reached very few of the front line soldiers, is popularly connected with the near rout of Gough's 5th Army on the Somme but it was more likely prompted by the situation in Flanders.

On 12 April General Plumer assumed command of General Horne's 1st Army (responsible for Ypres) in addition to his own, the Third (responsible for the area south of the Lys) as the British attempted to co-ordinate their response to what was becoming a very confused struggle. Haig brought up the Australians from the Somme, his reserves dwindling. Formations and units fought for every inch of ground, often reduced to bullet and bayonet. Rear areas were prepared for defence and civilians and non-combatants were evacuated from Poperinghe. Ludendorff drove north-west, straight for Neuve Eglise en route for the Flanders Hills – Kemmel, Mont Noir, Mont Rouge and Mont des Cats – knowing that if he had them the British and Belgian positions between Ypres and the sea would become untenable and that the way to the Channel Ports would be open. The tired troops of 34th Division struggled backwards and the 2nd Worcesters held the Germans for a while in Neuve Eglise before the village fell.

But Ludendorff was confused too and, short of the hills, changed the direction of his attack towards Langemarck and then switched again this time towards Kemmel which fell on 25 April, the French who had taken over the hill just nine days earlier from the British, putting up little resistance. Meanwhile Plumer, in order to shorten his line, withdrew from the hard-won Passchendaele Ridge in the first phase of a movement that called for the evacuation of the Ypres Salient – Foch vetoed it.The protagonists were like two tiring boxers, ducking and weaving, looking for gaps in the other's defences, but Ludendorff was now at a disadvantage. His lines of supply were longer and his deep salient into the Allied lines left his troops open to fire on three flanks. Back at home dissatisfaction with the conduct of the war had spawned endless strikes, food riots and the beginnings of armed revolution. Ludendorff himself was worn out and had never recovered from the death of his youngest son, Erich, in March. Finally, on 29 April, once again a finger's touch from success, the German commander ended the campaign. Ypres and the Channel Ports had been saved.

THE BATTLEFIELD TOUR

[Inevitably the route goes through some sites of 1st, 2nd and 3rd Ypres as well.]

• **The Route:** The tour begins at Ploegsteert, visits Underhill Farm CWGC Cemetery; Neuve Eglise Churchyard and CWGC Plot; Dranoutre Churchyard and CWGC Plot; Locre No 10 CWGC Cemetery, Locre South Demarcation Stone, Hospice CWGC Cemetery & Redmond Memorial, Locre Churchyard and CWGC Plot; Mont Noir Mil Cemetery & 34th Div Memorial; Westoutre Churchyard & Churchyard Extension CWGC Plots, Brit Cemetery; Locre East Demarcation Stone; Kemmel Hill: French Ossuary, French Memorial, Belvedere; Kemmel Château Mil CWGC Cemetery; La Laiterie CWGC Cemetery; American Memorial; Suffolk CWGC Cemetery; Godezonne Farm CWGC Cemetery; French 32nd Div Memorial; Vierstraat Demarcation Stone; Kemmel No 1 & Klein Vierstraat Brit CWGC Cemeteries; Dickebusch Group of Cemeteries and Dikkebus Lake; Menin Gate. If possible travellers should return to the Menin Gate by 2000 hours (any and every day of the year) for the Last Post ceremony.

• **Total time:** 5 hours   20 minutes
• **Total distance:** 32.6 miles
• **Distance from Calais to start point:** See 1st, 2nd and 3rd Ypres Tour
• **Base town:** Ieper
• **Maps:** Major & Mrs Holt's Battle Map of the Ypres Salient plus best of all are *the Carte de Belgique* 1:25,000 Nos. 20/5-6, 28/1-2, 28/3-4, and 28/5-6. *The Carte de Belgique* No. 28 IEPER 1:50,000 is coloured and covers the whole area and shows the road changes, including the motorway up to 1979. IGN 2 Lille/Dunkerque 1:100,000 covers the area.

Set your mileometer to zero.
From the Ploegsteert Memorial drive in the direction of Ieper and take the first left signed Underhill Farm CWGC Cemetery. Continue to the cemetery on the right.

• *Underhill Farm CWGC Cemetery/.7 miles/10 minutes/Map 16/3*

Started in June 1917 during the Battle of Messines and used until 1918 when it fell into German hands in the spring (it was recovered in September 1918), this cemetery at the foot of Hill 63 (Rossignol, or Nightingale, Heights) contains 102 UK, 47 Australian, 1 Canadian, 39 New Zealand, 1 unknown burial and 5 special memorials. The cemetery was designed by G.H. Goldsmith. From the back of the cemetery Niewkerke (Neuve Eglise) Church spire can be seen.

The ruined Château de la Hutte on the heights was defended by the 19th Hussars and 1st Dorsets in 1914. In 1918, 25th Division held the position.

Continue along what was known as 'Red Lodge Road' to the T junction and turn right along 'Leinster Road' (Zuidlindestraat). After entering Nieuwkerke (Neuve Eglise), turn left at the T junction and continue to the car park by the church.

MAP 16: FOURTH YPRES (BATTLE OF THE LYS) 7-29 APRIL 1918

Legend

1. Hyde Park Corner CWGC Cem
2. Ploegsteert Mem & Berkshire CWGC Cem
3. Underhill Farm CWGC Cem
4. Neuve Eglise Churchyard CWGC Plot
5. Dranoutre Churchyard CWGC Plot
6. Locre No 10 CWGC Cem
7. Demarcation Stone Locre South
8. Locre Hospice CWGC Cem
9. Willie Redmond Mem
10. Locre Churchyard CWGC Plots
11. French 17/18th Cavalry, 4/12th Dragoons
    & 23rd Inf Regt Mems
12. Mont Noir CWGC Cem
13. 34th Div Mem
14. Westouter Churchyard & Extension
    CWGC Cems
15. Westouter Brit CWGC Cem
16. Demarcation Stone Locre East

17. French Nat Cem & Ossuary, Kemmel
18. French April 1918 Mem
19. Belvedere Kemmel
20. Kemmel Château CWGC Cem
21. Demarcation Stone Kemmel
22. La Laiterie CWGC Cem
23. American 27th & 30th Div Mem
24. Suffolk CWGC Cem
25. Godezonne Farm CWGC Cem
26. French 32nd Div Mem
27. Demarcation Stone Vierstraat
28. Kemmel No1 CWGC Cem
29. Klein Vierstraat CWGC Cem
30. Dickebusch Group Cems

© TVH 2004

• *Neuve Eglise Churchyard, CWGC Plot/3.6 miles/10 minutes/Map 16/4*

On the morning of 13 April 1918, the Germans pushed the tiring troops of 34th Division back towards Neuve Eglise broadly from the direction of Hyde Park Corner and in response to their pleas for help 100th Brigade sent forward their 'Battle Reserve', the 2nd Worcesters. By late afternoon the Worcesters were forced northwards up the N331 into the village, the CO, Colonel Stoney, losing contact with A, C and D Companies. He set up his HQ in the *Mairie* and with help from two rifle platoons of B Company barricaded the windows, made improvised loopholes and prepared the area for defence. (The *Mairie* has been rebuilt opposite the church. At the time of the action described, it was on the right hand side 200 yards up the Dranouter Road from the junction ahead.)

Belgian Veteran's Plaque, Neuve Eglise Churchyard.

At dawn the *Mairie* was surrounded and mortar shells were falling on it, causing many casualties. Machine guns were firing at it on three sides, from the church where you now are, from the crossroads to the south and from the open high ground to the west. Something drastic had to be done and 26-year-old **2nd Lt Anthony Johnson**, who in the previous two days had carried messages between the companies, volunteered to set out for help, but was killed, winning a bar to his MC for his bravery. He is buried in Kandahar Farm CWGC Cemetery.

The adjutant Captain J. J. Crowe asked for volunteers to go with him to silence one of the machine guns, which was successfully done, CQMS Trotman joining him. However, enemy reinforcements continued to enter the village and the ammunition at the *Mairie* was running out so, at about 1330, Colonel Stoney gave the order to withdraw. Under covering fire from Private F.R. Bough the whole force retired safely along the Dranouter Road. For this action Private Bough and CQMS Trotman were awarded the DCM, Lt Colonel Stoney the DSO and **Captain Crowe** the **VC.**

While this was going on, the other companies of the Worcesters were engaged in isolated actions with the enemy. Just beyond Neuve Eglise to the north east, about half a mile on the road past the church, Lt C.S. Jagger (qv) rallied the

Dranoutre Military CWGC Cemetery.

remnants of D Company and held up the German advance from the east. Gathering stragglers of other regiments he set up defensive positions in the buildings at La Trompe Cabaret (now called Trompe) and held on until relieved. As they were moving back, Jagger was badly wounded, but survived, both to receive the MC and to become a famous sculptor.

At the entrance to the churchyard is an impressive local War Memorial. The CWGC plot, with its Cross of Sacrifice, contains 69 UK, 5 Australian, 1 Canadian, 1 Indian, 1 New Zealand and 1 unknown burials from WW1 from 1914, 1915 and 1918 and a World War II plot of 11 UK, 3 Belgian and 1 French burials. The cemetery which had been used by fighting units and field ambulances at intervals during the war was captured by the Germans on 14 April 1918 and retaken by the 36th (Ulster) Division on 2 September and there is a row of 7 RIR burials from 2/3 September 1918 along the side.

Continue to the junction and turn right direction Dranouter on the N322. Turn left at the T junction and continue to the church.

• Dranoutre Churchyard Cemetery and CWGC Plot/6.2 miles/10 minutes/Map 16/5

This contains 19 UK burials and 2 unknowns who still lie in this small plot, 19 graves having been moved in 1923 to the nearby Military Cemetery. The churchyard was used for burial by the British from October 1914 until the Military Cemetery was opened in July 1915. In the far left corner is a memorial in the form of a Belgian soldier, erected by the Flemish Old Soldiers' Association with the Joe English 'AVV-VVK' (qv) insignia. Beside it is a World War II memorial in the shape of an aeroplane tail to **Capt Flyer B. de Hemptinne**, 5 May 1942. In the right-hand British plot (all burials from 1914) is the grave of **Norbert D'Hussar, age 9**, an innocent victim of the war. His headstone is non-standard. Just inside the hedge to the right is a long row of 1915 headstones in single file. At the front is the grave of **2nd Lt Geoffrey Staniland**, Lincolnshire Regt, 13 April 1915, age 31. Three months later the body of his brother, **Capt Meaburn Staniland**, 29 July 1915, was brought here for burial in the nearest space – the third from the end of the row. [The remarkable story of the Boston brothers is told in Martin Middlebrook's, *Captain Staniland's Journey*].

Continue round the church to the right and then turn left on Vierstraat following signs to Dranoutre Mil Cemetery.

• Dranoutre Military CWGC Cemetery/6.5 miles/15 minutes/Map 16/6

This is approached by a track that passes alongside the local timber yard where you should park and walk up the grass path to the left. The cemetery was in use from July 1915 until the German assault of March 1918. There are 421 UK, 17 Australian, 19 Canadian, 1 New Zealand, 3 unknown and 1 German burials. Many of those from April-June 1916 were of the 72nd Bde of 24th Division. The entire back row is from September 1918. Buried here is a member of the Australian YMCA, the **Rev Thomas George Trueman**, attd 5th Bn Australian Inf, killed on 22 March 1918, age 30, and **Pte Frederick Broadrick** of the Royal Warwickshires who deserted from his billets in Locre on 1 July 1914. He was arrested in Calais five days later and, as he was already serving a suspended death sentence for a previous desertion, was executed on 1 August at Dranoutre.

The cemetery, designed by Charles Holden, has a most pleasing lay-out. A newly planted beech hedge surrounds the area and one enters onto a generous lawn then ascends a few steps cut into a fine low grey dry stone wall to the graves area and Cross of Sacrifice. In mid-summer there is a joyous mixture of flowers.

Dranoutre was captured by the Germans under the Crown Prince of Bavaria on 25 April 1918. The depth of the German advance in this area during Fourth Ypres was formidable and can be readily seen by using a pencil to join the marker stones K13, L1, L5 and L13 on the Holts' Ypres Map.

Continue to the cemetery on the left.

• Locre No 10 CWGC Cemetery/6.9 miles/10 minutes/Map 16/6a

This was originally started by the French during the German offensive of April 1918. After the Armistice the French graves were removed (probably to the Kemmel Ossuary) and British and German dead were reburied here from the surrounding battlefield. There are 55 UK burials, mostly of the 2nd London Scottish and the 2nd S Lancs, and some 75 Germans lie under a number of headstones with multi-burials. There are 14 unknowns. There are many burials from 21-23 August 1918, among them, **Pte J. Pickup**, S Lancs, 21 August 1918, age 20, whose headstone bears the message, 'Some day we'll understand.'

Continue to the Demarcation Stone on the left.

• Locre South Demarcation Stone/7.2 miles/5 minutes/Map 16/7

Continue into Loker and turn right just before the Church and right again in about 100m. Continue to the sign to the right to Locre Hospice Cemetery and park. Walk up the grass path beside a new building.

• Locre Hospice CWGC Cemetery & Private Memorial to Major Redmond /8.1 miles/20 minutes/Map 16/8, 16/9

This was opened in June 1917 (during the Battle of Messines) and used until April 1918 when the Germans attacked. It lies near the Hospice, now also a school and a convent, and was the scene of fierce battles in 1918. The Germans took the area in April and the French counter-attacked on 20 May 1918. They failed to retake the position, which was only regained in July.

The cemetery contains 238 UK burials, amongst them 28 year old **Pte Denis Jetson Blakemore** of the 8th N Staffs, who was arrested in Boulogne 18 days after he deserted whilst already serving a suspended sentence for the same offence. He was shot on Mount Kemmel on 9 July 1917, and his grave bears the inscription, 'Thy will be done'. Also buried here is **Pte William Jones** of the 9th RWF, a stretcher bearer who absconded whilst taking a wounded man to a dressing station on 15 June 1917. Jones gave himself up to the assistant Provost-Marshal at Bristol on 4 September and was shot on Kemmel Hill on 25 October. He, too, was already under a suspended sentence for desertion. Who now can blame these men for reaching the end of their tether under unspeakably horrific conditions? Tragically their supposed 'crimes' were committed in an age when there was little understanding of the reasons why. Their sentences were imposed 'For the Sake of Example' and in his forthright book, *A Brass Hat in No Man's Land*, Brig-Gen F.P. Crozier wrote, 'I should be very sorry to command the finest army in the world on active service without the power behind me which the fear of execution brings.' There are also 2 Australian, 1 British West Indies, 1 Canadian, 1 New Zealand and 2 German burials with 12 unknown.

Beside the cemetery entrance a path leads to the **Private Memorial** grave of **Major William (known as 'Willie') Hoey Kearney Redmond** (now maintained by the CWGC). Redmond was the Irish Nationalist MP for Wexford, then for North Fermanagh and finally for East Clare. Born in 1861 he was a fervent Irish nationalist and was imprisoned as a nationalist 'suspect' in 1881. With his brother John, the MP for Waterford, who was Charles Parnell's successor as leader of the Nationalist Party 1890-1916, he went on a political mission to Australia and America in 1883. He joined the Royal Irish Rifles and was a well-loved officer. Wounded in the attack on Messines on 6 June, the 54 years old Redmond's injuries proved fatal. He was taken to the 36th (Ulster) Division Dressing Station at Dranouter where he subsequently died. His body was originally buried in the Nuns' garden, in a spot personally chosen by Colonel Rowland Feilding (qv) who had described him as 'a charming fellow'. On 20 October the Mayor of Wexford, accompanied by 'a red-hot Sinn Feiner', came from Dublin with special masses to visit the grave.

Private Memorial to Major Redmond with Locre Hospice CWGC Cemetery and Kemmel Hill behind.

Turn round and return to Loker Church. Turn right past the local War Memorial and stop.

• *Locre Churchyard French Memorials & CWGC Plot/7.7 miles/10 minutes/Map 16/11, 16/10*

On the churchyard wall are plaques to three French units who succeeded in repulsing the Germans from the village in April 1918: the **17th/18th Light Cav of 2nd Bde, the 4th/12th Dragoons and the 23rd Inf Regt**. In the churchyard are the two plots, one either side of the church, of **Locre Churchyard Cemetery**. Here are 184 UK burials, including the sad graves, side by side, of two young Privates of the 1st Royal Scots: **Andrew Evans and Joseph Byers** (the first Kitchener Volunteer to be executed and who was not represented at his trial). Both were shot at Locre on 16 February 1915, for 'attempting to desert'. In the next row lies 20-year-old **Pte George Collins** of the 1st Lincolns, shot on 15 February for desertion – also undefended at his trial. Here is also buried **2nd Lt C. Hawdon**, Yorkshire Regt, age 20, 27 June 1916, whose two brothers also fell in the war. There are 31 Canadian and 2 unknown burials.

Headstone of 2nd Lieutenant C. Hawdon whose two brothers 'also fell'. One was a Captain, RGA, and the other a Chaplain. Both died in November 1918.

Headstone of Pte J. Byers, first Kitchener Volunteer to be executed.

In the church on Sunday 17 December 1916, Col Rowland Feilding, commanding the 6th Connaught Rangers, arranged a special Church Parade and High Mass for his Irish troops. The men marched through the village with pipes and drums and three priests officiated. 'All was very impressive,' wrote Col Feilding to his wife, 'and, considering that they are only out of the trenches for a few days' rest, the smart and soldierly appearance of the men was very remarkable.' Rowland Feilding was the very best kind of Regimental officer. He had a genuine love of and respect for his men and commanded the same in return. In a typical gesture, Feilding got his wife to obtain miniature crucifixes, have them blessed by the Pope and brought back from Rome by a Cardinal. They were presented to the men (each of whom kissed the crucifix as he received it) at another splendid Church Parade on 22 April 1917. The Mass was conducted by Father O'Connell 'for Mrs. Feilding's intention'. 'I may admit that the devout reverence of these soldiers, redolent of the trenches, as they filed towards the altar, affected me, too, very deeply,' reported the Colonel.

Continue to the junction with the N372.
This is Canada Corner.

34th Division Memorial, Mont Noir.

Turn left on the N372, signed Zwarteberg and Rodeberg, and continue uphill over Rodeberg.

You are now driving through the most scenic and popular tourist area of Flanders, with many hotels, hostels and restaurants, including the Hotel Kosmos, popular with student groups.

Continue to the junction with the D223 just over the French border.

This is a bustling and busy area of souvenir shops, restaurants, snack bars and hotels.

Turn first left and continue to the sign to Mont Noir Mil Cemetery to the right. If it is not too wet and muddy the final track is negotiable by car, but there is no turning area at the end.

• *Mont Noir Military CWGC Cemetery/11.1 miles/10 minutes/ Map 16/12*

The cemetery was started in April 1918 during the First Battle of the Lys and used again in the Second Battle of September 1918. At the Armistice it contained 96 British and 33 French graves (all of the 26th Dragoons or the 88th Infantry Regiment). It was enlarged afterwards by the concentration of 57 more British graves (including some from November 1914) from the surrounding battlefields and more French graves (from March-May 1915 and April-May 1918), one Australian and two Newfoundlanders. There are 2 graves from WW2. The traditional CWGC Cross of Sacrifice is mirrored by a French Cross to the *Morts Pour La Patrie* 1914 1915 1916 1917 1918. The cemetery lies in a disused sandpit.

Turn round and return to the junction with the D318/N372. Turn left and continue uphill to the memorial on the right past the old Hotel du Mont Noir.

• *34th Division Memorial, Mont Noir /11.5 miles/5 minutes/Map 16/13*

Mont Noir was captured by the Cavalry Corps on 13 October 1914. In November 1914 3rd Division set up their HQ in Mont Noir Château and 'Billy' Congreve (qv), ADC to General Haldane, reported in his diary on 25 November 'We are going to keep the Château as our night headquarters and use the Scherpenberg Hill as a day headquarters'. It was held throughout the 1918 Battles of the Lys (Fourth Ypres) but there were anxious moments when it looked as if the Germans were going to break through. The advanced HQ of 34th Div came to Mont Noir on the afternoon of 12 April and on 15 April General Nicholson, the divisional commander who was having trouble maintaining contact with his brigades in the confusion of the battle, brought the brigade HQs together in a large dugout on the hill and co-ordinated his artillery support from there. On 21 April the fighting in the immediate area died down and the division was relieved by the French 133rd Division while 34th Division went back to Abeele. In the period 8-21 April 1918, the division lost almost 200 officers and over 4,700 soldiers. A New Army division, the 34th had as its first commander Major General E.C. Ingouville-Williams (Inky Bill) who was killed on 23 July 1916, and is buried in Warloy Baillon CWGC Cemetery on the Somme.

This handsome memorial of a victorious female figure, the Angel of Victory, is similar in style to the Division's memorial at La Boisselle on the Somme, but there the figure no longer holds her laurel wreath. On the base is the Division's black and white checkerboard insignia and the Division's ORBAT. The memorial commemorates the officers and men 'who fought near this spot October-November 1918 and is on the site of the Divisional Headquarters during the Battles of the Lys' when the Germans captured Kemmel Hill, little more than 5km ahead, just over the Belgian border.

It bears the legend, 'On the eastern slopes of this ridge the 34th British Division finally stopped the German advance from Armentières 9-21 April 1918.'

Behind the old hotel building, on private ground, is a bunker dating from 1938 with a Maginot Line style metal cupola.

Turn round and continue downhill, passing a well-preserved, ivy-covered bunker on the right.

N.B. Some 3 miles to the southwest lies the village of Meteren. In this village on 13 October the 1st Bn the Royal Warwickshires made an attack on the enemy. One platoon was led by its lieutenant with drawn sword, who ran it through 'a large German' and then took him prisoner. He was then shot through the chest and saved by one of his soldiers who ran to put a field dressing on the wound. The soldier was then shot in the head by a sniper, collapsing over his officer, and thereby saving him. The lieutenant was taken back to an ADS, where he looked in such bad shape that a grave was dug for him. He survived, however, to be transported back to base hospital and thence to the UK, returning to the front in early 1916 as a brigade-major. That 26-year-old lieutenant, who had joined the regiment in 1908, was none other than Bernard Law Montgomery, who led the British to victory at El Alamein in 1942, and was promoted to Field Marshal on 1 September 1944. There is little doubt that Monty's horror at the loss of life in World War I led to the cautiousness that was sometimes criticised by his American colleagues in World War II.

Cross the border into Belgium and take the first (sharp) left signed Westouter on the D398 and continue into the town.

Westouter. This was another behind-the-lines area where tired troops went to get some rest before being sent into the front line once more. The 3rd Division rested here for four days from 22 November 1914, exhausted from their participation in the First Battle of Ypres.

Continue to the church and park.

• *Westoutre Churchyard & Churchyard Extension CWGC Cemeteries/13.1 miles/5 minutes/Map 16/14*

The local churchyard and then the extension were used by the British from November 1914 until April 1918. The extension contains 64 UK, 1 Australian, 15 Canadian, 1 New Zealand and 3 German burials.

Continue, direction Poperinge. On the right is

• *Westoutre British CWGC Cemetery/13.3 miles/10 minutes/Map 16/15*

Thus was begun in October 1917 during the Third Battle of Ypres. It contains 166 UK, 4 Canadian, 3 New Zealand and 3 Chinese burials. There is one French WW2

Headstone of Maj E.S. Dougall, VC, MC, Westoutre British CWGC Cemetery.

burial. **Maj Eric Stuart Dougall VC, MC**, 'A' Bty 88th Bde RFA, 14 April 1918, age 32, is 'believed to be buried' here. Dougall won his VC on 10 April at Messines when he managed to maintain his line of gunners throughout the day, under intensive fire, thereby delaying the German advance. Among many moving inscriptions in this cemetery, Dougall's says, 'A man greatly beloved.'

Turn round and return to Westouter. Turn left after the church signed Ieper. Continue to the N375 and turn left signed Kemmel. Continue to the Demarcation Stone on the right.

• *Locre East Demarcation Stone/16.6 miles/5 minutes/Map 16/16*

Continue uphill, over the next crossroads signed Belvedere, to the cemetery on the right.

• *French National Ossuary, Kemmel/17.4 miles/10 minutes/Map 16/17/OP*

The cockerel (emblem of France) standing on an elongated pyramid marks the ossuary where 5,294 officers and soldiers lie buried, most of whom fell in the April 1918 battle of Mount Kemmel. Of these only fifty-seven have been identified. The bodies were concentrated here between 1920 and 1925. On the right of the pyramid are inscribed the French units which fought in Belgium and on the left the names of their commanders. Standing in front of the memorial and taking the cockerel as 12 o'clock, the wireless aerial of Mont des Cats can be seen at 11 o'clock on the horizon. To the right of it the abbey is visible in the dip between Mont Noir to the left and Mont Rouge to the right. Just inside the entrance is an Information Board giving the history of the French 4th Army in the battles of April-19 October 1918 with a plan of the 1918 Flanders Battles.

French National Ossuary, Kemmel.

Continue uphill on a cobbled road, evocative of '14-'18, to the memorial on the right.

• Memorial to French Soldiers 1918/17.5 miles/5 minutes/Map YP L4 and Map 16/18

This 60ft high column with its winged figure commemorates those who fell in the battles on the Flanders Hills during the German assault of April 1918. Until 1970, when it was struck by lightning, the column was capped with a French casque. It was unveiled by General Pétain in 1932. The French plaque on the Cloth Hall commemorates in general the French who fell in the Salient. This monument commemorates the units who fought in this sector and whose names are inscribed around the column.

Continue uphill.

To the right is signed the 3-star Hostellerie Kemmelberg with 16 bedrooms, gourmet restaurant and superb views from its terrace. Tel: + (0) 57 45 21 60. E-mail: info@kemmelberg.be

Continue to the tower and car park on the right.

• Kemmel Hill and Belvedere/18.0 miles/15 minutes/Map 16/19/RWC

The tower, which is a rebuilt and different version of the original which was destroyed during the war, is open from the end of April to the end of September and may be climbed for a small fee. On a clear day it provides superb views over the Salient to Ypres and beyond as well as south to Armentières. The pleasant restaurant has a bar and can offer snacks or full meals during the season. Tel: + (0) 57 44 54 13.

French Memorial, Kemmelberg.

Headstone of Lt R Lightburn, La Laiterie CWGC Cemetery, with moving personal message.

Entrance with Register Box, Kemmel Château Military Cemetery.

The hill was in Allied hands until Fourth Ypres. The French had taken it over on 17/18 April 1918, by which time the Germans had stormed through Armentières and pushed the front to a line running from Dranouter to Wijtschate. On 25 April, preceded by a savage artillery barrage of high explosives and gas that one French soldier described as 'worse than anything at Verdun', three and a half German divisions attacked the six French regiments holding the hill. By 0710, the Alpine Corps, leading the assault, reached the summit taking 800 prisoners. Before 0730 Kemmel village fell to the German 56th Division which took 1,600 prisoners. French infantry tumbled in confusion down the far side of the hill, their failure to hold the height adding to the distrust that was growing between the Allied politicians as to what each others' true defence priorities were – Paris or the Channel ports. German faith in victory and determination to carry on had reached their zenith and commanders and soldiers began to lose heart. Early in August there were rearward movements in the south and the Allies kept up a constant pressure so that, on the night of 29 August, withdrawal began along the whole front, the British 34th Division retaking Kemmel on 31 August.

Continue downhill.

As you turn right out of the car park there is an unreadable concrete and brick **memorial** on the bank to the right to a **French Regiment.**

Continue to the bottom of the hill, turn left downhill into Kemmel past the bandstand and turn left again on the N304 signed to Poperinge and then immediately right following signs to Kemmel Château Mil Cemetery on the right.

• *Kemmel Château Military CWGC Cemetery/18.9 miles/10 minutes/Map 16/20*

An early cemetery, begun in December 1914, it was used until the German offensive of March 1918 and again from September of that year when the village was retaken. It contains 1,030 UK, 24 Australian, 80 Canadian, 1 New Zealand, 21 unknown and 1 French WWII burials. Many men from the Sherwood Foresters and from Irish Regiments lie here. Also buried in the cemetery is **Lt Col Guy Louis Busson du Maurier, DSO**, of the 3rd Bn the Royal Fusiliers, killed on 9 March 1915, brother of the novelist Gerald du Maurier. A professional soldier, who had fought in the Boer War, (where, so sensitive a man was he that his hair had turned white when the man next to him had been killed) du Maurier went out to the front in January 1915. Guy was the uncle of George Llewelyn Davies (the original 'Peter Pan') also newly out.

Nothing of the Château, which was badly damaged in August 1918, now remains but Sir Edwin Lutyens' elegant design retains some of its grace and its grandeur is reflected in the two arches at the entrance.

Return to the N304 turn left and at the roundabout turn left on the N331. Continue to the cemetery on the left

• *La Laiterie CWGC Cemetery/20.2 miles/10 minutes/Map 16/22*

The cemetery contains 468 UK, 7 Australian, 197 Canadian, 1 Newfoundland and 78 unknown burials. It was used throughout the War and enlarged with concentrations after the Armistice. Against the right hand hedge is a row of April/May 1918 graves. **L/Cpl J.G. Munro**, KO Scottish Borderers, age 19, 25 April

1918, has the message, 'Gone to meet his mother.'

The cemetery, which got its name from a dairy farm that was located here, was designed by Sir Edwin Lutyens.

Continue to the memorial on the right.

• American 27th and 30th Divisions Monument/20.7 miles/5 minutes/Map 16/23

When the war began America was firmly neutral, but the activities of the belligerents at sea began to interfere with American maritime trade and when, on 4 February 1915, Germany declared that she would regard the waters around Great Britain and Ireland as part of the war zone in which even neutral vessels could be targeted, America protested. The stories of German atrocities in Belgium (many, if not all, the products of the Allied propaganda machine), their use of poison gas which was considered an 'evil' weapon, and patently false German propaganda being produced by the Washington embassy, contributed to an atmosphere in which America became sympathetic to the Allied cause. The event that more than any other prompted American entry into the war was the torpedoing of the liner *Lusitania* on 7 May 1915, with the loss of 1,100 lives, some American, although it was two years before war was declared – on 6 April 1917.

Urged on by the Allies, whose armies were hard pressed and anxious for fresh troops, the Americans created the 1st Division from existing formations and sent it to France, the first units landing at the end of July 1917 at St Nazaire. General Pershing established his HQ at Chaumont on the Marne and was soon visited by Clemenceau, the French Prime Minister, who as a schoolmaster had been in Richmond, Virginia, during the American Civil War when General US Grant marched into the city. Clemenceau wanted the Americans to be under the total command of the Allies. Pershing would have none of it. Nevertheless, to accustom the Americans to the 'new' European type of war, some were attached to different Allied formations. The divisions commemorated here, the 27th and 30th, arrived in Europe in May 1918 and served with the British until the Armistice, initially as small units and finally as divisions. In August 1918 the 27th Division took over the sector from, but excluding, Kemmel to here, the 30th Division from here to the area of Lankhof, the front lines being roughly parallel to this road and 700yd west of it (i.e. to the left of the road – the memorial area was behind the German lines). On 31 August 27th Division attacked towards where you are now standing and the following day the 30th followed suit. Both the villages up ahead, Vierstraat and Voormezele, were taken with advances of up to 2,000 yards. Some of the American casualties from the operations here are buried in the Flanders Field cemetery near Wareghem (qv). By the time that the two divisions were relieved three days later the 27th had suffered nearly 1,300 and the 30th some 800 casualties.

The memorial is a rectangular white block with a soldier's helmet in front resting on a wreath. The architect was George Howe of Philadelphia.

Taking your direction of travel as 12 o'clock, Mont Kemmel and its belvedere (which you have recently visited) are on the horizon at 7 o'clock.

Continue to the large Goudezeune Prefab building on the left and a group of CWGC signs on the right. Immediately turn left along Vierstraat. Continue to the next small crossroads and turn left. Continue to the cemetery on the left.

• Suffolk CWGC Cemetery/21.4 miles/10 minutes/Map 16/24

This tiny cemetery, approached up a grassy path, containing 47 UK and 8 unknown burials, was begun by the 3rd Suffolks in March 1917. There is a row of York & Lancs burials from April 1918.

Continue to the next cemetery on the left.

• Godezonne Farm CWGC Cemetery/21.7 miles/10 minutes/Map 16/25

In the back row of this tiny cemetery are graves from April/May 1918.

Continue to the junction ahead.

Just beyond is the **French 32nd Division Memorial (Map 16/26)**, commemorating the battles of Wytschaete 1914, Kemmel 1918 and the Canal de Charleroi to Dunkerque 1940. Its insignia is in the form of a bunch of grapes.

Turn round and return to Vierstraat and turn left, signed Dikkebus.

As you drive along here the Flanders Hills are clearly visible to the left.

Continue following signs to Dikkebus. On the left is

• Vierstraat Demarcation Stone/22.6 miles/Map 16/27

Immediately afterwards on the left is

Suffolk CWGC Cemetery.

The American Memorial, Vierstraat.

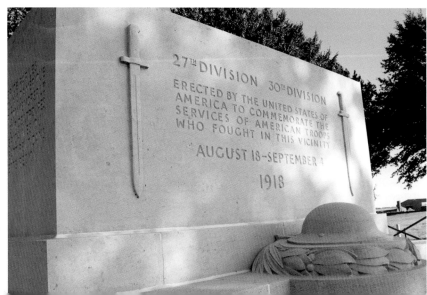

• Kemmel No 1 French CWGC Cemetery/22.7 miles/15 minutes/Map 16/28

Originally started by the French, who later removed their burials to the Ossuary at Kemmel or the French National Cemetery at St Charles de Potijze, the plot was taken over by the British. It contains 277 UK, 12 Australian, 3 Canadian, 3 New Zealand, appproximately 250 German in a mass grave and 1 unknown burial. It is approached by an imposing, but fairly steep, flight of stairs. Behind it is

• Klein Vierstraat British CWGC Cemetery/ Map 16/29

The cemetery contains 777 UK, 8 Australian, 1 British West Indies, 8 Canadian, 7 New Zealand, 1 South African, and 1 Chinese Labour Corps burials. It was begun in January 1917. All of this area was involved in the fierce fighting during the German April 1918 assault of Fourth Ypres.

Continue and at the next junction keep right up Kerkstraat towards the church. Stop by the cemetery on the right.

Monument to French 32nd Division, Vierstraat.

• The Dickebusch Group of CWGC Cemeteries/23.9 miles/20 minutes/Map 16/30

The cemeteries were designed by Sir Edwin Lutyens. In the summer of 2003 the inscriptions on the headstones in the group were very difficult to read.

• Dickebusch New Military Cemetery Extension

This was begun in May 1917 in succession to the other Dickebusch cemeteries and used until January 1918. It contains 520 UK, 24 Australian, 2 Canadian, 1 South African and 1 German burials.

The Last Post Buglers with the authors.

On the right is

• *Dickebusch New Military Cemetery*

The cemetery, begun in 1915 and used to May 1919, contains 528 UK, 11 Australian and 84 Canadian burials, including the poet and classic scholar **Lt R.W. Sterling** of the 1st Royal Scots Fusiliers. He was killed on 23 April 1915, after holding a trench all day with fifteen men in the Second Battle of Ypres in 'the storm and bitter glory of red war', to quote from one of his short poems, *Lines Written in the Trenches, 1915.*

Beside the church is

• *Dickebusch Old Military Cemetery*

A front-line cemetery from January to March 1915, it contains 41 UK, 2 Canadian and 1 German burials.

Continue to the T junction with the N375.

N.B. Some 2.5 miles down the N375 to the left is Klijte (La Clytte), where the future Prime Minister Anthony Eden served during the winter of 1916/17 as Adjutant of 21st Bn, KRRC. His older brother 'Jack' had been killed in the Salient in October 1914, his cousin 'Bill' (the Hon WAM) Eden, also of the KRRC, had been killed on 3 March 1915 and his younger brother, Nicholas, was killed as a 16 year old Midshipman when the *Indefatigable* went down in the Battle of Jutland. Anthony's sister Marjorie served on a hospital train in France. To complete this aristocratic family's contribution to the war, Eden's maternal Uncle, Robin Grey, a pilot with the RFC, was shot down, taken prisoner and suffered solitary confinement as he was a cousin of the Foreign Secretary, Sir Edward Grey. The family seat, Windlestone, in County Durham, was used as a war-time VAD hospital.

Turn right and after approx 0.8 miles right again following signs to Dikkebus Vijver/Etang (Lake). Stop in the restaurant car park.

• *Dikkebus Lake/25.2 miles/10 minutes/RWC*

The name Dickebusch means 'thick forest' and dates from the era when this area was dense woodland. On the right of the path leading from the car park to the lakeside restaurant, which has a bar and offers snacks, is an old Vauban watchtower and from it around the edge of the water are ramparts dating from 1678 which may be walked. The lake has been artificially enlarged and is a leisure resort for fishing and boating. The patio railings posts are shells and behind them over the water is Kemmelberg.

Neither the village nor the lake was ever taken by the Germans, although in the May 1918 fighting they reached the edge of the water. Rest camps of temporary huts and tent lines were set up here and T. E. Hulme (qv), serving with the 1st Bn, the HAC, was billeted here in March/April 1915. The Liverpool Scottish were also here and stayed through May. In 'the Black Hut' in Dickebusch their MO, Noel Chavasse (qv), held his sick parade and he sent home for sweet pea, nasturtium and other seeds to brighten up the huts area (Ann Clayton *Chavasse Double VC*).

Return to the main road and turn right following signs to Ypres.

After some 1.5miles the sign to Belgian Battery Corner Cemetery is passed on the left.

Continue to the Ieper Ring Road and turn left signed Andere Richtingen, then turn right signed Centrum and park in the Grand' Place. Walk up Meensesstraaat.

• *The Last Post Ceremony, Menin Gate/New Model for the Blind/ 32.6 miles/20 minutes/ Map 6/3*

This is where the echoes still remain, under the Menin Gate at 2000 hours every evening when the call of the Last Post rings out under the impressive arch. Just before 2000 hours two policemen arrive, stop the traffic and stand guard at each end of the gate. The buglers, just two in civilian clothes on most nights, or as many as six in uniform on special occasions, stand at the side of the road by the north-east pillar and, as the Cloth Hall clock strikes eight, they march together into the centre of the road, face the town and play the Last Post.

It is the very simplicity of the occasion that makes it poignant, the absence of martial organisation. Here are people gathered together in an orderly and respectful manner to remember, not because they have been told to do so but because they wish to do so. Now and again a particular regiment may bring a colour party to the occasion, a Legion branch or school cadet force may come, and so the ceremony may be extended by the laying of wreaths, the recitation of Binyon's words of Exhortation, the playing of the Reveille. There are, too, the growing number of conducted battlefield tours groups, but each bows to the Gate's tradition. This is not a ceremony extolling the glories of war. This is remembrance, acknowledgement of a debt by those that remain to those who sacrificed, together with the hope that knowledge of war's legacies might increase the chance of future peace. In our view it is not appropriate to applaud. When the ceremony is over, do thank the buglers. They are dedicated people from the local fire brigades and, often, Commonwealth War Graves gardeners. They take it in turns to play the nightly ceremony and they are proud and long-serving. Daniel Demey has been playing for well over thirty years and two others – Antoon Verschoot and Albert Verkouter – are not far behind. Marciel Verschoot is relatively new compared with them, but the youngest are the twins, Rik and Dirk Vandekerchkove – they are so alike that we joke they cannot tell each other apart. The ceremonies are co-ordinated by the Last Post Association whose dedicated Chairman is Mr Guy Gruwez and the idea for the ceremony was that of Pierre Vandenbroembussche, Commissioner of Police in 1927. From 1 May 1929 the Last Post was sounded every day until interrupted by the Second World War, when the ceremony was continued at Brookwood cemetery near Pirbright. Twenty-four hours after the liberation of Ypres in September 1944 by the Poles the ceremony recommenced. On 8 October 1960 the Last Post was played for the 10,000th time. On 12 July 1992, the 75th Anniversary year of the Battle of Passchendaele, the 65th anniversary of the Menin Gate was celebrated, once more by the presentation of new bugles.

Walk up the steps on the left hand side (facing the Cloth Hall). At the top is

Model of the Menin Gate

This 1.9m long, 1.05m wide bronze model stands on a socle of Portland Stone and has a Braille text in 4 languages. It was cast by Dirk de Groeve and funded by the local Kiwanis Club (who also sponsored the Cloth Hall model in the Grand' Place). It was unveiled on 20 September 2003 by the blind Belgian singer, Séverine Doré.

• *End of Fourth Ypres Battlefield Tour*

ALLIED AND GERMAN WARGRAVES & COMMEMORATIVE ASSOCIATIONS

THE AMERICAN BATTLE MONUMENTS COMMISSION (ABMC)

'Time will not dim the glory of their deeds.' Gen John J. Pershing

The Commission was established by Congress in March 1923 and has been responsible for commemorating members of the American Armed Forces where they have served overseas since 6 April 1917 (the date of the US entry into WW1). Its task was to erect suitable memorials and cemeteries. It now administers 24 permanent burials grounds (in which there are 30,921 WW1 burials, in 8 cemeteries, of a total of 116,516 killed in the war), 21 separate monuments and three 'markers', as well as 4 memorials in the USA.

Its first chairman was Gen John J. Pershing who served until his death in 1948. The current Chairman is Gen Frederick F. Woerner. After WW1 families were allowed to choose to have their loved ones repatriated (at Government expense) or to be buried near where they fell by the War Department for the Dead. In each of the 8 beautifully landscaped WW1 cemeteries at Brookwood, Surrey; Flanders Field, Waregem; Somme, Bony; Aisne-Marne, Belleau; Oise-Aisne, Fère-en-Tardenois; Meuse-Argonne, Romagne; St Mihiel; Thiaucourt and Suresnes, near Paris, there is a non-denominational chapel (although the atmosphere is predominantly Christian). The land for the cemeteries was given free of charge by the various host countries. The graves are surmounted by brilliant white marble crosses, interspersed by Stars of David for Jewish servicemen. There is no appropriate symbol for men and women of other denominations or for atheists and when the authors queried how a Star of David came to be placed on the grave of an Unknown in Flanders Field the Superintendent explained that the percentage of Jewish servicemen was known and the Unknowns were deemed to be Christian or Jewish in that same proportion. Unknown graves bear the legend, 'Here rests in honored glory an American soldier known but to God.' Identified graves bear the name, unit, date of death (but not of birth), and the home State. Headstones of Medal of Honour winners bear a gold star and the wording is picked out in gold. The pristine grave markers are laid out in perfectly symmetrical lines on immaculately manicured emerald green grass. There are no flower beds in front of the rows but the graves areas are surrounded by beautiful shrubs and trees. Each cemetery contains a luxuriously-appointed Visitor's Room with a Superintendent's office where information about the burials may be obtained and in which there is always a Visitor's Book, an example of the Purple Heart medal and photographs of the current President of the USA and of other American cemeteries.

The American flag flies proudly and is lowered when the cemetery closes (now a standard 1700 hours in each cemetery throughout the year, opening time 0900) when *Taps* (the American equivalent of the Last Post) is played. There are rest rooms and good parking. The overall impression is one of pride and glory, with gilded seals and mosaics much in evidence giving the feeling that no expense should be spared to honour the dead.

A progressive programme of installing carillons with pealing bells and a sequence of patriotic and wartime songs in ABMC Cemeteries is underway and is funded by the McCormick Tribune Foundation (www.rrmtf.org) who donate the necessary funding to AmVets National Service Foundation (www.amvets.org). The first carillon was installed in 1985 in the Manila Cemetery. Of the WW1 Cemeteries the Aisne-Oise, Meuse-Argonne, Oise-Aisne and Somme (Bony) already have their carillons.

As well as the cemeteries the AMBC maintains the impressive WW1 memorials at Audenarde, Kemmel, Bellicourt, Château-Thierry, Cantigny, Sommepy, Montfaucon, Montsec and Brest (Naval).

There are also some 700 Private American Memorials in Europe which are presently being located and listed, often by the Superintendents in the nearest ABMC Cemetery. Many of them are in a neglected state but local authorities are being encouraged to help maintain them and there is now a Private Memorials Administrator at Garche, Lillian A. Pfluke. Tel: + (0)1 47 01 32 50. E-mail: privatemonuments@abmc-er.org

In Flanders Field ABMC Cemetery.

Headstone of an Unknown
American Soldier.

Memorial Day programmes are held on different days near to the actual Memorial Day date at the end of May in each ABMC Cemetery. Then each grave is decorated with the flag of the United States and that of the host nation (who donated the ground for the cemetery). There are speakers, usually including the appropriate American Ambassador, and the laying of wreaths with ceremonies that include military bands and units.

The American dead of the Salient are buried in Flanders Field Cemetery at Waregem (off the A19 motorway, direction Kortrijk). It contains 368 burials, the majority being of the 37th and 91st Divisions, 21 of which are unknown. Here is buried **Lt Kenneth MacLeish**, USNR, 15 October 1915, brother of the American Pulitzer Prize-winnning poet, social critic and educator, Archibald MacLeish. Tel: + (0) 56 60 11 22.

Head Office: Courthouse Plaza II, Suite 500, 2300 Clarendon Boulevard, Arlington, VA22201, USA. Tel: + 703 696 6897. Fax: + 703 696 6666. Website: www.abmc.gov.

European Office: 68 rue du 19 janvier, 92380 Garches, France. Tel: + (0)1 47 01 19 76. Fax: +(0)1 47 41 19 79.

BELGIAN WAR GRAVES

There is no Belgian War Graves Commission as such, and the cemeteries are maintained either by the military or by the local commune. The nearest Belgian Military Cemetery to Ieper is in the Forest of Houthulst, (to the north of Poelkapelle on the N301) with 1,704 Belgian, 146 French and 81 Italian burials.

There is also a Belgian Military Cemetery at Westvleteren. From the road which passes the church in the direction of Poperinghe is a sign *Militaire Begraafplats* leading to the cemetery up a narrow road. This concentration cemetery contains 1,100 graves. Other Belgian Military Cemeteries are at Keiem, to the north of Diksmuide, with 628 burials, and Ramskapelle near Nieuwpoort, with 623 graves, 400 of which are unknown. There are two data bases for the Belgian 32,000 named and 10,000 missing dead of WW1 – one 'official' and one 'unofficial, not yet completed.

The Wereldoorlog I in de Westhoek website, www.westhoek.be, an initiative of the Province of West Flanders, gives details of cemeteries, memorials and other preserved sites in the Province.

Individual Belgian graves, with their distinctive yellow, black and

Headstone at Houthulst
Belgian Cemetery.

red enamelled flag roundel, are to be found in several CWGC and French cemeteries on the routes in this book.

Contact: Kabinet van de Chef v. Defensie, Kwartier Koningen Elisabeth, Blok 1, Everstraat 1, 1140 Brussel 1 Evere, Belgium. Tel: + (0) 27 01 61 05, Fax: + (0) 27 02 66 25.

CANADIAN VIRTUAL WAR MEMORIAL

This searchable database contains information about the more than 116,000 Canadians and Newfoundlanders who have lost their lives since 1884 in major conflicts. It is searchable by family name and gives, where available, service number, age, date of death, unit, force, rank and regiment, citations, honours and awards, burial information and any additional information known. It has been created with the support of Canada's Digital Collections, a programme of Industry Canada. Veterans Affairs Canada are also calling on Canadians to provide photos, documents and other memorabilia to help build up the Virtual War Memorial.

Contact: www.virtualmemorial.gc.ca

COMMONWEALTH WAR GRAVES COMMISSION (CWGC)

'Their name liveth for ever-more' *Ecclesiasticus 44.14*

[Many detailed and different aspects of the origins and work of the CWGC have been covered in other *Major & Mrs Holt's Battlefield Guidebooks.*]

The Commission was the brainchild of Major Fabian Arthur Goulstone Ware, the 45-year old volunteer leader of the Red Cross Mobile Unit that came out to Lille on 19 September 1914 to care for the wounded. Once out on the Western Front he more and more concerned himself with identifying the dead, registering the deaths and ensuring a standard, well-marked burial for them. By the end of October 1914 31,300 graves had already been registered and by March 1915 the army acknowledged the importance of Ware's work and he was given sole responsibility for registering graves. The next task was to negotiate with the French Government to protect the land in which soldiers had been buried. It was not an easy task as the French preferred the concept of mass graves or '*ossuaires*' as being more economical and also easier for relatives to locate than small, sometimes isolated, burial places.

In March 1916 a National Committee for the Care of Soldiers' Graves was established, with the Prince of Wales as President. On 21 May 1917 he became President of the Imperial War Graves Commission when it was established, with Fabian Ware as its Vice-Chairman. Its Charter, (extended on 8 June 1964 to include the dead of World War II), was to mark and maintain the graves of the members of the forces of the Commonwealth who died in the war, to build and maintain memorials to the dead whose graves are unknown and to keep records and registers. Each of the dead were to be commemorated individually by name, either on the headstone on the grave or by an inscription on a memorial: the memorial should be permanent: the headstones should be uniform: there should be no distinction made on account of military or civil rank, race or creed. Ware's egalitarian wish that the wealthy and/or high ranking would get equal treatment in their burial with the poor and/or low ranking was fulfilled. The terms of the Charter should be maintained 'in perpetuity', but as with the agreement with the French above, the question arises, 'How long is perpetuity?' There is no doubt that the answer today is 'As long as the Member Governments are prepared to fund the Commission's work'.

The seemingly indefatigable Ware, who was knighted in 1922 and became a titular Major-General, returned to the War Office as the Director of Graves Registration during World War II, while still fulfilling his duties as Vice-Chairman of the Commission, a post he held until his retirement in 1948. He died in 1949 in his eightieth year.

The saga of the post-war years is described in Philip Longworth's book *The Unending Vigil*, which has an Introduction by Edmund Blunden (qv) who became literary adviser to the Commission on the death of Rudyard Kipling (see below) in 1936.

Today, as the Commonwealth War Graves Commission, it looks after the 1,694,714 commemorations on graves or memorials from two world wars, and later conflicts such as the Falklands, in 147 countries. The cost of maintaining them and of administration runs at nearly £35,000,000. The current long-serving President is the Duke of Kent.

CWGC Cemeteries

The tall white Cross of Sacrifice with its inset bronze-coloured sword was designed by Sir Reginald Blomfield and is found in most cemeteries world-wide. Larger burial grounds also have a white sarcophagus-shaped 'Stone of Remembrance' designed by Sir Edwin Lutyens, whose inscription, 'Their Name Liveth for Ever More' was chosen from Ecclesiasticus by Rudyard Kipling, who was on the Commission's Committee and who became involved after his only son, John, went missing in the Battle of Loos in September 1915. The headstones marking the graves are a standard 2ft 8in high, normally of white Portland stone (although now stones are usually replaced with Italian, smooth Botticino limestone) and bear, where possible, the rank, name, regimental number, regimental crest, unit, age, date of death and religious emblem (e.g. Latin Cross, Jewish Star of David, blank for agnostic etc.) At the bottom is a space for an inscription to be chosen by the family (a facility never offered to New Zealand soldiers). Headstones for foreign and enemy soldiers buried in Commission cemeteries have slightly differently shaped tops – e.g. the tops of the German headstones are straight, instead of slightly curved as are the British and Commonwealth, and civilians – such as CWGC workers – have varyingly shaped headstones. The inscriptions on the headstones and on the memorials are in a standard, pleasingly open and legible style of lettering designed by MacDonald Gill.

Headstones marking unidentified bodies have the inscription, also chosen by Kipling: 'A Soldier of the Great War. Known Unto God'. On graves whose markers were later destroyed but whose rough location was known, he chose the epitaph, 'Their glory shall not be blotted out'. These are known as 'Kiplings'. Kipling was also responsible for the poetic name, 'Silent Cities' for the many war cemeteries he visited in his work for the Commission. The name may have been taken from the Urdu for cemeteries: Shahr-e-Khamosham. In most cemeteries there is a bronze box containing the Cemetery Report, complete with plan, a concise description of the origins of the burials and actions in the area and an alphabetical list with full personal details of all the burials – a mine of useful information for the researcher.

It also contains a Visitors' Book and a visit to a cemetery should always be commemorated by a signature in the book. The aim of the original designers, such as Sir Edwin Lutyens, Sir Reginald Blomfield and Sir Herbert Baker, was to create the impression of an English country garden (the original choice of plants and shrubs had been made by advisers from the Royal Botanical Gardens at Kew and Lutyens worked closely with the garden designer, Gertrude Jekyll) and today, despite severe cuts in personnel, the cemeteries are usually immaculate, and places of great beauty and peace. The gardeners are dedicated people, many of them being grandsons or great-grandsons of soldiers who came out with the Commission after the war. They can be a useful source of local information.

Memorials to the Missing

In 1918 Sir Frederick Kenyon, the Director of the British Museum and Chairman of the Committee advising on cemeteries and memorials, proposed that those men who were missing and had no known grave should be commemorated as near as possible to the spot where they had died.

However, there was an inherent difficulty in such a proposal. If it was not known where a man had died how could a memorial be placed near the spot? A counter-idea to the geographical commemoration was that members of regiments should be commemorated together in allocated cemeteries without reference to where they actually died.

Then there was the matter of 'National' memorials. At the end of 1919, at the suggestion of Winston Churchill, a 'National Battlefield Memorials Committee' was created to report on 'the forms of National War Memorials and the sites on which they should be erected, together with estimates of costs.' These abstract memorials were to be the responsibility of the Office of Works and quite separate to the work of the Imperial War Graves Commission that was concerned with the cemeteries and the memorials to the missing. The Cabinet was becoming apprehensive about

LE DIANORWIFON
RUSSIAN FORCES
11H NOVEMBER 1918

Russian Headstone, Mons General Cemetery.

the impending costs of the two commemorative authorities and it was agreed that a suitable compromise would be to combine the national memorials with memorials to the missing and to transfer the responsibility for them to the Commission. This would also solve the problem of trying to commemorate the missing on a geographical basis since it could now be done according to the dates of major actions.

New Zealand refused to agree to the idea and declined to be included when in 1921 it was decided that the memorial to the missing in Ypres (later to be known as the Menin Gate) should also be a national monument. The New Zealand forces had remained together throughout the war and complete lists were held of where they had fought and where casualties had fallen and so there was no problem in separating the known dead from the missing. Thus the New Zealand missing are commemorated on a number of memorials near the spot where they were lost according to the idea originally put forward by Kenyon in 1918. In a further departure from the general policy New Zealand also decided that the headstones of her soldiers would not carry personal inscriptions.

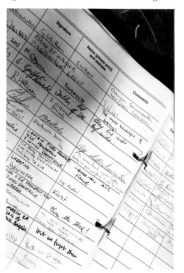

It is a rewarding and informative exercise to sit down with the Cemetery Report of one of the larger cemeteries and read through the entries from beginning to end. The words of the entry were chosen by the family and represent their attempt to perpetuate their lad. Often the full names, addresses (the name of a pub or village store, for example) and posts held by grieving parents or wives and children are given; sometimes there are academic, career or sporting achievements; the fact that a father or brother had also been killed in the war; the manner of death (e.g. 'died of wounds, gas'); previous service (in South Africa, on the *Lusitania*); occasionally an American is shown as having gone to Canada to enlist; a man has chosen to serve under another name ... A rounded picture of the diversity of the social classes that made up the British and Commonwealth Forces of 1914-18 emerges.

Visitors' Book, St Symphorien Cemetery, Mons with signature of Geoffrey Hoon, then Secretary of State for War, in January 2003.

CWGC SERVICES TO THE PUBLIC

The Commission holds records of 1.7 million Commonwealth War dead and its Enquiries Section can provide details of the place of burial or commemoration and where possible, directions to the cemetery or memorial. Enquiries are taken by letter, telephone or e-mail and, increasingly, searches can also be made using the online Debt of Honour Register at www.cwgc.org

The Commission's website is being continuously developed as a platform from which information on its history, publications, events, work in progress and other items of interest can be disseminated. Recent improvements to the database allow the public to access cemetery as well as casualty information, with plans and photographs of the larger sites.

A range of printed material is also available including guides to various cemeteries, memorials and campaigns, most of which can be downloaded from the website. Superbly produced Information Sheets cover subjects such as Fabian Ware; Sportsmen and Women; War Poets; Horticulture, Water, a Mobile Team etc. A new Michelin map book showing the location of WW1 cemeteries on the Western Front, and WW2 cemeteries, including those in Normandy, will be available in early 2004.

The beautifully landscaped Prowse Point Military CWGC Cemetery.

No charge is made for enquiries requesting information on one or two casualties but more detailed reports to specified criteria listing casualties from a regiment, ship, squadron or locality may be charged for according to size.

The Commission now has a higher profile about the magnificent work it achieves. For instance it had a stand at the Chelsea Flower Show in 2003 and its beautifully-produced Annual Report, with its superb coloured illustrations, is a mine of information about the never-ending maintenance work it continually undertakes. Now, over 85 years since the end of the Great War, masonry is beginning to crumble in a daunting number of cemeteries and a major programme of refurbishment is underway. Vandalism is another unfortunate headache and the 2002-2003 Report highlighted the horrific graffiti (as in the large cemetery at Etaples at the outbreak of the war in Iraq), broken headstones and defaced Crosses of Sacrifice, not only in cemeteries in France, Northern Ireland, Papua New Guinea but shamefully on the home mainland as well.

Head Office: Commonwealth War Graves Commission, 2 Marlow Road, Maidenhead, Berks SL6 7DX , UK. Tel: + (0) 1628 634221. Fax: + (0) 1628 771208.

Website: www.cwgc.org E-mail Casualty & Cemetery Enquiries: casualty.enq@cwgc.org. **Area Office in France**: rue Angèle Richard, 62217 Beaurains, Tel: + (0)3 21 21 77 00. Fax: (03) 21 21 77 10. E-mail: france.area@cwgc.org

Area Office Northern Europe: Elverdingsestraat 82, B-8900 Ieper, Belgium. Tel: + (0) 57 20 01 18. Fax: + (0) 57 21 80 14. E-mail: neaoffice@cwgc.org

MOD PS4(A) Non-War Graves Casualty/Compassionate Cell

Working closely with the CWGC, MOD PS4(A)Cas/Comp, operating from Upavon in Wiltshire is now responsible for identifying the newly discovered remains of British Army personnel from the two World Wars and other past conflicts when sufficient evidence is found with the remains.

If a soldier is identified (DNA testing is not used) the NWG Section then becomes involved not only in co-ordinating a military funeral in a CWGC cemetery near to where they are found, but also in trying to trace any surviving family of the soldier.

The most famous and well-documented recent find was at St-Laurent-Blangy near Arras when in January 2001 excavations began for a business site called Actiparc over the sector where in 1917 five different British units were facing the Germans during the April offensive. Then human remains were discovered, notably a trench containing twenty-three soldiers, with badges of the Lincolnshire Regiment (the Grimsby Chums). Poignantly their arms appeared to be linked together. The CWGC at Beaurains were informed and working with the Arras Archaeological Service and a forensic scientist from MOD PS4 stringent efforts were made to further identify the men. Unfortunately no identifications could be made and the soldiers were buried in nearby Point du Jour CWGC Cemetery in June 2002. (This cemetery still has space, as the French remains originally buried here in a significant plot were later removed.) A video for television was made of the incident called *Bodyhunt Search for the Unknown Soldier.*

Other well-publicised discoveries of remains have been to the north of Ieper in the excavations for the new industrial estate and exploratory archaeology for the continuation of the A19 motorway (qv). **Contact:** PS4(A) NWG, Tel: + (0) 1980 618824. Fax: + (0) 1980 615563. E-mail: cascomcoord@hotmail.com

FRENCH MINISTERE DES ANCIENS COMBATTANTS ET VICTIMES DE GUERRE

On 29 December 1915 a law was passed to guarantee a perpetual grave at State expense to every Frenchman or ally *'mort pour la France'*. On 25 November 1918 a National Commission of *Sépultures Militaires* was formed to create cemeteries with standard concrete markers (Christian crosses, shaped headstones for Muslims, rounded headstones for Jews and non-believers) on graves laid out in plots, ossuaries, monuments, enclosures and gateways. On 31 July 1930 the cemeteries were declared 'national' and the *Service des Restitutions de Corps'* was created. The *Tricolore* flies in every French cemetery. Many of the damaged wartime cemeteries were concentrated into larger graveyards. On 29 June 1919 each signatory to the Versailles Treaty agreed to respect and maintain the graves of foreign soldiers on their land. On 11 July 1931 generous finances were allocated to the cemeteries and memorials, permitting the rapid completion of important sites such as Notre-Dame de Lorette, Douaumont etc. After the defeat of 1940 the burial of victims of war was left to municipalities, to private individuals or to the enemy. Once WW2 was over new cemeteries were created, several inaugurated by Gen de Gaulle. Between 1983 and 1990 many of the cemeteries were planted with flower beds (in most case with pinky-red polyanthus roses) and in recent years a programme of erecting Information Boards describing the combats in the region at the cemetery entrances has been undertaken. The standard of maintenance varies, however, and it has to be said that some French cemeteries in their homeland provide a neglected contrast to nearby immaculate ABMC or CWGC cemeteries.

On French soil there rest 997,000 Germans, 450,000 British and Commonwealth, 56,000 Americans, 5,719 Italians, 3,450 Belgians, 21,836 Poles, 1,060 Portuguese, Rumanians, Russians, Serbians etc.
Head Office: 37 rue de Bellechasse, 75007 Paris 07 SP. Tel: + (0)1 48 76 11 35.

VOLKSBUND DEUTSCHE KREIGSGRÄBERFÜRSORGE (VDK)

The German War Graves Organisation provides a similar service to that of the ABMC and the CWGC in looking after the German war dead and in assisting relatives to find and, in many cases, visit the graves. In 1925 a treaty was signed between Germany and Belgium to organise care of the German dead from the Great War. Until then the German dead lay scattered in 678 burial places.

In Belgium many were exhumed and concentrated in cemeteries at Langemarck and Roeselare. In 1954 a new convention granted more land and the dead from the remaining 128 small cemeteries were transferred to Langemarck, Menin and Vladslo. Hooglede remained as it was. Langemarck (the only German cemetery which is actually in the Salient) contains 44,294 burials, 25,000 of which are in the communal grave surrounded by bronze panels bearing the names of the missing. Hooglede (on the Roeselare-Ostende road) contains 8,247 burials. Menin (on the Franco-Belgian border) contains 47,864 burials. Vladslo (on the Diksmuide-Beerst-Torhout road) contains 25,664 burials and the famous statuary group of Grieving Parents by Käthe Kollwitz. Further landscaping work was undertaken between 1970 and 1972, mainly by volunteer students during their vacations. Work in Langemarck was finally completed in the late 1980s.

The German cemeteries present a stark contrast to those of the ABMC or CWGC. The predominant colours are dark and sombre and a strong feeling of grief for the dead is present. The grave markers are not standard like those in American and British cemeteries and vary from stark black metal crosses, to grey or reddish stone crosses, sometimes laid flat as in Langemarck. They bear, when known, only the soldier's name, rank and dates of birth and death. Usually there are several burials beneath each marker, symbolising comradeship in death as well as in life and because less space was available to the vanquished nation. Most cemeteries contain mass graves for the unidentified with tablets listing the missing. Sometimes there is a small chapel, an entrance/reception chamber with a WC and a dramatic piece of mourning sculpture is often present. Also symbolic is the presence of oak trees, which signify strength but there are no flower beds in front of the rows of graves (although flowering shrubs are sometimes planted on the mass graves).

Similar programmes of progressive concentration and landscaping took place in the German cemeteries in France visited on the battlefield tours in this book. The German plots in St Symphorien Cemetery at Mons and the Le Cateau International Cemetery are particularly diverse and interesting, and also contain German monuments. The German Cemetery at Fournes-en-Weppes has been cruelly vandalised and has to be kept locked.
Contact: *Volksbund Deutsche Kriegsgräberfürsorge*, Werner Hilperstrasse 2, D-34117 Kassel, Germany.
French Office: rue de Nesle Prolongée, 80320 Chaulnes. Tel: + (0)3 22 85 27 57.

THE NATIONAL MEMORIAL ARBORETUM

This site which stands on 150 acres of land reclaimed from gravel workings at Alrewas near Lichfield was the brainchild of its director, David Childs, influenced by conversations with Gp Capt Leonard Cheshire, VC. It was envisaged as a tribute to the war-time generations of the twentieth century, a gift in their memory for future generations to reflect upon and enjoy and in order that the debt that was owed to those who died in the wars should not be forgotten. It was officially opened on 16 May 2001 by the Duchess of Kent.

Financially the project was supported by Redland (who donated the original land), the armed services and veterans' organisations, a grant from the National Forest and the Millenium Fund. Enough money was raised to build the Visitor Centre and the Millenium Chapel (the country's only one). The Chapel contains some beautiful wood carvings and at 1100 each day the Last Post is played inside it and a minute's silence observed.

Since March 1977 over 40,000 trees have now been planted and the site is divided into dedicated plots (plans can be obtained from the Visitor Centre), such as 'The Garden of the Innocents', a tribute to all the young lives lost in the wars; 'War Widows' Wood'; The Dunkirk and Normandy Veterans; 'The Beat', an avenue of chesnuts funded by the Police Force and many more regimental and non-military plots. The 'Shot at Dawn' section where stark stakes laid out in the form of a Greek amphitheatre surround the blindfolded statue by Andy DeComyn of Pte Herbert Burden, age 17 of the 1st Northumberland Fusiliers, executed at Ypres on 21 July, is particularly moving. There is a stake for every soldier executed in the First World War other than for the crime of murder. Stakes can be 'adopted' at a cost of £20.

Contact: National Memorial Arboretum, Croxall Road, Alrewas, Staffs, DE13 7AR. Tel: + (0) 1283 792333. Fax: + (0)1283 792034. E-mail: nmarboretum@btconnect.com
Website: www.nationalmemorialarboretum.co.uk
Open daily: 1000-1700 (or dusk if earlier). Closed Mon Nov-March. Admission fee payable. Group guided visits by appointment. Allow 90 minutes to cover the whole area. Parking, shop, pleasant restaurant and WCs.

Antiq'Air Flandre-Artois
Research on and erection of memorials to wartime pilots brought down in the area.
Contact: Jocelyn 'Joss' Leclercq, 51 Route de Fromelles, 59249 Aubers, France.
Tel: + (0)3 20 50 27 25. E-mail: JossLeclercq@aol.com

Association for Battlefield Archaeology in Flanders (ABAF)
A scientific Association of historians, archaeologists and technicians was founded in 1999 to research, survey, chart and preserve the pillboxes, bunkers and underground remains of WW1 in the Ypres Salient. Important finds include Beecham Dugout, Cryer Farm *Sanitätsunterstand* and work is now in progress in Bayernwald.
Contact: President Franky Bostyn, Sint Elooisweg 14, Voormezele 8902, Belgium. Tel: + (0) 51 77 04 41

Aubers *Cercle Historique*
Contact: M Pierre Descamps, 109 le Haut Pommereau, 59249 Aubers, France. Tel: + (0)3 20 50 26 56.

Association des Musées et Sites de la Grande Guerre
A grouping of museums and preserved sites of the Western Front from Ieper in the north, through Notre-Dame de la Lorette, Vimy, the Somme, Compiègne, Blérancourt, Chemin des Dames, the Champagne, Meuse-Argonne, Verdun, St Mihiel and into the Vosges in the south-east. The VDK, CWGC, AMBC and WFA are associates. The aim is to preserve and promote international sites of the '14-'18 War.
Contact: Secretary Jean-Pierre Thierry, O.A.M., c/o Historial, B.P. 63 – 8201 Péronne Cedex.
Tel: + (0)3 22 83 14 18. E-mail: df17@Historial.org

Diggers, The
A team of local amateur enthusiasts formed in the 1980s who came into prominence in 1992 with their find of a 1917 British dugout (the most intact ever found in the Salient) which came to light

German Plot, St Symphorien Cemetery, Mons.

during the digging of foundations for the industrial estate beside the Ieperlee Canal north of Ieper in the parish of Boezinge. Subsequent discoveries culminated in the now-preserved site of Yorkshire Trench (qv). A booklet called "The Diggers" is on sale locally and the proceeds go towards future projects.

Contact: Aurel Secu, Bloemendale 11, B-8904 Boezinge, Ieper, Belgium. Tel: + (0) 57 42 27 25. E-mail: aurel.sercu@pandora.be Website: www.diggers.be

Durand Group
Organisation for historical research into subterranean military features run by well-qualified military, ex-military and other professional members (surveyors, archaeologists, engineers etc.). They have done a great deal of work in the tunnels at Vimy Ridge.

Contact: Lt Col Mike Dolamore, 5 Wentworth Ave, Temple Herdewyke, Southam, Warks CV7 2VA. E-mail: mike@dolomore.demon.co.uk

Friends of In Flanders Fields Museum
This organisation was formalised by the election of a Committee on 23 October 2001. The Hon President is Governor Paul Breyne, the Vice-Chairman is Freddy Rottey and Johan Lottegier of Langemarck is the secretary. Benefits include free entrance to the museum, organised trips to places of military interest. There is also a Museum magazine.
Contact for information about subscriptions: Tel + (0) 57 22 85 82.

Friends of St George's Church
From 1933 the Old Comrades of the Queen's Own Royal West Kent Regiment were encouraged by ex-CQMS Len Dawson to support the upkeep of the Church and to make an annual pilgrimage to it which continued until 1939. In 1945 the Royal British Legion restored the slight damage that St George's Memorial Church had suffered during World War II, but it was soon apparent that on-going funds would be needed to provide for the maintenance of the church. In 1955 the Association of the Friends of St George's Memorial Church was formed under Les Dawson, Col Donald Dean, VC and Maj-Gen Raymond Biggs, CB, DSO. Its objects were to promote interest in the life and work of the church, to provide a link between members in the UK and overseas and the local community, to co-operate with bodies such as the RBL and the CWGC for the benefit of the church and to provide funds to help maintain the fabric of the church and its life.
Contact the Hon Sec: Mr K.A.E. Sears, 41 Winstanley Road, Sheerness, Kent ME12 2PW.

Fromelles *Association Souvenir de la Bataille de Fromelles*
Contact: M. Francis Delattre, 42 rue Lammeries, 59249 Fromelles, France. Tel: + (0)3 20 50 64 26.

Guild of Battlefield Guides

Launched on 28 November 2003 the Guild aims to provide a 'kite-mark' for Battlefield Guides in the form of a badge which the public can trust and which it will be deemed an honour to wear. **Mission Statement**: *"To analyse, develop and raise the understanding and practice of battlefield guiding."* To gain the Badge prospective applicants are 'validated' by other qualified and experienced Guild Validators. Applicants are required to prepare nine pieces of work including giving a presentation on a battle or action of their choice, produce progressive maps of a battle, design a battlefield tour route, solve practical problems, identify 'difficult' situations etc to demonstrate their battlefield knowledge, presentational skills and duty of care. The Guild is an inclusive organisation, not a regulatory body. Future plans aim to engender a 'Club' environment with a magazine and educational and social meetings. Patron: Prof Richard Holmes. The authors are Hon Members. **Contact:** Guild Secretary (and Founder), Major Graeme Cooper, Coopers Court, Moreton, Ongar, Essex, CM5 OLE, UK. Tel: + (0) 1277 890214.
E-mail: secretary@battleguides.org Website: www.battleguides.org

In Flanders Fields Documentation Centre

This incorporate the Rose Coombs and Dr Caenepeel (founder of the Salient Museum) libraries, contains much fascinating information, documents, records, photographs, trench maps about the Great War in the Salient. It is in the Stedelijke Musea, opposite St Martin's Cathedral, at 9 Janseniusstraat.
Contact: Dominiek Dendooven. **Open** Wednesdays from 0800-1200 and 1300-1700 or by appointment. Tel: + (0) 57 23 94 50. Fax: + (0) 57 23 94 59. E-mail: Stedelijk.Musea@ieper.be

Royal British Legion (RBL)

The UK's foremost Association for the welfare of ex-servicemen, formed in 1921 through the energetic efforts of Earl Haig, received its Charter in 1925 and its 'Royal' prefix in 1971. Amongst its functions is the organisation of pilgrimages to battlefields.
Contact: Piers Storie-Pugh, Pilgrimage Dept., Aylesford, Kent ME20 7NX, UK.
Tel: + (0) 1622 716729. E-mail: remembrancetravel@britishlegion.org.uk
National HQ, 48 Pall Mall, London W1Y 5JY
Ypres Branch: Chairman David Beattie, Tel/Fax: + (0) 57 44 53 06.

Ross Bastiaan Commemorative Plaques

A series of beautifully designed, durable and informative plaques erected by Australian dentist, Ross Bastiaan, on sites where Australian Forces were engaged with distinction.
Contact: Website: www.plaques.satlink.com.au

Souvenir Français

An Association founded in 1872 after the Franco-Prussian War and revived after WW1. Its aim is to keep alive the memory of those who died for France, to maintain their graves and memorials in good condition and to transmit 'the flame of memory' to future generations.
Head Office: 9 rue de Clichy, 75009 Paris.

Victoria Cross Society

The Society, which aims 'to educated, enlighten, stimulate and further interest and knowledge in the history and personalities associated with the Victoria Cross', has an excellent Journal.
Contact: Brian Best, Secretary and Editor, Kintons, Harlequin Place, Crowborough, E. Sussex TN6 1HZ.
Tel: 01892 664234. E-mail: secretary@victoriacrosssociety.com Website: www.victoriacrosssociety.com

Western Front Association (WFA)

Formed by John Giles in 1980 to further the interest in WW1 to perpetuate the memory, courage and comradeship of all who fought in it. Two excellent publications: *Stand To* and *The Bulletin*.
Contact: Hon Sec Stephen Oram, Spindleberry, Marlow Road, Bourne End, Bucks SL8 5NL
Website: www.westernfrontassociation.com

TOURIST INFORMATION

It is the ironic fate of a guide book that some information given in it will inevitably become out of date as soon as it is published. For instance, and perhaps somewhat surprisingly after some 90 years since the Armistice of 11 November 1918, new memorials are still being erected on the battlefields. Established ones are often dramatically altered by new landscaping by the Commonwealth War Graves Commission or to make way for new motorways or high-speed trains which have completely altered navigation across the battlefields of Belgium and France over the past quarter century.

Print a direction using road numbers and the authorities may decide to alter the system of numbering or send the pilgrim on interminable diversions *(déviations)*, which often abandon the driver part way along. Recommend a restaurant and the brilliant chef may have departed in a huff. Advise on a hotel and the *patron* may have done a moonlight flit. Give opening hours for tourist offices and they may well have invented new, rare 'off season' times.

The information and advice we will, therefore, give here will mostly be of a general, rather than a particular, nature – with the exception of a few favourite haunts we cannot resist mentioning which are conveniently sited close to the battlefield and are sometimes mentioned in the actual itineraries rather than in the section below. But please do not blame us if you should be faced with the dreaded 'Under New Management' sign.

The very best advice if you are well organised is to go carefully through the itineraries that you intend to follow in this book, then **contact the appropriate national tourist offices in London or New York well before you leave.** Give them, if possible, at least one month, list all the major towns you intend to visit, and request the following information, with relevant brochures (tourist literature is now of a generally high and helpful standard):

1. Addresses and phone numbers of local tourist offices with likely opening times. In smaller towns or villages these can be erratic, and we have found that whatever the information you may be given about them, the optimum time for getting in is 1000-1200 and 1400-1600 during the summer time. The most reliable and helpful offices in the battlefields areas are listed below.
2. Listings of local hotels, bed-and-breakfast homes, self-catering lets, restaurants, museums, camping sites, etc, also maps and town plans. Staff are often discouraged from giving personal recommendations, but you can smile and try.
3. Specific information about battlefield routes: in both France and Belgium there are well-marked *circuits*, signed *Route '14-18'*, or *Circuit de Souvenir*, etc., often with useful accompanying literature.
4. General tourist information/local attractions/cultural events/festivals, etc. The serious student of the battles may well wish to avoid the latter – the area will be congested, local hostelries full.

BELGIUM

Note: When phoning Belgium add the following prefix: ex-UK and USA 00 32, indicated by '+' in the phone numbers listed.

FLANDERS TOURIST OFFICES

UK Tourism Flanders-Brussels, 31 Pepper Street, London E14 9RW. Tel: 0800 954 5245. Fax: 020 7458 0045. E-mail: info@visitflanders.co.uk
USA 745 5th Avenue, New York, NY 10151 Tel: 00 1 75881 30
They produce some attractive and helpful booklets – but not one composite one like the French – with details of how to get to Belgium, on local museums and attractions – and hotels (a new list every year). **Beware** – the French and Belgian versions of place-names are very different. You can be driving through France heading for Lille and when you cross the border into Belgium it disappears from the signposts to be replaced with Rijsel. Other traps are: Ypres-Ieper; Anvers-Antwerpen; Courtai-Kortrijk; Tournai-Doornik; Warneton-Waasten. Flemish is generally spoken in the main tourist areas of Flanders today, but English is widely understood and spoken.

LOCAL TOURIST/INFORMATION OFFICES

Ypres. **The Ieper/Westhoek Tourist Office** is handily situated in the Cloth Hall (Stadhuis), Grand Place, B-8900 Ieper. Tel: + (0) 57 22 85 84. Fax: + (0) 57 22 85 89. E-mail: toerisme@ieper.be The staff are very helpful; and they produce their own booklet of tourist information in English, which is very comprehensive. They also sell guidebooks, maps and souvenirs in an attractive and well-stocked boutique. There is a separate leaflet for hotels and restaurants. It is difficult to have a bad meal in the cafés and restaurants around the Grand' Place, but if you choose an environment with starched tablecloths, gleaming cutlery and glass, it can take a long time.

Around the square are to be found the following: the three-star Regina Hotel, reopened under new ownership on 11 November 2002 with 17 refurbished bedrooms, and two restaurants (one of which is 'gourmet'). Tel: + (0) 57 21 88 88, Fax: + (0) 57 21 90 20. E-mail: info@hotelregina.be Nearest to the Cloth Hall is the **In't Klein Stadhuis**, Tel: + (0) 57 21 56 86 and next is **The Anker** restaurant where a fine meal can be had, Tel: + (0) 57 20 12 72, but allow plenty of time. **The Trompet** (which serves a superb mixed salad and chips), Tel: + (0) 57 20 02 42, is very convenient and popular, especially for lunch. The **Kolleblume** (Cauliflower) Tel: + (0) 57 21 90 90, and the **Café Central**, Tel: + (0) 57 20 17 60, are reasonably priced and serve snacks as well as full meals. The **Vivaldi** tearoom/restaurant has undergone a major enlargement but still provides the same mix of snacks and full meals, Tel: + (0) 57 21 75 21. **The Old Tom** (one-star, Tel + (0) 57 20 15 41) and the refurbished **Sultan** (three-star, Tel + (0) 57 20 01 93) are restaurants that also have some hotel beds.

The superb **Hostellerie St Nicolas** restaurant that used to be in Boterstraat has now moved to 532 Veurnseweg, Elverdinge, Tel: + (0) 57 20 06 22.

Local specialities are on offer in most of these restaurants. There are several hundred varieties of beer to choose from to wash them down, from thick dark brown almost treacley black concoctions like that brewed by the Trappist monks to light (*blonde*) lagers or even raspberry flavoured! A few hundred grammes of the renowned Belgian hand-made chocolates – on sale in half a dozen or so outlets in the square – make a perfect end to a calorific spree. You must not leave Belgium without sampling some of their legendary *frites* – quite irresistible with mayonnaise. Mussels are very popular – especially for family treats at lunchtime on Sunday. Pepper steak is also a favourite and the pancakes are yummy, as are leek flans and chicken stew. In fact Belgian cuisine is very good indeed.

If really pressed for time, buy a carton of those crisp *frites* and a sausage from one of the *frituur* windows and eat them on the hoof. If you want the maximum time on the battlefields, then there is a choice of shops/supermarkets around the square, along Coomansstraat or Meninstraat to buy the makings of a picnic. Along Coomansstraat/A Vandenpeereboomplein is the **'t Ganzeke** (Goose) restaurant with a varied menu. Worth a visit to see the superb posters of Ypres from post-World War I to the 1950s. Tel: + (0) 57 20 00 09. Further along, if you want a change, is the large, elegant Chinese Restaurant, **Shanghai City**, where the food is excellent – and copious! Tel: + (0) 57 20 06 52.

*Continue past the Theatre (by which there is a **Mié Tabé Peace Post**) on your right opposite St George's Church to the right-hand corner of the square and continue along the small Boezingestraat and Veemarkt.*

Ahead is the four-star, **Hotel Ariane**, Tel: + (0) 57 21 82 18. Fax: + (0) 57 21 87 99. E-mail: info@ariane.be. It is within an easy stroll of the Menin Gate and the Grote Markt and the best hotel in Ypres for battlefield tourers. It has a smart new wing opened in 2002 with spacious rooms, a superb restaurant, an attractive foyer with WW1 exhibits and book stall, bar, sauna and jacuzzi and a warm welcome by owners Natasja and chef Johann. There is a large car park.

The **Novotel** group has opened a smart, 122 bedroom modern three-star hotel in Sint-Jacobsstraat just off the Grote Markt and near the Menin Gate. It has underground parking, fitness room and sauna. Tel: + (0) 57 42 96 00. Fax: + (0) 57 42 96 01. E-mail: H3172@accor-hotels.com Opposite the Novotel is **The Old Bill Pub** whose pub sign, a Bairnsfather cartoon, originally hung outside the Regina Hotel in whose cellar a pub and private club was opened on 8 March 1969. The distinguished historian Dr Caenepeel made a speech about Bruce Bairnsfather and his links with the Salient on the occasion.

Agriculture thrives again in the fields around Ieper and there is a growing industrial estate in the northern suburbs (see the 'Diggers' entry). This is served by a modern hotel, the three/four-star **Best Western Flanders Lodge** (formerly the Rabbit), Tel: + (0) 57 21 70 00. Fax: + (0) 57 21 94 74. E-mail: bw-ieper@skynet.be. It is built in wood like a Swiss Chalet, with thirty-nine rooms with en-suite bathrooms, jacuzzi, restaurant and attractive bar, which is also used by visitors to the battlefields. It has been completely remodelled.

The Bairnsfather cartoon on the Old Bill Pub sign.

The ideal lunch in Belgium, plus, of course, the famous chips!

In Poelkapelle, some 7 miles from Ieper, is **Varlet Farm** (the original farm was named by the British and taken by the Hood Bn of the RND in October 1917), rebuilt in 1920. This B & B is popular with Battlefield tourists who are warmly welcomed by owners Dirk and Charlotte Cardoen-Descamps, Wallemolenstraat 43, 8920 Poelkapelle. Tel/Fax: + (0) 51 77 78 59. E-mail: info@varletfarm.com

The Shell Hole
One of the best selections of World War I books, magazines, maps, ephemera and collectables available can be found at The Shell Hole run by Falklands Para veteran John Woolsgrove at 54-56 d'Hondstraat, Ieper, Tel + (0) 57 20 87 58. The completely refurbished building has a cosy bar and restaurant and nine modestly priced bedrooms with en-suite bathrooms. It is very popular with British visitors and makes an ideal base for touring the Salient. Hondstraat leads off the Grote Markt, from mid-way along the side opposite the Cloth Hall.

The British Grenadier
Another well-stocked book and map shop with a battlefield resource centre and computer facilities for looking up burials. 5 Meensestraat, Ieper. Tel/Fax: + (0) 57 21 46 57.

'T Klein Rijsel
This is a welcoming pub for all battlefield tourists – they even stock 'Peace Beer' served in special peace pots. Behind it is the excellent **Ramparts War Museum** with life-like scenes of trench life and original artefacts.. By the Lille Gate.
Open 1030-2200 (closed Wed). Tel: + (0) 57 20 02 36.

Battlefield Tours
Battlefield tourism is a vital part of the economy of West Flanders – with visits by the British still among the most important – and the Westhoek, which covers the three 'Front Towns' of Ieper, Diksmuide and Nieuwpoort, produce a booklet entitled *The Great War in Flanders* describing the most obvious WW1 sites, website www.westhoek.be/toerisme. They also produce booklets covering two battlefield routes – *The Ijzerfronte* (around Diksmuide) and *In Flanders Fields Route* (around Ieper). They are available for a small fee from the appropriate tourist offices.
Guided Battlefield Tours
In addition to the tours by qualified guides offered by the Ieper Tourist Office there are two locally based commercial organisations which run regular English-speaking tours in comfortable mini-buses: **Flanders Battlefield Tours** (which is based in the Ariane Hotel). Tel: + (0) 57 36 04 60. Fax: + (0) 57 36 06 60. E-mail: info@ypres-fbt.be
Salient Tours. Tel: 0475 910223. UK head office 01994 484717. E-mail: info@salienttours.com.

Once more the Grote Markt has become the scene of a bustling market each Saturday morning and in 1994 it received a major facelift when it was repaved and trees were planted, thus restoring it more to its pre-1914 aspect, so superbly documented in the photographs of 'Anthony of Ypres'. Some extremely 'modern' fountains were constructed at the same time which contrast strongly with the otherwise medieval appearance of the square. Nearby in May 1995 the Kiwanis erected a small bronze model of the Cloth Hall with raised features so that blind people can experience its shape.

There is also a series of interesting events to attract the visitor throughout the year. The Flemish have a capacity for enjoyment of their festivals and fairs which belies their somewhat dour image and these events are fun to attend. The medieval custom of throwing live cats from the Cloth Hall Belfry (the symbolic killing of evil spirits as personified by the cat) has been revived – with toy cats – in the Festival of the Cats, a colourful and popular carnival which takes place on the second

Sunday in May every third year (next in 2006). Other regular events are the 100 Kilometres Ieper March on the weekend after Ascension, the 24 Hours Ieper Automobile Rally on the last weekend in June, the Thuyndag Fair, on the first Saturday and Sunday of August, the four days of the Ijzer March in mid-August, the Tooghedagen Craft and Antiques Fair on the second weekend in September and The Procession of St Martin on 10 November. Armistice Day is always celebrated on 11 November, whatever day of the week it falls on (not the nearest Sunday as happens now in Britain) and it is a public holiday. On that day there is a Belgian Memorial Service in St Martin's Cathedral and an English one in St George's Church, a 'Poppy Parade' and special ceremony at the Menin Gate. Hundreds of pilgrims come from the UK for this event and it is as well to apply early for tickets in the church – usually there is a 'spillover' service in the Cloth Hall with TV relay. This commemorates the sacrifice of all those who fought and, in particular, those who gave their lives, many willing and proud volunteers, in the Great War in Flanders.

Diksmuide. Tourist Office, 28 Market Square, Diksmuide. Tel: + (0) 51 51 91 46.
Market day is on Monday, Cheese and Butter Fair on Whit Monday, Ijzer Tower Pilgrimage last Sunday in August, Flemish Day of Peace 11 November.
Accommodation etc:
Pax, brand new 4-star, 2 Heilig Hartplein. Tel: + (0) 51 50 00 34.
De Vrede, 3-star, convenient situation in Grote Markt, traditional restaurant. Tel: +(0) 51 50 00 38.
Several restaurants round the attractive Market Square.

Koksijde. Tourist Office, 24 Zeelaan, 8670 Koksijde. Tel: + (0) 58 53 30 55. Fax: + (0) 58 52 25 77, e-mail: toerisme@koksijde.be.
End June Shrimp Festival. Flower Parade 4 August.
Accommodation: A range of 3-star to modest 1-star and B & Bs. List from Tourist Office.

Nieuwpoort. Tourist Office, 7 Marktplein, 8620 Nieuwpoort. Tel: + (0) 58 22 44 44. Fax: + (0) 58 22 44 28, e-mail: nieuwpoort@toerismevlaanderen.be
End March-beginning April The Fourteen French-Flemish Days. 20 May Blessing of the Fishing Fleet. On 4 August is the Day of Honouring King Albert I and the Heroes of the Yser.
Accommodation: A range of 3-star to B & Bs. List from the Tourist Office.

Poperinghe. Tourist Office, Stadhuis, B-8970 Poperinghe. Tel: + (0) 57 33 40 81, Fax: + (0) 57 33 75 81, e-mail: poperinge@tourismevlaanderen.be
The annual Hop Festival is in September, and there is a signed, 54km 'Hop Route' around the area. Market day is on Friday (as it has been since the Count of Flanders granted permission for a market in 1187). They produce a leaflet called *Poperinge in the First World War* as well as the *POP.Route* booklet (for which there is a fee).
Accommodation etc:
Talbot House (qv), 43 Gasthuisstraat. Self-catering, clean and simple accommodation in this marvellously evocative setting. Tel: + (0) 57 33 32 28.
Hotel *Amphora*, 3-star, attractive décor, Market Square. Tel: + (0) 57 33 88 66.
Hotel *Belfort*, 3-star, good restaurant, Market Square. Tel: + (0) 57 33 88 88.
Hotel *Palace*, 3-star, good restaurant, 34 Ieperstraat. Tel: + (0) 57 33 30 93.
Hotel *Recour,* Luxe, gourmet restaurant Pegasus, 7 Guido Gezellestraat. Tel: + (0) 57 33 57 25.
There are several good restaurants and cafés around the main square wich are convenient for a lunch break, including the old WW1 favourite the De Ranke.

Zonnebeke. Tourist Office, Zonnebeke, Ieperstraat 5, 8980 Zonnebeke. Tel + (0) 51 77 04 41, Fax: + (0) 51 78 07 50, e-mail: cultuur.zonnebeke@belgacom.net. A new attraction is the Old Cheese Factory. This go-ahead commune has many sites of WW1 interest within its boundaries (e.g. Tyne Cot Cemetery, the new Memorial Museum, Bayernwald, Zandvoorde etc) and often organises events with a WW1 interest, especially round the 11 November period.

The Proposed Extension of the A19 Motorway.

There has been much opposition from historians and battlefield enthusiasts to the plan (which has, however, some considerable local support) to extend to Ostende the existing motorway which currently ends just above Sint Jan just beyond Mousetrap Farm (qv). The new road would cross the historic battlefield, over the Pilckem Ridge and pass very close to several CWGC cemeteries (such as Buff's Road, Track X, No Man's Cot, Colne Valley, Welsh Cemetery (Caesar's Nose), Dragoon Camp and Artillery Wood. The project was put 'on hold' in 2002 when the Institute for the Achaeological Heritage (Flemish Community) was asked to conduct excavations along the length of the proposed extension to ascertain the 'archaeological potential' (i.e. the historical importance of the area and what might be destroyed in the building of the road). First of all contemporary trench maps and aerial photographs were studied in detail and the archaeologists walked the area minutely. Nine potentially important sites were then pinpointed for detailed excavation. By the end of 2003 work had been undertaken in three areas:

1. 'High Command Redoubt' or 'Mauser Ridge near the Pilkem Ridge. This is high ground which from October 1914-April 1915 was in Allied hands until it was lost to the enemy in the first gas attack. The Germans then constructed an elaborate stronghold with a trench system and solid wooden structures (thought to be platforms for mortars or other artillery) and dozens of blockhouses. They held the position until 1917 when they were forced to pullback.

2. 'Turco Farm' some 100m further south along the same road. Excavations here revealed Allied trenches, artefacts such as rum jars, ammunition and some human remains which were thought to be those of a French soldier (red cloth such as the French pantalons worn at the beginning of the war were made of was clinging to the leg that was found in a boot). The remains of an unidentified British soldier were also found and he was buried in Track X CWGC Cemetery. After the gas attacks and the construction of the German stronghold on Mauser Ridge the trenches here were reorganised but remained in Allied hands until July 1917 when the troops who held them took part in Third Ypres (Passchendaele).

3. 'Cross Roads', on the old 'Track X' site. This important site is closest to the end of the existing A19. It was being excavated in November 2003, around the period of the Armistice, and received much media coverage. Several human remains were discovered and, unusually, there were possible means of identification with at least one of them. The CWGC and MoD(PS4) (qv) take great pains to confirm identifications and to trace any family members before releasing any names. Unfortunately *The Times* newspaper prematurely published the name of L/Cpl William Stephen Storey of the Northumberland Fusiliers, died 26 October 1917, before that process was completed. Three other remains were identified as belonging to the Royal Sussex Regiment, deduced to have been a machine-gun crew. Regimental insignia of the Buffs (E. Kent) Regt and the RHA were found, as well as shells, grenades, an ammunition dump (or perhaps a sump intended to pump the groundwater away and to keep the trenches dry), remains of a Lee Enfield Service Rifle, entrenching tools, barbed wire, an elaborate trench system and defensive earthworks.

Future plans include the excavation of the remaining six zones, or their investigation by a new technique by which the subsurface structures are traced by measuring the resistivity of the surface soil.

Mons. Tourist Office in the Grand Place, No. 20, 7000 Mons. Tel: + (0) 65 33 55 80.
They produce literature, usually available in English, on the battlefield, hotels and restaurants.
Typically the Grand' Place has a huge variety of restaurants and cafés serving good, hearty Belgian cooking. Mons is very fond of folkloric pageants, parades and festivals (e.g. the Lumecon – the Combat between St George and the Dragon on Trinity Sunday; St Waudru, Mons' Patron Saint, who has her own procession when a relic is carried through the streets in a golden carriage, normally housed in the St Waudru Church's Treasury). The proximity to **SHAPE,** with its mixture of nationalities, gives Mons a cosmopolitan flavour.
The 4-star Best Western Lido Hotel, 112 rue des Arbelestiers (at the bottom of the hill leading to the Grand' Place) is very smart and conveniently placed. Tel: + (0) 65 32 78 00, Fax: + (0) 65 84 37 22. Near the station is the 2-star Ibis Centre, 27 Bvd Charles Quint, Tel: + (0) 65 84 74 40. On the Route d'Ath at Nimy are the attractive 3-star Le Monte Cristo, Tel: + (0) 65 36 42 99, Fax: + (0) 65 40 37 17 and the Château de la Cense au Bois, Tel: + (0) 65 31 60 00, Fax: + (0) 65 36 11 55. Both the latter have excellent restaurants. See also Maubeuge on page 282.

FRANCE

Note: When phoning France add the following prefixes: ex-UK and USA 00 33, indicated by '+' in the phone numbers listed.

FRENCH GOVERNMENT TOURIST OFFICES

UK 178 Piccadilly, London W1J 9AL. Information line, Tel: 09068 244123. Open Mon-Fri 0830-2000 (calls charged at 60p per minute), e-mail: info@mdlf.co.uk
USA 444 Madison Avenue, New York, NY 10022. Tel: 00 1 212 838 78 00. Fax: 00 1 212 838 78 55, e-mail: http://info@francetourism.com
The French produce a marvellous booklet, *The Traveller in France: Reference Guide*. This is updated every year. It contains just about all the basic information you need to know before going to France: on currency, passports/visas, medical advice, electricity, metric measurements and sizes, banking and shopping hours, phoning, motorways, driving, caravanning, camping, hotels, self-catering, *Gîtes de France*, local tourist offices *(syndicats d'initiative)* signed 'i' for information, maps, food and drink, etc., how to get there by car, ferry, rail and air, car hire, with relevent phone numbers. It is absolutely essential. Please send a large SAE and £1 in stamps.

ACCOMMODATION IN FRANCE

The largest group serving the whole area is the **Accor Group**. This includes the 4-5 star Sofitel, the 3/4-star Mercure, the 3-star Novotel, the 2-star Ibis and the 1/0-star Etap and Formule 1. They are reliable, if somewhat predictable, with well-equipped bedrooms (usually standard and identical throughout the hotel) and bathrooms, restaurants, parking (some with swimming pool). Size of room decreases with the star rating. The ambience and quality of food in the restaurants of the 3-star hotels has greatly improved of late. They are conveniently sited on motorway access roads, with a few in city centres.
Central booking: UK Tel: 0870 609 0961. **N AMERICA** Tel: 1 800 221 45 42 Toll Free.
The 2-star **Campanile Hotels** are to be found near many of our battlefields. Usually run by a husband and wife team they have small but well-equipped rooms and specialise in good value buffet style meals. **Central booking:** Tel: 0 825 003 003. **UK** Tel: 0207 519 5045.
New hotels are springing up in France like mushrooms – especially in the 2 and even 1or 0-star category: chains like Balladins, Fasthotel, Mister Bed, Première Classe, 1-star Plus. Often conveniently sited on access roads to main towns, they are functional, with private bathrooms – the lower the star rating, the tinier the space – and the basic essentials; usually very clean, and good value for money but with little atmosphere or personality. Most are listed in *The Traveller in France*.
For something more individual, with character and personality, often privately owned, the hotels grouped under the banners *Relais & Châteaux* (Central booking UK Tel: 0207 630 7667), *Logis de France* **(Central booking:** Paris Tel: + (0)1 45 84 83 84), *Relais du Silence* **(Central booking,** Paris Tel: + (0)1 44 49 90 00) and those marketed under the **Best Western group (Central booking: UK** Tel: 0800 39 31 30. **N AMERICA** Tel: 800 528 1234) are worth investigating. Not all have restaurants, but when they do they are normally very good. Not all rooms have en-suite bathrooms (although this is becoming far more prevalent) and may vary in size and furnishing – check carefully when you book. Because of this non-standardization they vary from 2 to 4 stars. More hotel groups are listed in the *Traveller in France Reference Guide.*
The words *auberge* or *hostellerie* often indicate a patron-run establishment with superb restaurant but more basic accommodation.
Self-catering accommodation can be booked through the reliable *Gîtes de France.* **Central booking** UK Tel: 0990 360360.
A selection of **Bed and Breakfast** *(Chambres d'Hôtes)* establishments are listed in the *Traveller in France.* Lists of Camping Sites can be obtained from local tourist offices.

LOCAL INFORMATION/TOURIST OFFICES

Lille Area.
Comité Departmental de Tourisme du Nord, 15-17 rue du Nouveau Siècle, 59800 Lille. Tel: + (0)3 20 57 00 61. Fax: + (0)3 20 57 52 70. This has full hotel, restaurant and attractions listings.

Lille and its surroundings make an alternative base for touring the Ypres Salient and even Mons, Neuve Chapelle, Aubers and Fromelles. It is an interesting, lively, garrison city, with many WW1 associations too, with some superb restaurants. But beware, navigation is complicated and the traffic heavy and fast-moving.

There is a variety of hotels in the Accor group (qv) in the Centre and at the Airport and the more distinctive, centrally situated Best Western Grand Hôtel Bellevue (Tel: + (0)3 20 57 45 64) and Hôtel Arts Deco Romarin (Tel: + (0)3 20 14 81 81). Well-placed for the above battlefields at Englos, just off the D71 or the N41 to la Bassée are the 3-star Novotel Lille-Englos (Tel: + (0)3 20 10 58 58. Fax: + (0)3 20 10 58 59, outdoor pool, parking) and the economy Etap (Tel: + (0)3 20 93 06 45).

Maubeuge
There are a Campanile (Tel: + (0)3 27 64 00 91) and Formule 1 (Tel: + (0)8 91 70 53 04) which are convenient for the Mons tour.

Artois/Pas de Calais
Béthune. Tourist Office: In the ground floor of the belfry. **Open** every day 0930-1230 and 1400-1830. Tel: + (0)3 21 57 25 47.
This delightful town would make an ideal base for the Loos, Neuve Chapelle, Aubers Ridge, Fromelles and Festubert Tours. The picturesque main square is everything you imagine a northern French *Place* should be. After the almost total destruction of the war it was rebuilt with style and verve in a mixture of architectural styles, incorporating the new *Art Deco* fashion with the traditional Flemish. It has the statutory belfry tower (originally dating from 1346, twice burned and thrice rebuilt) with bells that ring out each hour.

Béthune is famous for its beer CH'TI (nickname for the people of Northern France). It boasts a 2-star Michelin restaurant (the only one in the Nord Pas de Calais), le Meurin, with chef Marc Meurin, 15 Place de la République, Tel: + (0)3 21 68 88 88 (but there are four other 1-star restaurants and a plethora of cheap and cheerful eateries around the square – pick up a restaurant guide from the Tourist Office.). There is an equal array of hotels – from the Meurin (see above) and the 4-star Chartreuse du Val St Esprit at nearby Gosnay, Tel: + (0)3 21 62 80 00, to chains like Campanile (near Exit 6 from the A1) Tel: + (0)3 21 57 76 76 and conveniently situated hostelleries like the Hôtel du Vieux Beffroi in the Grand' Place. Tel: + (0)3 21 68 15 00 (more details from the Tourist Office).

Le Cateau. Tourist Information: *Mairie.* Tel: + (0)3 27 84 10 94 They have a list of the small local hotels (2-star Logis de France Le Florida, rue Théophile Boyer, Tel: + (0)3 27 84 01 07 and 2-star Hostellerie du Marché, rue de Landrecies, Tel: + (0)3 27 84 09 32) and variety of restaurants from *friteries* and pizzerias to traditional fare.

There are 3-star Novotel Hotels at **Henin-Douai-Lens** (Tel: + (0)3 21 08 58 08. Fax: + (0)3 21 08 58 00, on the A1-E15) and at **Valenciennes** (Tel: + (0)3 27 21 12 12. Fax: + (0)3 27 21 06 02, on the A1) and a 2-star Campanile at Valenciennes (Tel: + (0)3 27 47 87 87. Fax: + (0)3 27 28 95 25 off the A23) and **Lens** (Tel: + (0)3 21 28 82 82. Fax: + (0)3 21 42 41 33 (off the A23) which could be useful for Loos, Cambrai, Neuve Chapelle.

La Bassée. Tourist Information: *Mairie.* Tel: + (0)3 20 29 90 29. Fax: + (0)3 20 29 21 40. Here an annual guide to la Bassée with useful telephone numbers and listings of restaurants is available. There are no hotels in la Bassée, but it is a useful lunch stop, with a selection of restaurants and brasseries with local, North African, oriental and Italian specialities.

Arras. Tourist Office: *Hôtel de Ville.* Tel: + (0)3 21 51 26 95 . Fax: + (0)3 21 71 07 34.
E-mail: arras.tourisme@wanadoo.fr
This makes the best base for Vimy, and is convenient for Neuve Chapelle, le Cateau and Cambrai too, if

you prefer not to move and don't mind a bit of daily motoring. You could even do the Somme from Arras. It is also an ideal place to eat. All around the station square is a variety of restaurants and cafés – from 'quick snack' (and what better for lunch than a *Croque Monsieur* or half a *baguette* with *jambon de Paris* or *Camembert*) to gourmet. The 'Astoria', 10-12 Place Maréchal Foch, is a good compromise. Highy recommended is La Coupole, 26 Boulevard de Strasbourg, Tel: + (0)3 21 71 88 44, with a great Parisian brasserie atmosphere and décor and fine seafood specialities. The only 4-star hotel in Arras is the Hotel d'Angleterre, Place Maréchal Foch, Tel: + (0)3 21 51 51 16. Fax: + (0)3 21 71 38 20. A Conference Centre has been built in the square with a 3-star Mercure Hotel, Tel: + (0)3 21 23 88 88. Fax: + (0)3 21 23 37 07. The 3-star Hotel Moderne, Bvd Faidherbe Tel: + (0)3 21 23 39 57. Fax: + (0)3 21 71 55 42 is opposite the station. There is a 2-star Ibis, 11 rue de la Justice, Tel: + (0)3 21 23 61 61. Fax: + (0)3 21 71 31 31, and on the outskirts there is a Campanile, ZA les Alouettes, Tel: + (0)3 21 55 56 30. Fax: + (0)3 21 55 46 36. The *Places* (squares) with their picturesque Flemish baroque arcades also offer a variety of eating possibilities. Beneath the Grand' Place is a huge car park. Beneath the Gothic Town Hall and Belfry Tower are the *Boves* (qv) – underground tunnels and chambers much-utilised in the First World War and visited from the Town Hall.

Remember that the Western Front can be very wet and muddy!

ACKNOWLEDGEMENTS

During our long 'recce and research' phase of this book we renewed many old friendships and made many new ones who were generous with their knowledge and their time.

As always we express our admiration for the dedicated work of the **CWGC** and for the assistance we have had from staff at Maidenhead, notably David Parker and Peter Francis, at Ieper from Jerry Gee and at Beaurains, notably from Tim Reeves, Roy Hemington and Colette Vandeville. In Ypres Peter Slosse from the Tourist Office and Dominiek Dendooven from the Documentation Centre have been helpful as always, as has Aurel Sercu of 'The Diggers'. Natasja and the Staff of the Ariane Hotel looked after us extremely well during 'recces'. Marc DeWilde of the Archaeological Heritage (Flemish Community) provided detailed information about the excavations on the route of the proposed A19 extension. In **Zonnebeke** we have received much help from the enthusiastic Franky Bostyn. In **Poperinge** Jan Louagie and Jacques Ryckebosch of Talbot House provided us with ongoing information. On **the Yser** the expert Lt Col Roger Verbeke gave us generously of his time with the able help of guide Kristin de Meyere and at the **Raversijde Domein** curator Alecks Deseyne was particularly helpful. In **La Targette** David Bardiaux answered some useful questions. In **Aubers and Fromelles** we were courteously assisted by dedicated and knowledgeable local historians, *Maire* of Aubers and President of the Historical Circle, Pierre Descamps, ex-*Maire* of Fromelles Francis Delattre and young enthusiast 'Joss' Leclercq. For permission to reproduce the poem *The Next War* from *Selected Satires and Poems*, Osbert Sitwell and Macmillan. For reading the manuscript, Mr R.M. Loosmore and to all the team at Pen & Sword Books for their patience. Our thanks go to them all and to Elaine and Ian Parker for keeping us 'on the road'.

PICTURE CREDITS

For the pictures of the Atlantic Wall Museum on pages 86 and 87 we are grateful to the Domein Raversijde (Ostende); for the pictures of the Menen Gate Buglers on page 263, Foto Daniel; for the pictures of the Vimy Memorial on page 187, the kind permission of Veterans' Affairs, Canada.

INDEX

FORCES

These are listed in descending order of size, i.e. Armies, Corps, Divisions, Brigades, Regiments... then numerically and then alphabetically. Many more units are mentioned in the Cemetery descriptions throughout the book.

MEMORIALS

MUSEUMS

WAR CEMETERIES

GENERAL INDEX